Eisenhower, Science Advice, and the
Nuclear Test-Ban Debate, 1945–1963

EISENHOWER,

SCIENCE ADVICE,

and the

NUCLEAR TEST-BAN DEBATE,

1945-1963

Benjamin P. Greene

Stanford University Press, Stanford, California, 2007

Stanford University Press
Stanford, California
© 2007 by the Board of Trustees of the
Leland Stanford Junior University

Library of Congress Cataloging-in-Publication Data

Greene, Benjamin P.
  Eisenhower, science advice, and the nuclear test-ban debate,
1945–1963 / Benjamin P. Greene.
    p. cm.
  Includes bibliographical references and index.
  ISBN-13: 978-0-8047-5445-3 (cloth : alk. paper)
    1. United States—Military policy. 2. Nuclear weapons—United
States. 3. Nuclear Test Ban Treaty (1963) 4. United States—Politics
and government—1945–1989. 5. Science and state—United States—
History—20th century. 6. United States—History—1953–1961.
I. Title.

UA23.G7879   2007
327.1'747097309045—dc22   2006008798

Printed in the United States of America
on acid-free, archival-quality paper.

Typeset in 10/12.5 Sabon

In memory of G. Gordon Greene

The Stanford
Nuclear Age Series

Conceived by scientists, delivered by the military, and adopted by poli-
cymakers, nuclear weapons emerged from the ashes of Hiroshima and
Nagasaki to dominate our time. The politics, diplomacy, economy, and
culture of the Cold War nurtured the nuclear arms race and, in turn,
have been altered by it. "We have had the bomb on our minds since
1945," E. L. Doctorow observes. "It was first our weaponry and then
our diplomacy, and now it's our economy. How can we suppose that
something so monstrously powerful would not, after forty years, com-
pose our identity? The great golem we have made against our enemies is
our culture, our bomb culture—its logic, its faith, its vision."

The pervasive, transformative potential of nuclear weapons was
foreseen by their creators. When Secretary of War Henry L. Stimson
assembled a committee in May 1945 to discuss postwar atomic energy
planning, he spoke of the atomic bomb as a "revolutionary change in
the relations of man to the universe." Believing that it could mean "the
doom of civilization," he warned President Truman that this weapon
"has placed a certain moral responsibility upon us which we cannot shirk
without very serious responsibility for any disaster to civilization."
In the decades since World War II that responsibility has weighed heavily
on American civilization. Whether or not we have met it is a matter of
heated debate. But that we must meet it, and, moreover, that we must
also prepare the next generation of leaders to meet it as well, is beyond
question.

Today, over half a century into the nuclear age the pervasive impact of the nuclear arms race has stimulated a fundamental reevaluation of the role of nuclear armaments and strategic policies. But mainstream scholarly work in strategic studies has tended to focus on questions related to the developments, the deployment, and the diplomacy of nuclear arsenals. Such an exclusively managerial focus cannot probe the universal revolutionary changes about which Stimson spoke, and the need to address these changes is urgent. If the academic community is to contribute imaginatively and helpfully to the increasingly complex problems of the nuclear age, then the base of scholarship and pedagogy in the national security–arms control field must be broadened. It is this goal that the Stanford Nuclear Age Series is intended to support, with paperback reissues of important out-of-print works and original publication of new scholarship in the humanities and social sciences.

Martin J. Sherwin
General Editor

Contents

x   Contents

Preface

This study examines the debate over the pursuit of a nuclear test-ban agreement during the Eisenhower presidency. It connects the disagreements amongst the scientific community to the policy deliberations within the administration, focusing on the influence of Eisenhower's scientific counsel on his decisions. The complex interaction of public and private debates among governmental officials and scientists required me to make some difficult choices on the organization and the scope of this work. Developments within the administration and the scientific community often occurred in parallel, at times converging at critical junctures. My analysis within each chapter thus weaves back and forth between the public and the private debates and developments within the scientific community. The chapters appear chronologically and are organized thematically within. The only exceptions are Chapters Three and Four, which assess developments from 1954 through 1955 within the administration and the scientific community separately.

Since it was necessary to limit the scope of my research, I chose which scientists to examine in greater detail based upon their influence on the internal debate within the administration, as well as the availability of primary sources that illuminated their roles. A full-length examination of the role of all scientists on the public test-ban debate warrants a separate study. I focused my analysis on the consideration of the test ban from within the Eisenhower administration and the community of atomic scientists within the United States. Since previous studies emphasized the public debate within the United States and the international pressures on the administration to ban testing, I limit my discussion of those factors to provide the context that, at times, influenced the internal debate. I examined British archival sources to investigate the discussions between Great Britain and the United States on the test-ban issue. I only briefly speculate on Soviet motives and objectives in the test-ban discussions.

There are many people I would like to acknowledge for their assistance in the completion of this work. My doctoral advisor, Barton J. Bernstein of Stanford University, introduced me to this subject and guided me throughout the course of this study. He has been the perfect teacher and mentor, providing a constant source of encouragement. I would not have completed this study without his wisdom, guidance, and support. Gordon H. Chang has been a steady source of generous and practical counsel. A paper written for his graduate research seminar served as the basis for a chapter in this book. I am also thankful for David Holloway's assistance and advice in the completion of my dissertation. Several staff members and fellow graduate students at Stanford provided me with a great deal of encouragement and support: Matthew Booker, David Holland, Lynn Kaiser, Andy Koloski, Hyung-Suk Lee, Sean Malloy, Gertrud Pacheco, Margo Richardson, Cecilia Tsu, and Monica Wheeler.

I am also grateful for the assistance of several individuals from the Department of History at the United States Military Academy (USMA), where I taught for three years while preparing this manuscript. Lt. Col. Gian P. Gentile reviewed early drafts of my work and sagely guided me away from several potential pitfalls and missteps along the way. I am also deeply indebted to Col. Gary J. Tocchet for our numerous discussions about the challenges of interpreting Eisenhower's leadership and his approach to arms control. Brig. Gen. (ret.) Robert A. Doughty, Col. Lance A. Betros, and Lt. Col. Dana M. Mangham each provided useful advice and constant encouragement. Several junior faculty members at USMA were helpful in both large and small ways. My thanks go especially to Jim Isenhower, Matt Morton, George Sarabia, and Glenn Voelz.

The *Journal of Strategic Studies* (http://www.tandf.co.uk.) published an early version of my research in an essay that incorporated some themes and events that I analyze in greater detail in Chapters Two, Four, and Five. An anonymous reviewer from the *Journal of Strategic Studies* offered helpful comments on Eisenhower's efforts toward arms control.

Grants from the USMA Dean's Faculty Development and Research Fund paid for a number of research trips. I received invaluable assistance at several archival collections across the country. Heather Bischof at the

USMA library efficiently processed my constant stream of inter-library loan requests. Tom Branigar and the entire staff at the Eisenhower Library made my several weeks in Abilene fruitful and enjoyable. Elaine Kistiakowsky provided a great deal of encouragement and granted me access to her husband's papers at the Harvard University Archives. Dusty Sue Hellmann at Cornell University assisted me with Hans Bethe's papers. Nora Murphy at the MIT Archives and Matthew Schaefer at the Herbert Hoover Presidential Library were particularly helpful in searching for specific documents. Jim and Robin Lloyd provided me a home away from home during my research visit to West Branch, Iowa. Muriel Bell and Kirsten Oster of Stanford University Press provided wise and diligent counsel throughout the preparation of the manuscript.

My family supplied me with unending support during my completion of this study. I owe a lot to my mother, Marynelle, and to Ned Sharp for their constant encouragement and for the memorable weekends that I was able to spend at home one summer in between weekly research trips to Abilene. I am grateful for my wife, Marion, for her loving companionship and her patience and understanding throughout the preparation of this manuscript. I owe the most to my father, a teacher who instilled in me a passion for history at a very early age. He was the greatest influence on my life and continues to be the inspiration for everything that I do.

Abbreviations

ACDA	Arms Control and Disarmament Agency
AEA	Atomic Energy Act
AEC	Atomic Energy Commission
DOD	Department of Defense
GAC	General Advisory Committee
JCAE	Joint Committee on Atomic Energy
JCS	Joint Chiefs of Staff
MIT	Massachusetts Institute of Technology
NAS	National Academy of Sciences
NATO	North Atlantic Treaty Organization
NSC	National Security Council
OCB	Operations Coordinating Board
ODM	Office of Defense Mobilization
PSAC	Presidential Science Advisory Committee
SAC	Science Advisory Committee
UNDC	United Nations Disarmament Commission

Eisenhower, Science Advice, and the
Nuclear Test-Ban Debate, 1945–1963

Introduction

> We must be alert to the equal and opposite danger
> that public policy could itself become the captive of a
> scientific-technological elite.
> —Eisenhower's Farewell Address, 17 January 1961

President Dwight D. Eisenhower's farewell address is most remembered for its warning against the unwarranted influence of the "military-industrial complex." Eisenhower issued a second warning, since overshadowed by the first, that is seldom quoted and even less understood. The departing president cautioned Americans that the growing influence of government-sponsored scientific research risked making public policy the "captive of a scientific-technological elite." This second warning, combined with an eloquent expression of his disappointment over the lack of progress on disarmament, suggests Eisenhower's frustration with his inability to conclude a nuclear test-ban agreement and the forces that opposed his efforts. This book examines the test-ban debate within the Eisenhower administration, focusing on the centrality of scientific counsel for determining the course that the president pursued. It argues that Eisenhower, for part of his presidency, allowed his policy on nuclear testing to become the captive of those who controlled the presentation of scientific advice within his administration.

Eisenhower's efforts to reach a nuclear test-ban accord with the Soviet Union continue to be a source of historical dispute. According to a leading Eisenhower revisionist, biographer Stephen Ambrose, the test ban became the major goal of Eisenhower's presidency. In Ambrose's view, the test ban for Eisenhower was to be "the capstone to his half century of public service, his greatest memorial, his final and most lasting gift to his country."[1] Subsequent analyses of the test ban, however, question Eisenhower's commitment to reach an agreement with the Soviet Union.

The most recent full-length examination of the test-ban debate during the Eisenhower presidency concludes that "the administration never seriously pursued an accord to ban nuclear testing."[2] Two conflicting truths suggest an explanation for such contradictory conclusions. Eisenhower spoke passionately, publicly and privately, about banning nuclear tests, but often moved indecisively and inflexibly toward a goal he ultimately failed to achieve. Yet the explanation for such sharply contrasting conclusions lies deeper than the differences between words and actions and between desires and decisions. Scholars examining the test-ban debate within the Eisenhower administration encounter a confused historical record rife with official government secrecy, clever public dissembling, bitter personal conflicts, vigorous bureaucratic infighting, sharp partisan politics, tense allied negotiations, and complex technical problems that often defied scientific understanding and solutions. Participant's efforts to settle old scores and recast their own role in the most favorable circumstances have only clouded rather than clarified the historical record.

Initial accounts of the pursuit of a test-ban agreement assess only the final years of the Eisenhower presidency, minimize Eisenhower's interest in a ban, and fault the president for his poor leadership on the issue.[3] Since the mid-1970s, three important studies of the test-ban debate throughout the Eisenhower presidency have appeared, each differing from this study in scope, analysis, and interpretation. Robert A. Divine assesses Eisenhower's commitment to a test ban more favorably, yet he too faults the president's leadership for failing to achieve the results that he desired. Writing when many of the salient documents on the test-ban issue remained classified, Divine speculates, correctly as it turns out, that Eisenhower considered pursuing a test ban much earlier in his presidency. With only limited access to the relevant documents, Divine focuses on the public test-ban debate, providing what remains as its most comprehensive account.[4]

Richard G. Hewlett and Jack M. Holl's official history of the Atomic Energy Commission (AEC) during the Eisenhower administration views Eisenhower's leadership and his interest in the test ban even more favorably. According to them, Eisenhower developed a deep moral commitment to reach a verifiable test-ban agreement as a step toward his "cardinal objective" of nuclear disarmament. In their view, the complex issues related to inspection and control prevented Eisenhower from achieving his cherished goal. Their important study, with access to many documents that remain classified, uncovers a great deal about the internal test-ban debate. The test ban, however, is just one of many atomic energy issues that they explore. As a result, they are not able to focus sharply on the test-ban issue or venture far beyond those scientists affiliated with the AEC.[5]

Martha Smith-Norris, in her doctoral thesis and an essay in *Diplomatic History*, reverses the historiographical trend portraying Eisenhower as genuinely committed to the pursuit of a test ban. She faults Eisenhower for failing to resolve the bureaucratic divisions within his administration or to use his popularity to build public and congressional support for a comprehensive test ban. In her view, Eisenhower did not take a decisive stand on the issue because he never seriously desired a test ban. Smith-Norris's study, which draws upon a substantial number of British sources, underscores the international implications of the Eisenhower administration's test policy, focusing on its impact on relations with Great Britain and Japan. Her conclusions, however, often rely perilously upon contemporary British interpretations of the secretive debate within the Eisenhower administration.[6]

This study combines extensive research in government archival sources with several untapped collections of private papers to shed new light on the test-ban debate. While recent scholarship questions the sincerity of Eisenhower's efforts to ban nuclear testing, this study concludes that Eisenhower since 1954 was favorably inclined to accept a test-ban agreement.[7] Several contributing factors explain why Eisenhower's decisions, which were at times deferred, tentative, or both, often failed to support an objective that he strongly desired, but failed to achieve. Eisenhower's leadership style, which sought a consensus among his closest advisors, inhibited him from overruling the strong internal opposition to a test ban. The absence of pressures from Congress, key allies, and the American people for a test ban permitted the administration to delay continuously its policy decisions. Eisenhower's mistrust of the Soviet Union made him unwilling to accept a test-ban agreement that did not include adequate safeguards against Soviet evasion. Most importantly, Eisenhower's understandable confusion with the complex technical issues, such as the seismic detection of underground testing, compelled him to rely heavily on his scientific counsel, which was strictly limited to those who opposed a test ban for the first half of his presidency.

As one or more of these factors faded in significance, others rose at critical junctures during internal policy debates and international negotiations to inhibit the president's actions and frustrate his goals. In sum, they combine to explain why Eisenhower failed to secure an accord to cease testing and consequently why he felt compelled to confess in his farewell address that he ended his presidency "with a definite sense of disappointment."[8] For Eisenhower, the test ban was an essential first step toward significant progress on disarmament and an initial move toward a lasting peace.

While examining the test-ban debate over the course of the Eisenhower presidency, this study also illuminates several broader themes. To place the debate in the proper context, this study explores Eisenhower's attempts to grapple with the implications of nuclear weapons, which inspired his efforts at arms control.[9] Previous scholarship focuses on Eisenhower's "Chance for Peace" speech and his "Atoms for Peace" and "Open Skies" proposals during his first term as his main arms control initiatives.[10] Less emphasized are the secret considerations in 1954 and 1956 of a test ban. An examination of those episodes reveals that Eisenhower in his first term had already begun to consider a test ban as a means of controlling the nuclear arms race.[11]

Much of the scholarship on the test-ban debate identifies a lack of presidential leadership as a principal reason for the administration's failure to achieve a test-ban agreement.[12] This study examines and evaluates Eisenhower's leadership and decision-making style. Although revisionists might be correct to portray the president as a strong, decisive leader in times of crises, this image is often inaccurate on less pressing matters, as this study reveals, where Eisenhower sought a consensus among his most trusted advisors.[13] For him, the testing of nuclear weapons that fueled the spiraling arms race was a central anxiety, but never a crisis. Despite his own inclinations, he allowed his administration to remain divided over disarmament in general, and a test ban specifically, for much of his presidency.[14]

Yet contrary to a recent post-revisionist interpretation, Eisenhower did act increasingly without a consensus beginning in 1956.[15] His first decisions provided goals rather than actions, but in 1958 Eisenhower overruled the staunch internal opposition to separate a test ban from general disarmament, to unilaterally declare a test moratorium, and to pursue negotiations toward a comprehensive test ban. His willingness to overrule his dissenting advisors on these occasions suggests that Eisenhower's tentative leadership provides an appropriate explanation of the failure to pursue a test-ban agreement only for the first four years of his presidency. Moreover, this study reveals that Eisenhower's hesitance to seek a ban during the first part of his presidency was at times less a reflection of his leadership style than it was an illustration of Eisenhower's reliance upon a narrow range of scientific advice.

Previous studies identify the powerful opposition of key figures within the AEC and the Department of Defense (DOD) as a second prominent reason why the Eisenhower administration failed to conclude a test-ban accord.[16] This study examines the bureaucratic opposition in greater depth, exploring the hidden tactics of test-ban opponents within the administration to convince Eisenhower, Congress, and the American public that a test cessation would perilously threatened the nation's security. Lewis L. Strauss, Eisenhower's powerful AEC chairman, was the administration's most vehement test-ban opponent. Strauss effectively filtered until 1957 the technical advice on nuclear matters that reached the president. A staunch cold warrior, Strauss was convinced that the nation's survival depended upon its ability to maintain its nuclear superiority through continuous testing. He successfully delayed serious negotiations toward a test-ban agreement by presenting powerful scientific conclusions to Eisenhower that undermined the president's reasons for pursuing a ban. Strauss repeatedly insisted that atmospheric testing did not pose any significant health hazards. Moreover, the AEC chairman often depicted scientists that argued to the contrary as dupes of a worldwide communist propaganda campaign to cease testing. Most importantly, Strauss maintained that that there was no foolproof means to enforce a test-ban agreement. In his view, the Soviet Union would certainly clandestinely test during a ban and surpass the United States in advanced nuclear weaponry.

Such arguments succeeded for several years in delaying Eisenhower's pursuit of a test ban because they drew upon the president's mistrust of the Soviet Union. Eisenhower shared Strauss's fear that the Soviet Union would secretly continue testing. Yet contrary to Strauss and other test-ban opponents, the president did not consider a foolproof monitoring and inspection system as a prerequisite for signing a test-ban treaty. Eisenhower was willing to accept a system that provided sufficient controls and safeguards to deter the Soviet Union from attempting to test clandestinely. Nevertheless, the president's willingness to accept an accord to cease testing hinged upon a technical assessment that stated a high probability of detecting Soviet nuclear detonations. As much as Eisenhower worried about the lasting implications of the arms race, these concerns never completely overcame his immediate fear of Soviet deceitfulness.

Although Eisenhower was slow to realize Strauss's monopolization of scientific advice, he increasingly expressed apprehension about the growing influence of the AEC's scientists on his public policy. Frustrated that the AEC's incessant demands for additional testing conflicted with his efforts to slow the arms race, Eisenhower lamented that his "statecraft was becoming a prisoner of scientists." Curiously, he ignored calls for the use of scientific expertise from outside of the administration until the launch of *Sputnik*.[17]

The creation in 1957 of a Special Assistant for Science and Technology and the formation of the President's Science Advisory Committee (PSAC) became crucial for broadening the range of the president's scientific counsel. Both of Eisenhower's science advisors, James R. Killian, Jr. and George B. Kistiakowsky, as well as a vast majority of PSAC members shared Eisenhower's desire for a test ban. PSAC served as a powerful counterweight to Strauss and the test-ban opponents within the AEC, convincing Eisenhower that a test-ban agreement would be strategically advantageous and technically feasible to enforce. The powerful technical arguments of this new body of scientific expertise finally provided the president with the confidence to act upon his inclination to overrule Strauss's arguments and pursue a test-ban agreement.

Although PSAC propelled Eisenhower to open talks with the nuclear powers toward a test-cessation agreement, negotiations quickly bogged down over several political and technical disputes. In fact, the technical questions were so complex that some of the nation's top science advisors reversed their positions on the test-ban issue as the debate raged within the administration and the scientific community.[18] With the issues confounding the leading scientists in the country, it is not surprising that Eisenhower became confused on the matters and relied heavily upon his technical counsel.

The source of scientific advice was the central variable that explained Eisenhower's decisions during his second term in office and a critical factor for understanding the evolution of his approach to a test ban throughout his presidency. The central theme of this study is Eisenhower's dependence on scientific advice and the pivotal role of scientists inside and outside of government in shaping the test-ban debate. Although several previous accounts address Eisenhower's approach to science at specific stages and his relationship with his science advisors, none focuses on the implications of these issues for the test-ban debate and traces them throughout his presidency.[19]

Finally, and to a lesser extent, this study also examines the influence of foreign and domestic public opinion, domestic politics, and alliance diplomacy on the course and the outcome of the test-ban debate. None of these ever became the prevailing factor that barred a test-ban agreement, but each served to reinforce more dominant factors to inhibit Eisenhower's actions. Although public opinion in Great Britain strongly favored a test ban, the British government privately opposed a cessation of testing for much of the Eisenhower presidency.[20] The British sought to prevent a ban until Congress amended the Atomic Energy Act in 1958 to allow greater sharing of nuclear information. The tension between the domestic political pressure in favor of a test ban and the private opposition of the British government strained the Anglo-American relationship. Private British opposition to a test cessation, however, was not as decisive as Eisenhower once suggested in blocking an earlier test-ban initiative.[21]

Although public pressure to cease testing was lower in the United States than in Great Britain, public opinion and domestic politics in the United States still played an important role in the test-ban debate.[22] Democrat Adlai Stevenson made the test ban a dominant theme of his presidential campaign in 1956, prompting the Eisenhower administration to respond with heated rhetoric, clever arguments, and disingenuous statements that further confused the American people about the issues and concealed from them Eisenhower's own commitment to pursue a test-ban agreement. Criticism of the administration's national security posture and its handling of complicated scientific matters after the launch of *Sputnik* led to increased skepticism in the Democratic-controlled Congress about the ability to verify a test ban. Domestic politics thus played an important role in the congressional hearings in 1960 that cast doubt on the Senate's willingness to ratify a comprehensive test-ban agreement as Eisenhower prepared for the Paris summit and the test-ban discussions at Geneva reached a critical stage.

At the close of his presidency, these final factors increased the challenges confronting Eisenhower, but did not prove decisive for his inability to reach a test ban. In the end, Eisenhower's mistrust of the Soviet Union and the complex technical matters related to detection undermined an accord to cease testing. Despite their efforts, negotiators failed to agree on an inspection and control system that eased both the Soviet Union's fears of foreign intrusion and Eisenhower's concerns with Soviet evasion. The technical uncertainties of the adequate control system defied agreed upon scientific solutions. The lack of conclusive scientific data on these complex issues prompted many scientists on both sides of the debate to use their scholarly credentials to advance exaggerated political arguments rather than sober technical assessments. After the scientific debate on an inspection and control system spread from the White House to

Congress to the American public, Eisenhower became deeply troubled that scientists could not agree.

As the test ban talks stalled and the end of his presidency approached, Eisenhower lamented that his science advisors had failed him. Eisenhower clearly assigned partial blame for his failure to make significant progress on disarmament to the opposition of powerful scientists. It is one of the great ironies of the Eisenhower presidency that the twentieth century president with the greatest amount of military experience became so dependent upon scientific advice to determine a major component of his national security strategy. Eisenhower painfully and belatedly realized that scientific expertise often trumped military experience in the nuclear age.

Eisenhower and the Atomic Age
(1945-1952)

> The reports that reached us after the first one [atomic
> bomb] was used at Hiroshima on August 6 left no
> doubt in our minds that a new era of warfare had
> begun.
> —Eisenhower, 1948

Between the close of the Second World War and his inauguration as the
nation's thirty-fourth president, Dwight D. Eisenhower served at the
forefront of the military's response to the atomic age. His wide-reach-
ing responsibilities as the army chief of staff, the chairman of the Joint
Chiefs of Staff (JCS), and the commander of NATO involved him in
many of the monumental decisions related to the nation's approach to
atomic energy. Eisenhower often participated, albeit never decisively, in
the Truman administration's decisions toward the international control
of atomic energy, the testing of atomic weapons, the decision to accelerate the quest for the H-bomb, and the integration of atomic weapons
into the nation's arsenal and war plans. In each case, Eisenhower largely
approved of the Truman administration's atomic energy policies. Eisenhower's duties between 1945 and 1952 provided him a powerful vantage
point to consider the implications of the atomic age.

Several other issues, though less pressing at the time, also had a lasting influence on Eisenhower's later approach to the nuclear-testing issue.
Eisenhower, from the end of the Second World War to his inauguration
as President, developed strong attitudes on disarmament and the peaceful
uses of atomic energy. In the course of his various duties in the military
and as president of Columbia University, Eisenhower forged lasting relationships with some of the powerful scientists and administrators who
would play prominent roles in the test-ban debate during his presidency.
These personalities, debates, analyses, and controversies during the first
eight years of the atomic age shaped Eisenhower's approach toward
atomic energy as president.

I

Eisenhower, despite his tremendous satisfaction with the defeat of Germany in the Second World War, became deeply depressed following the war at the human and societal cost of the conflict in Europe. After witnessing the unprecedented devastation caused by the Second World War, Eisenhower feared that civilization would never recover from another global conflict. In this context, Secretary of War Henry Stimson in July 1945 informed Eisenhower of the successful test of an atomic bomb at Alamogordo. Eisenhower in 1948 asserted in his wartime memoirs, *Crusade in Europe*, that he had immediately expressed to Stimson "the hope that we would never have to use such a thing against any enemy because I disliked seeing the United States take the lead in introducing into war something as horrible and destructive as this new weapon was described to be."[1]

The absence of corroborating evidence of this conversation where Eisenhower, very uncharacteristically, firmly offered unsolicited advice to a superior raises serious doubts that Eisenhower reacted in such a manner.[2] In fact, Eisenhower knew so little about the atomic bomb project at the time that it is highly unlikely that he understood the implications of the information that Stimson may have provided him. Eisenhower's account in *Crusade in Europe* thus perhaps better serves as an indication of Eisenhower's thoughts on the A-bomb in 1948 than it does as a record of his reaction in 1945 when so much remained unknown about the capabilities and implications of atomic weapons. What remains clear is that the unparalleled destruction of the Second World War convinced Eisenhower that there must not be another global conflict. The development of the atomic bomb merely served to underscore an argument he was already committed to presenting to the public: The United States must use its military strength as a deterrent to war.

Although it remains unclear if Eisenhower in 1945 opposed the forthcoming use of the atomic bomb on Japan, after the war he clearly supported the continued testing of atomic weapons and the incorporation of them into the nation's arsenal. As chief of staff, Eisenhower backed the Truman administration's decision to conduct in July 1946 two tests of atomic bombs on ships off Bikini.[3] Eisenhower informed a national radio audience that the Second World War had taught him, "moral nations must forever remain so strong that another war would be impossible." In a veiled threat issued during this period of the U.S. atomic monopoly, Eisenhower warned that in the "atomic age" the safety of the nation depended, in part, on the knowledge that the United States would use its "strength" to control "any world gangsters who may threaten world peace."[4]

Eisenhower as army chief of staff did not face the public concerns related to fallout that dominated the public debate over nuclear weapons testing during his presidency. Scientists had only begun to assess the hazards of radiation, and atomic tests generated much less radioactive fallout than the massive hydrogen bomb tests that followed. Yet even at this early stage of the atomic era, Eisenhower recognized the political implications of atomic testing and became aware of the potential health hazards that atmospheric testing posed beyond the immediate target area. Stafford Warren, the former chief medical officer of the Manhattan Project, cautioned Eisenhower in April 1947 that tests of atomic weapons generated potentially hazardous levels of radioactive materials that passed into the atmosphere. According to Warren, the radioactive materials would eventually return to earth, contaminate the food supply, and cause a significant number of genetic mutations within a few generations. The lack of experimental data at the time, however, meant that Warren's concerns remained theoretical.[5]

Other scientists at the meeting responded to Warren's claims with skepticism. One of them was chemist and Harvard University president James B. Conant, who served as one of Roosevelt's science advisors and was a principal architect of the wartime quest for the atomic bomb. Eisenhower accepted Conant's counsel and the advice of one of his staff officers to keep Warren's "theory" private, fearing that its release would adversely affect public support for continued testing.[6] As president, Eisenhower witnessed how fears of radioactive fallout could create strong opposition to the administration's atmospheric test program. Despite the effort to keep secret the potential hazards of testing, Warren's concerns soon circulated throughout the scientific community and spread throughout the world after a massive H-bomb test in 1954 showered Japanese fishermen and Marshallese Islanders with radioactive ash. Eisenhower in 1947 could not have known that the privately dismissed theory would turn into an ominous cloud that hovered over his decisions on nuclear testing throughout his presidency.[7]

II

Eisenhower's approach to the postwar effort to place atomic energy under international control foreshadowed some of the competing objectives that greatly complicated his efforts as president to reach a test-ban accord with the Soviet Union. His conflicting objectives included maintaining the nation's strategic superiority, preventing an atomic arms race, and insisting upon stringent inspection provisions in any disarmament agreement. As the army chief of staff, Eisenhower recognized that the U.S. atomic arsenal provided a powerful deterrent to war. Yet he also understood that a failed effort to place atomic energy under international control would increase tensions and spur an atomic arms race. Although hopeful of reaching an agreement to prevent this outcome, Eisenhower, mindful of the shortcomings of previous efforts at disarmament, insisted upon adequate inspection and enforcement provisions. As president, his effort to reach a test-ban accord and slow the arms race stalled over the definition of adequate inspection. Late in his presidency, Eisenhower's anxiety about the spiraling arms race grew so great that he was willing to accept some limited risks in the area of inspection. While Eisenhower served as chief of staff from November 1945 to February 1948, the atomic arms race remained a dangerous possibility for the future; thus, his paramount concern was with the importance of rigid inspection provisions. The conflict between Eisenhower's hopes for progress on disarmament and his deep concerns about control measures made his support for an agreement on international control qualified and ambiguous. As a result, interpretations remain divided over the sincerity of Eisenhower's publicly stated support for the Truman administration's efforts at the United Nations.[8]

Eisenhower played only a minor role in the Truman administration's attempt to place atomic energy under international control. Although consulted on the matter, Eisenhower's views did not shape the outcome of any decisions. His views aligned closely with the decisions already made by Truman, Secretary of State James Byrnes, and Bernard Baruch.[9] The Truman administration's proposal, which evolved from the Acheson-Lilienthal Report into the Baruch Plan, required the Soviet Union to submit to international inspection before the United States would destroy its atomic weapons or share any secret information.[10] If anything, Eisenhower supported even more stringent inspection provisions than Baruch, whose proposal already included control measures that most administration officials believed offered little chance of Soviet acceptance.[11] Eisenhower's role was thus limited to building congressional and public support for a policy that he agreed with, but had little influence in developing. Although Eisenhower's attitude toward the international control of atomic energy did not shape the Truman administration's policy, this episode reveals his early thinking on the implications of atomic energy and his general approach toward disarmament.

Between April and June 1946, Eisenhower revealed his thoughts on the control of atomic energy in private consultations with Baruch and in his congressional testimony. Eisenhower's comments reveal his distrust of the Soviet Union, his penchant for secrecy, and his insistence upon rigid inspection provisions that inhibited his willingness to negotiate a test-ban agreement during his presidency. Eisenhower agreed with Baruch in a meeting in April 1946 that the United States should continue its production of atomic weapons until the Soviet Union reached an agreement. Further, they concurred that the United States would not relinquish any secret atomic energy information until the Soviet Union implemented strict inspection provisions. They acknowledged, however, that the Soviet willingness to accept international inspection and control posed the greatest obstacle to reaching an agreement.[12]

Despite his recognition that the matter of inspection would be the most contentious issue, Eisenhower revealed no willingness to compromise on the matter in order to reach an agreement. Testifying in June before the House Committee on Appropriations, Eisenhower maintained that he favored the idea of placing atomic energy under international control, but that he was "very, very fixed" in his opinion that any agreement must "include full, free, and complete inspection."[13]

The following week, Eisenhower sent Baruch a formal recommendation detailing his strongly qualified support for the international control of atomic energy. His letter simply reiterated the views that Eisenhower had discussed informally with Baruch the previous two months. Eisenhower clearly stated that the U.S. monopoly served as a deterrent "to aggression in the world." To preserve this capability, he cautioned against prematurely limiting the nation's capability to produce atomic weapons. Although Eisenhower emphasized the short-term advantages of the U.S. atomic monopoly, he also acknowledged that the effective international control of atomic energy provided the only lasting hope for preventing atomic war. Yet, Eisenhower's fears that another nation could violate the agreement with impunity overrode his hopes for reaching an agreement. His letter to Baruch echoed his congressional testimony in his emphasis on the importance of inspection. For Eisenhower, the essential first step was to install and test "a system of free and complete inspection."[14]

At this stage, Eisenhower feared the perils of inadequate inspection and control more than the consequences of an atomic arms race. Eisenhower's belated formal analysis emphasizing inspection had no bearing on the torturous debates within the United Nations on international control. The failed effort to control atomic energy unleashed the atomic arms race that became a central anxiety for Eisenhower during his presidency.

The prolonged debate over the control of atomic energy deferred any substantive discussions on comprehensive disarmament measures. Eisenhower in 1946 acknowledged that it was "premature and futile" to undertake disarmament negotiations until talks on atomic energy concluded, but he encouraged his staff to begin considering the issue.[15] Eisenhower's approach toward general disarmament paralleled his thoughts on the control of atomic weapons. Although Eisenhower expressed his hopes for peace and stressed the necessity of working toward disarmament, he insisted that strong inspection provisions must accompany any agreement.[16]

Eisenhower in January 1947 commented to the JCS: "Neither publicly nor in our own thinking must we ever fail to support every honest proposal toward world disarmament. The tone of our own messages and replies must not be negative; we should embrace the object and continuously point out constructive paths toward its attainment."[17] Yet qualifying comments on the importance of inspection inevitably accompanied Eisenhower's remarks supporting disarmament efforts. Eisenhower instructed his staff: "The one point of importance to us is inspection and verification and this is what we should insist upon whether we are talking about atom bombs or infantry soldiers."[18]

Eisenhower's comments in this tumultuous period reveal a remarkable consistency in emphasizing the importance of disarmament combined with the imperative of inspection. Neither the Soviet detonation of an atomic bomb nor the conflict in Korea altered Eisenhower's approach to disarmament. Eisenhower in 1952 asserted that the U.S. "should use every influence open to us to bring about a progressive program of disarmament," but insisted that it be accompanied by "full and free inspection."[19] As president, Eisenhower continued his struggle to reconcile his hopes for making progress on disarmament with his fears of Soviet evasion of an inspection system.

III

In his memoirs, Eisenhower suggested that he immediately recognized after the bombing of Hiroshima that atomic weapons ushered in a "new era of warfare."[20] In fact, despite such a conclusion, his focus on the immediate problems of administering postwar Germany and his struggles mediating budget disputes and the controversies related to the postwar reorganization of the military left him with little time to give atomic matters sober study.[21] Instead, he relied upon staff agencies and civilian analysts to examine the far-reaching political and military implications that he knew must exist, but had little understanding of what they might be. Eisenhower, himself unsure about what he was looking for, was rarely satisfied with their conclusions.

As the army chief of staff, Eisenhower directed his planning staffs to consider the implications of atomic weapons on the nation's wartime strategy. The historical record thus reveals his response to the theories and thoughts of others, but does not indicate any original systematic analysis. Eisenhower's predecessor, General George C. Marshall, ordered studies in August 1945 to assess the role that atomic weapons would play in future military operations.[22] On 3 December, Eisenhower's first day as the chief of staff, he reviewed the report initiated by Marshall. Eisenhower agreed with the general conclusion that atomic weapons would change some of the techniques of warfare, but would not alter the importance of the conventional ground, naval, and air forces. He noted, however, that the report failed to consider the advantages of the nation's atomic monopoly, which he considered transitory. Eisenhower requested further examination of this matter as well as additional study on the specific effect of the atomic bomb on strategy.[23]

Eisenhower in January 1946 responded critically to later drafts that minimized the impact of atomic weapons. He was concerned that one statement, prepared for presentation to members of congress, portrayed the military as reactionaries who feared that atomic weapons would lead to the elimination of the conventional armed services.[24] Eisenhower remained frustrated that initial analyses within the military minimized the implications of the bomb.

Two months later, Eisenhower received a manuscript of a collection of essays that provided a depth of analysis that was lacking within the War Department.[25] The essays, edited by Bernard Brodie and collectively entitled *The Absolute Weapon: Atomic Power and World Order*, provided one of the first systematic analyses of strategy and deterrence in the atomic age. Brodie's two essays contended that the destructiveness of atomic bombs fundamentally changed the character of war. In perhaps the most oft-quoted passage of his essays, Brodie wrote: "Thus far the chief purpose of our military establishment has been to win wars. From now on its chief purpose must be to avert them. It can have almost no other useful purpose."[26] Eisenhower clearly read several of the essays, including Brodie's, where he recorded his reactions with comments in the margins. Although he did not agree with all of Brodie's conclusions, and rejected his central argument that wars were no longer winnable, Eisenhower considered the analysis so important that he made it available to his staff and senior members of the War Department.[27]

Eisenhower's own views fell between his staff's minimalist assessment and Brodie's revolutionary conclusions. Although he frequently commented in public that the new weapons swept away the old concepts of war, his private postwar strategic vision essentially incorporated atomic weapons as more powerful bombs in the nation's arsenal. For Eisenhower, atomic weapons made war neither inconceivable, nor did they make a meaningful victory unimaginable. He rejected the extreme views that atomic weapons made conventional forces obsolete and sharply dismissed suggestions that the nation could use its atomic monopoly to impose a *Pax Americana*.[28]

With the apparent failure of the Baruch Plan to bring atomic energy under international control, Eisenhower in the spring of 1947 directed his strategic planners to incorporate the unrestricted use of atomic weapons in the nation's war plans.[29] In his view, there was a "considerable probability, if not a certainty" that atomic weapons would be used in the next major conflict.[30] War plans envisioned a central role for atomic weapons to blunt a Soviet offensive and counter their vast superiority in ground and tactical air forces.[31]

Despite the general agreement within the JCS to incorporate atomic weapons into the nation's war plans, considerable disagreement remained over how decisive they would be in a future conflict. The contentious debate involved broader issues related to postwar budgets, missions, and resources.[32] Eisenhower held a moderate view in the debate within the Pentagon on the effectiveness of atomic weapons. As chairman of the JCS, Eisenhower in 1949 believed that a "sudden and powerful" atomic strike provided a critical capability to retard or even cripple a Soviet surprise offensive. He regarded the use of atomic weapons as essential to reduce "the capacity of the enemy and the time needed by us for his eventual subjugation." He cautioned, however, that atomic weapons alone would not end a war.[33] Similarly, Eisenhower as the commander of NATO planned to use atomic weapons to help thwart a Soviet invasion of Western Europe, but believed that they were insufficient to ensure victory.[34]

Already convinced by the wartime destruction that he witnessed in

Europe that the world should spare no effort to avoid another global conflict, Eisenhower in public drew upon the general fear of atomic warfare to underscore his reasons for avoiding a future global conflict. For this purpose, he emphasized in his public comments how the development of such terrifying new weapons transformed the nature of warfare.

In private, Eisenhower downplayed the significance of atomic weapons and simply incorporating them into his broader strategy of maintaining the nation's military strength as a deterrent to war. If deterrence failed, Eisenhower continued to believe that the United States would win a future conflict, but it would do so because of its superior industrial capacity, not its possession of an absolute weapon. The nation's atomic arsenal would provide distinct advantages, but these were not sufficient to bring victory alone. For Eisenhower, atomic weapons provided neither a guaranteed deterrent nor an assured victory.[35]

IV

After the Soviet Union detonated an A-bomb in 1949 and President Truman decided in early 1950 to accelerate the development of the H-bomb, Eisenhower temporarily retreated from his public comments emphasizing the horrors of atomic weapons. Eisenhower, who had considered the military budget too small in the years immediately following the Second World War, feared that the new developments would lead to public hysteria and support within the government for dangerously high defense expenditures. He sought to soothe anxieties by assuring the public that scientists had predicted years ago that another nation would soon develop an atomic bomb. Since scientists anticipated that other nations would develop an A-bomb four or five years after the success of the Manhattan Project, Eisenhower saw no reason for "any revolutionary change in our thinking or in our actions."[36] He cautioned that the Soviet possession of that A-bomb did not require a radical change of the defense budget and criticized the media for exaggerating the threats posed by A-bombs and H-bombs.[37] Nevertheless, Eisenhower publicly declared his full and unqualified approval of Truman's decision to speed the effort to develop the H-bomb. In Eisenhower's view, ignoring the possibilities of acquiring such a weapon with the hope that the nation's adversaries would do the same would be like burying "our heads in the sand."[38]

Yet Eisenhower's public comments in this period that minimized the threat of nuclear weapons overshadowed the slow transformation under way in his thoughts about confronting the perils of the nuclear age. The

Soviet detonation of an A-bomb caused Eisenhower to reverse his previous opposition to releasing information to the public on the capabilities
of atomic weapons and on the nation's ability to defend and protect its
citizens against them. Eisenhower initially opposed the release of information since significant uncertainty remained about the capabilities and
consequences of atomic weapons. After the Soviet Union detonated an
A-bomb, Eisenhower changed his mind. In his view, an informed and
enlightened public was essential to avoid hysteria or defeatism spread by
the Soviet acquisition of atomic weapons.[39]

Eisenhower also attempted to calm public fears of the Soviet threat
by emphasizing the potential peaceful uses of atomic energy. He urged
an audience at Columbia in March 1950 to free themselves of the terror
that newspapers had associated with atomic weapons. In his view, "no
matter how strong may be that hydrogen bomb . . . it can be produced
for good or for evil."[40] Eisenhower, emphasizing the "good" uses of the
powerful new discoveries, publicly supported efforts to finance research
into the peaceful applications of atomic energy.[41] As president, Eisenhower's interest in the peaceful uses of atomic energy developed in 1953 into
his Atoms for Peace proposal. Throughout his presidency, Eisenhower
expressed great interest in the peaceful applications of atomic energy as
a means of calming the public's fear of the atom.

V

Between the end of the Second World War and his inauguration as president, Eisenhower became acquainted with several important scientists
and administrators who became influential in the test-ban debate within
his administration. Eisenhower in 1950 wrote to his brother Edgar that
he became interested in the peaceful applications of atomic energy because he had been "intimately associated with one or more scientists
who were engaged in the development of nuclear fission" ever since he
returned from the war.[42] Central among them were Roosevelt's wartime
science advisors, Vannevar Bush and James Conant. Both continued to
play important roles within the government following the war in the
debates over matters such as the international control of atomic energy
and the pursuit of the H-bomb. Although Eisenhower took positions
opposite Bush and Conant on some of those issues, he still valued their
opinions. Eisenhower, as the army chief of staff, specifically requested
Conant's views on the vast implications of atomic weapons.[43]

As president of Columbia, Eisenhower broadened his relationship with Conant, a chemist who had been the president of Harvard since 1933. Eisenhower valued Conant's advice on matters ranging from medical education to national security. Conant advocated universal military service of two years for all able-bodied youth. Eisenhower, whose efforts to institute universal military training failed following the war, applauded Conant's proposal, which he realized risked alienating their counterparts at elite universities.[44] Conant and Eisenhower differed on other matters. Conant supported the release to the public of additional information on the capabilities of atomic weapons, which Eisenhower initially opposed.[45] Through periodic interaction on a range of issues, Conant felt secure enough in his relationship with Eisenhower to meet privately with him in 1954 to strongly protest his administration's handling of the loyalty-security hearing of J. Robert Oppenheimer.[46]

Eisenhower did not always accept Conant's position and remained concerned that scientists' desires to share knowledge clashed with the imperative of keeping secrets in the atomic age. Nevertheless, Eisenhower learned through his relationship with Conant that scientists could offer valuable counsel. In fact, Eisenhower soon learned that he would have to rely heavily upon science advice because the complex technical issues related to atomic warfare reached well beyond his limited scientific background.

As president of Columbia, Eisenhower became acquainted with several additional influential scientists and administrators. He developed a particular fondness for I. I. Rabi, a Nobel prize–winning experimental physicist who served with Conant on the Atomic Energy Commission's (AEC) General Advisory Committee (GAC).[47] Eisenhower's duties at Columbia also brought him into greater contact with the influential presidents of other elite East Coast universities. As the president of the United States, Eisenhower brought several of them into government service: Conant of Harvard, James R. Killian of MIT, and Harold Stassen of Penn.[48] Significantly, Rabi, Killian, and Stassen each strongly supported Eisenhower's pursuit of a test-ban agreement in spite of considerable opposition from the AEC and the Department of Defense.

Born in Austria, I. I. Rabi immigrated as an infant to New York City. The son of a grocer, Rabi excelled in New York's public schools and studied chemistry at Cornell and physics at Columbia, where he received his Ph.D. in 1927. Rabi completed two years of postdoctoral studies at the most prestigious research institutions in Europe. The gregarious Rabi became acquainted with many of the leading European physicists, including Otto Stern, Niels Bohr, and Hans Bethe. After completing his studies,

Rabi returned to Columbia to join the faculty, becoming the first Jewish member of the physics department. He received in 1944 the Nobel Prize in physics for his pioneering atomic research. During the Second World War, Rabi concentrated on the development of microwave radar technology at MIT's Radiation Laboratory. At the same time, he routinely consulted with scientists working on the Manhattan Project at Los Alamos.

Eisenhower's tremendous appreciation for Rabi's counsel originated at Columbia. Eisenhower's respect for Rabi grew not only from his impressive scientific credentials, but also from his willingness to speak his mind openly. In his first meeting with the new university president, Rabi reportedly corrected Eisenhower's reference to the faculty as university "employees." The five-foot, two-inch-tall Rabi firmly stated that the faculty were not simply employees of the university, they *were* the university.[49] One year later, Rabi again challenged his powerful university president. Rabi was one of six faculty members representing different departments who sent a letter to Eisenhower protesting his practice of making appointments and polices affecting their departments without soliciting the faculty's opinion. *Newsweek* reported that Eisenhower's actions upset the faculty so much that some wanted to petition for his resignation.[50] Eisenhower quickly met with Rabi and the other five professors and began to consult more frequently with the faculty on major decisions.[51]

Eisenhower, recognizing Rabi's value as an advisor and his importance to the reputation of Columbia, was determined to keep him at the university. Eisenhower later recalled how he convinced Rabi to decline an offer to join the prestigious Institute for Advanced Study (IAS) at Princeton.[52] Eisenhower recalled in a memoir, *At Ease*, that he could not possibly match the financial offer of the IAS. Instead, he stressed to Rabi that his departure would irreparably damage the morale and prestige of Columbia's science programs and appealed to Rabi's sense of loyalty to convince him to stay.[53] The university had previously lost in the 1940s to the University of Chicago two Nobel–prize winning scientists who had worked on the Manhattan Project, chemist Harold Urey and physicist Enrico Fermi. Rabi remembered the conversation quite differently, recalling that Eisenhower simply directed the university provost to exceed the IAS's financial offer and eliminate Rabi's teaching duties.[54] Although the precise nature of Eisenhower's appeal to the distinguished scientist remains unclear, Rabi ultimately stayed at Columbia.

Through their battles at Columbia, Eisenhower and Rabi developed a strong mutual admiration that made Rabi's trusted counsel particularly influential after Eisenhower entered the White House. Rabi's refreshing candor and keen intellect convinced Eisenhower that he could be a valuable consultant on a range of issues. He recognized Rabi's advisory potential as early as 1948 when he asked Rabi to join him on a blue ribbon panel created by the Council on Foreign Relations to examine the requirements for economic aid in Europe.[55] As president of the United States, Eisenhower continued to place a great deal of confidence in Rabi's counsel. Rabi and James Killian were instrumental in convincing Eisenhower to expand the range of scientific advice that he received. The expertise within a new science advisory committee provided Eisenhower the confidence on the complex technical issues related to nuclear testing that he needed to pursue his inclinations.

In the eight years before his presidency, Eisenhower became acquainted with influential individuals, explored implications, and waded his way through controversies that prepared him, in part, to confront the test-ban issue as president. Eisenhower's atomic age apprenticeship remained incomplete, however, because an event on the eve of his election dramatically changed the strategic situation that he inherited as president. On 1 November 1952, three days before the presidential election, the United States detonated the world's first thermonuclear device, at Enewetak Atoll in the Pacific. Several days later, Eisenhower, as president-elect, received a top-secret briefing from AEC officials on that successful test in the Pacific. Eisenhower learned that the nation possessed the capability to explode devices five hundred times more powerful than the fission bomb that destroyed Hiroshima. Within a year, Eisenhower as president feared that the Soviet Union possessed the same capacity.[56]

Similar to his response to the advent of the A-bomb, Eisenhower struggled for a time to grapple with the implications of the H-bomb. In the end, the A-bomb altered Eisenhower's thinking about the nature of war in only a strictly limited sense. The H-bomb, however, fundamentally transformed his view of warfare. Whereas Eisenhower viewed war as winnable in the atomic age, he eventually considered the concept inconceivable in an era of thermonuclear weapons delivered by intercontinental ballistic missiles (ICBM).[57]

Although the development of thermonuclear weapons eventually transformed Eisenhower's approach to warfare, his views remained largely unchanged on other matters related to atomic energy. While the horrific new strategic environment heightened Eisenhower's concern with the spiraling arms race, his insistence on the imperatives of inspection and control remained unchanged. Despite the exponentially greater destructive powers of an H-bomb, Eisenhower also continued to look toward the peaceful applications of atomic energy as a means to calm the fears of an anxious public.

For Eisenhower, the complexity of the issues related to atomic energy almost seemed to match the exponential growth in their destructive force. As president, he slowly discovered the powerful influence of scientific advice on shaping his nuclear test policies. In time, the relationships that Eisenhower forged in the eight years before his presidency proved critical in expanding his range of scientific advice and supporting his efforts to negotiate a nuclear test-ban agreement.

2 ■

The Dawn of the
Thermonuclear Age (1953)

> We, as scientific men, have no claim to special
> competence in solving the political, social, and mili-
> tary problems which are presented by the advent of
> atomic power.
> —Report of the Scientific Panel, 16 June 1945

> Science seems ready to confer upon us, as its final gift,
> the power to erase human life from this planet.
> —Dwight D. Eisenhower,
> Inaugural Address, 20 January 1953

Eisenhower's first year in office was one of hope mixed with fear. The former Supreme Commander of Allied Forces in Europe pledged during his 1952 campaign for the presidency that he would "go to Korea," raising expectations that he would find a solution to the lengthy stalemate on the Korean peninsula. The death of Stalin in March 1953 not only improved prospects for a negotiated settlement in Korea, it also raised hopes for an early end to the Cold War. Eisenhower responded the following month with his "Chance for Peace" speech, one of the most eloquent expressions of the human and economic costs of the nuclear arms race. Although these words and events raised hopes for a reduction in Cold War hostilities, other events served only to increase tensions and arouse fears of a catastrophic world conflict. Days before Eisenhower's election in 1952, the United States detonated the world's first thermonuclear device. The Soviet Union tested a thermonuclear device of their own the following August. Thus, Eisenhower entered office at the dawn of the thermonuclear age. He struggled to grapple with the implications of this new strategic environment throughout his first year in office.

Eisenhower's thoughts on science and his relationship with science advisors greatly shaped his approach to the nuclear age. He entered office deeply skeptical of scientists who drew political conclusions from their inventions. Moreover, he was convinced that the scientists' unyielding quest to discover and disclose newfound knowledge would not only lead to the development of ever more dangerous weapons, but also result in disastrous security leaks that would spread the danger to America's enemies.

Lewis L. Strauss, initially Eisenhower's advisor for atomic energy before adding the position of Chairman of the Atomic Energy Commission (AEC), served to reinforce these often false perceptions. Most importantly, Strauss meticulously filtered the scientific advice made available to the president, severely restricting the views of atomic scientists who sought arms control measures from reaching Eisenhower. The case of physicist J. Robert Oppenheimer, director of the wartime Los Alamos laboratory, provides only the best known example of Strauss's influence. Eisenhower's first year in office began with Oppenheimer serving as a government consultant, but ended with his security clearance suspended and the beginning of the procedure that would culminate in his loyalty-security hearing in 1954. The administration's excessive secrecy on nuclear matters, its rejection of proposals to expand the scope and range of science advice, and its initiation of the loyalty-security case against Oppenheimer deeply troubled many leading atomic scientists. These actions, along with residual conflicts over the control of atomic energy and the pursuit of the H-bomb, fostered increasingly sharp divisions within the scientific community.

Eisenhower remained largely unaware of the growing concerns and bitter conflicts among scientists as he developed a strategy for containment that relied heavily on the ability and willingness to use nuclear weapons. His "New Look" national security strategy sought to contain the expansion of communism through threats of a massive retaliation from the nation's growing atomic arsenal. Privately, Eisenhower appeared favorably inclined to use tactical atomic weapons in Korea, while his administration publicly claimed its atomic threats against China were decisive in convincing the Chinese to accept an armistice. The month after the July 1953 armistice in Korea, the Soviet detonation of a thermonuclear device prompted Eisenhower's effort to slow the arms race that culminated in December with the "Atoms for Peace" proposal.

The president's leading advisors clearly recognized that Atoms for Peace was a one-sided program that the Soviet Union was likely to reject. Yet a Soviet rejection of any peaceful proposal would still provide the United States with a tremendous propaganda victory. Although Eisenhower clearly understood the one-sided nature of the proposal, he remained hopeful, perhaps naively, that the Soviets would not reject it. For Eisenhower, Atoms for Peace would be a first step toward the building of mutual confidence necessary for resolving political issues and agreeing upon tangible steps for slowing the arms race.

I

On 20 January 1953, a crisp winter day in Washington, sixty-two-year-old Dwight D. Eisenhower placed his left hand on the bible his parents had presented him in 1915 upon his graduation from West Point, raised his right hand, and repeated the presidential oath of office.[1] The thirty-fourth president's initial remarks as head of state are much less remembered than his farewell address in 1961. His inaugural address focused almost entirely on foreign affairs, foreshadowing his primary engagement and interest for the next eight years.

Embedded within this otherwise unremarkable twenty-one minute speech was an insightful passage that illustrates his skepticism of science and his horror at the nuclear age: "Yet the promise of this life is imperiled by the very genius that has made it possible . . . Science seems ready to confer upon us, as its final gift, the power to erase human life from this planet." Eisenhower did not dwell on this point. Instead, he moved on to discuss a nine-point plan for maintaining peace through strength and allied unity. Media comment on this passage at the time simply noted that it was a single, but ominous reference to the newly tested hydrogen bomb. While it certainly reflects Eisenhower's recognition that the world had entered the nuclear age, it also reveals his thoughts about science. The passage indicates Eisenhower's view that scientists considered their discoveries as a "gift," without considering moral implications or social responsibilities. It also suggests his frustration that the decisive factors of warfare had shifted from the expertise of military planning and mobilization to a new generation of weapons understood only by the scientists who created them.[2]

Less than a month later, Eisenhower privately expanded upon his views on science after reviewing a report, initiated by the previous administration, from an advisory panel on disarmament. Frustrated with the lack of progress within the United Nations Disarmament Commission (UNDC), Truman's Secretary of State, Dean Acheson, formed in April 1952 the five-member Panel of Consultants on Disarmament. Acheson instructed the panel to examine the problem of "arms limitation in the context of a general study of the political meaning of modern weapons in the present deeply divided world." The panelists included two of the nations' most experienced science advisors, J. Robert Oppenheimer and Vannevar Bush. Oppenheimer was a prominent theoretical physicist, the director of the Los Alamos laboratory during World War II, and the chairman of the AEC's General Advisory Committee (GAC) until 1952. Bush had played a critical role in persuading Franklin D. Roosevelt to develop the A-bomb. He was Roosevelt's top World War II science advisor and served as the director of the wartime Office of Scientific Research and Development (OSRD). Joining the two scientists on the panel were two former diplomats, John Dickey, the president of Dartmouth College, and Joseph Johnson, the president of the Carnegie Endowment for International Peace. Allen Dulles, deputy director of the Central Intelligence Agency and brother of John Foster Dulles, joined this impressive group of scientists, educators, and diplomats as the fifth panelist. The panel chose Oppenheimer as its chairman (thus the group was often referred to as the Oppenheimer Panel) and appointed McGeorge Bundy, then a junior member of the faculty at Harvard, as its executive secretary. The panel met periodically throughout the remainder of the year and submitted its final report the week before Eisenhower's inauguration with the hope that the incoming administration would consider its final report, entitled "Armaments and American Policy."[3]

Eisenhower himself expressed his "high opinion" of the report and directed the members of the National Security Council (NSC) to read it and "become thoroughly familiar" with its conclusions and recommendations.[4] He also revealed his hope that "when we finally achieved a sufficient stockpile of weapons, it would be possible to turn the atomic energy program to peaceful uses."[5] This seed of an idea eventually developed into his Atoms for Peace proposal after a torturous bureaucratic effort to follow the candid disclosure of the perils of the nuclear age with a message of hope. Moreover, this early expression of interest in the peaceful uses of atomic energy endured beyond Eisenhower's first year in office and his Atoms for Peace proposal. His strong interest in peaceful uses became a consistent theme throughout his presidency with significant implications for his approach to nuclear testing. Recognizing Eisenhower's interest in peaceful applications of the atom, test-ban opponents stressed the need for more tests to develop bombs that could create harbors and access oil reserves without spreading hazardous radiation. Raised at critical stages in negotiations and policy reviews in 1957 and 1960, these arguments had a significant, if not always decisive, influence on Eisenhower's hesitancy to pursue a test-ban accord. Thus, the peaceful use of atomic energy became the centerpiece of Eisenhower's first effort at limiting atomic arms, but served thereafter to challenge his efforts to pursue a test ban as a first step toward greater arms control measures.[6]

Of the panel's five recommendations, Eisenhower focused on the first: adopting "a policy of candor toward the American people . . . in presenting the meaning of the arms race."[7] Eisenhower agreed with the Oppenheimer Panel that the American public must understand the horrific implications of the latest weapons in order to respond to the threat intelligently.[8] Committed to informing the American public, Eisenhower initiated a program called "Operation Candor." The implementation of a policy of candor, however, required the resolution of two dilemmas: how to reveal the peril of the nuclear age to the public without creating hysteria, and how to inform the American public about the realities of the arms race without releasing secrets to the Soviet Union. Eisenhower directed his advisors to find some way to disclose the dangerous new situation to the American people while providing an overall message of hope. Eisenhower's advisors struggled for several months to resolve these dilemmas.

Although Eisenhower responded favorably to the Oppenheimer Panel's efforts, he expressed concerns about the role of scientists as advisors. According to records of NSC discussions on the report, Eisenhower thought that it was "strange that two eminent scientists had been put on the Panel." He observed that Bush and Oppenheimer had "immediately moved out of the scientific realm into the realms of policy and psychology." Eisenhower not only suggested that the scientists lacked the appropriate background in politics and diplomacy to provide sound policy advice, but he also observed that their professional norms posed a potential threat to national security. Eisenhower commented that his experience as president of Columbia convinced him that "most scientists concerned with atomic problems had no real grasp of the security issue and were generally anxious to reveal what they knew to any and all of their fellow scientists."[9] Specifically related to the panel's report, he was concerned that any attempt to describe the reality of the current and growing dangers of the nuclear age would necessarily expose military secrets. Thus, Eisenhower believed that scientists lacked the requisite breadth of knowledge to provide sound policy recommendations and the discipline to keep their advice private. Although Eisenhower shared Bush and Oppenheimer's concerns about the implications of the nuclear age and their desire to relate this somehow to the American public, he remained skeptical that scientists could and should offer advice on such important matters of national security.

The advisor most responsible for shaping Eisenhower's subsequent approach to scientific advice, classified information, and all atomic affairs was AEC Chairman Lewis L. Strauss. The fact that Strauss exerted a dominant influence on Eisenhower's views on atomic affairs, jealously guarded his jurisdiction over those matters, and aggressively fought for the AEC's bureaucratic interests is neither surprising nor even exceptional. What made Strauss uniquely influential and powerful was his ability to monopolize the information that Eisenhower received on matters of tremendous disagreement and his willingness to employ almost any means to do so. Unable to reconcile opposing points of view, Strauss remained utterly convinced of the rectitude of his beliefs and considered it his patriotic duty to advance them at all costs. In the end, Strauss's excessive secrecy, deviousness, and self-righteousness raised the enmity of powerful members of congress and the scientific community. Nevertheless, Strauss dominated Eisenhower's approach to atomic energy for the first three and a half years of his presidency.

The son of a Virginia shoe wholesaler, Lewis L. Strauss rose from a comfortable middle-class upbringing with little more than a high school education to earn a fortune on Wall Street and amass substantial power in Washington.[10] Strauss convinced Herbert Hoover in 1917, then head of the Food Administration, to hire him as a research assistant. Within a month, Hoover was so impressed with Strauss's hard work, intelligence, and organizational skills that he made him his private secretary. As Hoover's talented administrator, Strauss impressed several powerful international figures in government and finance, including Felix Warburg of the Wall Street investment banking firm Kuhn, Loeb, and Co. After Warburg arranged an interview, Strauss, a religious Jew, went to work for the firm in 1919, married the daughter of a Kuhn, Loeb partner, began to amass tremendous wealth, and became in 1929 a partner of the firm.[11]

The Second World War returned Strauss to government service and into closer contact with his first passion, science. Strauss, who received a commission as a naval reserve officer in 1925, entered active duty in 1941 and soon became an assistant to James V. Forrestal, then the under secretary of the navy. Although not a scientist by profession, Strauss had acquired an early fascination for science and was planning to study physics at the University of Virginia at the time he joined Hoover's staff. Thereafter, Strauss, who never attended college, closely followed scientific achievements and even provided financial support to several research efforts. Possessing a scientific inclination but lacking expertise, Strauss served as the navy's representative on an interdepartmental committee on atomic energy, gaining a valuable education in atomic affairs.[12]

President Truman appointed Strauss in 1946 to the newly formed Atomic Energy Commission, a position he held until 1950. During his tenure as a commissioner, Strauss played a powerful role in establishing a long-range surveillance system capable of detecting Soviet atomic tests. Significantly, he clashed with Oppenheimer over several issues facing the AEC, including the detection system, peaceful atomic power, security of information, and the pursuit of the H-bomb. Their disagreements turned particularly heated in 1949 over the authorization of a shipment of radioisotopes to Norway. During a hearing on the matter before the Joint Committee on Atomic Energy (JCAE), Oppenheimer presented technical arguments that belittled Strauss's objection that the shipment of radioisotopes would release valuable atomic secrets. Depicting Strauss's concerns as paranoid and uneducated, Oppenheimer testified that a beer bottle provided as much information on atomic energy as the radioisotopes that troubled Strauss. Oppenheimer's comments generated loud laughter from many people attending the proceedings. The humiliating episode fueled Strauss's deep personal animosity toward Oppenheimer that only intensified after Strauss returned to the AEC as a member of the Eisenhower administration.[13]

Eisenhower did not know Strauss well before appointing him in 1953 as his primary advisor on atomic energy matters. Eisenhower commented in a private letter that he had only met Strauss briefly and "could not claim him as a friend."[14] In fact, Strauss did not even back Eisenhower's 1952 quest for the Republican nomination for the presidency, supporting instead Ohio Senator Robert A. Taft. Following Eisenhower's victory in the 1952 presidential election, his advisors sought to broaden the incoming administration's support among Republicans by offering positions to individuals representing the various factions within the party. Strauss's Jewish faith and his backing by the Taft wing of the party made him an appealing figure to add a measure of diversity to Eisenhower's appointees, who primarily represented the internationalist wing of the party.[15]

Strauss's reputation as a staunch anti-communist and his obsession with guarding the nation's atomic secrets also made him an appealing choice to join the administration.

Eisenhower's military experience fostered an emphasis on deception and secrecy that continued into his presidency. As the commander of

Allied forces invading Normandy in World War II, Eisenhower oversaw what was perhaps the most comprehensive deception plan in military history, which his planners designed to confuse the Germans of the size, location, and date of the assault. Because maintaining strict secrecy over the actual details was essential to the success of the deception plan, Eisenhower displayed no tolerance for security lapses. When Major General Henry J. Miller, a West Point classmate and friend of Eisenhower's, talked freely about details of the invasion at a cocktail party in Great Britain, Eisenhower acted swiftly to demote Miller and send him home in disgrace.[16]

As he presided over the nation's nuclear arsenal, Eisenhower continued to place a premium on maintaining secrecy. For Eisenhower, Strauss, and others within the administration, the fate of the nation depended upon clandestinely developing and mass-producing the most advanced nuclear weapons. This Cold War imperative sharpened Eisenhower's obsession with secrecy, as he believed that the Soviet Union would obtain and benefit from any information on the nation's nuclear capabilities leaked to the American public.

As he entered office, Eisenhower was deeply troubled that the Truman administration had lost so many atomic secrets to the Soviet Union. Less than a month after his inauguration, Eisenhower was outraged that John A. Wheeler, a Princeton physicist who was an AEC consultant, had lost top-secret documents containing detailed technical descriptions of the development of thermonuclear weapons. In June, Eisenhower had declined to intervene to halt the executions of Julius and Ethel Rosenberg, who were convicted of giving atomic secrets to the Soviets. In this context of espionage and security lapses, which Eisenhower feared had led to the narrowing of the technological gap between the Soviet Union and the United States, Eisenhower depended upon Strauss's vigilance safeguarding the nation's secrets.

In many ways, Strauss's meteoric rise was typical of the self-made men that Eisenhower preferred to associate with in his leisure. Although Eisenhower did not consider Strauss a friend when he appointed him as his advisor on atomic energy, they soon developed a friendship that extended beyond Eisenhower's presidency. Strauss quickly learned Eisenhower's interests and proved especially adept at courting and pleasing the president, presenting him gifts ranging from books to bovine. Sharing an ascent from obscurity and a distrust of the Soviet Union, Eisenhower and Strauss forged a lasting personal friendship built upon their interest in their Angus cattle herds, their memories of political battles, and their concern with protecting the legacy of Eisenhower administration policies.[17]

Eisenhower and Strauss shared many interests and inclinations, which served to strengthen the president's early reliance on Strauss's technical counsel. A man of deeply held convictions, Strauss held a Manichean view of the world, wholeheartedly accepting the premise that the Cold War was a conflict between religious, political, and economic systems inimical to each other. He considered the maintenance of nuclear superiority as the only means to prevent a Soviet takeover of the United States and the free world. Although Eisenhower held misgivings about Soviet intentions, Strauss's suspicions bordered on paranoia. He foreclosed any possibility of honest negotiations with the Soviet leaders, whom he characterized as "cold blooded murderers."[18] Strauss's rigid anti-communism, obsession with secrecy, and ability to take a broader view of technical issues than the scientists that he represented served as the basis of Eisenhower's growing dependence on the advice of his AEC chairman.

The Oppenheimer Panel provided one of the first challenges to Strauss's protection of information on atomic energy. Strauss's objections added to the difficulties Eisenhower's advisors faced in resolving the dilemmas posed by the Oppenheimer Panel's suggested policy of candor. As Eisenhower's advisors struggled for several months to resolve them, Oppenheimer and Bush expressed their frustrations that the administration had not implemented their recommendations. While Oppenheimer publicly presented his arguments for candor, Bush privately criticized the administration for subverting the original intent of the panel's recommendations.

Oppenheimer on 17 February presented an unclassified version of the panel's report to a closed session of the Council on Foreign Relations.[19] He published a version of his remarks as an essay entitled, "Atomic Weapons and American Policy" in the July issue of the influential journal *Foreign Affairs*.[20] Although the administration cleared both the speech and the essay in advance, the opponents to candor within the government quickly moved to redirect Oppenheimer's original purpose for candor. In a telephone conversation with Eisenhower on 22 July, Strauss strongly criticized Oppenheimer for advocating the release of information on the U.S. atomic stockpile, its production rate of weapons, and the administration's estimate of enemy capabilities. Eisenhower agreed with Strauss and insisted, "I am at least the one person more security-minded than you are."[21] Eisenhower's comments reveal why he had begun to place so much trust in the ally of his political rival. After Strauss effectively used this incident to sharpen Eisenhower's mistrust of scientists as advisors, the AEC chairman moved to discredit Oppenheimer in the eyes of the public. Strauss collaborated with *Fortune* and *Life* writer Charles J. V. Murphy, an Air Force Reserve officer with close ties to the Air Force leadership, in an article sharply critical of Oppenheimer's *Foreign Affairs* arguments for candor. Strauss likely coordinated the similar attacks on the influence of Oppenheimer and other scientists on national security strategy that appeared in *Time* and *Life* magazines over the next few months.[22]

While Oppenheimer advocated greater candor publicly, Vannevar Bush privately protested the administration's delay to a less-than-sympathetic Strauss. According to Strauss, Bush criticized Eisenhower at a dinner held by the British Ambassador to honor Lord Cherwell, Winston Churchill's science advisor. Speaking loud enough for others to hear, Bush told Strauss that he was "very much disappointed" in Eisenhower. In Bush's view, the president had "forfeited the confidence of the people by his lack of leadership." Bush was especially upset that Eisenhower did not follow the advice of the Oppenheimer Panel to release more information on "the atomic weapon situation." In an only slightly veiled rebuke of Strauss himself, Bush criticized Eisenhower for allowing "his underlings who are making fools of themselves" to act as the spokespersons for the administration on atomic weapons issues. Although the strength of Bush's critique may also reflect his frustration with his decline in status and his feeling of neglect in comparison to his position in the Roosevelt administration, it certainly illustrates his frustration that Eisenhower had ignored the advice of two of the nation's most experienced science advisors and instead relied upon Strauss.[23]

Thus, the Eisenhower administration had isolated itself from two of the nation's top science advisors. Presented with the panel's conclusions for greater candor in February, by October the administration had still failed to implement its recommendations. Oppenheimer and Bush reacted to this snubbing quite differently. While Oppenheimer presented his case to the public, building the enmity of Strauss in the process, Bush confined his outspoken views to private dinners. In a relatively short time, Strauss effectively marginalized Oppenheimer and Bush, then consolidated his own role within the administration as the president's most trusted advisor and the administration's official spokesperson for all atomic energy matters.

II

The difficulties that Oppenheimer and Bush experienced in advancing their views within the Eisenhower administration reflected several developments and concerns within the scientific community that Eisenhower himself was unlikely aware of at the time. Atomic scientists remained deeply divided over the decision to accelerate efforts to develop the H-bomb. Concerned that H-bomb proponents had won this debate and had subsequently dominated the science advice reaching the president, several scientists tried unsuccessfully to broaden the range of science advice provided at the highest levels of government. Atomic scientists troubled by the nuclear age debated how to most effectively influence the nation's atomic policies. Some, such as I. I. Rabi, believed that the best approach was to retain their ability to offer candid advice within the government, even though their opinions rarely reached the highest levels. Maintaining the confidence of the decision-makers, however, required being quiet and loyal bureaucrats, operating within the mid-level channels of government. Others, such as Oppenheimer, sought to present their views to the public to exert public pressure to reach their goals.

Whichever tactic they chose, the scientists faced a formidable obstacle in Lewis L. Strauss. Strauss insisted that subordinates address him as "Admiral," extending the recognition of the temporary rank he acquired as a Naval Reserve officer in World War II. The Admiral effectively imposed a blockade on scientific advice reaching the president that differed with his own. He vigorously discouraged efforts to expand the range of science advice reaching Eisenhower and initiated FBI investigations and loyalty-security hearings against top scientists who opposed his views on the role of the nation's nuclear arsenal and efforts at arms control.

Some scientists working on the wartime Manhattan Project privately debated the morality of their work well before the first test of the A-bomb at Alamogordo and the combat use of the A-bombs at Hiroshima and Nagasaki. The most well known example of this is the Franck Report, named after one of its authors James Franck, a Nobel Prize winner and director of the Chemistry Division at the Manhattan Project's Chicago laboratory. Signed by seven scientists working on the project at the Chicago lab, the report appealed to Secretary of War Henry Stimson to conduct a demonstration of the A-bomb before its planned surprise combat use on Japan. Though partly inspired by military reasons, the report recommended a demonstration primarily out of political rather than moral concerns. The scientists feared that the surprise combat use of the weapon would intimidate the Soviet Union, eliminate the possibility for international control of atomic energy, and propel an atomic arms race.[24]

Stimson forwarded the report to a group of scientists advising the Interim Committee, a special committee appointed to provide recommendations about the use of the bomb and future atomic policy. The committee's Scientific Advisory Panel, composed of physicists Arthur Compton, Enrico Fermi, Ernest Lawrence, and Oppenheimer, only briefly discussed the matter.[25] They concluded: "We can propose no technical demonstration likely to bring an end to the war; we see no acceptable alternative to direct military use." Significantly, these four prominent physicists not only rejected the conclusions of the Franck Report, but they also cast aside the report's assumption that scientists should have a role in deciding how to use the weapons they invented. The Scientific Advisory Panel's report to the Interim Committee began with the caveat, "We, as scientific men, have no claim to special competence in solving the political, social, and military problems which are presented by the advent of atomic power."[26]

Debates about the nation's atomic policy and the role of scientists in shaping it continued after the war. A vocal minority of scientists that included Albert Einstein, Leo Szilard, James Franck, and Eugene Rabinowitch publicly condemned the use of the A-bomb against Japan.[27] Even more atomic scientists criticized the Truman administration's seemingly half-hearted efforts to place atomic energy under international control. These festering divisions within the scientific community exploded over the Truman administration's decision to accelerate efforts to develop the H-bomb.

The divergence of prominent physicists Edward Teller and Hans Bethe, who were friends and fellow refugees, illustrates the magnitude of the debate. Teller combined a sharp mind and an intense loyalty toward his friends with a fragile ego and intolerance with those who failed to agree with him. Teller's European accent and obsessive promotion of expanding the nation's nuclear arsenal as its only means of survival fueled speculation that he served as the inspiration for the title character in Stanley Kubrick's 1964 film, *Dr. Strangelove*.[28] Teller, a Hungarian Jew, was a talented and energetic theoretical physicist who fled his research position at the University of Göttingen following the Nazi's rise to power in Germany. Along with fellow countrymen Leo Szilard and Eugene Wigner, Teller convinced Albert Einstein in 1939 to sign a letter they had drafted to warn President Roosevelt of the possibility that Nazi Germany could develop an atomic bomb.

Teller enthusiastically joined the wartime project to develop the bomb. He and Hans Bethe had met briefly as graduate students in Germany, then became good friends in 1937 as they traveled throughout the western United States. Their families shared an apartment in Berkeley during the summer of 1942 while the two physicists attended a seminar Oppenheimer had organized on bomb physics. Although Teller advocated focusing on the development of the H-bomb, Bethe and Oppenheimer considered the atomic bomb much more feasible. Teller became deeply disappointed when Oppenheimer selected Bethe over him to head the Theoretical Division at Los Alamos. Tensions between Bethe and Teller grew in the summer of 1944 after Teller twice refused Bethe's request as the division director to assist in calculations associated with the atomic bomb. Oppenheimer transferred Teller out of the division, permitting him to work on the H-bomb on his own.[29]

Following the war, Teller opposed placing atomic energy under international control and continued to seek the enormous resources necessary to develop the H-bomb. Teller, recognized by his prominent eyebrows and his brooding persona, became in the 1950s the most visible of scientists who were convinced that the nation's security remained dependant upon the ability to develop and produce the most powerful weapons possible.

Many other scientists who assisted in the development of the A-bomb to counter the threat of Nazi Germany, such as German refugee and Cornell physicist Hans A. Bethe, considered the development of the H-bomb unnecessary from both a moral and military standpoint. Morally, they felt it was wrong to develop such a powerful weapon whose sole purpose could only be to target cities populated by civilians. Militarily, they felt that the Soviet Union's dispersed population offered few targets that could not be destroyed by less powerful A-bombs.

Hans Bethe, who initially opposed the accelerated development of the H-bomb, was one of the most remarkable physicists of the twentieth century. In an era of ever-increasing specialization, Bethe's expertise and path-breaking contributions spanned nearly all of the subfields of physics. Bethe, the son of a German physiologist, displayed an early talent for mathematics. Decades later in the computer age, Bethe amazed students with his rapid and accurate calculations of sophisticated problems, assisted only by his ever-present slide rule. Bethe earned in 1928 a Ph.D. in theoretical physics from the University of Munich. He produced several important articles, quickly establishing himself as one of the most talented theorists of his generation. The Nazi party's rise to power forced Bethe, who had two Jewish grandparents, to leave Germany. After spending a little over a year in England, Bethe joined the faculty at Cornell University, where he remained professionally active well into his nineties.

Following the outbreak of the Second World War, Bethe joined Rabi and others working on the development of radar at MIT. He accepted in 1943 Oppenheimer's offer to join him at Los Alamos to lead the theoretical physics division. Bethe worked intimately with Oppenheimer and remained close to him following the war. Bethe in 1945 returned to Cornell, but spent portions of each summer at Los Alamos, where he closely followed the efforts, which he initially opposed, to develop the H-bomb.

Five months after the Soviet Union detonated their first A-bomb, Truman decided in January 1950 to provide the budget and resources necessary to accelerate sharply the nation's efforts to develop the H-bomb. The debate and divisions within the scientific community intensified in the wake of this decision. Teller, worried that H-bomb opponents who worked at the Los Alamos lab would sabotage his pursuit of the H-bomb, promoted the development of a second weapons laboratory. The debate over the second laboratory resulted in the construction of Livermore Laboratory in California. Los Alamos and Livermore subsequently became rivals over several issues ranging from the design of weapons to the requirements for testing.

The Oppenheimer Panel secretly entered the debate over the H-bomb just before the first test of a thermonuclear device. Both scientists on the panel had favored international control of atomic energy. Privately, Bush beginning in 1944 unsuccessfully advocated making an approach to the Soviets for international control of the atom. Following the war, Bush and Oppenheimer served on the special committee that devised the Acheson-Lilienthal plan (which soon became the Baruch plan) for international control of atomic energy. Perhaps convinced by the failure to control the A-bomb that there was no possibility for international control once a weapon had been tested, the Oppenheimer Panel recommended approaching the Soviets on control before testing the H-bomb. At a minimum, the panel urged a delay in the test until after the presidential election of 1952 to allow the new administration to consider the matter.[30]

The panelists accepted the Truman administration's rejection of their views as loyal bureaucrats; they did not release their spurned recommendations to the public. Yet rumors of efforts by some atomic scientists, most prominently Oppenheimer, to slow the nation's H-bomb development coalesced in an article in the May 1953 issue of *Fortune* magazine.

It is now known that the anonymously authored article was crafted by Charles Murphy with the assistance of Lewis Strauss. The article accused Oppenheimer of sabotaging the H-bomb program by blocking resources, by opposing Teller's proposal for a second weapons laboratory, by opposing efforts in 1949 and 1950 to accelerate development of the H-bomb, and by discouraging scientists from working on the project after 1950.[31]

Some leading scientists were outraged at the *Fortune* article, fearing that it was part of an anti-intellectual campaign fueled by McCarthyism and accusations of atomic espionage. Eugene Rabinowitch, editor of the *Bulletin of the Atomic Scientists*, considered reprinting the entire *Fortune* article to counter its gross inaccuracies and oversimplifications. Hans Bethe, chairman of the *Bulletin's* Board of Sponsors, agreed that the article was a reflection of the climate of anti-intellectualism, but opposed reprinting the article, convinced that would simply "spread the misinformation" within the deeply flawed article.[32]

Concerns that the administration was only receiving the views of one side of the divided scientific community led to several proposals to expand the scope of science advice reaching the highest levels of government. These efforts failed until the launch of the Soviet satellite *Sputnik* in 1957 finally prompted Eisenhower to appoint a special assistant for Science and Technology and create a science advising committee. When Eisenhower took office, the Science Advisory Committee (SAC) of the Office of Defense Mobilization (ODM) served as the formal science advisory body for the administration. After the president and Congress rejected a proposal to appoint a presidential science advisor, the Truman administration in April 1951 approved the establishment of SAC. Although its charter authorized SAC to report directly to the president, it rarely did so. Instead, most reports went through the director of the ODM, Arthur Flemming, who had been the president of Ohio Wesleyan University for five years before joining in 1953 the Eisenhower administration. Despite its marginalized position within the government, SAC included some of the most prominent figures in the scientific community, including administrator James R. Killian of MIT; Robert Oppenheimer; physicist I. I. Rabi of Columbia; and James Conant, chemist and president of Harvard University.[33]

By May 1953, members of SAC, perhaps still frustrated by Truman's neglect of science advice and hopeful that Eisenhower would be more receptive, sought to assign permanently a science advisor to the NSC staff. Eisenhower's Special Assistant for National Security Affairs, Robert Cutler, an attorney who had worked for Secretary of War Henry Stimson during the Second World War, rejected the initiative. Cutler contended that the NSC staff did not need a science advisor because most problems it considered were "not technical."[34] With direct access to the president still essentially blocked in practice, scientists had to work through Flemming to present their views. This arrangement was critical in the outcome of the test-ban consideration in the NSC in 1954. Since Eisenhower directed only the Secretary of Defense, the Secretary of State, the Atomic Energy Commission Chairman, and the Director of the CIA to conduct analysis and present recommendations on the pursuit of a test ban, Flemming and SAC had no direct influence on the interagency policy deliberations. Flemming, likely influenced by SAC, urged Eisenhower in a separate memorandum to seek a test-ban agreement. His detachment from the policy-making process, however, meant that he could not prevent a unanimous recommendation against pursing a test ban from reaching the president. Flemming's support of the president's own inclination to pursue a test ban in 1954 proved too isolated to influence the outcome.[35]

Several months after Cutler rejected the assignment of a science advisor to the NSC staff, Strauss opposed an effort to broaden the range of science advice within the Department of Defense. Donald Quarles, the Assistant Secretary of Defense for Research and Development, sought to establish a Scientific and Technical Advisory Committee and appoint Oppenheimer and Bethe as members. Strauss demurred, asserting that federal statutes limited contacts between the AEC and DOD. Moreover, he emphasized that the DOD would have plenty to do outside of atomic energy, leaving that to the statutory body (AEC) established for that purpose. After preserving his control over advice on atomic energy matters, Strauss carefully endorsed the technical competence of Oppenheimer and Bethe, but implied that they would not be appropriate advisors if they were asked to consider matters of policy.[36]

Although Bethe initially opposed the accelerated development of the H-bomb, the outbreak of the Korean War convinced him to change his mind.[37] Thereafter, he assisted with the H-bomb project, but then privately sought to delay the initial test.[38] Bethe later became the head of a committee responsible for assessing evidence from Soviet atomic detonations to ascertain the probable yield and the design of the device tested.

Bethe, likely unaware that three months earlier Strauss had discouraged Quarles from expanding the physicist's advisory role, criticized not only the excessive secrecy imposed by security constraints, but also the narrow range of scientific advice reaching the government. In a private letter to Strauss, Bethe in December 1953 expressed his concern that government officials crafting defense policy rarely sought the counsel of scientists who were capable of assessing the political implications of their technical conclusions. Moreover, he criticized the security restrictions placed on his committee's findings and proposed bringing in U.S. scientists not affiliated with the U.S. weapons program to assess test debris.[39]

Strauss quickly responded by not only blocking Bethe's efforts to establish an advisory body of scientists from outside of the weapons laboratories, he also initiated an FBI investigation on Bethe. Just a month after playing a leading role in launching the Oppenheimer loyalty-security case, Strauss asked FBI Director J. Edgar Hoover to investigate Bethe. Apparently, the FBI's investigation found nothing for Strauss to use to incriminate or discredit Bethe.[40]

As several efforts failed to bring scientific expertise to the highest levels of government, those scientists who held an advisory role at the intermediate levels debated how they could best influence policy. I .I. Rabi was one of the most active scientists within the Eisenhower administration. Rabi was a member of SAC and served as the Chairman of the General Advisory Committee (GAC) of the AEC.[41] During the H-bomb debate, Rabi and another Nobel Prize–winning physicist on the GAC, Enrico Fermi, represented a compromise position. They advocated continuing thermonuclear research, but not fully developing the weapon unless atmospheric detection revealed that the Soviet Union had violated a pledge and tested a device.[42] While Rabi's position at Columbia earned him Eisenhower's confidence, his position on the H-bomb drew Strauss's suspicion.

After the *Fortune* article skewered Oppenheimer for serving as a government advisor but then openly criticizing the administration's policies, scientists became concerned about how they could express their views freely without isolating themselves within the administration. Most chose to keep their views within the private channels of the government. Frustrated that such an approach allowed popular periodicals to shape the debates about atomic energy matters, *Bulletin of the Atomic Scientists* editor Eugene Rabinowitch asked Rabi to comment on the dilemma that "the men most competent to discuss this matter [the implications of the development of thermonuclear weapons] among scientists, such as yourself, are also the most reluctant to do so because of their official connections." Rabi responded that "the fundamental difficulty is that the scientists who may know what the situation is cannot speak, because they are closely involved in matters which are highly classified or of such political significance that they dare not speak out lest they lose whatever influence for the good of the country they may have." For Rabi, presenting confidential opinions through bureaucratic channels had a better chance of influencing administration policy than direct appeals to the public.[43]

Less than a month after Rabi responded to Rabinowitch, the initiation of the Oppenheimer loyalty-security case raised deep suspicions among atomic scientists that they would face a similar fate if, in serving as government advisors, they criticized administration policies. Strauss's actions in 1953, whether driven by security concerns, personal animosity, or simply a desire to advance his strongly held views, had already severely limited the range of atomic energy advice within the Eisenhower administration. According to Strauss, he agreed to accept Eisenhower's appointment as Chairman of the AEC on the condition that Oppenheimer would not be "connected in any way" to the commission. Moreover, Strauss desperately sought to prevent Oppenheimer from meeting privately with Eisenhower in May 1953. When Oppenheimer refused to share with Strauss the purpose of the meeting, the AEC chairman had the FBI trail Oppenheimer in an attempt to ascertain his purpose for meeting with the president. Strauss then met with Eisenhower before the scheduled meeting with Oppenheimer to warn him of his suspicions of the physicist. By the end of 1953, Strauss had collaborated in several articles that attacked Oppenheimer and his views, discouraged the creation of additional scientific advisory bodies within the administration, discredited Oppenheimer and Bethe as possible administration consultants, initiated proceedings to revoke Oppenheimer's security clearance, and requested an FBI investigation on Bethe. Regardless of Strauss's motives, the effect of his actions was to widen the divisions within the atomic scientist community and limit severely the range of scientific advice reaching the highest levels of government.[44]

III

As divisions among scientists widened over the role of atomic weapons and their own ability to shape related policy, Eisenhower himself grappled with the question of how to incorporate atomic weapons into his national security strategy. Eisenhower's vigorous containment strategy that emphasized the threatened massive retaliation with nuclear weapons appears at odds with his oft-stated desire for peace. This pairing poses an interpretive challenge for historians. For some, such as Eisenhower biographer Piers Brendon, this conflicting approach indicates that Eisenhower was "a man divided against himself."[45] For others, such as Robert Bowie and Richard Immerman, Eisenhower's dependence on atomic superiority and his efforts to slow the arms race were natural and essential elements of his strategy known as the "New Look."[46]

Unlike his predecessor's administration, Eisenhower rejected the conclusion of NSC-68 that 1954 would be the "year of maximum danger." For him, the nation faced not a year of exceptional peril, but an age of enduring peril. His challenge was thus to prepare the nation's defense for waging a Cold War indefinitely. This required a strategy that not only prevented communist expansion and deterred the outbreak of a catastrophic nuclear war, but also avoided the destruction of the nation's economy in a costly arms race. In practice, this meant issuing atomic threats to China to contain communist expansion in Asia. The administration believed that the expressed willingness to use atomic weapons there enhanced its ability to deter a nuclear conflict with the Soviet Union in Europe. At the same time that it threatened China to pursue its first two objectives, the administration launched efforts directed toward the Soviet Union to reduce tensions, slow the arms race, and lower defense expenditures. In this manner, the New Look relied upon less-expensive nuclear weapons that contained communism and effectively deterred war without destroying the economy. "Massive retaliation" is the most emphasized aspect of the New Look, but the strategy included several other components designed to promote collective security and reduce the requirements for costly U.S. conventional forces; the expanded use of covert operations, the formation and maintenance of regional security pacts, and the increased use of military advisors. Thus, Eisenhower's New Look was neither entirely inflexible, nor inherently contradictory to his stated quest for peace.[47]

Although not the sole component of the New Look, massive retaliation was an essential element of Eisenhower's national security strategy. Contemporaries, participants, and historians have especially focused on atomic threats during crises in Korea and the Taiwan Strait. As these examples suggest, the administration directed the most prominent applications of atomic threats against Communist China. Eisenhower was much more cautious in handling crises in Berlin, Poland, and Hungary that directly involved Soviet forces. Moreover, the least ambiguous threats occurred before the Soviets developed greater retaliatory capability. Although there were always fears that the Soviet Union would come to the aid of China or retaliate against Japan, Eisenhower's conviction that Soviet leaders did not seek a direct conflict with the United States convinced him that he could manage the risks associated with threatening the Chinese. Whether Eisenhower was willing to follow his atomic threats against China with actions and whether those threats were decisive in the outcome of those crises are complex issues with rich scholarly dialogues that fall beyond the scope of this study. These issues do merit a brief summary and comment, however, because they illuminate Eisenhower's complex thinking on nuclear weapons and his efforts to shape his historical legacy. Eisenhower credited his publicly issued threats with promoting an armistice in Korea and preventing a broader conflict in the Taiwan Strait, yet he remained silent in other cases where he perhaps more seriously considered using atomic weapons.[48]

As his administration launched the lengthy reevaluation of its approach to waging the Cold War that resulted in the New Look, Eisenhower faced the immediate decision of how to fulfill his implied campaign pledge to break the stalemate in Korea. Eisenhower's contention in *Crusade in Europe* that he opposed the dropping of the A-bomb on Hiroshima suggests that he would reject the use of atomic weapons in Korea.[49] The documentary record, however, reveals that Eisenhower privately appeared exceptionally willing to use A-bombs in Korea. On at least two occasions Eisenhower himself suggested using "tactical" atomic bombs in Korea against the Kaesong sanctuary (a region of massed troops and equipment) and against North Korean airfields. His military advisors, primarily his West Point classmate and Chairman of the Joint Chiefs of Staff Omar N. Bradley, countered that these were not appropriate targets for A-bombs and their use risked isolating the nation's allies.[50] Eisenhower assured them that allied reaction was an important consideration, but he also agreed with John Foster Dulles that the administration should break down the taboo associated with atomic weapons and consider them as any other weapon in the nation's arsenal.[51] Most importantly, the president remained convinced that the United States could effectively use atomic weapons to destroy fortified defensive positions, even in the mountainous Korean terrain.[52] The record of these private NSC discussions between February and May 1953 clearly reveals that Eisenhower was one of the strongest advocates within his administration for using atomic weapons in Korea.[53]

Eisenhower's recollection of his attitude toward employing atomic weapons in Asia differs from the archival evidence. In a post-presidential interview by Stephen Ambrose, Eisenhower recalled his reaction to a recommendation Robert Cutler presented him in 1954 to use nuclear weapons during the siege of Dien Bien Phu in French Indochina. According to Eisenhower, he responded emphatically, lecturing Cutler, "You boys must be crazy. We can't use those awful things against Asians for the second time in less than ten years. My god."[54] Eisenhower's recollection to Ambrose presents a line of thinking at odds with Eisenhower's documented inclination to use nuclear weapons against Asians in Korea the previous year. His remembrance cultivates the image of a cautious president rejecting the belligerent counsel of his advisors, which is contrary to the record of the careful military restraining a president willing to use atomic weapons in Korea. Eisenhower's remembered negative attitude toward atomic weapons is also inconsistent with the fact that he seriously considered using atomic bombs against Asians during the Taiwan Strait crisis the following year. Overlooking these inconsistencies, some biographers have uncritically cited this remembered private conversation with Cutler as evidence of Eisenhower's reluctance to actually employ atomic weapons.[55]

In his presidential memoirs, Eisenhower does not address his inclination to use atomic weapons in Korea during the first half of 1953. Instead, he perpetuates the officially sponsored myth, likely originally fostered to justify the viability of the New Look, that threats to use atomic weapons proved decisive in convincing the Chinese to conclude an armistice that summer.[56] Eisenhower's arguments in his memoirs closely follow several comments by John Foster Dulles, most notably his 1956 interview in *Life* magazine. In it, Dulles asserted that his "unmistakable warning" to China compelled them to reach a negotiated settlement.[57] Several studies of the episode conclude that it is far from clear that the threats, which were much more discreet than Dulles suggested, proved more decisive than other factors. The death of Stalin and uprisings in Eastern Europe certainly eroded Soviet support for the war. Communist China also sought an end to the conflict to continue the recovery from its own civil war and prepare for a possible assault on Taiwan.[58] Yet Eisenhower does not address these factors in his memoirs, choosing instead to reinforce Dulles's earlier public arguments that atomic threats were decisive. Significantly, Eisenhower's assessment ten years later differs from the documentary record; the minutes of an NSC meeting on 23 July reveal that Eisenhower himself did not believe that the threats were responsible for the Chinese agreement on the armistice.[59]

Veiled nuclear threats also played an important role in the Taiwan Strait Crises. The threats took the form of discreet diplomatic exchanges, visible military deployments and exercises, and ambiguous public comments (or as James Reston of the *New York Times* termed them, "calculated imprecision"). One of the most prominent examples of the latter occurred during the Taiwan Strait crisis of 1954-1955. At the height of the crisis, a reporter asked Eisenhower at a press conference if the United States would use tactical atomic weapons in a general war in Asia. Eisenhower replied, "I can see no reason why they [tactical atomic weapons] shouldn't be used just exactly as you would a bullet or anything else . . . yes, of course they would be used."[60] When a reporter pursued the matter further a week later, Eisenhower responded with a classic performance of semantic wanderings to "confuse" his audience that has become a staple of Eisenhower revisionism.[61]

Although the purpose of Eisenhower's ambiguity is now quite clear, the advisability of his tactics remains in dispute. Was Eisenhower's handling of the Taiwan Strait crisis, as Stephen Ambrose describes it, "a tour de force . . . of deliberate ambiguity and deception" or was it a reckless and unnecessary case of brinkmanship in an area not vital to U.S. national security?[62] Eisenhower cultivated the former interpretation in his memoirs. According to Eisenhower, his administration maintained its freedom of action, kept control over a complex series of events, rejected extreme recommendations, and thread its way with "watchfulness and determination, through narrow and dangerous waters between appeasement and global war."[63] Leading Eisenhower revisionists largely concur with Eisenhower's interpretation. In their analysis, Eisenhower shrewdly issued veiled public threats that maintained his flexibility and halted the adversary without actually jeopardizing his credibility or needlessly risking a broader conflict.[64] The documentary record, however, reveals that Eisenhower's memoirs minimized how close he came to employing atomic weapons against Communist China. This evidence suggests that Eisenhower was committed to using nuclear weapons if the Chinese called his bluff. Moreover, his ambiguity came dangerously close to provoking his enemy rather than giving them sober pause.[65]

These examples illustrate the challenges of assessing Eisenhower's approach to atomic weapons. Eisenhower carefully cultivated the image that his atomic diplomacy in crises in Korea and the Taiwan Strait were measured, necessary, and successful. Eisenhower's efforts to recast his past are not exceptional. Memoirists often succumb to the natural human tendency to place their actions in the most favorable light. After the fact, Eisenhower recalled providing prescient counsel on the Bonus Army March, the A-bomb decision, and relations with the Soviet Union that appears at odds with his character, his attitudes at the time of the events, or both. The archival evidence to support Eisenhower's remembrances is weak on the first two cases, and contradictory on the third. Thus Eisenhower's self-serving recollections of his uses of atomic diplomacy are neither exceptional to memoirists, nor to Eisenhower's remembrances of other episodes.

There is one other significant explanation, in addition to his desire to construct his history, for the inconsistencies in Eisenhower's post-presidential writings and interviews on his atomic diplomacy. His remembrances reflect, consciously or not, the dramatic evolution of his thinking on nuclear weapons between 1953 and 1961. Consequently, his recollections claim remarkable prescience on matters that he simply did not possess when the events occurred. His later understanding of the consequences of nuclear warfare, his awareness of the growing Soviet nuclear arsenal and his cognizance of the implications of intercontinental ballistic missiles likely shaped the memory of his willingness in 1953 to use tactical atomic weapons. Similarly, the awareness that the crises did not escalate provides his memoirs with a sense of confidence he and other participants did not possess at the time.[66]

IV

Although Eisenhower's first year in office included atomic threats aimed at China, it concluded with his Atoms for Peace proposal that illustrates his efforts to promote peace and reduce tensions with the Soviet Union. Thoroughly briefed on the results of America's first H-bomb test that occurred just days before his election in November 1952, Eisenhower entered office horrified at the thought of nuclear warfare.[67] His fears grew throughout 1953, intensifying after he viewed a top-secret movie of that American test, then again after receiving indications that the Soviets detonated a thermonuclear device just nine months after America's first test.[68] In March 1954, Eisenhower wrote Winston Churchill that his "principal preoccupation" throughout his first year in office was to find ways to lessen the dangers presented by the appalling new methods of mass destruction.[69] In order to confront the dangers intelligently, Eisenhower agreed with the Oppenheimer Panel that the administration must adopt a policy of candor in presenting the implications of the nuclear age to the American people. For several months, his advisors struggled with a way to present this information without creating hysteria or releasing sensitive information. Despite their focused efforts, it was Eisenhower's own atomic pool idea that ultimately provided a measure of hope to balance the sober component of candor. The result was his "Atoms for Peace" speech, delivered at the United Nations on 8 December 1953. For Eisenhower, that speech provided a forum to reveal the dangers of the nuclear era, while at the same time proposing a first step to put a break on the arms race and lessen the threat of mass destruction.

The Oppenheimer Panel's recommendation for a policy of candor faced several challenges from within the administration. When Oppenheimer discussed the report with the NSC on 27 May, he assured the president that a simple disclosure of the basic facts of the arms race would not reveal any sensitive matters.[70] While this eased Eisenhower's skepticism, others criticized candor as a whole. Secretary of Defense Charles E. Wilson commented earlier that it would be foolish to unnecessarily "scare our people to death" without offering a solution. Treasury Secretary George Humphrey feared that providing such information would raise demands for increased defense spending, conflicting with the administration's effort to restore a peacetime economy upon the conclusion of the Korean conflict.[71] To avoid an overreaction, Eisenhower directed the drafting of a speech that would emphasize vigilance and sobriety, not panic.[72] Balancing a description of the staggering destructive power of the latest weapons with a message of hope proved extraordinarily difficult in practice; the administration struggled over the next several months to craft such an address.

Meanwhile, events soon reinforced the dangers of the nuclear age to Eisenhower. On 1 June, Eisenhower assembled the Cabinet, the NSC, the JCS, and the AEC Commissioners in the White House East Wing theater to view the uncut, top-secret film of the first hydrogen device detonated the previous fall. Eisenhower, who had visibly paled when he heard a description of the magnitude of the first test, was profoundly moved by the image of an entire island disappearing into the Pacific. Eisenhower directed the AEC to create a shorter, secret version to allow a wider audience to view it.[73] The president received a second jolt on 12 August when the administration received the first fragmentary evidence that the Soviets had detonated a thermonuclear device.[74] Deeply distraught, Eisenhower began to push his primary speechwriter, C. D. Jackson of Time-Life, to complete the candor speech so that he could inform the American people about the new nuclear equation. Although the president personally made revisions, the absence of a hopeful conclusion led a frustrated Eisenhower to admit on 24 August that the speech remained "far from being a finished document."[75]

As he vacationed in Colorado, removed from the daily crises of Washington, Eisenhower continued to grapple with the implications of the

Soviet test. Vacationing with the president in Colorado, Eisenhower's Special Assistant for National Security Affairs, Robert Cutler, described how the president's mind "very frequently" turned to the explosion of the thermonuclear device.[76] Lamenting the potentially devastating economic burden of a long-term arms race, Eisenhower suggested to John Foster Dulles that the Americans might owe it to a future generation to consider *initiating* a war at "the most propitious moment."[77] The following day, the president asked AEC Chairman Lewis L. Strauss for an estimation of the Soviets' capability to produce thermonuclear devices over the next two to three years.[78]

Was Eisenhower assessing the window of opportunity for a preventive war? Eisenhower never seriously considered a first strike against the Soviet Union as a viable option. He opposed preventive war because he believed that initiating a war was against the nation's traditions and that its allies would oppose it. Further, the president insisted upon first securing the approval of the Congress and of the American people, which precluded a surprise preventive strike. Finally, he did not believe that any nation could claim victory in a nuclear war that destroyed civilizations.[79]

Rather than indicating an inclination to launch an attack upon the Soviet Union, Eisenhower's private rumination of preventive war illustrates how deeply the implications of the detonation of the Soviet thermonuclear device troubled him. Clearly struggling with the realization that the destructive force of the H-bomb was now in Soviet hands, the president sought alternatives to an extended, economically crippling nuclear arms race. Rejecting preventive war, Eisenhower, in time, began to view a test-ban agreement as an essential first step toward controlling the arms race while maintaining the nation's nuclear superiority. The president in September 1953 suggested to his advisors that the United States and the Soviet Union could donate fissionable material from their nuclear stockpiles to the United Nations for peaceful uses, such as atomic power generation.[80] Convinced that the world was "racing toward catastrophe," Eisenhower believed that diverting fissionable material would slow the arms race without jeopardizing America's strategic advantage.[81]

Yet Eisenhower's advisors did not immediately recognize the advantages of his proposal. Strauss deemed Eisenhower's idea "novel" and possibly valuable for "propaganda purpose," but Strauss thought it had "doubtful value as a practical move."[82] Expressing similar reservations, Dulles developed specific criteria that he believed any initiative should meet: it should contain new proposals which should be acceptable to the Soviets "if they possess a shred of co-existential reasonableness or desire;" if the Soviets accepted, it must not seriously impair or jeopardize the Western strategic position; if rejected, it should set world opinion and blame for the arms race against the Soviet Union.[83] With Dulles's framework, the administration began to develop Eisenhower's idea into a program that would solve many problems at once. It would replace despair over the atom with hope; it did not require on-site inspection, a stumbling block in previous arms control proposals; and it would not threaten America's strategic superiority because its fissionable material stockpile was believed to be two to three times that of the Soviets.[84] Combining the sober reality of candor with a hopeful atomic pool initiative, the administration prepared a speech for Eisenhower to present before the United Nations General Assembly. Complex issues related to the atomic pool proposal and a desire to consult with the British and French at the upcoming Bermuda Conference delayed the speech until early December 1953.

Although gaining a propaganda victory was the central objective of Dulles and Strauss, Eisenhower had much broader purposes in mind.[85] At Bermuda in early December 1953, he emphasized that his proposed speech was not intended "just for the sound and fury, but would have a serious proposal to make."[86] Underscoring his seriousness, Eisenhower became increasingly involved in the enterprise, resolving internal staff objections and vigorously revising several speech drafts; he was certainly not exaggerating when he later wrote his childhood friend Swede Hazlett that he had personally spent "a tremendous amount of time" on it.[87] For several weeks after his 8 December 1953 speech, Eisenhower elaborated on his purposes for Atoms for Peace in his diary, at a press conference, and in his private correspondence. He hoped that informing the American public and the world of the general size and strength of its atomic capability would prompt them to think about the world situation to help devise means to avoid "the possible disaster of the future."[88] Moreover, Eisenhower thought that the "gradual approach" of the atomic pool proposal would bring some hope to replace the prevalent fear in the world and possibly open up additional opportunities for reducing Cold War tensions.[89] At a press conference on 16 December, he emphasized that his proposal did not automatically require inspection, eliminating an automatic reason for the Soviets to reject it.[90] He referred to this important aspect again in the letter to Hazlett. The president saw his proposal as a way to escape the impasse in negotiations to control atomic energy created by "Russian intransigence in the matter of mutual or neutral inspection of resources."[91] Most importantly, Eisenhower hoped that his initiative would "put a break" on the world's race "toward catastrophe."[92]

Much like Eisenhower and his advisors, atomic scientists supported Atoms for Peace for widely divergent reasons. Edward Teller, similar to Lewis Strauss and John Foster Dulles, was very enthusiastic about Atoms for Peace because he was convinced that the Soviets would have nothing to do with it. In his view, a Soviet rejection of Atoms for Peace would convince the world that only the strength of continued U.S. nuclear superiority would maintain the peace. Therefore, the assured Soviet rejection would spur the U.S. weapons development program.[93] Differing from Teller, Hans Bethe strongly supported the president's proposal because he hoped, like Eisenhower, that the Soviet Union would accept Atoms for Peace. Bethe and Eisenhower shared the desire that the president's proposal would result in a world organization that fostered mutual confidence and slowed the arms race.[94] Unfortunately for Eisenhower, the attitudes of Dulles and Strauss prevailed in the efforts to implement Atoms for Peace; Bethe and other scientists who shared the president's hopes for Atoms for Peace remained outside of his inner circle of advisors.

Internationally, Eisenhower's 8 December speech itself won applause in the United Nations and an overwhelmingly positive world reaction outside of the communist countries. The Soviet Union, however, stalled negotiations. By the time that the United Nations created an International Atomic Energy Agency in 1957, the arms race had accelerated to new levels beyond that agency's ability to control it. The delay was decisive and tragic. But this outcome should not obscure the great hopes that Eisenhower attached to Atoms for Peace. Far from a mere propaganda gesture, Atoms for Peace represents Eisenhower's sincere attempt to slow the arms race after his year-long struggle to grapple with the implications of the nuclear age.

The Eisenhower administration did not consider a test ban in 1953 as it developed the nation's approach to waging a Cold War indefinitely in the nuclear age. Indeed as the year ended, the AEC and DOD prepared for a test series in early 1954 that included one that remains the most powerful weapon the United States has ever tested. Despite this initial movement in the opposite direction, Eisenhower's first year in office remains essential for understanding the origins of several critical themes that shaped his administration's later approach to a test ban. Test-ban opponents within the administration quickly identified both Eisenhower's skepticism of scientists who sought to provide advice on policy and his interest in the peaceful uses of atomic energy. They used those two observations during the test-ban debate to discredit contrary science advice and promote tempting applications of "peaceful" atomic detonations that required additional testing. Finally, the administration's torturous bureaucratic struggle to transform the Oppenheimer Panel's recommendations into Atoms for Peace reveals that Eisenhower was very much alone in his commitment to seek measures to slow the arms race.

A passage frequently cited to indicate Eisenhower's early commitment to arms control is his directive to Lewis Strauss on his first day as AEC Chairman. According to Strauss, Eisenhower privately instructed him, "My chief concern and your first assignment is to find some new approach to the *disarming* of atomic energy." If this conversation transpired as Strauss recalled, it not only indicates Eisenhower's early interest in slowing the arms race, but also reveals how the president showed uncharacteristically horrible judgment in selecting the person responsible for pursuing his goals.[95] An avid cold warrior, atomic energy enthusiast, and a shrewd bureaucrat, Strauss moved in the opposite direction of this initial guidance to advocate aggressively the expansion of the nation's nuclear arsenal. Far from finding ways to slow the arms race, Strauss was one of the most powerful opponents to a test ban within the administration. As with Atoms for Peace, he supported only gestures that he considered essential for favorable propaganda that would allow him to continue to develop and test additional weapons. In this view, Strauss was not alone as it appears only Eisenhower himself believed Atoms for Peace was anything more than a propaganda gesture. If Eisenhower genuinely sought disarmament at this stage, he could not have picked a worse person to advance that goal.

Lewis Strauss took advantage of Eisenhower's suspicions of scientists to manage effectively the range of advice reaching the president. Eisenhower entered office skeptical of scientists, considering them unqualified to provide advice on matters of policy and dangerously prone to sharing the classified information of their discoveries. The fissures between atomic scientists, already deeply divided over nuclear issues, widened the following year as a result of the Oppenheimer hearing. Eisenhower was unaware of the growing divisions among scientists and, most importantly, the desires of many of them to slow the arms race. He remained convinced as late as 1957 that scientists would provide the strongest opposition to a test ban because they possessed an unyielding desire to invent without consideration of the moral implications. Skeptical, shielded, and unaware, Eisenhower remained isolated from the powerful opinions of prominent scientists who shared his desire for progress in arms control.

The *BRAVO* Shot and the Rise of the Test-Ban Debate within the International and Scientific Communities (1954-1955)

> It is quite clear that something must have happened
> that we have never experienced before, and must
> have surprised and astonished the scientists.
> —Eisenhower, Press Conference, 24 March 1954

> Before very long, the Eisenhower Administration is likely
> to have to answer a short, highly practical question: "Do
> we really need scientists, or can we just make do with
> Lewis Strauss?"
> —Joseph and Stewart Alsop, October 1954

Eisenhower's Atoms for Peace proposal raised the hopes of many for an easing of tensions and a slowing of the arms race. Three months later, the detonation of the largest thermonuclear device the United States has ever tested, code-named *BRAVO*, underscored the perils of the thermonuclear age. The spread of unprecedented amounts of radioactive ash from the horrific *BRAVO* shot in the Pacific led to increasing international pressure for the nuclear powers to cease testing. Concerned that the political fallout from the *BRAVO* test was driving the nation's allies away, Eisenhower directed his closest advisors to consider seeking a test-ban agreement with the Soviet Union. Although Eisenhower was favorably inclined to pursue a test ban, he reluctantly accepted the unanimous recommendation of his advisors against seeking a test accord. Atomic scientists, many of whom were preoccupied with the Oppenheimer loyalty-security case and lacked access to Eisenhower and his top advisors, played no role in the administration's secret consideration of a test ban.

The administration, after secretly rejecting a test cessation, focused its efforts on convincing its allies and neutral nations to support continued testing. It mounted a global public relations campaign that minimized the health hazards of testing and emphasized the necessity of tests to maintain the nation's nuclear superiority for the defense of the free world. Despite this focused effort, international opposition to testing remained particularly strong, even in such allied nations as Japan and Great Britain. Within the United Nations, the United States faced difficult challenges to its testing program from neutral nations and the Soviet Union. U.S. representatives in the United Nations narrowly averted the passage of resolutions that limited testing; it became increasingly clear that the administration's attempts to justify its test program remained unconvincing to much of the world.

As the international debate rose over the administration's test program, the American scientific community, bitterly divided by the Oppenheimer case, presented contradictory interpretations of the health hazards from radioactive fallout and the necessity of testing for the nation's security. The complex issues related to fallout and testing had confounded even the nation's top experts. With scientists themselves sharply divided, Congress and the American public tended to trust the views of the AEC that testing posed insignificant hazards compared to the risk of ceasing tests and possibly falling behind the Soviet Union.

I

The horrifying level of destruction and radioactive fallout from *BRAVO* in March 1954 led to widespread public anxiety, if not near-hysteria, in Japan and Great Britain. As a result, nuclear testing became an international political liability, launching the Eisenhower administration's first serious consideration of a test ban. While the appalling destructive force of the *BRAVO* device alone could be cause for such alarm, the public first discovered only the effects of its fallout; it was the fate of the Japanese fishermen aboard the *Lucky Dragon*, who were 80 miles from "ground zero," that aroused public anxiety.

Showered with a "snowfall" of radioactive white ash, the fishermen began to suffer from horrendous symptoms consistent with radiation exposure: burns, skin discoloration, a lowering of blood counts, and a loss of hair. Panic broke out in Japan several days after the test when the crew, with worsening symptoms of radiation exposure, returned to the ship's home harbor.[1] After this news spread to Great Britain, Prime Minister Winston Churchill sent a message to Eisenhower, informing him of the "widespread anxiety" about the H-bomb there.[2] The following day, over one hundred Laborite members of Parliament signed a motion demanding a ban on further H-bomb tests.[3] International pressure continued to rise after Prime Minister Jawaharlal Nehru of India made a public appeal, later referred to the United Nations, for a moratorium on testing H-bombs.[4]

Initial reports of the powerful *BRAVO* shot had caused considerable, albeit short-lived, concern within the United States. Eisenhower did little to calm an anxious public when he remarked at a press conference: "It is quite clear that something must have happened that we have never experienced before, and must have surprised and astonished the scientists."[5] Eisenhower's comments only fed the impression that the power of the H-bomb and resulting fallout had gotten out of control. After this initial blunder, he wisely withheld further comments until Strauss returned from the test site in the Pacific.

Upon his return, Strauss appeared at his first press conference, held jointly with the president, to discuss the tests in the Pacific. The AEC chairman carefully read from a prepared statement, which was designed to reassure the public that the test went according to plan. Strauss explained that a sudden shift in wind direction led to the regrettable spread of fallout beyond the forecasted danger area, but he emphasized that the U.S. response was rapid and that everyone exposed to fallout would suffer no lasting ill effects. He comforted consumers that the test did not cause widespread contamination of tuna or other fish.

Venturing beyond his prepared statement, Strauss stumbled. When asked how powerful the AEC could build an H-bomb, Strauss replied, large enough to destroy a large city. When pressed further, Strauss stunned the press corps with his acknowledgment that this included a city the size of metropolitan New York.[6] According to Eisenhower's press secretary, James Hagerty, the president told Strauss after the press conference, "Lewis, I wouldn't have answered that one that way . . . But other than that I thought you handled it very well." Unwittingly, Strauss's response shifted public attention from the current hazards of fallout from testing to the possible horrific consequences of nuclear warfare.[7]

Strauss's comments provoked only fleeting interest in the test issue within the United States. Thereafter, domestic public opinion was not a decisive factor in the administration's consideration in 1954 of a test ban. News of the destructive force of the *BRAVO* test and the fate of the fishermen aboard the *Lucky Dragon* only briefly raised public concerns about further testing within the United States. The *BRAVO* test established a pattern which would be repeated throughout the 1950s—sudden concern with nuclear tests, sharp debate and public discussion, and then the equally abrupt disappearance of the issue from all but scientific circles. Public attention in the spring of 1954 shifted from the *BRAVO* test to the Army-McCarthy hearing, the siege of Dien Bien Phu, and the *Brown* case before the Supreme Court.[8] A Gallup Poll in April 1954 found that 71 percent of Americans supported continued testing; concern over the health hazards of fallout from testing was limited to a small but vocal minority. Another poll in March 1955 found that only 17 percent of Americans could even correctly describe fallout.[9]

While the general public focused on other matters, only a few attentive scientists raised concerns to the administration about continued testing. Arthur Compton, a Nobel prize–winning physicist and one of the four scientists on the advisory panel that rejected in 1945 the Franck Report, urged Eisenhower in a telegram on 8 April to cancel the remaining shots in the current series. Compton feared that the U.S. tests were causing even allies to questions its motives and trustworthiness. In his view, additional shots in the Pacific could create "lasting widespread antagonisms." He urged a postponement and an effort to reach an international agreement on further tests.[10]

David Inglis, a physicist from the Argonne National Laboratory, wrote at least five letters to top officials within the administration advocating a test ban. Asserting that international stations could effectively monitor a test ban from outside of Soviet territory, Inglis argued that a ban on H-bomb tests would halt the development of more powerful offensive weapons and prevent other nations from acquiring nuclear arms. Although Dulles's atomic affairs advisor, Gerald Smith, agreed to receive Inglis's views, the physicist received no encouragement elsewhere within the administration.[11]

After these private, direct appeals failed to halt the ongoing Pacific test series in 1954, test-ban advocates within the atomic scientist community began to seek public support. Inglis, after his quiet letter-writing campaign failed, focused his efforts on promoting a test ban in commentaries in *Nation* and the *Bulletin of the Atomic Scientists*.[12] Challenges from Inglis and others provoked a vigorous response from scientists who considered continued testing essential to maintain the nation's strategic superiority. The administration's test-ban policy soon became the focus of an emotional public debate within the bitterly divided community of atomic scientists.

II

The *BRAVO* shot and resulting concern among informed scientists with the administration's test policy coincided with the Oppenheimer loyalty-security hearing, which widened the schism that had split the scientific community over the development of the H-bomb.[13] Scientists sharply divided between those supporting Oppenheimer, who many felt was being persecuted for his opposition to the H-bomb, and his accusers, led by the "father of the H-bomb," Edward Teller. With the impression widespread that Oppenheimer's opponents in the AEC and DOD were attacking him for his opinions, the case had important implications for the relationship between science and government.

Among the greatest concerns was that the case against one of the most revered atomic scientists in America would prompt scientists to depart the weapons laboratories in droves, greatly impeding progress in military research and development.[14] As the *New York Times* pointed out, about half of the country's scientists and engineers were working directly or indirectly on government projects.[15] The Oppenheimer case dominated conversations at laboratories and scientific conferences across the country. At Los Alamos, scientists lined up to read a transcript of the hearings. Yet the judgment against Oppenheimer did not provoke a widespread exodus from the AEC's laboratories as Strauss and others had feared. Instead, it inspired several prominent scientists to caution the president, Strauss, and the American people about the implications of the case for the relationship between science and government.[16]

Eisenhower's greatest concern about the case was keeping Senator Joseph McCarthy away from it. He emphasized that the administration must handle the hearing "so all of our scientists are not made out to be Reds. That goddamn McCarthy is just likely to try such a thing."[17] The administration succeeded in keeping the Oppenheimer case away from Joseph McCarthy, who was already preoccupied with his climactic hearings against the army. It failed, however, to keep the case against the prominent physicist out of the press or prevent it from alienating many atomic scientists.

Although Eisenhower clearly recognized that only negative consequences could arise from McCarthy taking the case, he failed to understand that even a closed and careful handling of the matter would have lasting implications for the relationship between government and science. With the case already under way, James Conant, whom Eisenhower had appointed as the U.S. High Commissioner to Germany, visited the president at the White House to express his deep concerns about the Oppenheimer case. Like Oppenheimer, Conant had opposed the accelerated development of the H-bomb. Conant cautioned Eisenhower of the general impression among atomic scientists that the administration was prosecuting Oppenheimer simply for his outspoken opinions on the H-bomb. Eisenhower drafted a letter to Conant later that day, assuring him that Oppenheimer's charges were not related to his opinions. The president insisted that the charges were based upon Oppenheimer's alleged actions that sought to hinder the development of the H-bomb after Truman had decided to make it a priority effort.[18]

Despite Conant's warnings, Eisenhower curiously did not appear to understand the potential implications of the case for governmental science advising. Eisenhower, after the board voted not to renew Oppenheimer's security clearance, suggested to a shocked Lewis Strauss that perhaps the administration could enlist the eminent physicist's assistance in declassified projects, such as desalination efforts. Eisenhower's belief that Oppenheimer would continue to serve the administration was remarkably at odds with the dire warnings among scientists and the media that the case had irreparably damaged the relationship between science and government.[19]

As the Oppenheimer hearing was under way, Bethe, likely unaware that Strauss had requested an investigation of him months earlier, sent a concerned telegram to the AEC commissioners. Bethe cautioned that the implication scientists drew from the Oppenheimer case was "that scientific integrity and frankness in advising the government on policy matters of a technical nature can lead to later reprisals against those whose earlier opinions have become unpopular."[20]

Strauss's reply, clearly crafted for public release, attempted to justify the decision against Oppenheimer. He then assured Bethe that the AEC did not wish "any Government servant-scientists or engineer or administrator to slant his advice or temper his professional opinion because of apprehension that such advice or opinion might be unpopular then or in the future. We certainly do not want 'yes men' in the employ of the Commission."[21] Strauss's words likely did little to comfort Bethe and ease the concerns of others that Strauss would not tolerate contrary views.

Other scientists and influential columnists raised the private concerns of Bethe and others to the attentive public. Journalists Joseph and Stewart Alsop's critical essay in the October 1954 issue of *Harper's* on the Oppenheimer hearing skewered Strauss in particular for "equating disagreement with disloyalty."[22] The Alsops blamed Oppenheimer's ordeal on the vindictive Lewis Strauss and part of an anti-science, anti-intellectual crusade waged by air force "zealots" who mistrusted Oppenheimer's opposition to their doctrine of strategic attacks using atomic weapons. Recognizing that the administration was ignoring the advice of top scientists and relying upon Lewis Strauss to provide and filter advice, one of the Alsop's columns commented, "Before very long, the Eisenhower Administration is likely to have to answer a short, highly practical question. 'Do we really need scientists, or can we just make do with Lewis Strauss?'"[23]

Vannevar Bush, president of the Carnegie Institution and one of the nation's most experienced government science advisors, wrote a lengthy article in the *New York Times Sunday Magazine* about the implications of the Oppenheimer case. Bush lamented that the Oppenheimer case had "gravely damaged" the partnership between government and science. According to Bush, scientists concluded that Oppenheimer was "being tried for his opinions." In a possible veiled reference to Strauss, Bush related the impression of scientists that the government would "exclude anyone who does not conform completely to the judgment of those who in one way or another have acquired authority."

Bush's cautionary article also included an appeal for the importance of science advising. For Bush, one of the most troubling aspects of the case was the board's admonition of scientists to be modest and restrained when they offered opinions that stepped beyond their special fields. In Bush's view, scientists possessed the depth beyond their field to provide counsel on military strategy and tactics (something in which Eisenhower in 1954 would sharply disagree). On the other hand, Bush argued that the military was beyond their depth in considering how the trends in science and its applications would change the future of warfare. Bush was already deeply troubled that the administration considered complex technical issues without the proper range of scientific advice. After the Oppenheimer matter, Bush feared that the administration had alienated itself further from powerful scientific expertise.[24]

The immediate impact of the loyalty-security case was the end of Robert Oppenheimer's government advisory role just as the test-ban debate began. As many of the nation's most prominent scientists took opposing positions on the public test-ban debate, Robert Oppenheimer remained conspicuously silent.[25] The outcome of the security hearing ensured that Oppenheimer played no role in the internal consideration of a test ban. Perhaps believing that the government persecuted him for publicly stating his views on the H-bomb, Oppenheimer offered few public comments on the nuclear test-ban debate. Early in 1955, Oppenheimer presented his private views in a memorandum of a conversation in January 1955 with a French diplomat that he provided to the State Department.

In his record of the conversation with M. Jacques Tiné, a member of the French delegation to the United Nations, Oppenheimer revealed skepticism over the purpose and possibilities of reaching a test-ban agreement and uncertainty over the hazards from testing. Oppenheimer believed that the dangers from testing alone "were perhaps not serious" and expressed optimism that improvements would reduce the hazards further. He cautioned, "there was a difference of opinion and that many contrary expressions by competent people had been made public."[26] Oppenheimer in May 1955 expressed a similar view in a rare interview with a French newspaper. Addressing the hazards of radioactive fallout, Oppenheimer commented that "there are many opinions and hypotheses but no certainty . . . Physicists don't know. Specialists in genetics don't know. Nobody knows, and we must take account of this ignorance."[27] To resolve this uncertainty and assess whether concerns over testing merited an approach to a test ban, Oppenheimer recommended to Tiné that the United Nations sponsor an international scientific study of the hazards from testing.

Although a test ban appealed to Oppenheimer as a means to decrease tensions and slow the proliferation of atomic weapons, he remained pessimistic that the nuclear powers could reach an agreement. In his view, both sides would seek to reach an advantageous position before the ban took effect, making the timing of a ban exceedingly difficult. Oppenheimer agreed that detection devices could police a ban from outside of the Soviet Union, but he doubted that this provided a firm basis for an international agreement. The physicist informed Tiné that the methods and analysis of interpreting this evidence were so secret that the United States would not agree to share its techniques with an international body. Oppenheimer thus was unconvinced that testing posed significant health hazards, unimpressed with arguments that a test ban would lead to progress on arms control, and uncertain that the nuclear powers could resolve the timing and control issues necessary to reach an accord on testing. This rare glimpse at Oppenheimer's private thoughts on the test ban contrasts sharply with the expanding public commentary from a deeply divided scientific community.[28]

Beyond this insightful indication of Oppenheimer's thoughts on the test-ban debate, the administration's handling of Oppenheimer's correspondence reveals Strauss's deep concern that Oppenheimer was seeking to ease back into his former advisory role. In Oppenheimer's letter to

Dulles on 11 January he offered to meet with State Department officials to discuss his conversation with Tiné.[29] Dulles sought Strauss's advice on how to handle this approach from Oppenheimer. The AEC chairman interpreted the letter as "a fairly transparent attempt to get the Secretary of State to send for him so that with something of a fanfare, it could be announced that he had been sent to confer with the State Department on disarmament." To counter this, Strauss suggested a reply from a mid-level bureaucrat that simply requested a memorandum of the conversation from Oppenheimer.[30] The State Department heeded Strauss's advice and Oppenheimer complied with the request of the State Department.[31]

If this was, as Strauss feared, an effort by Oppenheimer to return to government advising, Strauss effectively ended it. Oppenheimer remained outside of both private government advisory channels and the public debate over a test ban.[32] The significance of the loyalty-security case for the test-ban debate extends beyond the removal of Oppenheimer as an important actor. The case widened the schism between an already divided scientific community. In many cases, the existing divisions over the H-bomb and the Oppenheimer case simply extended to the test-ban debate. Some of Oppenheimer's strongest defenders, such as Bethe and Rabi, became staunch test-ban advocates, while the martyred physicist's most powerful detractors, Edward Teller and Ernest Lawrence, became the most visible advocates for continued testing. In the absence of conclusive scientific data on the complex issues related to nuclear testing, bitter personal rivalries from these recent policy disputes often punctuated the technical dialogue.

III

Despite the diverted attention of scientists and the waning of public anxiety about testing within the United States, the Eisenhower administration continued to face pressures from allies and neutral nations to limit or cease testing. Public opinion in Great Britain and France strongly favored a test ban. Although both governments privately feared that an international test-ban accord would prevent them from developing their own nuclear deterrent, domestic political challenges prompted them to moderate their public position on testing, straining relations with the United States. Secretary Dulles in 1954 and 1955 personally urged representatives from Great Britain and France not to alter their public positions on testing or present any international proposals that limited testing.[33]

In Japan, the slow U.S. response to the fallout from the *BRAVO* shot and the lack of sympathy with the impact of continued testing on the

health of the Japanese population and the prosperity of its fishing industry greatly strained U.S.–Japanese relations. For the Japanese, the *BRA-
VO* test also raised horrific memories of the atomic bombs dropped on
Hiroshima and Nagasaki.[34] For some Eisenhower administration officials,
the irradiated Japanese fishermen aboard the *Lucky Dragon* raised more
suspicion than sympathy. Lewis Strauss was convinced that the fishermen were Soviet agents who were covertly collecting information on
the U.S. tests while creating animosity toward continued testing. Strauss
confided to Eisenhower's press secretary, James Hagerty, "If I were the
Reds I would fill the oceans all over the world with radioactive fish. It
would be so easy to do!"[35] Although Strauss did not openly discuss his
theory of planted irradiated tuna, he did publicly blame the fishing ves-
sel for entering the AEC designated danger area, when he knew that it
had remained outside of it. Even a CIA investigation in 1954, which
concluded that the crew was not attempting to collect anything other
than fish, failed to convince Strauss.[36] As late as 1966 Strauss wrote CIA
Director Richard Helms, urging the reopening of an investigation into
the matter.[37] Strauss was certainly one of the most suspicious officials
within the administration, but he was not alone in believing that the
Soviet Union played a role in the mounting calls for a test cessation. The
FBI investigated hundreds of letters urging an end to testing that flooded
the White House after the *BRAVO* test, believing that only communist
organization could raise such widespread concern.[38]

The U.S. response to Japanese concerns over radioactive fallout and
the fears of nuclear warfare included such sensitive plans as the construction an atomic power generator in Hiroshima to convince the Japanese of the "peaceful" applications of atomic power.[39] Privately, Dulles
firmly counseled the U.S. Embassy in Japan that the importance of the
U.S. nuclear testing program "to national and world security outweighed
the concerns of the Japanese fishermen."[40] Publicly, the United States
belatedly and quietly expressed its regret for the incident and eventually
compensated the victims, but refused to discontinue the use of its Pacific
testing grounds or move their tests to areas less disruptive to the Japanese fishing industry. As an ally dependant upon the powerful United
States, the Japanese government restrained its criticism of testing, duti-
fully cracking down on extreme protests within Japan against U.S. testing.[41]

Neutral nations, such as India, felt no such inhibitions on protesting
U.S. tests in the Pacific. India's Ambassador to the United States cautioned U.S. officials that the nation's testing policy made the people of

Asia feel that the United States "did not value coloured people's lives as much as [it] did white people's."[42] India later submitted Prime Minister Nehru's proposal for a "standstill agreement" suspending nuclear tests to the United Nations for consideration.

While the United States successfully referred Nehru's proposal to the United Nations Disarmament Committee (UNDC), strictly limiting its consideration to a few nations, the Eisenhower administration could not avoid a broader debate over the legality of conducting tests in areas the United States administered under a United Nations trusteeship. Fallout from the *BRAVO* shot forced the evacuation of 236 inhabitants of the Marshall Islands, two long chains of atolls stretching east of the Pacific Proving Grounds that the United States governed under a United Nations trusteeship. Officials from the AEC initially predicted that the evacuees would be able to return safely to their home islands within a year, but the contamination proved so great on the island of Rongelap that the inhabitants could not return for over three years. The Marshallese petition to the United Nations modestly requested that the United States cease testing in the Pacific unless it was absolutely necessary. Otherwise, the petition simply sought compensation for those inhabitants evacuated, along with additional precautionary information and safeguards for future tests. India and the Soviet Union, however, moved beyond the modest Marshallese to challenge the right of the United States to test in an area that it had pledged to protect, as part of the United Nations trusteeship agreement, from ill effects. U.S. officials shrewdly argued in 1956 that its tests served the purpose of maintaining international peace and security, and thus they were consistent with its trustee responsibilities.[43]

While the United States effectively submerged Nehru's proposal in the UNDC and cleverly avoided actions in the Trusteeship Council to curtail its use of the Pacific proving grounds, it was less successful silencing Pope Pius XII. The month following the *BRAVO* test, the Pope's Easter message urged a ban on nuclear war to spare the world the hazards of radiation.[44] Although these comments addressed the consequences of fallout resulting from nuclear war, the Pope's later messages expressed concern with the hazardous effects of radiation from testing alone. The Eisenhower administration responded by sending in November 1955 Harold Stassen, whom Eisenhower had appointed as his special assistant for disarmament, to explain their position on testing to the Pope. Stassen stressed that U.S. tests were essential to maintain the peace, that they did not entail serious health hazards, and that an effective disarmament agreement must contain inspection and control measures.[45]

Stassen's presentation did not fully produce the desired results. The Pope's Christmas Eve message in 1955 urged the nuclear powers to cease testing, warning that continuing them could "cause increased density of radioactive products in the atmosphere" and generate "conditions very dangerous for many living beings."[46] The Pope acknowledged that a test cessation required inspection and control mechanisms, which comforted Stassen. Strauss, however, was deeply troubled that it was unclear if the Pope advocated a test moratorium before those mechanisms were in place to police broader disarmament measures. Dulles rejected Strauss's pleas to send an administration official to Rome to explain this essential point to "his holiness."[47]

The administration's careful approach to convince the Pope of its test policy reflected the multiple sources of criticism of its test policy. The administration at times coaxed, threatened, and even paid off its allies. Within the United Nations, the administration emphasized that its tests were essential to create a superior force that would maintain the peace at best, and defend the free world at worst. Although its arguments failed to comfort the international community, the administration succeeded in shifting discussions out of the General Assembly and into the Disarmament Commission and the Trusteeship Council, which were both dominated by nations friendly to the United States. These arguments and tactics only temporarily slowed international pressures to limit testing as the uncertainties over the hazards of testing became more apparent.

IV

The mounting criticism abroad from allies and such symbols of peace as the United Nations and the Pope compelled the Eisenhower administration to respond to mounting criticism of its testing program. The Operations Coordinating Board (OCB), an interagency organ created to coordinate the implementation of NSC decisions, identified in December 1954 international concerns over testing as a "major emerging problem."[48]

Within the United States, a vigorous debate among many of the nation's leading atomic scientists baffled the public on the complex issues related to nuclear testing. Although test-ban advocates and opponents confused the public enough with their sharply contrasting interpretations, even proponents disagreed over the primary necessity of a test ban, rendering an informed opinion on the matter for laymen even more difficult.

For some test-ban advocates, the greatest peril facing the world remained the consequences of nuclear war. In Hans Bethe's view, nuclear testing heightened tensions and increased the capacity of the nuclear powers to destroy "industrial civilization." This threat of destruction, rather than the potential genetic hazards of fallout from testing, represented the greatest danger to Bethe.[49] For him, a test ban provided an essential step toward easing tensions and slowing the nuclear arms race.

For other critics of the administration's test policy, the health hazards of radioactive fallout from testing alone provided the most pressing concern and necessitated an immediate test cessation. Yet even those most concerned with fallout differed in their emphasis on local or global fallout. For California Institute of Technology (Cal Tech) chemist Linus Pauling, the global effects of fallout from testing presented an immediate concern. For Ralph Lapp, a physicist who had worked on the Manhattan Project at Los Alamos, the local fallout from tests or a nuclear exchange posed the deepest peril and the fundamental reason for pursuing a test ban.

The administration countered these critics with the technical views of such prominent scientists as Ernest Lawrence and Edward Teller, who remained absolutely convinced of the necessity of further tests to maintain the nation's superiority over the Soviet Union. The administration embarked upon a vigorous public relations campaign to counter the test-ban advocates. The campaign emphasized that nuclear tests alone did not pose significant health hazards, that a test cessation would erode the nation's nuclear superiority and increase the likelihood of a Soviet nuclear strike, and that the U.S. testing program was essential for the defense of the free world.

The concerns of the international community and the simmering scientific debate within the United States prompted the administration to respond to the increasing concern over fallout as the AEC prepared to conduct the next test series. Unlike the test series in 1954, which was held in the Pacific, the *TEACUP* series in 1955 was to be conducted at the AEC's Nevada Proving Grounds, sixty-five miles north of Las Vegas. The AEC feared that an announcement of the forthcoming tests would stoke the memories of the *BRAVO* test unless a reassuring report of the fallout hazards from the massive shot in the Pacific the previous year preceded it. The administration considered the matter of such importance that it solicited the advice of one of the top public relations minds in the country, Coca-Cola president and former *New York Herald Tribune* executive William E. Robinson, to craft the most reassuring public statement possible.[50]

Contrary to some interpretations, Strauss, who favored an early press release to forestall a challenge to tests within the continental United States, was not responsible for delaying the issuance of a report on the human effects of radioactive fallout.[51] Instead, Dulles and the State Department feared that releasing the report before an important meeting on European defense would erode support for the European Defense Community (EDC) and the extension of the U.S. nuclear deterrent to western Europe.[52] Despite the true reasons for the delay, the timing of the report's release fostered the impression that the AEC resisted issuing the report to the public until domestic and international pressures compelled them to respond. The report appeared just after Ralph Lapp strongly criticized the delay in the *Bulletin of the Atomic Scientists* and on the same day as a British assessment of fallout.[53]

Strauss issued a statement accompanying the report that offered assurances that continental testing, involving weapons much less powerful than those tested in the Pacific, presented no serious public health hazards. Emphasizing defensive purposes, his statement asserted that additional testing was essential for gathering information for U.S. civil defense authorities to determine how to protect the American public from a Soviet nuclear attack. The report itself, entitled "The Effects of High-Yield Nuclear Detonations," downplayed genetic risks, but acknowledged that its conclusions were incomplete and that further study was necessary.[54]

Congress also responded to the growing concerns about continental testing to defend the administration's test program. The Joint Committee on Atomic Energy (JCAE) held hearings in the spring of 1955 on the matter. The committee chairman, Senator Clinton P. Anderson (D-N. Mex.), stated that the purpose of the hearings was to clear up the "public misapprehension and unwarranted concern" about the upcoming test series to be held at the Nevada test site.[55] Anderson's selection of witnesses ensured that the hearings met his purpose. Rather than subject the administration's testing program to a rigorous analysis from a representative body of scientific opinion, the JCAE only called witnesses affiliated with the AEC.

Strauss's congressional testimony falsely asserted, "so far as we are aware, no American had ever been injured as a result of these tests" within the continental United States.[56] Two other AEC witnesses testified that the possibility of harmful genetic effects resulting from these tests were "remote" and "unlikely," while a meteorologist dismissed the wild rumors that nuclear tests were responsible for the ongoing drought and the sudden increase in tornadoes. Strauss closed his testimony by reminding the committee that the tests were essential to maintain the American technological advantage over Soviet nuclear weapons. According to Strauss, the weapons tested were "essential to our national security and that of the free world; they have been and may well continue to be a deterrent to devastating war."[57] The hearings thus focused on dismissing only the most outlandish claims, while ignoring or providing one-sided testimony on issues where there were divisions among responsible scientists.

The AEC report and JCAE hearings served their immediate purpose of preventing a delay of the test series in Nevada, but they did little to forestall the growing debate about the possible hazards of testing. While Lapp's warnings initially appeared in scientific publications, more dire warnings began to seep into the popular press. Linus Pauling warned that radiation from tests could be fatal to persons whose resistance to cancer was low.[58] Geneticist Alfred H. Sturdevant, also of Cal Tech, predicted that H-bomb tests would inevitably increase birth defects, estimating in 1955 that 1,800 children born worldwide were already genetically affected.[59]

The conclusions of Pauling and Sturdevant differed sharply from those of AEC Commissioner Willard Libby. Libby was a chemist known internationally for his discovery of the ability to date ancient rocks with radioactive carbon-14, an accomplishment that led to his awarding in 1960 of the Nobel Prize in chemistry. As the lone scientist on the five-member AEC, Libby became the administration's chief spokesperson on the radiological effects of fallout. Libby asserted that the hazards of all testing thus far contributed less radiation than that of a single chest x-ray. Libby's reassuring conclusions, however, failed to convince the skeptical scientific community. A *New York Times* editorial in April 1955 drew broader public recognition to the fact that there was sharp disagreement and exaggerated claims among scientists on a number of issues related to the health hazards of radiation from testing.[60]

The recognition of conflicting assessments of the health hazards pressured the administration to sanction further study by scientists unaffiliated with the AEC. Dean Rusk, president of the Rockefeller Foundation and future secretary of state under Presidents Kennedy and Johnson, wrote Eisenhower in 1955 to offer funding for a National Academy of Sciences (NAS) study of radiological hazards.[61] The challenge, however, was that studies of the effects of atomic blasts required the examination of classified information. The ever-security-conscious Strauss thus opposed outside non-governmental studies due to fears of security leaks as well as concerns that independent scientists would present politically motivated conclusions that erred on the side of caution. For the same reasons, he opposed expanding the NAS study to include scientists from abroad, which the OCB and the State Department deemed essential for the credibility of its conclusions.[62]

By this time, the international community had grown increasingly skeptical of the AEC's reassurances. Strauss's arguments failed to block the NAS study and only briefly forestalled an international scientific inquiry on the harmful effects of radioactive fallout. The United Nations voted in December 1955 to establish an international panel of scientists to collect data on the radiological effects of testing. The UN resolution instructed the group to report annually but did not expect it to issue its conclusions until the summer of 1958. Strauss was unable to halt this action, but succeeded in securing the appointment of a sympathetic ally, Shields Warren, as the U.S. representative. Strauss knew that he could count on Warren, former director of the AEC's division of biology and medicine, to discount the harmful effects of radiation.[63]

The radioactive fallout from the massive *BRAVO* shot generated international pressures on the Eisenhower administration to reconsider its test policy. The political fallout from the *BRAVO* test soon dissipated within the United States where public attention quickly shifted to other matters, but it lingered internationally as allies and neutral nations pressured the United States to halt the spread of hazardous radioactive fallout. The administration responded with a vigorous public relations campaign that minimized the potential health hazards of radioactivity from testing and emphasized the necessity of improving the nation's nuclear arsenal to defend the free world. The administration prevented the passage of UN resolutions calling for a test cessation, blocked challenges to its ability to conduct tests in the Pacific, and delayed the formation of an independent international study into the health hazards of fallout. Yet despite the administration's energetic campaign of soothing speeches, calming congressional testimony, and reassuring scientific reports, it failed to convince an increasingly critical international community, and a vocal minority within the United States, that nuclear weapons testing was innocuous.

Many of the nation's atomic scientists, already bitterly divided over the H-bomb issue and the Oppenheimer case, took opposing sides during the public debate over testing. The scientists themselves, confronted with inconclusive data on a range of complex issues, clashed over the degree of hazards from fallout, the ability to monitor a test-ban accord, and the effect of a test moratorium on the nation's technical superiority in nuclear weapons. Even those who advocated a test ban did so for different reasons; some emphasized the hazards of radioactive fallout, while others minimized this aspect, supporting a test ban to reduce the greater threat of nuclear war. Most disturbingly, many scientists entered the public debate as impassioned advocates, rather than detached analysts. Flouting their scholarly credentials to advance their views, these scientists failed to furnish the objective advice both the public and the government expected them to provide. Scientists on both sides of the debate were guilty of exaggerating their claims.[64]

Part of the difficulty of countering exaggerated claims was the fact that assessing the hazards of radioactive fallout defied objective analysis. Scientific examination of widespread exposure to radiation was relatively new, and the genetic implications took years, if not generations, to manifest itself. The emotional issues that dwelt on much that remained unknown fostered a festering debate among scientists that served to confuse the public, the press, and, ultimately, the president.

Fallout from the *BRAVO* Shot: The Test-Ban Debate within the Eisenhower Administration (1954-1955)

> Everybody seems to think that we're skunks, saber-rattlers, and warmongers.
>
> —Eisenhower, 6 May 1954

International criticism, which increased after the *BRAVO* shot, shaped the Eisenhower administration's secret debate over testing for the following two years. The initial reaction to *BRAVO* in 1954 prompted Eisenhower to launch his administration's first serious consideration of a test ban. Although Eisenhower was initially inclined to pursue a moratorium on testing, he ultimately acceded to the unanimous recommendation of his closest advisors in 1954 to not seek a test-ban agreement with the Soviet Union.

Following Eisenhower's June 1954 decision, AEC commissioner Thomas E. Murray struggled to keep the test-ban issue alive within the administration. The following year, Eisenhower appointed a disarmament advisor, Harold E. Stassen, who looked favorably upon a test ban as an important first step toward a disarmament agreement. Murray and Stassen, however, both possessed liabilities in personality and politics that limited their effectiveness in advocating a test ban to Eisenhower and his closest advisors.

Most importantly, neither Murray nor Stassen proved to be a match for Lewis Strauss. Because Eisenhower limited his administration's deliberation of the test issue to a few close advisors, Lewis Strauss exerted a powerful influence over the private debate. Strauss carefully framed the technically complex issues related to the testing of nuclear weapons to ensure that Eisenhower's advisors reached a negative conclusion on the issue. Over the next two years, the AEC chairman effectively marginalized Murray, who favored a ban on H-bomb tests, and closely managed the scientific advice provided to Stassen. Moreover, Strauss vehemently opposed any of Stassen's proposals that offered to cease testing separate from a broader agreement on disarmament. After the NSC's rejection in June 1954 of a separate test ban, the administration linked any future limitations on testing to a comprehensive disarmament agreement.

As Stassen's disarmament review turned into a torturous bureaucratic struggle over goals and tactics, the administration's policies remained static. Meanwhile, the nation's nuclear weapons test program continued. As a result, the administration became more susceptible to international criticism of its testing and to Soviet propaganda that underscored the U.S. inflexibility on disarmament. Eisenhower's Open Skies proposal in 1955 only temporarily relieved pressures for the administration to soften its approach. By the end of 1955, even officials within the AEC and Department of Defense (DOD) recognized that the negative world opinion against testing made it politically necessary to express at least a willingness to limit, but not cease, testing.

I

As the administration struggled through talks with the Soviet Union to implement Eisenhower's Atoms for Peace proposal, the testing of megaton H-bombs continued, leading to international pressure to cease testing.[1] Although some scholars address Eisenhower's willingness to consider the test-ban issue in 1954, none examine the depth of his desire for a test ban, the strong private British support for a ban, or the delay of Prime Minister Winston Churchill's visit to the United States to accommodate a joint public announcement of a test-ban agreement.[2] A closer examination of the Eisenhower administration's secret consideration of a test ban in 1954 reveals that the opposition of Eisenhower's advisors frustrated his own desire to seek a test moratorium agreement. With the AEC and DOD arguing that any limits on testing would threaten the nation's strategic superiority, the position of Secretary of State Dulles was decisive. For Dulles, a test moratorium initially appeared to present an opportunity to reap a great propaganda victory. Yet when he realized that the United States could lose this advantage during the negotiation process, Dulles withdrew his support of an initiative, eliminating the president's only significant ally inside the administration.

Although Eisenhower also recognized possible political benefits from a moratorium, his concerns were much broader. For the president, a test moratorium presented an opportunity to ease Cold War tensions and slow the arms race. As with Atoms for Peace, none of Eisenhower's closest advisors shared his broad perspective. He, in turn, was unwilling to override their unanimous opposition to a test moratorium agreement. Despite his reluctance to decide against his advisors' recommendations, it is clear that Eisenhower was initially favorably inclined to seek a test moratorium agreement in 1954.

News of the dangerous radioactive fallout from the *BRAVO* shot prompted bitter criticism against the United States, even from such allies as Japan and Great Britain. Neutral nations also pressured the United States to halt its test program after India submitted Prime Minister Nehru's call for a cessation of H-bombs tests to the United Nations. Assessing this international reaction from Washington, Dulles complained to Strauss that the "wave of hysteria" over tests was "driving our allies away from us."[3] Believing that a test moratorium would protect America's strategic superiority and provide a great propaganda victory, Dulles suggested privately to Eisenhower that the United States could advantageously agree to Nehru's proposal. After Dulles reassured him that they could effectively monitor a moratorium from outside of the Soviet Union, the president directed Strauss to study the issue.[4]

Dulles received additional encouragement for a test moratorium from the British. In London, Dulles discussed a possible moratorium on large tests with Churchill and British Foreign Minister Anthony Eden, both of whom, according to Dulles, "spoke approvingly of the idea."[5] After returning from Great Britain, Dulles discussed the H-bomb moratorium again with the president, who was vacationing in Augusta, Georgia. Eisenhower firmly believed that the Americans should advocate a test moratorium on all further nuclear tests (H-bombs and A-bombs). The president directed the completion of the ongoing technical studies "as rapidly as possible" to allow a potential late-May test moratorium announcement.[6]

With Eisenhower's solid support, Dulles began to develop his idea into a specific proposal in talks with the British. He discussed a moratorium in great detail with Eden when they met in Geneva in early May 1954. British scientists, studying the matter, concluded that it would be feasible to verify a test moratorium on weapons over 50 kilotons (kt), the equivalent of three or four Hiroshima bombs. According to the scientists, seismic detection observatories could be located in neutral countries, such as Switzerland or Sweden, thus eliminating the contentious issue of inspection infringements on Soviet national sovereignty, which had blocked previous arms control initiatives.[7]

Supported by Eisenhower and the British, Dulles presented his proposal to the NSC on 6 May. A record of that meeting indicates that

Eisenhower and Dulles both spoke with great conviction in favor of an international test moratorium agreement, while Strauss, Wilson, and Admiral Arthur Radford, Chairman of the JCS, expressed grave concerns. Dulles emphasized Great Britain's strong support for a moratorium and reiterated that it would give the Americans a tremendous propaganda victory while freezing America's strategic superiority. Strauss, Wilson, and Radford did not question the political advantages of a moratorium, but strongly challenged Dulles's assessment that an agreement would be militarily advantageous and easily policed.

Although these issues concerned Eisenhower, he spoke "with great emphasis" on the necessity to gain some significant psychological advantage in the world. Concerned that "everybody seems to think that we're skunks, saber-rattlers, and warmongers," the president thought that a test moratorium would make "our peaceful objectives clear," placing America in a better position before the world.

Picking up on this theme, Dulles argued that even the allies were making comparisons between the American defense establishment and Hitler's military machine. He insisted that America could not continue to develop bigger bombs without regard for its influence on world opinion. When Strauss charged that the Soviets would probably cheat on any agreement, Eisenhower remarked that the prospect of nuclear warfare was now more terrifying to the American people than the memory of the long list of Soviet violations of agreements.

Perhaps feeling the strength of Eisenhower's convictions, Radford and Strauss both cautioned against making a hasty decision without further study. Strauss requested at least thirty days to evaluate the results of the ongoing *CASTLE* test series, suggesting that the evaluation might indicate that no further tests would be necessary for "perhaps a year's time." Eisenhower agreed that the complex issues merited additional study and directed the AEC, the Department of State, and the DOD to study the moratorium "as a matter of urgency" and report back to the NSC before 3 June.[8]

Curiously, the NSC directive did not request the analysis of Eisenhower's statutory science advisory body, SAC, of an issue of such scientific complexity. In fact, several members of SAC had met shortly after the *BRAVO* shot (but *before* Eisenhower secretly directed a study of a test ban) and discussed the implications of the test. For I. .I. Rabi, the detonation of a 15-megaton weapon underscored the immediacy of pursuing disarmament. In his view, an early agreement could freeze the U.S. advantage before the Soviets developed a similar capability.[9]

Rabi, who in 1957 played an essential role in convincing Eisenhower to overrule his advisors and pursue a test-ban agreement, quietly expressed a different opinion in the months that followed. Although Rabi was known for his refreshing candor behind closed doors, he was also adept at working within the channels of government. Rabi, then Chairman of the GAC, reaffirmed to Strauss in 1954 that tests were "necessary to maintain our lead and defensive posture in the field of atomic weapons." He recommended, on behalf of the General Advisory Committee (GAC), "that no arbitrary limitation should be imposed on the number of tests in any given period." It remains unclear if Rabi actually changed his views, was expressing the majority view within the GAC, or simply thought twice about challenging Strauss on the matter in the midst of the Oppenheimer hearing, which he considered an attack on the physicist's opposition to the H-bomb.[10]

Despite being left out of the official directive to study a test ban, ODM director Arthur Flemming, perhaps with the encouragement of the advisory committee's scientists, privately wrote to Eisenhower, urging him to announce a test ban without delay.[11] Although Eisenhower and Dulles shared Flemming's inclination to pursue a test ban, they agreed that a delay in announcing a test ban was necessary to coincide with Churchill's visit.[12]

With the opinions and expertise of SAC left out of the process, the advice of the AEC's scientists monopolized the technical assumptions supporting the administration's decision on a test ban. Lewis Strauss sought the opinions of Edward Teller and Norris Bradbury, director of Los Alamos, during the test-ban deliberations. Strauss cited their concerns about the difficulties of detecting low-yield weapons as part of his arguments against a test ban. Scientists thus had little influence, beyond bolstering Strauss's arguments, on the administration's consideration of a test ban in 1954. Strauss's presentation, which was entirely pessimistic, failed to mention to the NSC Bradbury's hope that "some positive approach toward international agreement will ultimately be possible."[13]

Despite the firm opposition of Strauss, Radford, and Wilson that challenged many of Dulles's initial assumptions, the prospects for a decision to pursue a test moratorium still appeared favorable in early May. When Dulles and Eisenhower discussed the matter again on 11 May, Dulles suggested that Eisenhower and Churchill could make a "spectacular" joint announcement of a test moratorium from the White House in late May. After Dulles noted that Churchill's visit was scheduled before the NSC study was due at the beginning of June, Eisenhower suggested that the British Prime Minister should come in June, rather than May. Churchill's visit was delayed until late June.[14]

Originally Eisenhower's strongest ally in favor of a moratorium, Dulles in late May began to question his initial assumptions for supporting a test moratorium. The AEC and DOD expanded on their arguments that a moratorium on high-yield weapons would not be to America's technical advantage beyond 1957 and that there were no infallible means to detect violations of a ban on high-yield tests. More importantly, Dulles began to fear that negotiating an agreement might "boomerang" in the propaganda field. Although the United States would gain an initial propaganda advantage for proposing a ban on *detectable* explosions (with the threshold set at 100 kt), he feared that this advantage could be lost if the United States were forced to reject a Soviet counterproposal that banned *all* tests. For Dulles, propaganda considerations were paramount. Once this potential advantage appeared tenuous, he began to reconsider his position on the matter.[15]

At a meeting of the NSC on 27 May, Dulles reported that the three central agencies needed more time to study the propaganda and military implications of negotiating a test moratorium agreement before presenting a recommendation to the council. He touched on his own fears of securing a propaganda advantage when negotiating a threshold agreement, then raised the AEC and DOD's technical concerns over the ability to measure accurately the size of tests within the Soviet Union.

The record of the meeting indicates Eisenhower's deep frustration with the presentation of issues opposing a test moratorium. The president stressed that it was wrong for them "merely to take a negative view of this terrible problem." He urged his advisors to find a "positive answer," something that "would require more imaginative thinking than was going on at present in this government." Eisenhower apparently spoke so forcefully that Strauss thought that the president had already made up his mind to pursue a test moratorium agreement, but he calmed Strauss's fears, indicating that he had no intention of "making an impulsive decision on so grave a matter." Yet, Eisenhower lamented that they "were now pursuing a course which had no future for us." For Eisenhower, a test moratorium meant much more than a mere propaganda victory; it presented an opportunity to slow the economically crippling nuclear arms race and reduce the threat of catastrophic warfare.[16]

Despite Eisenhower's forceful appeal for a positive solution, Dulles completed his decisive shift toward the AEC and DOD positions on testing, eliminating the support of the president's only significant ally in the bureaucratic struggle. At the NSC meeting on 23 June, Dulles recommended against a moratorium. He reported that the three-man "committee" of himself, Strauss, and Wilson had "virtually been forced" to a unanimous negative recommendation. He asserted that the conclusions "illustrated the power of reason against the power of will, since all members of the committee had desired to reach a different conclusion but could not succeed in so doing." Yet he was certainly speaking only for himself; Wilson and Strauss never wavered in their opposition to a limitation on testing. Dulles's withdrawal of support was decisive; Eisenhower was unwilling to override the unanimous recommendation of his advisors. Deeply disappointed, the president decided "at this time" not to seek a separate test moratorium agreement.[17]

Two days later, Eisenhower and Dulles discussed the matter with Churchill and Anthony Eden. According to a record of the conversation, there was "general agreement" that it would be unwise to agree to a moratorium on H-bomb testing in light of the difficulties in detecting and determining the size of any explosion. Ironically, Churchill's visit, initially delayed to accommodate a "spectacular" joint announcement on a test moratorium, marked the end of the administration's first serious consideration of limiting nuclear weapon experiments. In fact, Churchill's visit signaled not a freeze in nuclear weapons development, but proliferation. During the same visit, Churchill informed Eisenhower that he had decided to move forward with the British development of their own H-bomb.[18]

Initially favorably inclined to seek a test moratorium in 1954, Eisenhower had ultimately yielded to the unanimous opposition of his advisors. Although united in opposition, his advisors opposed a test moratorium for different reasons. For Dulles, propaganda considerations were central. For Strauss, Radford, and Wilson, technical matters were paramount; they considered a test moratorium unenforceable and were thus concerned that a moratorium would erode the United States' strategic superiority. For the president, his reliance on his advisors and his unwillingness to carve his own path was decisive. Eisenhower had an inclination, but not an answer to the testing dilemma. Confronted with the opposition of his advisors, a series of complex technical issues, and a range of crises elsewhere, the president was unable to transform this central anxiety about testing into a central issue of his presidency in 1954. With his range of scientific counsel strictly limited, he had yielded, albeit reluctantly, to the counsel of his top advisors and to the weight of the objections they had presented.[19]

II

Much to Lewis Strauss's chagrin, the test-ban issue within the administration did not die with Eisenhower's decision in June not to pursue a moratorium on testing. Strauss, so successful in filtering the scientific opinions that reached the president, was unable to prevent his greatest personal and political rival within the AEC from periodically advancing his case for a test ban directly to the president. AEC commissioner Thomas E. Murray was in 1954 the strongest advocate for a ban on H-bomb tests among top administration officials. Murray, an industrial engineer who ran New York City's subway system during World War II, became deeply interested in the peaceful uses of atomic power. Appointed as a commissioner in 1950, Murray by the end of 1954 was the sole remaining Democrat and Truman appointee on the commission. Murray and Strauss clashed over issues ranging from atomic power contracts to nuclear testing. Their quarrels over substantive issues developed deep personal animosities that resulted in petty bickering over trivial issues and accusations of dishonesty. Woodford B. McCool, the secretary of the commission, occasionally cleared the AEC conference room of all staff members to allow Murray and Strauss to conduct their heated verbal exchanges in private.[20]

Murray especially infuriated Strauss by appealing directly to the president to overturn one of Strauss's decisions. In early January, 1954, Murray wrote directly to Eisenhower, asking him to override a majority vote by the commission not to allow United Nations observers at the upcoming nuclear tests. Eisenhower referred the proposal to Strauss for a draft reply. Strauss's response, appropriately characterized by Sherman Adams's secretary as "awfully strong," castigated Murray for taking the privilege of appealing directly to the president against a majority decision of the AEC, "particularly since the majority included the Chairman of the Commission." Although the brusque reply was never sent to Murray, it illustrates Strauss's efforts to prevent contrary views from reaching the president.[21]

Strauss must have been deeply angered when Murray sent another suggestion directly to the president a month later. In February 1954, the month before the *BRAVO* shot that launched international efforts toward a test ban, Murray proposed an effort to negotiate an agreement to limit testing as an extension of Atoms for Peace. Murray argued that since large yield detonations were easily detectable, the "self policing" agreement would not infringe on Soviet sovereignty. This feature appealed to Eisenhower, who identified during deliberations on his Atoms for Peace proposal Soviet intransigence on inspection provisions within their territory as the primary reason for failing to reach previous disarmament agreements. In Murray's view, a ban on H-bomb tests could decrease world tension and slow, or even halt, the development of nuclear weapons, thus freezing the U.S. superiority.[22]

Again, Eisenhower asked Strauss to draft a response to Murray. Strauss's draft rejected Murray's argument that tests were easily detectable. The pessimistic reply simply informed Murray that the president would discuss the subject with Dulles and Strauss. Strauss's curt reply only temporarily delayed a consideration of the issues Murray raised; allied and international opinion after the *BRAVO* shot, rather than the views of a maverick commissioner, initiated a thorough examination of a test ban. During that deliberation, Strauss kept Eisenhower's directive to study a test ban secret from the other commissioners for over a month. Furious that Strauss did not inform him that the issues he originally raised were receiving a thorough examination without his input, Murray belatedly submitted his separate views to the NSC. His minority arguments did nothing to sway the minds of those firmly opposed to a test ban in the June 1954 deliberations.[23]

After Murray's direct appeals to Eisenhower drew the ire of Lewis Strauss, the commissioner attempted to press his test ban views upon John Foster Dulles. Murray and Dulles were personal friends who served together on the board of trustees of a New York bank.[24] Despite their friendship, Dulles, ever concerned with bureaucratic jurisdiction and proper procedure, insisted that Murray first inform Strauss of his visit. Although this caused Murray to become "very angry," he complied and met with Dulles five days later.[25] In a five-minute conversation on 14 December 1954, Murray presented his familiar arguments that the United States could easily monitor a ban on the H-bomb from outside of the Soviet Union and that a ban would freeze the U.S. advantage. Dulles, preparing for another engagement, simply thanked the commissioner for his ideas.[26] There is no evidence that suggests Murray's presentation altered Dulles's views on a test ban. The following week, Dulles reiterated his acceptance of Strauss's assessment that a ban was technically unfeasible.[27]

Rebuffed by Dulles, Murray in March 1955 again appealed directly to Eisenhower. The AEC commissioner expanded his arguments that remained based on his central assumption that the United States was currently "far ahead" of the U.S.S.R. in nuclear weapons technology. In

Murray's view, a U.S. proposal for a moratorium on tests over 100 kt would extend the period that the United States maintained its superiority, slow proliferation, serve as a first step toward disarmament, and reap a tremendous propaganda victory whether the Soviet Union accepted it or not.[28] Although Eisenhower expressed an interest in Murray's recommendation, Strauss effectively countered his technical assumptions with Eisenhower and the interagency workgroup that he directed to study the proposal.

Eisenhower instructed his national security advisor, Robert Cutler, to have Murray's proposal "thoroughly studied."[29] Two days later, Eisenhower had a rare opportunity to discuss the matter with scientists beyond Strauss's orbit of AEC-affiliated test advocates. The scientists briefed Eisenhower on the conclusions of the Technological Capabilities Panel (known as the Killian Committee after its chairman, MIT president James R. Killian, Jr.), an ad hoc group of scientists and engineers from government, industry, and universities tasked with assessing how to use advances in science and technology to minimize the threat of surprise attack. After receiving the committee's report, Eisenhower asked several probing questions of the scientists that revealed his deep interest in Murray's test proposal and his solid understanding of the assumptions underlining the AEC commissioner's conclusions. Eisenhower asked whether a moratorium on tests over 100 kt would freeze the U.S. technical advantage. James Fisk from Bell Laboratories challenged the assumption that the United States was well ahead of the Soviet Union. In his view, more U.S. tests were essential to "tailor nuclear weapons to a variety of military needs." Others challenged Eisenhower's suggestion that tests were easily detectable.[30]

With Murray's central assumptions refuted, Eisenhower moved on to thank the scientists for their advisory efforts and suggested that scientists serve on a continuing advisory panel. Significantly, the purpose Eisenhower envisioned was not to provide technical advice on policy, but to consider what technical information on nuclear weapons the administration could release to the public. Thus this rare meeting with scientists did not prompt Eisenhower to expand immediately the scope of presidential science advising or seek additional technical counsel on the test-ban issue. Instead, it confined the scientists to provide advice on Eisenhower's previous policy of candor.[31]

Failing to recognize this distinction, Eisenhower's neglected body of scientific expertise, SAC, attempted to use the president's favorable response to the Killian Committee's report to expand its advisory role.

Perhaps disappointed in its limited role and eager to present favorable views on a nuclear testing, SAC offered to study and present conclusions on a test ban.[32] SAC extended its offer just after Eisenhower appointed Harold Stassen as his disarmament advisor. Rather than consulting with SAC, Stassen relied instead upon Lewis Strauss and physicist Ernest O. Lawrence, a longtime political ally of Strauss's since the late 1930s, to provide him expertise on nuclear matters.[33] Thus, SAC's effort to expand Eisenhower's range of science advice failed in the short run. Two years later, however, Eisenhower appointed Killian as his first special assistant for science and technology and entrusted him with reorganizing the presidential science advisory system. Both developments had critical implications for providing Eisenhower the confidence to pursue his inclination to seek a test ban.

As the science advisory committee sought to expand its role, Strauss moved to impress upon Eisenhower the need to prevent any limitations on testing. Alarmed by Eisenhower's close reading of Murray's proposal and the president's suggestion that he was considering broadening his exposure to technical counsel beyond AEC scientists, Strauss met with the president the Monday following the Killian Committee's briefing. Strauss strongly refuted each of Murray's technical assumptions, arguing that continued testing above 100 kt was essential to develop warheads for missiles, that there were great difficulties detecting the yield of tests, that a moratorium would "imply some admission of fault" or some recognition that testing of large yield weapons was "reprehensible," and that a proposal for a ban on large yield tests would only increase pressures for a ban on all tests or perhaps even all nuclear weapons themselves. Strauss feared falling into "an international political trap" that would erode the principle of linking nuclear weapons to an inspected agreement on general disarmament. Strauss and Goodpaster's memoranda of this conversation reveal little about Eisenhower's response to Strauss's arguments beyond recording the president's understanding from Murray's proposal that a moratorium would be to the "relative advantage" of the United States.[34]

The scientists' replies to his questions in the NSC meeting and Strauss's private intervention appear to have temporarily convinced Eisenhower against pursuing a ban. Although administration officials did assess Murray's proposal as the president directed, an ad hoc panel of representatives from each agency, rather than the heads of those agencies as in 1954, conducted the analysis. The interagency working group, consisting of representatives from the FCDA, CIA, AEC, NSC Staff, and the Departments of State and Defense, met only once, in March 1955, to consider the subject. As in 1954, the administration did not consult the Science Advisory Committee as part of its consideration of a test ban. Of the participating agencies, only the State Department representative, Dulles's atomic affairs advisor Gerald Smith, recommended supporting a test moratorium. Smith made it clear, however, that his support was contingent upon the validity of Murray's technical assumptions. The AEC and DOD opined that they were not, ensuring a unanimously negative reply to Murray's proposal.[35] After the NSC spurned another of Murray's personal proposals, the commissioner began to expound his views to Congress and the public, presenting embarrassing conclusions that greatly complicated the administration's efforts to manage the information related to the test-ban debate.

III

With the exception of the brief considerations of a separate test-ban initiative in 1954 and 1955, the administration linked the question of limiting tests to its comprehensive disarmament policy, the subject of a torturous bureaucratic review. From the time that the NSC ordered a review of disarmament in September 1953, the participating agencies (the AEC, CIA, DOD, and Department of State) struggled to reach an understanding on even the broad issues.[36] As a result, Eisenhower in February 1955 decided to appoint a talented individual to focus solely on developing a disarmament policy. After requesting nominations from key agencies within the NSC, Eisenhower shocked his advisors when he selected an individual that none of them had recommended. Instead, he appointed Harold Stassen in March 1955 to a cabinet-level position as his special assistant in charge of disarmament. The president instructed Stassen to complete the disarmament policy review and to address arms control issues on a full-time basis.[37]

Stassen, a politically ambitious Republican, received the nickname "boy governor" for being the youngest elected governor of Minnesota. His failed bid in 1948 for the party's presidential nomination was only the first of several runs for the presidency. Stassen, who was president of Penn while Eisenhower was the president of Columbia, carried a loyal following among young Republicans and delivered critical delegates to Eisenhower during the 1952 Republican National Convention. As a reward, Eisenhower placed him in charge of the administration's foreign aid program.

Eisenhower's appointment of Stassen reflected the president's realization that only an aggressive advocate for disarmament could broker the consensus he desired among his advisors, most of whom were deeply pessimistic, if not hostile, to any disarmament negotiations. Known for his keen judgment in placing the right personalities in the appropriate positions, Eisenhower erred miserably in this case. He failed to foresee that Stassen's overweening ambition would quickly isolate him within the administration rather than forge the consensus that he desired.

Stassen clashed almost immediately with John Foster Dulles over policy and procedural issues. The president's new disarmament advisor enthusiastically promoted the title "Secretary of Peace" that the press had coined. This drew the immediate ire of Dulles, who jealously guarded his jurisdiction over foreign policy and despised the insinuation that his foreign service officers in the State Department were not committed to seeking peace.[38] Stassen subsequently infuriated many other administration officials for his efforts to remove Nixon from the 1956 Republican ticket and his violation of diplomatic protocol in negotiations with the Soviet Union the following year. The fact that Eisenhower appointed Stassen as his disarmament advisor and retained him for three years, in spite of the persistent efforts of John Foster Dulles and Sherman Adams to remove him from the administration, illustrates the president's strong dedication to the pursuit of disarmament.

One of Stassen's first tasks was to meet with the top officials in each key agency to receive their views on disarmament. Stassen's meeting with AEC officials in June provided him a first-hand impression of the powerful views of Strauss and Libby and the isolation of Murray. Murray immediately presented his now familiar arguments in favor of a test ban; it would freeze the U.S. lead (but stressed that "time was essential") and did not require intrusive inspection mechanisms on Soviet soil. While Libby agreed that the United States was "far ahead" of the Soviets in nuclear technology, he disagreed that a moratorium would freeze the U.S. lead. In his view, the Soviets would cheat during any agreement, and thus a moratorium would allow them to catch up more quickly.

Differing from the two commissioners, Strauss cautioned that the United States was not as far ahead. He forcefully pointed out that Murray's views "were not shared by the Commission, by State, or by Defense." Although Stassen became a leading advocate for a separate test ban within the administration two years later, the predominant views of Strauss in 1955 swayed him initially. Stassen assured the AEC chairman that his current policy envisioned a test-ban agreement only as part of a comprehensive disarmament agreement and that it would go into effect only after "inspectors were in place."[39]

Recognizing that one of the most contentious issues in previous disarmament discussions with the Soviet Union was that of inspection, Stassen established eight task forces to consider requirements and methods of effective international inspection and control. Stassen selected Ernest O. Lawrence, a strong advocate of continued testing, to head his Task Force on Nuclear Inspection.[40]

Ernest Lawrence, the son of Norwegian immigrants who became South Dakota educators, earned in 1925 his Ph.D. in physics from Yale University. Three years later, Lawrence accepted a position at the University of California, where he soon after became the youngest full professor on the faculty. A tireless researcher and a master fund-raiser, Lawrence adeptly solicited funds from industrialists, financiers, and foundations to establish the Radiation Laboratory (known as the "Rad Lab") at Berkeley. Lawrence, who served as the laboratory director, drew scores of talented young physicists to Berkeley to participate in the group approach to research in physics. Lawrence developed the cyclotron, an invention that inaugurated a new era in big-machine physics and earned him in 1939 the Nobel Prize. Lawrence, supported by the financial contributions of leaders in business such as Lewis Strauss and by the intellect of talented theoretical physicists such as Robert Oppenheimer, transformed Berkeley into a center of nuclear research.[41]

During World War II, Lawrence's Rad Lab contributed to the successful development of the atomic bomb by developing techniques to separate uranium. Following the war, Lawrence championed expanding the nation's atomic arsenal and fully supported the accelerated development of the H-bomb, which he believed suffered from delays and missteps caused by the leadership at Los Alamos. Along with Edward Teller, Lawrence successfully lobbied the government to establish in 1952 a radiation laboratory in Livermore, California, that would be devoted to research on the H-bomb. The lab was eventual renamed the Lawrence Livermore Laboratory in honor of one of its most powerful advocates.

Lewis Strauss, who had eagerly supported Teller and Lawrence's campaign to open the Livermore lab, volunteered McKay Donkin to be the AEC's liaison to Lawrence's Task Force on Nuclear Inspection. Donkin, who delighted in uncovering derogatory information on Oppenheimer for Strauss, essentially served as Strauss's spy on the inspection panel. Strauss also packed the panel with those he believed shared his aversion to any limitations on testing. Eight scientists from Livermore, including

Edward Teller, comprised a powerful majority on Lawrence's original twelve-member panel.[42]

As the number of panelists grew to twenty-one, however, Strauss became alarmed that even Lawrence would embrace Stassen's disarmament objectives and propose a plausible inspection system that could threaten his test program. Strauss drafted a strongly worded letter to Lawrence attempting to shape his work on the nuclear inspection task force. Although Strauss admitted that his letter constituted an "indiscretion," he cautioned Lawrence that he was "uneasy" about the physicist's assignment to design an effective nuclear inspection system. Strauss feared that the public would expect that an eminent scientist such as Lawrence, like a magician pulling a "rabbit out of the hat," could develop a workable and foolproof inspection system for nuclear disarmament "whether you wish it or not." He warned that the public hope for disarmament was so great that they would overlook any reservations Lawrence issued about the search for "a foolproof, all-embracing method."[43]

Strauss's letter proved unnecessary. At a meeting of the panelists in Stassen's study, Lawrence and Teller "protested strongly against any proposal which would attempt to limit future scientific advances." Lawrence's task force concluded that the Soviet Union could and would clandestinely test during a moratorium, resulting in the loss of U.S. superiority in nuclear weapons technology. Based upon these fears, the inspection system that the panel prepared included over 40,000 inspectors on Soviet soil. Some administration officials recognized that the inspection requirements to police nuclear disarmament were unrealistic. Although a State Department representative criticized the task force's "exaggerated idea" of what constituted a reasonable verification of a test-ban agreement, the views of the AEC scientists faced no technically competent challenges.[44]

Stassen's rigorous analysis of inspection and control systems sought to prepare background studies to probe recent shifts in Soviet disarmament policy. The Soviet Union achieved a propaganda victory in May 1955 with a proposal that accepted for the first time the presence of an international arms control organ within its territory at key ports, railroad junctions, and airdromes. James J. Wadsworth, deputy head of the U.S. Delegation to the UN Disarmament Commission negotiations in London, quickly realized that the Soviet proposal included "tremendous concessions" that risked "exposing [a] lack of U.S. policy" on several of the issues. Deeply concerned that recent instructions from Washington indicated that he could expect no decisions on substantive issues in the near future, Wadsworth urged the administration to "quickly take a position" on disarmament issues.[45]

The Eisenhower administration, drawing upon experiences in Korea with such fixed inspection sites, rejected the Soviet proposal's detection mechanism as insufficient. Rebuffing the Soviet proposal, however, placed the administration on the defensive on the propaganda front. Divisions between the key agencies on the multiple aspects of Stassen's comprehensive disarmament review remained so deep that agreement on a comprehensive proposal was nowhere in sight. The NSC had not directed Stassen to design an effective, reciprocally acceptable inspection system until the end of June, a full month after the Soviet proposal. Stassen did not expect his newly created inspection task forces to complete their work until October.

Unable to wait this long, Eisenhower countered the Soviet concessions with a partial measure, the Open Skies proposal in July 1955 at the Geneva Summit. The proposal combined an exchange of "blueprints" of each nation's military installations with the authorization to conduct aerial inspections. For Eisenhower, the purpose of his proposal was to reduce the possibility of a surprise attack, break the deadlock in on-site inspections, and "create mutual confidence" that would perhaps lead to broader arms control measures.[46]

Although Eisenhower privately acknowledged that Open Skies provided the United States with distinct advantages, he presented it as a compromise measure that responded to concerns of both nations. Countering the administration's rejection of fixed sites, Open Skies called for aerial inspection across the entire country. Responding to Soviet concerns about unleashing international observers throughout its country, Open Skies limited the ground presence of the international control organ within each country to the air facilities necessary to carry out the flights. In a revealing gesture that indicated who was rising to the top of the post-Stalin power struggle, Soviet First Secretary Nikita Khrushchev expressed his immediate skepticism of Open Skies as an intelligence ploy. His rejection of Eisenhower's proposal signaled the continued Soviet reluctance to allow the minimum inspection provisions within its territory that the Eisenhower administration deemed fundamental to any arms control accord. With the two sides deadlocked over the inspection issue, test-ban advocates such as Murray and Inglis continued to assert a powerful argument for an agreement to limit tests that would break this impasse; tests of large nuclear weapons could be detected from international monitoring stations *outside* of the United States and the Soviet Union.[47]

As 1955 came to a close, the rejection of Open Skies, the Soviet proposal for a separate test ban, and the continued stalemate in the administration's disarmament review led Dulles, Strauss, and Stassen to each recognize the importance of revising its test policy. Frustrated by the lack of response to his proposals within the administration, Murray in November publicly proposed a test ban. Two weeks after Murray's comments, the Soviet Union, after completing its own extensive test series, announced its willingness to ban further testing "if the other powers possessing such weapons agree to do the same." Although the Soviet proposal offered no inspection provisions, the suggestion of a test moratorium separate from a ban on all nuclear weapons represented a shift in Soviet policy.[48]

The administration began to feel pressure from the press to respond. A *Washington Post* editorial, reaffirming an idea it "ardently advocated" in February, urged the administration to explore the Soviet offer "with genuine interest and good will."[49] When asked about the Soviet proposal in a press conference, Dulles calmly stated that a test ban was a complex issue with "a great many highly technical elements." He insisted that a test ban "has been long considered" within the administration but despite their best efforts officials had failed to find a mutually acceptable "formula" to reach an agreement.[50] Privately, Dulles expressed his frustration to Stassen that the "period of grace is coming to and end." The United States could no longer defer, "without detriment to its international stature," discussions on disarmament. Dulles even asked Strauss if, due to debate in the United Nations over testing, the United States could delay an announcement of its upcoming test series in the Pacific.[51]

Strauss became increasingly concerned with the intensification of the political and propaganda campaign to limit testing. Troubled "by the fact that a number of our own people are falling for the bait," he dictated in December 1955 a long memorandum for Dulles and Eisenhower. Strauss cautioned that the Soviet proposal to cease testing was "a coldly calculated maneuver to overcome our nuclear weapons superiority, which now stands as the principle deterrent to aggressions by the Communists aimed at our subjugation and their domination of the world." Strauss concluded with his firm recommendation that the U.S. response to proposals for a test moratorium "should be one of aggressive opposition" except as part of a final phase of a comprehensive disarmament program.[52]

With domestic and international pressures mounting for a reconsideration of a test ban, the administration began to discover just how divided the scientific community had become on the matter. Noting the "increased agitation" on testing, Stassen asserted that they must give the administration's test policy further consideration.[53] But despite the mounting pressures, Stassen concluded less than two weeks later that the administration must postpone a decision on the test policy due to AEC and DOD objections and the fact that "the scientists were divided considerably" on whether a test ban would be to the nation's advantage.[54]

By early 1956, officials within the State Department cautioned Dulles that the administration's policy on testing, inflexible and outdated, was isolating the nation from the rest of the world. They requested an urgent reexamination of the administration's test-ban policy.[55] According to Dulles, he and Eisenhower had "a long discussion on disarmament and the difficulty of our present position."[56] Eisenhower was certainly aware of the mounting pressures, though unlikely aware of the bitter divisions among scientists on the issue.

The Eisenhower administration's first serious consideration of a test ban, which followed the massive *BRAVO* shot in 1954, highlighted two powerful themes that influenced the administration's approach to the test issue for the following two years. First, Eisenhower expressed a great deal of interest in seeking a test ban, but he refused to overrule the opposition of his advisors. Second, Lewis Strauss deftly controlled the scientific conclusions that supported the administration's rejection of a ban.

Although favorably inclined to pursue a test-ban agreement with the Soviet Union, Eisenhower ultimately yielded to the counsel of his closest advisors. Outside of crises, Eisenhower preferred to support the consensus of his advisors, even when their conclusions clashed with his instincts. Eisenhower lamented toward the close of his presidency that he had acceded to the unanimous advice of his subordinates in authorizing additional U-2 flights rather than trusting his intuition and disapproving them.[57] The situation in 1954 was analogous. Eisenhower possessed strong instincts but lacked technical answers to chart his own course on the test ban.

While Eisenhower's decision had important implications for understanding his leadership style, it also exposed his dependence upon scientific advice on such complex issues. Eisenhower was devoid of supporting scientific conclusions to give him the confidence to overrule his advisors. Concerned about security breaches, Eisenhower confined the discussions on the test ban to a few close advisors. Significantly, this allowed Lewis Strauss to manage closely the scientific counsel provided on such a technically complex issue. Strauss effectively marginalized Thomas Murray, one of the strongest test-ban advocates within the administration, and successfully redirected the efforts of Harold Stassen, who increasingly looked toward a test ban as one way to break the impasse over disarmament.

Strauss's control over science advice in 1956 slowly began to break down as Eisenhower's frustrations with the international political implications of his administration's test policy grew. Eisenhower in mid-1956 received some rare scientific advice, supporting a test ban, from beyond Strauss's core of test advocates. As a result, he began to move his administration closer to pursuing a test ban. With domestic and international pressures mounting, the administration divided, and scientific opinion split, the administration in 1956 faced the challenge of a presidential election campaign, in which the nation's test-ban policy became a surprisingly salient issue.

The Election of 1956:
A Moratorium on Candor

> It [a system to detect nuclear tests] is in fact much too
> complex for me to understand. I am not a scientist
> or engineer. I have never studied in that field, and the
> whole thing is very much a mystery to me.
> —John Foster Dulles,
> Press Conference, 24 January 1956

Democratic Presidential candidate Adlai E. Stevenson made a ban on
H-bomb tests one of the central themes of the 1956 campaign for president. While Eisenhower deplored the injection of such a complex issue
of national security policy into a political campaign and attempted to
avoid discussing the issue in public, administration spokespersons and
Republican Party leaders bitterly attacked Stevenson's proposal as naive
and dangerous. As the election of 1956 neared, various rumors began
to circulate that President Eisenhower had reversed an earlier decision
either to halt testing or seek a test-ban agreement after Stevenson made
the test ban one of his major campaign positions.

In fact, there was a significant gap between the public presentation of
the issue and the private position of Eisenhower. Outside of Eisenhower's inner circle of advisors, few people could possibly have known that
Eisenhower himself was favorably inclined to seek a test ban in 1954,
antedating Stevenson's proposal by two years. Paradoxically, several
journalists and Democrats charged in 1956 that Eisenhower stood in the
way of a unanimous administration recommendation to seek a test ban.
Significantly, the historical record now shows that Eisenhower himself
was actually inclined to seek a test ban in 1954 and 1956, but faced the
near unanimous opposition of his advisors. Indeed, it was Eisenhower
himself who directed his advisors during the campaign to find an acceptable formula to limit testing that resolved complex issues involving
inspection and detection.

The Eisenhower administration responded to Stevenson's proposal by manipulating public understanding of the test issue to isolate the Democratic challenger and to conceal Eisenhower's own sincere desire to limit nuclear tests. These extensive measures had domestic and international political purposes. At first, the desire to maintain a favorable international negotiating position on a test ban motivated the administration's efforts; Eisenhower and his advisors feared that Stevenson's initial proposal would foster international pressure for a *unilateral* test ban that would preclude a *multilateral* agreement with inspection provisions that Eisenhower deemed fundamental. Yet as Stevenson's ever changing public test-ban proposals neared the conditions of Eisenhower's secret framework, domestic political motives predominated. Confronted with accusations that Eisenhower had issued a secret directive to formulate a test-ban proposal during the campaign, administration officials publicly lied to avoid an embarrassing domestic political revelation on the eve of the election. This episode reveals that the administration, initially dedicated to a policy of candor toward the American people on nuclear matters, ended its first term with an extensive campaign of deception.[1]

I

As the administration continued to struggle during the first half of 1956 to develop a comprehensive disarmament policy, international opposition to nuclear testing increased. With no new proposal immediately forthcoming, administration officials sought new methods to repackage its stale justifications for continued testing and detract attention from U.S. nuclear detonations in the Pacific. In Great Britain, public opinion remained heavily in favor of limiting testing, pressuring Prime Minister Anthony Eden to declare publicly his commitment to find a means to limit tests. Privately, the British government opposed any such proposals that could challenge its plans to test Britain's first H-bomb in the spring of 1957. Although some studies argue that the British began to shift away in 1956 from the U.S. position on testing, the record suggests that the British, with no intention to immediately alter their policy, carefully crafted their statements to defang domestic criticism.[2] Eden's government, privately confident that the Soviet Union would not agree to any limitations on testing, publicly announced a willingness to negotiate limits on testing though they privately did not expect or even desire to reach an agreement.[3]

During Eden's visit to Washington in January and February 1956, British officials proposed announcing a joint U.S.-U.K. study of the fea-

sibility of limiting nuclear tests. Foreign Secretary Selwyn Lloyd, assuring
Dulles that the proposal was "essentially a cold war exercise" as they
had no intention of limiting "United States or United Kingdom freedom
of action in the matter of testing," suggested that they expected the study
to reach a negative conclusion that a system was infeasible.[4] Despite
the anticipated and desired negative findings, Lloyd told Dulles that his
government needed, for domestic and international purposes, to indicate
a willingness to study the matter and to bolster their common position
against test limitations with a technical study that provided a "well-
buttressed conclusion." Dulles agreed that the trend of world opinion
made the administration's posture on testing "an unhappy one," but he
deferred to Strauss's advice on the matter.[5] Strauss adamantly opposed
the study, fearing that it would raise false hopes of nuclear disarmament
in the public. Although Dulles proposed adding to the combined com-
muniqué a commitment to regulate and control nuclear testing as part of
a general disarmament system, Strauss convinced him to eliminate any
references that suggested limitations on testing.[6]

Two months later, British and French representatives tabled a working
paper with a test-ban provision at the United Nations disarmament talks
in London. Although the provision limited tests at an earlier stage in a
comprehensive disarmament program than the United States desired, the
British privately indicated their proposal was purely propaganda, certain
that the Soviet Union would reject it. As domestic opposition to nuclear
testing increased, Eden struggled to present a public willingness to seek
limits on testing, while privately opposing limitations that would challenge his own test plans and clash with the Eisenhower administration's
policy. At one point, Dulles and Strauss pressured British Ambassador
Sir Roger Makins to ensure that Eden's comments in the House of Com-
mons maintained a common position on testing. Illustrating the powerful influence of Dulles and Strauss on British test policy, Eden's actual
comments were almost identical to the phrases that Dulles and Strauss
had earlier provided to Makins. Through June 1956, Eden maintained a
common policy with the Eisenhower administration: any test limitations
must be a part of a comprehensive disarmament agreement with adequate inspection safeguards. The following month, Eden, under tremendous pressure from the Labor Party and British public opinion, shifted
course, indicating his willingness to discuss a test limitation agreement
separate from a comprehensive disarmament program. Although this
public pronouncement presented the appearance of a firm break with
the Eisenhower administration's policy, private correspondence revealed

that the British, determined to proceed with their spring 1957 test series, did not intend to propose any immediate negotiations.[7]

Pressed by its closest ally, the United States faced even greater pressures on its test policy from other nations. Fallout from Soviet tests in 1955, combined with the AEC's announcement of a U.S. test series in the Pacific in 1956, heightened worldwide opposition to testing. Protests were especially strong in Japan, where many feared a repeat of the *Lucky Dragon* incident in 1954 that followed the last major test series in the Pacific. Within the United Nations, the United States faced fresh challenges in the trusteeship council, and India submitted another resolution for a complete ban on nuclear testing. The United States narrowly retained enough support in the United Nations to counter these challenges and proceed with the test series in the Pacific that spring. U.S. representatives cautioned, however, that they could not expect to prevent another test-cessation resolution from passing in the General Assembly in the fall of 1956 if the United States did not modify its test policy or at least present a viable disarmament proposal.[8]

With no agreed upon disarmament policy forthcoming in the foreseeable future, administration officials realized that they must do something to counter mounting opposition to testing. State Department officials complained that U.S. efforts to justify its test series by explaining the difficulties of test detection and minimizing the health hazards of atmospheric testing were unconvincing. Gerald Smith in June 1956 recommended conducting "a large-scale public information program to make the U.S. position more understandable around the world." Smith's recommendation came after the United States Information Agency (USIA) had been conducting such a campaign for the previous year, suggesting much about the effectiveness of that program. Part of the administration officials' frustration was that the U.S. tests continued to receive the brunt of worldwide criticism, though Soviet tests were also contributing to the spread of radioactive fallout. The United States received greater attention because it announced most of its tests, while the Soviet Union often attempted to test secretly. Yet, the United States could not simply disclose that it had detected Soviet tests without suffering from disadvantages as well. U.S. announcements of Soviet tests provided the Soviet Union with valuable intelligence on U.S. detection capabilities. Strauss feared that this practice allowed the Soviets to determine the threshold that they could test clandestinely under a test-limitation agreement.[9]

To solve this dilemma, administration officials turned once again to Coca-Cola president William Robinson, who frequently played golf and bridge with Eisenhower and was considered one of the president's closest personal friends. Recognized as one of the nation's foremost public relations minds, Robinson provided the AEC several recommendations on accentuating the positive aspects of the U.S. test policy, while drawing negative attention to Soviet testing. With Robinson's advice, the U.S. began to emphasize the clandestine nature of Soviet tests in an effort to deflect some of the international opposition to the Soviet Union. The administration also announced when it detected some, but not all, Soviet tests.[10]

For Lewis Strauss, deflecting negative attention to the nation's adversary was not enough. Strauss recommended offering the use of the AEC's Pacific Proving Grounds to the British for their upcoming tests series. Strauss suggested that this would provide the United States with valuable espionage opportunities about the nuclear weapons program of the nation's closest ally. Most importantly, it would shift animosity over nuclear testing in the Pacific away from the United States and toward its British allies. Determined not to let international pressure threaten the continued development of the U.S. nuclear arsenal, Strauss was willing to draw negative attention to friend and foe alike.[11]

II

The highly technical issues related to detecting nuclear tests and assessing the hazards of radioactive fallout brought scientists increasingly to the forefront of the test-ban debate. Asked in January 1956 if the administration had found a mutually acceptable formula to enforce a test ban, John Foster Dulles, admitting that he was "not competent" in the technical aspects of the problem, declined to provide a direct answer. Instead, he emphasized that "it [a system to detect nuclear tests] is in fact much too complex for me to understand . . . the whole thing is very much a mystery to me." Dulles's admission illustrates the tremendous technical complexity of the test-ban issue. The fact that Dulles, an international business lawyer, could not understand the details is not surprising; even the nation's most prominent scientists sharply disagreed on the hazards of testing and the ability to detect nuclear detonations.[12]

Despite the recognition that a growing number of issues related to national security policy contained such complex technical issues, the administration continued to decline scientists' proposals to provide decision makers with additional scientific expertise. Robert Cutler in 1953 rejected the recommendation of ODM's Science Advisory Committee

(SAC) to assign a science advisor as a permanent representative to the NSC, arguing that few matters reaching the NSC contained technical issues. Three years later, SAC scientists made a similar proposal to Cutler's successor, Dillon Anderson. Although Anderson was more sympathetic than Cutler, acknowledging that roughly a quarter of the issues reaching the NSC contained highly technical issues, he cited Eisenhower's determination to minimize the size of the NSC as his reason to deny SAC's recommendation to bring independent scientific advice to the council.[13]

Three months later, Sherman Adams blocked a separate suggestion from the director of the National Science Foundation, Alan T. Waterman, for Eisenhower to appoint a presidential science advisor.[14] Anderson's and Adams's efforts to minimize Eisenhower's advisory staff denied the president an independent source of scientific expertise at a time when national security affairs increasingly involved highly technical issues. As a result, Lewis Strauss essentially monopolized the scientific conclusions presented to the highest levels of the administration, exerting an often decisive influence on atomic energy matters.

One of the most contentious issues within the scientific community that the Eisenhower administration confronted was the level of danger posed by radioactive fallout from testing. The report of the National Academy of Science's study, "The Biological Effects of Atomic Radiation" failed to end the debate. The findings of the six committees of experts were generally reassuring; nuclear tests had thus far not produced dangerous levels of worldwide radiation. The report even bolstered one of the AEC's favorite arguments: medical x-rays posed greater immediate health risks than radioactive fallout from tests to date. The genetics committee, however, warned of potential problems in the future. Cautioning that all radiation caused genetic mutations, they viewed the depiction of a safe level of radiation as illusory. The committee on pathological effects, also concerned about future hazards, warned of the dangers of strontium-90, a substance with a half-life of twenty-eight years that is produced only through nuclear fission. High-yield blasts sent radioactive strontium-90 into the stratosphere. Scientists in 1956 believed that the radioactive strontium remained there for as long as a decade, spreading throughout the world before descending to earth and slowly contaminating the food supply. Strontium-90 then concentrated in human bone, potentially causing bone cancer. Although the committee concluded that existing levels were well below permissible doses, the unique qualities of strontium-90 made its future levels difficult to predict.[15]

Since the genetic hazards developed over generations and strontium-

90 possessed such a long half-life, the cautionary aspects of the report were limited to potential risks in the future from either increased testing or nuclear warfare. Thus, the inconclusive findings allowed test-ban opponents and advocates to each cite the report to support their arguments. Lewis Strauss accentuated the positives to Eisenhower and Commissioner Willard Libby referred to the report freely in his reassuring public comments on fallout. Ralph Lapp criticized Strauss and Libby for twisting and misstating the report's conclusions, citing the findings to bolster his arguments in the *Bulletin of the Atomic Scientists*. According to Lapp, strontium-90 could cause bone cancer fifty years after the last nuclear test. For Lapp, however, the greatest concern remained the catastrophic somatic and genetic damage caused by a nuclear war, rather than the much lower, yet troubling levels introduced by continued testing.[16]

Concerned that fears of fallout, even if unwarranted, would threaten the AEC's test program, Strauss began to emphasize that continued testing was necessary to develop weapons that produced less fallout. Some of the tests in the AEC's 1956 series in the Pacific, named *REDWING*, sought to develop weapons with reduced fallout. Although the level of fallout is a function of many variables, including the altitude of detonation and the mineralogical composition of the target area, Strauss emphasized the centrality of design improvements. When the combination of these factors resulted in reduced fallout in the Pacific, Strauss announced the development of clean bombs as a "humanitarian" victory. Critics from several corners skewered Strauss's depiction of this development. Ralph Lapp commented, "Part of the madness of our time is that adult men can use a word like humanitarian to describe an H-bomb." Eisenhower, who remained deeply interested in the peaceful applications of atomic energy, was greatly pleased with the development. Although the test series pleased the president, Strauss and Libby's exaggerated claims failed to reassure skeptical scientists within the United States and abroad that continued testing posed no unnecessary risks. The vast majority of the general public, however, continued to believe the reassuring words of administration officials. A State Department poll in March 1956 found that 83 percent of Americans supported the continuation of testing.[17]

The presidential election campaign brought unprecedented attention in the United States to nuclear testing. Although Adlai Stevenson initially emphasized the necessity of regaining moral leadership in the world as the primary reasons for a test ban, other test-ban advocates emphasized that a ban was necessary to halt the spread of fallout. By mid-October, Stevenson redirected the appeal of his test-ban proposal from exercising leadership and reducing tensions to preventing the spread of strontium-90, which he called "the most dreadful poison in the world." The campaign thus brought the complex and relatively new study of radioactive fallout, an issue that divided even the most competent scientists, into the arena of partisan politics. Both candidates vigorously publicized the endorsements of prominent scientists to support their cases.[18]

Stevenson's proposal received the support of many scientists and prominent figures, such as former Atomic Energy Commissioner Henry D. Smyth, a physicist, and former Secretary of the Air Force Thomas Finletter, a longtime Democrat. Stevenson also received endorsements from the Federation of American Scientists and scientists at prominent universities across the nation. His supporters included Nobel Prize winners, members of ODM's Science Advisory Committee, and participants in the NAS radiation study.[19] Newsweek's network of political analysts across the country estimated that though the general public supported Eisenhower's test-ban position by a five to two margin, scientists were evenly divided.[20]

Scientists who supported Stevenson did so for different reasons. David Inglis, a physicist at Argonne National Laboratory, and Eugene Rabinowitch, an editor of the Bulletin of the Atomic Scientists, criticized Stevenson's initial proposal, which called for a unilateral test ban. For them, the greatest appeal for a test ban was for its potential as a first step toward mutual nuclear disarmament.[21] When the Democratic challenger altered his position to advocate a multilateral test ban, they began to support Stevenson, though critical of his emphasis on the perils of radiation rather than disarmament. For others, such as geneticist Hermann J. Muller and biologist Bentley Glass, fallout from testing alone provided sufficient hazards to necessitate a test cessation. The divisions and mixed messages amongst Stevenson's supporters limited their ability to convince a broader segment of the general population.[22]

One scientist conspicuously absent from the public debate was J. Robert Oppenheimer. Oppenheimer privately expressed his support to Stevenson in April 1956, encouraging Stevenson to be critical and ask open questions during the campaign. Though Oppenheimer did not specifically mention the test-ban issue, he wrote his letter to Stevenson two days after Thomas Murray's well-publicized Senate testimony advocating a test ban. Stevenson, perhaps fearing that Oppenheimer's support would be a political liability, did not seek Oppenheimer's public support and did not even send a private reply to Oppenheimer for over four months.[23]

Even without Oppenheimer's endorsement, Stevenson's impressive roll of prominent scientists supporting his views troubled the Eisenhower campaign. Lewis Strauss worked closely on a response with Robert Cutler, who resigned as the president's national security advisor to focus on Eisenhower's reelection campaign. Strauss and Cutler solicited scientists to counter Stevenson's arguments and publicly endorse the administration's position. After Stevenson's advisors released the names of numerous scientists from prominent universities across the country who endorsed the Democratic challenger, Strauss and Cutler arranged for twelve scientists to defend the administration's position on the test ban. In a press release, the scientists argued that tests must continue until the Soviets accepted a comprehensive disarmament agreement. They cited the NAS study to support their contention that current testing levels posed no significant radiological hazards. Significantly, six of the twelve scientists were affiliated with the AEC, though the press releases only mentioned their academic institutional affiliations. Along with their endorsement, the scientists' statement expressed their concern at "the injection into a political campaign of statements and conclusions which extend beyond the limits of existing scientific evidence."[24]

Although these scientists endorsed Eisenhower, their final comments suggested that their conclusions remained tentative at best. Concerned with Stevenson's "continuous efforts to frighten the public," Strauss sought a completely reassuring statement that unequivocally denied that testing at the current levels posed significant health hazards. With Libby losing his credibility as a spokesperson for fallout because of his exaggerated his claims and his close affiliation with the administration, Strauss turned instead to Shields Warren. Strauss minimized Warren's past position as director of the AEC's division of biology and medicine and instead highlighted his participation in the NAS radiation study and his service on the United Nations scientific committee on radiation. Warren's public endorsement of the administration's position assured Americans that even if testing continued at the current rate for thirty years the genetic hazards would still be "insignificant."[25]

Although Strauss convinced Warren to speak out on behalf of the administration's position on the test ban, other scientists were much less willing to take a public position. Curiously, Strauss sought to gain I. I. Rabi's endorsement of Eisenhower's test policy. Rabi had recently resigned as the chairman of the AEC's General Advisory Committee and became the chairman of the ODM's Science Advisory Committee. In a letter to Strauss in August, Eisenhower reminded Strauss of his "tremendous confidence" in Rabi, then revealed that he had learned of Rabi's belief that it would be advantageous for the United States to stop testing.[26] Despite his awareness of Rabi's private anti-testing views, Strauss in October sought Rabi's public endorsement of Eisenhower's campaign position on testing. Strauss possessed too sharp a memory and a much too vindictive nature to forget that the Nobel Prize–winning physicist privately favored a test cessation. The intensely loyal Strauss apparently believed that Rabi's desire to support the reelection of a man he highly regarded would override his private beliefs on the ban. Strauss expressed "great surprise" when Rabi declined to endorse publicly Eisenhower's position against a test ban. Rabi did not tell Strauss that he opposed the president's position; he simply informed Strauss that he had decided "not to get into politics."[27] Rabi's campaign position is consistent with the views that he expressed to Rabinowitch in 1953 that an advisor to the government could not express his views publicly without risking the effectiveness of his private counsel.[28]

Rebuffed by Rabi, Strauss turned to two allies from previous battles over the H-bomb and the Oppenheimer case, Ernest Lawrence and Edward Teller. Strauss encouraged them to release a public statement in support of the administration's test policy. Although both were sympathetic to the administration's views, they wished to remain out of politics. Edward Teller, stung by his treatment from nuclear scientists after his crushing testimony against Oppenheimer in the loyalty-security hearing, hoped to remain out of "the public eye" and avoid taking a public position on another controversial matter. Yet Teller indicated to Strauss's secretary that he would be willing to do "almost anything" that Strauss wanted him to do to counter Stevenson's position. Teller told her, "if Lewis wants me to do something, he has only to ask."[29]

Lawrence was less easily convinced, believing that scientists should remain aloof from partisan politics. Despite his strong reservations, Lawrence issued a carefully crafted statement on the eve of the election, perhaps feeling indebted to Strauss since the physicist had not testified against Oppenheimer. Days before his scheduled appearance in 1954 before the Personnel Security Board reviewing the Oppenheimer case, Lawrence suffered a serve attack of colitis and returned to California before testifying. Still stung by Strauss' accusation that his failure to testify marked him as a coward who had lost his nerve, rather than a victim of a debilitating colitis attack, Lawrence drafted the endorsement Strauss desired the day before the election. Lawrence and Teller's joint statement emphasized the uncertainties of detecting tests, minimized the health hazards of fallout, and underscored the importance of tests to maintain the nation's strategic superiority. Their endorsement of Eisenhower's position appeared in newspapers the morning of the election. Lawrence and Teller's last-minute endorsement was certainly unnecessary to secure Eisenhower's reelection. It remains important, however, as an illustration of the powerful relationship between Strauss, Lawrence, and Teller. Significantly, the two scientists' endorsement broke down their inhibitions against taking a public position on the test-ban issue; Lawrence and Teller played critical roles in the public test-ban debate in the years to come.[30]

Although Stevenson was the most recognized loser in the election that day, the nation's trust and confidence in the objectivity of its scientists was also weakened during the campaign. In an editorial in the *Bulletin of the Atomic Scientists*, Eugene Rabinowitch lamented that the scientists' participation in the political campaign had "merely served to discredit scientists as objective advisors of public opinion." Scientific objectivity fared poorly in the realm of political propaganda and clever campaigning. Instead of providing the public sober assessments to make informed choices, prominent scientists on both sides of the debate issued emotional appeals that bewildered the public.[31]

III

As the administration struggled to counter mounting international challenges to its testing program, heightened concerns about fallout, and Stevenson's campaign proposal for a test ban, Stassen continued his ceaseless, but unfruitful efforts to forge a consensus a new disarmament policy.[32] Despite cabinet rank, the support of a large staff, and the creation of inspection tasks forces, Stassen failed to formulate a mutually acceptable policy that reconciled administration standards of inspection with the Soviet demands for a closed society. For Eisenhower, effective inspection was fundamental to any disarmament agreement, though his ideas of what constituted "effective" were less restrictive than the views of Strauss, Radford, and Wilson.

Thomas Murray continued to advocate a ban on H-bomb tests as a way to resolve the inspection dilemma that confounded Stassen's efforts. Murray, hoping to cancel the series of H-bomb tests in the Pacific in the spring of 1956, again pressed his views on Dulles on 9 January that a ban on H-bombs was easily enforceable and strategically advantageous to the United States.[33] Murray's views apparently did not sway Dulles, who met with Eisenhower the following day. According to Dulles, he and Eisenhower had "a long discussion on disarmament and the difficulty of our present situation."[34] In a diary entry written after meeting with Dulles, Eisenhower underscored the importance of inducing "the Soviets to agree to some form of inspection, in order that both sides may be confident that treaties are being executed faithfully."[35] The struggle over the disarmament policy thus centered on what constituted sufficient inspection safeguards. At this stage, Strauss successfully countered Murray's arguments that H-bomb tests were easily detectable without inspection posts on Soviet soil.

Privately rejected again, Murray began to air publicly in 1956 the arguments that he had been privately advancing within the administration for the previous two years. Murray presented his arguments for a ban on H-bomb tests in April to the Senate Subcommittee on Disarmament. In his testimony, Murray proposed a ban on multimegaton thermonuclear weapons, believing that the weapons then on hand were large enough. Significantly, Murray did not base his proposal on any concerns with fallout; he asserted that "the evidence presently available does not warrant stopping tests now for this reason." Curiously, Murray urged the accelerated testing of "small weapons." Test-ban advocates, split between those emphasizing disarmament and those concerned with fallout, thus found Murray's proposal both encouraging and troubling.[36]

Two weeks later, Adlai Stevenson, the front-runner for the Democratic nomination for President, cited Murray's proposal when he first advocated a ban on H-bomb tests in a speech on 21 April before the American Society of Newspaper Editors.[37] Eisenhower's dismissive response, and the counsel of Stevenson's advisors, silenced Stevenson on the issue temporarily. Yet the combination of Murray and Stevenson's proposals, which differed slightly, served to warn the administration that its test policy, already under intense attack from abroad, could soon face serious domestic challenges as well.

The rising pressures modified the views of some leading administration officials, yet several issues continued to confound efforts to reach a consensus on a new disarmament policy, simultaneously freezing the American position on testing. Stassen privately considered suggesting a separate test-ban agreement, but Lawrence and Teller persuaded him not to propose breaking the link between testing and a comprehensive disarmament agreement; Stassen's June 1956 draft disarmament policy maintained this linkage. As part of his policy review, Stassen in July 1956 conducted individual consultations with Eisenhower's inner circle of disarmament advisors. Appalled at the number of security leaks throughout his administration, Eisenhower had removed the detailed discussion of disarmament issues from the NSC to this much smaller group of Dulles, Strauss, Stassen, Radford, Wilson, and CIA Director Allen Dulles.[38]

Within this group, Stassen discovered that opposition to a comprehensive test *ban* remained strong, but there was a growing recognition that some form of test *limitation* might become politically necessary. Wilson and Radford maintained that nuclear tests should never be stopped, but conceded that tests could possibly be limited.[39] Strauss reiterated the administration's public position on the matter—any test ban must be linked to the implementation of a general disarmament agreement with an installed and effective inspection system that prohibited the production of fissionable material for weapons. Curiously, Strauss later sent additional comments to Stassen, acknowledging that there might be "over-riding political considerations" that would make it advisable to propose negotiations toward an agreement to limit the number, frequency, and size of weapons tested.[40] Although Gerald Smith, Dulles's advisor on atomic energy, identified this as a "radical change in AEC policy," it is clear that Strauss believed that the Soviets would never agree to the number of on-site inspections that he thought necessary to implement such an agreement.[41]

Dulles agreed with Strauss that ideally the cessation of testing should be inseparable from nuclear disarmament. Dulles advised Stassen in July that if the nuclear powers could not reach a broader agreement, the administration should consider a separate agreement to limit the numbers and size of tests with an inspection system to verify compliance. Two months later, however, Dulles believed that they could not wait any longer for a comprehensive agreement. He approved "as a basis of discussion" a Department of State proposal to halt unilaterally tests over 100kt.[42] Significantly, this framework differed little from the proposal that Stevenson, who had remained silent on the matter since April, would publicly inject into his campaign less than a week later. Dulles lectured Stassen on 5 September, the same day that Stevenson raised the issue, that a test-ban proposal "was an area in which we ought to get going." In Dulles's view, a test ban prevented proliferation and was essential for worldwide opinion; recent analysis concluded that the U.S. was "virtually isolated" on its opposition to any limitation on tests outside of a broader disarmament agreement.[43] While no member of Eisenhower's inner circle of advisors on disarmament advocated a comprehensive test ban, by the time Stevenson renewed his campaign proposal all were beginning to consider the political necessity of at least showing a willingness to discuss some form of test limitation.

Moving beyond expressing the willingness to negotiate merely for propaganda purposes, Eisenhower sincerely hoped for an agreement that would actually limit, if not end, testing. Largely dependent on the views of Strauss and leading AEC scientists, who emphasized the necessity to continue testing to maintain America's strategic advantage, Eisenhower received some rare scientific advice in late August from outside of the administration. The president learned that Rabi, a Nobel Prize–winning physicist whose views he deeply respected, questioned the need for further tests. Relaying Rabi's valued judgment to Strauss on August 30, Eisenhower reminded Strauss of their several previous conversations regarding the president's "hope that the need for atomic tests would gradually lift and possibly soon disappear." After reiterating that he shared Rabi's views on the matter, Eisenhower directed Strauss to discuss testing with him in the Oval Office soon.[44] Thus by the end of August both Eisenhower and Dulles had expressed a desire to reexamine the test issue, while those most opposed to a ban (Strauss, Radford, and Wilson) began to recognize the political necessity at least to indicate a willingness to negotiate a limit on testing.

Stevenson broke his lengthy silence and renewed his campaign pledge to end H-bomb tests six days before Eisenhower met with his disarmament advisors on 11 September to discuss Stassen's testing and disarmament proposals.[45] Lewis Strauss discussed his concerns about the State Department test limitation proposal with Dulles before the meeting. While Strauss opposed any limitations on testing, domestic political considerations made Dulles his temporary ally in opposing such measures.[46] Dulles, after recently approving the examination of a test limitation proposal, suddenly called Stassen two hours before the disarmament review began to oppose even discussing a test ban at the 11 September session. Dulles considered such a discussion "awkward from a political standpoint," because Stevenson was advocating a ban on H-bomb tests, while the administration sharply criticized it.

Stassen, however, argued that his own proposal and Stevenson's were "not in the same framework." Stassen recommended limiting testing as part of a broader disarmament agreement that included inspection provisions. At this point, Stevenson was advocating a unilateral test ban with the hope that the Soviets would also refrain from testing. If they did, Stevenson argued that long-distance detection was sufficient to detect any subsequent tests, thus on-site inspection was unnecessary. While Dulles remained unconvinced of this distinction in Stassen's argument, Stassen did not alter his plans to discuss the issue. Dulles's warning about possible political repercussions of the issue, however, proved prescient; rumors about the government's 11 September discussions soon surfaced and pestered the administration throughout the remainder of the campaign. Even more significant, this conversation reveals that Dulles, who had favored a test ban for its international political advantages, changed his position on testing when he perceived it as a domestic political liability.[47]

Dulles and Strauss could hardly have been pleased when a spirited discussion on the discontinuance of tests broke out during the 11 September meeting. Unlike 1954, when Dulles's opposition to a test ban proved decisive, Eisenhower ruled against the recommendations of his advisors in 1956. He demanded the development of an initiative to limit nuclear tests. Frustrated that his advisors found endless obstacles in Stassen's disarmament proposals, the president asserted that something had to be done to slow the arms race in order to prevent the proliferation of nuclear weapons and halt the spiraling expenditures of an ever-expanding nuclear weapons stockpile. Addressing testing specifically, Eisenhower insisted that the rising public concerns over radiation and the extreme nervousness over the consequences of a nuclear war compelled them to make some kind of initiative to limit or cease the testing of nuclear weapons. The president was willing to accept the risks of eroding America's strategic superiority involved in any test limitation agreement if they could be minimized with an effective inspection system. Frustrated with the disorganized individual arguments on this issue among his advisors, Eisenhower instructed Stassen to work out a collectively approved initiative with the AEC and the Departments of Defense and State for the "limitation or cessation of testing of nuclear weapons" under effective inspection and detection. Demanding a common position, Eisenhower instructed them to resolve the matter as soon as possible. The president approved a memorandum later sent to the participants that established 15 October as the latest date to report back with a staff recommendation. Stassen met with representatives at least nine times between the pivotal meeting on 11 September and the election on 6 November. Working under strict secrecy as the administration's test policy became a focal point of the ongoing campaign, they failed develop an effective inspection formula.[48]

Despite the lack of immediate results, Eisenhower's directive is significant for two reasons. First, it reveals that unlike 1954, Eisenhower was willing to overrule the unanimous opposition of his advisors and direct the formation of a test-ban initiative. Second, it suggests the critical role of independent science advice in giving Eisenhower the confidence to do so on such a highly technical issue. Rabi's expertise, which somehow evaded Admiral Strauss's screening of atomic energy opinions reaching the president, provided the assurance Eisenhower needed to overrule his advisors and follow his own inclination. The expanded range of scientific advice beyond Strauss's control during Eisenhower's second term was a decisive factor in explaining the president's stronger actions toward a test ban.

IV

While Eisenhower accepted the argument that any test-ban agreement entailed certain risks of eroding America's strategic superiority, he also emphatically believed by 1956 that the United States must somehow slow the arms race. Willing to accept the risks, the president directed his advisors to develop an initiative to halt or limit testing. Rejecting a unilateral test ban, Eisenhower insisted that some form of inspection and detection system that would minimize the risk of evasion was a prerequisite for any such agreement. This required the study and resolution of complex technical and political issues, which prevented the rapid development of his directive into a specific negotiating formula. As a result, the administration held only Eisenhower's basic framework for a possible test-ban agreement during the election campaign, but remained in the process of developing a complete proposal for negotiation.

Stevenson's own test-ban proposal changed often as the campaign progressed, causing a shift each time in the administration's strategy for isolating the Democratic challenger. Starting in April 1956, Stevenson initially proposed a unilateral ban on H-bomb tests, but dropped the issue after Eisenhower in a press conference noted a "paradox" in Stevenson's position that halted H-bomb tests but accelerated the development of missiles that could deliver them. The Democratic challenger avoided the matter for months before suddenly bringing a revised test moratorium proposal to the fore of his campaign in September. The administration initially used excessive rhetoric to isolate Stevenson, while quietly reaffirming Eisenhower's own commitment to limit tests under an agreement with proper inspection. As Stevenson shifted his proposal from a unilateral ban to a call for negotiations toward a multilateral agreement, narrowing the gap between his campaign proposal and Eisenhower's secret directive, the administration publicly raised some of the previously dismissed arguments of test-ban opponents within the administration. This political tactic used to counter Stevenson's campaign proposal misled the public with the impression that Eisenhower believed such risks did not outweigh the advantages of a test-ban agreement.[49]

With the election less than a month away, rumors circulated that Eisenhower had agreed to seek a test ban, but reversed his decision after Stevenson made his own proposal. The rumors initially differed just enough from fact for the administration to respond with a less than forthcoming, but not untruthful answer. Yet when ultimately confronted with the salient details of Eisenhower's directive to seek an acceptable formula for a test ban, an anonymous administration official flatly lied to conceal the president's views and directives. A review of the administration's techniques of countering Stevenson reveals the use of heated rhetoric, clever deception, and outright lies to manipulate public understanding of the test issue and to conceal Eisenhower's own sincere desire to limit, or even cease, tests.

As Eisenhower privately directed the development of a test-ban initiative, Stevenson transformed his test-ban proposal into a central theme of his campaign. Ironically, on the same day that an AEC Committee met to discuss possible test limitations should political considerations dictate them, Stevenson reinserted the test issue, dormant since Eisenhower ridiculed Stevenson's position in April, into the presidential campaign. Speaking at the American Legion's annual convention on 5 September, Stevenson proposed ending the draft and halting "further tests of large nuclear devices, conditioned upon adherence by other atomic powers to a similar policy." Press coverage of Stevenson's speech focused on the draft issue rather than the test ban. Interestingly, it was Vice President Richard M. Nixon's sharp response in a speech the following day that brought Stevenson's test-ban proposal to the headlines. Nixon criticized Stevenson's test-ban proposal as "naïve" and dangerous to our national security, comparing it to "telling police officials that they should discard their weapons provided the lawbreakers would offer to throw away the machine guns."[50]

In his clear reference to a lack of inspection and enforcement provisions in Stevenson's proposal, Nixon's response illustrates the administration's initial tactic for dealing with Stevenson's challenge; the administration used heated rhetoric in order to distance Stevenson's proposal from Eisenhower's own commitment to seek a test ban. Although Eisenhower secretly directed the formation of a test-ban initiative, he insisted on much more stringent conditions than Stevenson initially proposed. Eisenhower presently feared that the Democratic challenger, if unchallenged, might build support for a unilateral initiative, subsequently undermining the Eisenhower administration's negotiating position for a multilateral agreement with inspection provisions.

Eisenhower sought to avoid the issue publicly and, still recovering from his 1955 heart attack, spent little time on the campaign trail. Other party figures, such as Nixon and former governor of New York and presidential candidate Thomas E. Dewey, provided the bulk of the Republican campaign speeches, which included vigorous attacks on Stevenson's test-ban proposal. The Republican National Committee worked with Stassen to provide Nixon and the "Truth Squad" with material to counter Stevenson. Nixon and Dewey ridiculed Stevenson's H-bomb test-ban proposal as "naïve," "dangerous," "catastrophic nonsense," and even "the most dangerous proposal ever made by any American in our lifetime." While these charges provided headline material, the Republicans invariably followed their criticism of Stevenson with a quiet affirmation of Eisenhower's own desire for a test ban with adequate inspection provisions. As attention focused on the Republicans' sharp criticism of Stevenson, only the shrewdest observer could note the consistent, but inconspicuous statements of Eisenhower's own commitment to a negotiated test ban. Thus the exaggerated rhetoric served to separate the two candidates' position on testing in the public mind, without actually misrepresenting Eisenhower's privately held views.[51]

While Eisenhower was greatly troubled that such a complex issue had become part of the political campaign and he let others provide the most vocal criticism of Stevenson's H-bomb proposal, he did briefly address the matter in a radio and television broadcast on 19 September. The president criticized a unilateral suspension of H-bomb tests as a theatrical gesture, insisting that any limits of testing must be part of an "explicit and supervised" international agreement. Stevenson, asserting that "peace is not a partisan issue," criticized the president for brushing off his suggestion as a theatrical gesture. Despite the sharp Republican criticism and the contrary advice of his own campaign advisors, Stevenson continued to press the issue. In a speech in Minneapolis on 29 September, the Democratic nominee introduced two new components to his argument for an H-bomb test ban—the dangers of fallout from testing and the certainty of detecting large H-bomb tests. Previously, Stevenson focused on the horrific consequences of a nuclear exchange, proposing a test ban as a first step toward disarmament to reduce the possibility of catastrophic warfare. In Minneapolis, Stevenson emphasized the significant health hazards resulting from testing alone; fallout from testing poisons the atmosphere and possibly leads to the genetic damage of "unborn children."

In addition to his emphasis on the dangers of fallout, Stevenson also argued that H-bomb tests could be detected without on-site inspection, and thus that the United States would know if the Soviets continued to test H-bombs. Still proposing a unilateral initiative with the hope that the Soviets would also stop testing, Stevenson argued that if they did not then "at least the world will know we tried."[52]

By late September, it became clear that Stevenson would not drop the issue as he had done in April. Moreover, the addition of the complex and highly contentious issue of fallout hazards added a new, emotional component to the debate. The administration continued its sharp criticism but began to add arguments that the test-ban opponents within the administration had used in their attempt to convince the president not to seek a test-ban agreement. On 3 October, Nixon was the first to publicly argue that testing itself required lengthy preparations. Therefore, even if the Americans detected a Soviet violation of a test-ban agreement and wanted to resume immediately their own testing, the United States could still be months behind in the development of potentially decisive technological advances. This was a valid concern, one that AEC chairman Lewis Strauss expressed vehemently during secret discussions of a test ban. Its use in the campaign, however, was misleading, for it appears that Eisenhower was willing to accept the risk of a Soviet head start on testing if he could secure an international agreement with effective detection. Moreover, the administration likely exaggerated the time required to restart testing as its responses varied from one year to two years.[53]

Eisenhower himself contributed to the deception, presenting the same argument in his press conference on 5 October and elaborating on it even further in a written statement on testing released the same day. In his written statement, the president deplored the fact that such a sensitive matter of national security policy had become part of a political campaign. Without mentioning Stevenson by name, Eisenhower pointed out that the proposals have differed over time, leading to "confusion at home and misunderstanding abroad." The president then followed the same pattern for isolating the Democratic challenger; he strongly criticized Stevenson's proposal as "foolish," quietly reiterated his own "strong will" to restrict testing under a supervised international agreement, and then elaborated on the new test preparation time argument. Rather than directly counter Stevenson's emotional appraisal of fall-out dangers, the administration expanded their own argument that Stevenson's proposals presented too great of a national security risk, perhaps hoping to deflect public attention from the emotional fallout issue.[54]

If the administration sought to close the political debate over testing with Eisenhower's authoritative written statement, its hopes were surely dashed less than a week later. At his press conference on 11 October, the president was asked to comment on the "widely circulated reports" that Republican strategists were planning Eisenhower's own announcement to end the draft and halt H-bomb tests, but that Stevenson had proposed them first. The president replied, "I am being told things about my administration that I have never heard, and I am quite sure that it's not true." Shrewdly side stepping the test-ban issue, he stated, "No one had come up and had suggested to me that we eliminate the draft in my administration." Then he quickly preempted any further questions, announcing, "I have said my last words on these subjects." As Eisenhower publicly evaded the issue, his administration continued its secret examination of means to limit testing. That very same day, senior representatives from the AEC, Department of State, and Department of Defense met to discuss Stassen's disarmament policy, including limiting testing and effective inspection systems. Although Eisenhower sought to squash rumors of his secret consideration of a test ban and remove the testing issue from the campaign, he failed on both measures. The rumors persisted, as did Stevenson, who was actually emboldened by the president's "last words."[55]

Stevenson responded to Eisenhower's silence with a televised speech entirely dedicated to the perils of H-bomb testing titled, "The Greatest Menace the World Has Ever Known." Previously, many of Stevenson's campaign advisors thought it inadvisable to push the complex H-bomb question against Eisenhower's military prestige and superior experience. The strong response of audiences to Stevenson's proposals and Eisenhower's attempt to foreclose debate of the issue, however, altered their assessment. In one of the major speeches of the campaign, Stevenson changed his proposal yet again, calling for a multilateral agreement rather than a unilateral American initiative. Moreover, he pledged to continue both the testing of smaller weapons and the laboratory research on large weapons in order to resume testing as rapidly as possible if the Soviets violated an agreement. These changes significantly closed the gap between his public proposal and Eisenhower's secret views, leaving the matter of inspection as the only major difference.[56]

Unaware of this closing gap, the public debate focused on the contentious issue of fallout. Stevenson's speech included the strongest assertion thus far about the hazards of testing alone, especially the release of radioactive strontium, "the most dreadful poison in the world."[57] This emotional plea provoked an outpour of support. While Democratic

Party leaders and a number of prominent scientists sent their approval for a test ban to Stevenson's campaign headquarters, the White House mail was also running heavily in favor of a test suspension.[58]

The initial reaction to Stevenson's speech caused a great deal of concern within the administration, convincing the president that he must once again address the issue.[59] As Eisenhower campaigned on the west coast, his chief of staff, former New Hampshire governor Sherman Adams, called a meeting with Dulles, Stassen, Strauss, and Wilson to "consider various aspects of testing and the H-bomb which has been brought to the fore" by Stevenson.[60] The meeting resulted in a counteroffensive to Stevenson's speech across a broad front. Stassen provided Adams with six different versions of form letters expressing opposition to Stevenson's proposals for loyal "veterans" to sign and send to newspaper editors and representatives.[61] Eisenhower directed the compilation of a series of memoranda relating to testing, disarmament negotiations, and his Atoms for Peace and Open Skies initiatives.

Eisenhower's advisors believed that the president could no longer maintain his vow of silence on the test issue and allow only Nixon and Dewey to attack Stevenson; he would have to respond to Stevenson personally.[62] As his key advisors busily prepared a detailed response, Eisenhower attacked Stevenson's proposals in campaign speeches from Seattle to Los Angeles. The president criticized Stevenson's "strange new formula" for providing "pie in the sky" promises without effective safeguards, declaring that no political campaign justifies "the declaration of a moratorium on ordinary common sense." Although Eisenhower went on the attack, his main henchmen, Nixon and Dewey, provided even sharper criticism. Nixon chastised Stevenson for playing "dangerous politics" with national security, while Dewey charged the Democratic challenger with "the most irresponsible scaremongering" and referred to Stevenson's proposal as an "invitation to national suicide." Predictably, the Republicans followed their harsh criticism of Stevenson with statements of Eisenhower's own commitment to a test ban with effective safeguards.[63]

Just as Stevenson's proposal gathered momentum from a flood of endorsements from prominent scientists, Eisenhower received a fortuitous assist from a surprising source. Soviet Premier Nikoli Bulganin sent the president a letter, which he released to the press, expressing a willingness to reach an agreement prohibiting atomic weapon tests, a willingness that "certain prominent public figures in the United States shared," a clear reference to Stevenson. Yet Bulganin did not simply support Stevenson, he went on to sharply criticize Dulles for "direct attacks against the Soviet Union" and implied Eisenhower's bad faith in pursuing disarmament.[64] Dulles was particularly disturbed, noting, "there has never been a diplomatic note so crass as this one."[65] Upon further reflection, he began to consider how to take advantage of the letter. With Strauss's assistance, Dulles drafted Eisenhower's public reply that deplored the Soviet interference in American domestic political issues, repudiated the personal attack upon Dulles, and listed previous Soviet actions that broke or prevented previous agreements. Significantly, Eisenhower insisted that the response did not reject the idea of a limitation on weapons testing, leaving the option open to limit testing on his terms in the future.[66]

The administration seized the opportunity that Bulganin's letter presented to link Stevenson to the Soviets in the public mind. Nixon declared that Stevenson's test-ban proposal without inspection was "exactly what Khrushchev and Bulganin want us to do." Calling the Democratic proposal "dreadfully perilously wrong," Dewey charged Stevenson with adopting a suggestion that the Soviets made themselves ten years earlier. So successful was the administration's handling of the matter that the press concluded that Bulganin's letter might turn into "a political kiss of death," decreasing support for a test ban and destroying Stevenson's election hopes. James Reston of the *New York Times* reported after Bulganin's note that Republican chances for victory appeared brighter than at any time since the start of the campaign. Further, a *Newsweek* article concluded that "an astonishingly large preponderance" of Americans from all regions and walks of life were opposed to Stevenson's proposal to end H-bomb tests. Stevenson himself mishandled the issue, initially criticizing Eisenhower for rejecting Bulganin's proposal without "sober consideration" before later expressing his own "resentment" over the Soviet Premier's interference in the American election. Nevertheless, the Democratic challenger did not alter his position on ending H-bomb tests.[67]

As Nixon and Dewey completed their verbal barrage on Stevenson, Eisenhower sought to finally defuse the issue with a series of straightforward memoranda prepared following Stevenson's 15 October speech. Eisenhower insisted on this approach, concerned that excessive argumentation would tie his hands, preventing him in the future from achieving the test-ban agreement that he truly desired. Dulles agreed and expressed his concern that the AEC, which was "violently opposed" to any test limitations, was "trying to slip in some arguments" that would make it difficult to later publicly reverse course and pursue a test ban. Therefore, they decided that the language must simply state the diplomatic history of the administration's efforts. Eisenhower wanted it to be "so factual that it will be uninteresting except for the subject." The administration prepared a statement on testing with accompanying memoranda on disarmament negotiations, peaceful uses of the atom, fallout studies, and the long-range detection of nuclear explosions. Released together on 24 October, the memoranda fulfilled the president's intent; they received little scrutiny or attention at the time.[68]

The memorandum on disarmament negotiations, however, is of significant interest. It illustrates the degree of deception that was used to obscure Eisenhower's ongoing struggle to come to grips with the horrors of nuclear weapons and the strength of his own inclination to limit testing. The document reveals little of the intensive 1954 study of a test moratorium, simply stating that Eisenhower "adopted an interdepartmental recommendation that the United States should not at that time agree to a test moratorium." Thus, it does not reveal that Eisenhower was favorably inclined to agree to a test moratorium but the unanimity of his advisors dashed his hopes. Most significantly, the memorandum does not address the nature of the administration's own reexamination of testing during the election campaign.[69]

On 26 October, Stevenson himself raised the question whether Eisenhower had abandoned a move to halt H-bomb tests after he had "proposed such a course." A few days later, *Christian Science Monitor* correspondent William Frye contended that the administration was on the verge of deciding, or actually had decided, to suspend tests on large weapons for a year when Stevenson presented his proposal. According to Frye, the Eisenhower administration publicly denounced Stevenson's similar proposal in sharp language instead of moving forward with their decided upon policy. The following week, four Democratic Senators sent a telegram asking Eisenhower directly if he had received a staff recommendation for a ban on large bombs, if he had approved it or directed further study of the issue to determine specific details or limits, or if he had blocked a recommendation to negotiate a test ban with the Soviet Union.[70]

The administration issued a truthful but opaque reply that Eisenhower had never altered his basic view that any proposal for suspending tests must include "dependable safeguards." Neither the Democratic Senators nor the press accepted this evasive response. While Senator Clinton P. Anderson announced that he would ask the Joint Committee on Atomic Energy to investigate, the editors of the *Washington Post* called for a "full and frank explanation," insisting that "the country ought to know the whole truth." The following day, the *New York Times* reported the response of "a high official in a position to know the facts" who provided an answer that was neither full nor frank. This anonymous official flatly lied about the meeting held on 11 September, stating that the subject of ending H-bomb tests under an international agreement was not discussed. Further, the spokesperson stated that Eisenhower had never asked his advisors to review the subject or consider the details of an acceptable agreement, which is exactly what the president directed. This deceitful response, combined with international crises in Hungary and the Middle East, silenced the issue temporarily. The *Washington Post* observed that the Suez Crisis overshadowed this important domestic political issue. Similarly, Arthur Krock of the *New York Times* commented that the Democrats' attempt to revitalize the H-bomb as a campaign issue was "blown into reality by the bombs falling and the guns booming in Egypt."[71]

Eisenhower won his own battle on the political front in the United States with a landslide election victory on 6 November. But it was won at a cost. One of the first casualties was his policy of candor. The administration that began its term pursuing a policy of candor toward the American people on nuclear matters ended it with secrecy, deception, and lies. The growing domestic political challenge of Stevenson's evolving test-ban proposal during the election campaign provides one strong explanation for this abandonment of candor. Yet the strength and consistency of Eisenhower's commitment to seek a test ban two years before Stevenson's proposal suggests that international politics often played a more decisive role. Eisenhower never wavered in his insistence that a test ban must include inspection, and considered Stevenson's various proposals without inspection as terribly wrong-headed. Any attempt in the future to negotiate a test ban with inspection could be undermined if Stevenson built enough political and popular support for a test ban with less stringent conditions. To prevent this, the administration moved to the polar opposite of its initial policy of candor, replacing it with secrecy and deception to isolate the Democratic challenger and maintain its own freedom to negotiate a future test-ban agreement on Eisenhower's own terms.[72]

As Fred Greenstein has persuasively argued, Eisenhower went to great lengths to conceal the political side of his leadership. The election of 1956 supports this interpretation, revealing Eisenhower's use of Nixon and Dewey to provide the most outspoken criticism of Stevenson and the use of an anonymous official to deny the administration's secret test-ban consideration. The election of 1956 illustrates that the Eisenhower administration was not beyond manipulating and lying to the American public to achieve domestic political gain and retain Eisenhower's international negotiating position. The implications of these actions are significant. Instead of moving closer to a moratorium on nuclear testing that Eisenhower secretly desired, the election campaign of 1956 resulted in a moratorium on his policy of candor to the American people on nuclear issues.[73]

The Influence of Strauss, the Fall of Stassen, and the Rise of *Sputnik* (November 1956-October 1957)

> We are, however, up against an extremely difficult world opinion situation and he [Eisenhower] did not think that the United States could permit itself to be "crucified on a cross of atoms" [by continuing to test nuclear weapons].
>
> —Goodpaster, Memorandum of Conference with the President, 24 June 1957

> Eisenhower "indicated that our statecraft was becoming too much a prisoner of our scientists."
>
> —Memorandum of Conference, 9 August 1957

Eisenhower in 1956 made a pivotal decision to overrule the almost unanimous counsel of his advisors and secretly make a test ban a stated policy objective. Only his disarmament advisor, Harold Stassen, shared Eisenhower's deep conviction that something must be done to ease tensions and slow the arms race. Stassen in 1957 participated in the first serious discussions between the United States and the Soviet Union involving a nuclear test ban at the London meetings of the subcommittee of the United Nations Disarmament Commission (UNDC).[1] At the London meetings, both sides made important concessions, significantly narrowing the gap between them. Unfortunately, Stassen's provocative political activities and diplomatic gaffes isolated him at home and abroad, eliminating any possibility that he could broker a consensus on a test-ban proposal within Eisenhower's closest advisors and between the nation's allies.

Within the administration, Eisenhower continued to face the strong opposition of the AEC and DOD to any limitations on testing. Increasingly, he expressed frustration with their inflexible positions and incessant requests for additional tests. On several occasions, Eisenhower overruled their vehement protests and made tentative policy revisions toward a test ban. Lacking confidence in his understanding of the highly complex technical issues related to nuclear testing and detection, Eisenhower moved slowly until experts assured him that the scientific facts supported his inclinations.

Yet it was the most vehement opponents to a test ban, Strauss and some prominent AEC scientists, whom Eisenhower relied upon to assess the technical feasibility of his inclinations. For this reason, Lewis Strauss exerted a dominant influence on Eisenhower's approach to a test ban. Strauss strictly limited the range of scientific advice reaching the president, shielding him from scientific judgments that supported a test ban. Convinced that the nation's survival depended upon refining its nuclear arsenal through additional testing, Strauss misled the president on the necessity of additional testing, exaggerated the difficulties of policing a test ban, and dismissed the valid technical assumptions of test-ban advocates. At critical stages in the London discussions, Strauss publicly advanced powerful new arguments for conducting additional tests.

The dominant influence of Strauss and AEC scientists became apparent to other scientists, the press, and even the president himself. As the gap grew between Eisenhower's convictions and his administration's actions, Eisenhower expressed his bitter frustration that his statecraft was becoming a prisoner of the administration's scientists. Eisenhower did nothing, however, to broaden the spectrum of scientific advice that he received until the Soviet launch of *Sputnik* created a national sense of emergency that pressured him to revise the administration's relationship to science.

I

The significant public debate over testing during the 1956 presidential election campaign did not end the administration's private examination of the test issue. Soon after the election, Eisenhower secretly reaffirmed his desire to end testing. Reviewing Stassen's latest disarmament proposal in November 1956, Eisenhower overruled the objections of Strauss and personally altered the wording from Stassen's suggested objective "to strictly limit" nuclear testing to "limit or *eliminate*" nuclear tests.[2] Despite the president's clearly stated objectives, Strauss's relentless arguments for the necessity of additional tests received wide support from all of Eisenhower's key advisors but Stassen. Only one month after the president reaffirmed his goal to limit or eliminate tests, Strauss requested

Eisenhower's approval for conducting an extensive test series in 1957 at the AEC's Nevada test site. According to Dulles, Eisenhower "expressed his doubts as to the advisability" of conducting the tests. Dulles convinced him that since the United States would conduct the tests in Nevada there would be minimal international protest. Although hesitant, Eisenhower approved Strauss's request to proceed with planning for the next AEC round of tests scheduled for May 1957.[3]

As he secretly prodded his advisors to find an acceptable formula to limit or cease testing, Eisenhower emphasized his broader objectives to the British, the American public, and congressional leaders. At the Bermuda Conference in March 1957, Eisenhower endorsed a joint U.S.-U.K. pledge to limit testing to a safe level. At a press conference two months later, Eisenhower emphasized the importance of making certain that "we are not ourselves being recalcitrant, we are not being picayunish" about negotiating disarmament with the Soviets. Pledging to keep an "open mind," Eisenhower stated his willingness to meet the Soviets "halfway."[4]

In a letter the following week to Congressman W. Sterling "Stub" Cole (R-N.Y.), a member of the AEC's congressional oversight committee, the Joint Committee on Atomic Energy (JCAE), Eisenhower wrote, "the whole question of testing of atomic weapons has engaged my concern from the time I took office." Affirming his commitment to keep testing to "an absolute minimum," Eisenhower assured Cole, who had recommended a limitation on testing in number and yield, that he remained flexible on the matter. Moreover, the president expressed his hope that some form of test limitation, "or even a temporary test suspension" might result from the ongoing London negotiations.[5]

A series of meetings at the end of May to discuss Stassen's London proposals illustrated Eisenhower's disappointment with the disjunction between these public pronouncements and his administration's actions. According to the record of one meeting, Eisenhower "very forcefully" expressed the "absolute necessity" of slowing down the arms race for both moral and financial reasons. Eisenhower lectured his advisors that Stassen's ongoing disarmament review was "no mere intellectual exercise or empty debate." Frustrated with the lack of progress in his goals thus far, Eisenhower stressed that "we have got to do something" to slow the arms race.[6]

In a meeting two days later, Eisenhower overruled the inflexible position of Strauss to provide Stassen a more flexible negotiating position. Strauss strongly objected to Stassen's proposal for a temporary test moratorium, arguing that this would risk American qualitative superiority in weapons. Strauss then argued that a test cessation would lead to the loss of key scientists from the AEC's laboratories, despite the fact that he received Ernest Lawrence's assurance the day before that a temporary ban would not result in such a loss. Further, Strauss asserted that once a test moratorium began it would be hard to overcome public pressure against resuming testing even if they had failed to reach an agreement with the Soviets on a permanent inspection system. Eisenhower rejected Strauss's arguments, insisting that the United States must make some "tangible concessions" while expressing his confidence that Strauss could keep his weapons laboratories running during a temporary test ban. Dismissing Strauss's objections, Eisenhower approved Stassen's recommendation to reverse the sequence of the administration's disarmament policy, agreeing to a temporary test ban *before* an inspection system was in place to verify a comprehensive disarmament agreement. Significantly, the President sided with Stassen against Strauss, authorizing the former's proposal to pursue a temporary test-ban agreement during the London negotiations.[7]

As Eisenhower began to challenge the arguments of test-ban opponents within his administration and cautiously move closer to the Soviets' negotiating position, he increasingly questioned the necessity of future tests. In early June, Eisenhower called Strauss into his office to discuss his concern with the international fears of fallout from testing. With the latest test series already under way, the president questioned the need for additional tests. Moreover, he balked at Strauss's proposal for a large increase in nuclear weapons. Convinced that they already had "a pretty darn fine arsenal of atomic weapons," Eisenhower thought they could now reduce, rather than expand their program.[8] In fact, the United States in 1957 possessed over 6,000 atomic warheads, compared to 660 for the Soviet Union and 20 for Great Britain.[9]

Committed to finding a solution to slow the arms race, Eisenhower in the first half of 1957 pressed his advisors for agreement on greater flexibility in the administration's disarmament policy. Although the AEC and DOD remained opposed to any significant changes in Stassen's disarmament proposals, Eisenhower charted a middle course between the pliable views of his disarmament advisor and the rigid position of the defense establishment. Further, he increasingly challenged the AEC and DOD's arguments for additional tests. Yet even though his frustration with their incessant test requirements mounted, Eisenhower lacked the confidence in his technical judgment to do more than urge Strauss to limit the tests to those absolutely essential. Eisenhower, willing to take only partial steps beyond the static views of the AEC and DOD, nevertheless remained hopeful that his approved course would allow Stassen to produce results in London.

II

As Strauss continued to press Eisenhower for additional tests, Harold Stassen struggled to make progress on disarmament. Stassen was the only member of Eisenhower's inner circle of advisors who shared the president's commitment to arms control. In Stassen's view, Soviet negotiators at London genuinely desired a disarmament agreement. In fact, the Soviets made significant concessions during the London discussions, pressuring the Eisenhower administration to respond in kind. In his desperate efforts in 1957 to negotiate an agreement with the Soviet Union, Stassen isolated himself both within the administration and among the western allies.

Although deeply committed to making progress on disarmament, Stassen's political activities took precedence during the presidential campaign of 1956. Convinced that Vice President Richard M. Nixon would hurt the Republican Party's performance in the election, Stassen embarked upon a "Dump Nixon" campaign to prevent his renomination. Shockingly, Eisenhower merely granted his assistant a leave of absence through the Republican National Convention to oppose the nomination of Nixon as his running mate. Not surprisingly, Stassen's political miscalculation largely destroyed his remaining credibility within the administration and failed to prevent Nixon's nomination.[10]

Following the Republican convention, Stassen returned to his position as Eisenhower's disarmament advisor. Within the administration, Dulles and Eisenhower's chief of staff, former New Hampshire Governor Sherman Adams, frequently conspired to remove Stassen. While Dulles clashed with Stassen over diplomatic procedure and philosophy, Adams considered him a distinct political liability within the administration. In a late-December meeting with Eisenhower and Adams, Dulles argued that Stassen's activities had shaken confidence in him and recommended sending him temporarily to a diplomatic post in Europe.[11] Although Eisenhower recognized that Stassen's political motives brought him much criticism, the president considered him "head and shoulders above most people in the government" and sincerely devoted to the cause of disarmament.

The fact that Eisenhower retained Stassen when two of his most trusted advisors, Sherman Adams and John Foster Dulles, recommended his removal illustrates the president's hopes for progress toward disarmament. With his other advisors deeply suspicious of the Soviets and opposed to any disarmament measures, Eisenhower was unwilling to part with the one advisor who aggressively pursued his hope for an acceptable formula to slow the arms race. For the time being, Stassen tenuously held onto his position, but he lost his cabinet rank and his authorization to attend all NSC and cabinet meetings. Eisenhower, responding to Dulles and Adams's concerns over his ambitious disarmament advisor, placed Stassen under the control of Dulles and the State Department.[12]

Although Eisenhower continued to support Stassen in spite of growing unpopularity within the administration, the president lost confidence in him the following June when Stassen disrupted relations between the western allies. At the London Conference, Stassen committed what Eisenhower called "one of the most stupid things that anyone on a diplomatic mission could possibly commit." Eisenhower had just overruled the arguments of Strauss in order to seek an agreement on a temporary test ban before an international agency fully installed an inspection system. Sporting new proposals and bolstered with renewed confidence, Stassen returned to London with specific instructions not to undertake detailed negotiations until all of the interested U.S. agencies and the western allies concurred with Eisenhower's new policy. Despite previous admonitions from Dulles and explicit instructions from Washington the day before, Stassen shockingly provided the head Soviet negotiator, Valerin Zorin, with an "informal memorandum" that detailed the new disarmament policy before the western allies had a chance to respond to Eisenhower's new proposal. Not only did this violate the directives from Washington but it also breached diplomatic procedure; the NATO allies had not had time to review and comment on the new U.S. position. Within the administration, Dulles and Eisenhower worked feverishly to mend relations with the French and British, which the Suez crisis had already severely strained only months before.[13]

Stassen's inexplicable behavior meant different things to Eisenhower and Dulles. For Eisenhower, it finally eroded his confidence in his industrious disarmament advisor. For Dulles, it confirmed that Stassen's dangerous ambition might lead him to "reach an agreement on almost any terms and if necessary sell our allies down the river."[14] Stassen's tactics alone threatened to split the allies. After British Prime Minister Harold Macmillan wrote Eisenhower and expressed his "distress" at Stassen's actions, Dulles drafted a reply that revealed their humiliation over the incident. The reply stated that Eisenhower was "astonished and chagrined" at Stassen's actions, insisting that "everybody here deplores this occurrence as deeply as I do."[15] After he approved the draft, Eisenhower indicated that he was willing to accept Stassen's resignation even though the Soviets may use it as an excuse to break up the talks. He even asked Dulles to begin thinking about a replacement, something Dulles and Adams had been urging for at least six months. According to Dulles's record of the conversation, Eisenhower revealed that "for the first time his confidence in Stassen was seriously shaken."[16]

Upon reflection, Eisenhower decided not to demand Stassen's resignation, fearful that the Soviets would use the firing of the administration's strongest disarmament advocate as a reason to break off the negotiations that had thus far been productive. He did approve Dulles's request to "surround" Stassen with someone more dependable to ensure that he did not "go off on his own in the future." Stassen's actions illuminated the pecking order among Eisenhower's competing objectives. Although the president attached great hopes to Stassen's efforts to broker a disarmament agreement, his advisor's methods directly contradicted Eisenhower's condition that a consensus within his administration and the western allies must support the accord.[17]

Stassen's diplomatic blunder, which caused outrage within the administration and tensions between its allies, was ironically followed by major Soviet concessions. Soviet negotiators broke their insistence on a permanent test ban, proposing a two- to three-year ban instead. Most importantly, they indicated their willingness, for the first time, to accept international inspectors manning control posts on Soviet soil. Despite Strauss's urgings to treat the Soviet proposals as purely propaganda, the administration faced pressures to respond to the Soviet concessions with the flexibility that Eisenhower had publicly stressed.[18]

At this critical stage in negotiations, Stassen received some technical advice supporting a test ban that contradicted Strauss's pessimistic characterization of the ability to detect Soviet tests. Physicist Hans Bethe, after spending a year on sabbatical in England, resumed his work as the chairman of a scientific committee that worked with the AEC and the Air Force to evaluate evidence from Soviet tests. Encouraged by signs that "negotiations look[ed] more hopeful than at any time since the war," Bethe wrote Stassen on 11 June to inform him that his expert analysis differed from "prevalent official opinions" on detection. According to Bethe, the current monitoring system outside of Soviet soil could detect any atomic explosion above 100kt "with virtual certainty," which he defined as "99% or better."[19]

After detailing the nation's substantial detection capabilities, Bethe discussed several arguments in favor of a test ban based admittedly on "judgment and politics" rather than the technical facts of detection. Bethe discounted the dangers of fallout from testing and was troubled by test-ban advocates who emphasized this aspect. He lamented to Stassen that the Soviet ability to capitalize on these exaggerated fears presented a "psychological situation [that] irks me." For Bethe the strongest argument in favor of a test ban was as a first step toward disarmament. In his view, the United States could use the Soviets' desire for a test ban as leverage for an agreement on disarmament measures. According to Bethe, a test ban would also freeze the American advantage in nuclear weapons development and halt the proliferation of nuclear weapons to other nations. Bethe respectfully, though perhaps unwisely, sent Strauss a copy of his direct appeal of dissenting views.[20]

Strauss was likely horrified that Stassen possessed Bethe's powerful technical arguments supporting a test ban. Already critical of Stassen's test-ban proposals and negotiating tactics, Strauss expressed his concerns to Dulles that the "enfant terrible" would advance a personal proposal to the Soviet Union without allowing Strauss to counter it.[21] To prevent a test-ban agreement, which Bethe now identified as requiring minimal inspection, Strauss was adamant about linking it to a cutoff on the production of fissionable materials. Aware that policing a cutoff agreement required a substantial inspection system, Strauss was convinced the Soviets would never accept such a substantial international presence on their soil. For Strauss, maintaining the link between testing and other disarmament measures would block any progress toward an agreement, which would allow him to continue his test program.[22]

Strauss's conversations with Dulles convinced the AEC chairman that the secretary shared Strauss's commitment to retaining this linkage and that the State Department had regained firm control over Stassen. Strauss was more concerned, however, that Stassen would convince Eisenhower to break this link and seek a separate test-ban agreement. Although Strauss had thus far largely prevented Eisenhower from hearing the views of test-ban advocates, he could no longer be sure that Bethe's technical conclusions would not reach the president through Stassen. In case this happened, Strauss ensured that the president received the powerful views of scientists determined to continue testing.

In Congressional hearings the following week, three prominent physicists affiliated with the AEC provided an emotional argument for continuing testing. Joining Ernest Lawrence and Edward Teller was Mark Mills, the head of Livermore's theoretical division. The scientists described their efforts to develop a so-called "clean bomb" that would produce minimal radiation. A test ban would prevent the development of this weapon, which would sharply reduce the amount of radiation, subsequently reducing the number of casualties to friends and foes alike. According to Lawrence, "it would be a crime against the people" to stop testing before the perfection of such a weapon. In one bold reversal of logic, Lawrence elevated the argument to continue testing to a moral imperative no less forceful than the dire appeals to humanity of test-ban advocates such as Albert Schweitzer and Linus Pauling.[23]

Teller, describing to the JCAE the various ways that the Soviets could hide nuclear tests from detection, further undermined Stassen's efforts in London. The testimony occurred just as Stassen was sending optimistic reports about gaining the Soviet concessions on inspection and the time length of a temporary test ban. Yet everything that the scientists told the JCAE pointed to the absolute necessity of continuing testing. After considering recalling Stassen from London to testify, Congressman Cole instead arranged for the scientists to present the same information to the president the following Monday.

Alerted by Cole, Strauss spent the weekend preparing the three scientists for their meeting with Eisenhower. In their forty-minute meeting with the president, Lawrence repeated his argument that the failure to develop clean weapons would "truly be a crime against humanity." Eisenhower responded that naturally no one could oppose the development of clean bombs. The president also assured them that he would not stop tests without a broader agreement that included inspection provisions. He then stressed, however, that the strong worldwide public opinion against testing compelled them to limit testing. Eisenhower warned that the United States could not permit itself to be "crucified on a cross of atoms" for continuing to test without regard to world opinion. Eisenhower acknowledged that much of the worldwide opposition to testing was the result of intense Soviet propaganda, but also remarked that American opinion was divided over the harmful effects of testing. After Teller deprecated Linus Pauling's dire assessment of the test hazards and ridiculed the individuals who signed Pauling's petition, the president countered that they could not dismiss the fact of substantial public opinion against testing even if Pauling's analysis was erroneous. Teller concluded with a much more forceful argument that Eisenhower could not counter. Contradicting the analysis Bethe provided to Stassen, Teller restated his congressional testimony that the United States could not adequately police an agreement to stop tests.[24]

The meeting had an immediate impact on Eisenhower, temporarily shaking his commitment to a test ban. Eisenhower complained to Dulles that he was especially upset that Strauss and the scientists made "it look like a crime to ban tests." The president was drawn, however, to the potential of a clean bomb, but somehow conflated its development with the peaceful uses of nuclear explosions that he had previously championed. Most importantly, Eisenhower was deeply concerned with Teller's comments that they could hold tests without fear of detection. Assuming that the Soviets could do likewise, the scientists thought that the consideration of a test ban was "playing with fire."[25]

Eisenhower's "clean bomb" meeting had a profound impact on the London negotiations, undercutting Stassen's progress with the Soviets. At the suggestion of Robert Cutler, Dulles sent a private cable to Stassen, informing him that the scientists' testimony had shaken the confidence of the president and spurred opposition to a ban within Congress.[26] In his telegram to Stassen, Dulles revealed that since his meeting with the scientists Eisenhower "has had serious mental reservations as to the correctness of our proposal to suspend testing." Meanwhile, the Senate was also expressing "considerable skepticism" about the wisdom of suspending tests and the effectiveness of an inspection system. As a result, Dulles emphasized that testing was an area where "I do not think that any concessions can be made or the impression given that the kind of inspection required is simple and can be necessarily remote."[27]

Eisenhower's commitment to making progress, however, was only temporarily sidetracked by Teller, Lawrence, and Mills. A month after meeting with the scientists, he encouraged the London negotiators to show greater "flexibility" in negotiations on testing. At the same time, he remained concerned that the western allies, still distrustful of Stassen, had not yet accepted the latest U.S. proposals on aerial inspection zones based upon Eisenhower's earlier Open Skies initiative. In an effort to improve relations with the allies, Eisenhower sent Dulles to London to take charge of the negotiations from Stassen. Thus at the same time that Eisenhower sought greater flexibility in the negotiations in London, he suppressed his controversial advisor who was most likely to use it to advance the negotiations. Eager to shore up the western allies and assert his dominance over disarmament policy, Dulles extended none of the flexibility that Eisenhower desired, virtually eliminating the chance of any further progress.[28]

When Dulles arrived in London to "surround" Stassen, propaganda replaced progress. Nevertheless, the record of progress achieved earlier remained, as both sides made concessions that significantly narrowed their divisions. The Soviets had made two major concessions during the London talks that partly justified Stassen's optimism. First, they agreed to negotiate a two- to three-year test moratorium, dropping their previous demand for a permanent test ban. Second and most importantly, for the first time since nuclear disarmament talks began, the Soviets indicated a willingness to agree to the key American demand for on-site inspection. Eisenhower too made concessions, overruling the opposition of Strauss and the Department of Defense to agree to a temporary test ban before a comprehensive inspection system for broader disarmament was in place, then agreeing to extend this temporary moratorium from twelve to twenty-four months.[29]

After both sides showed greater flexibility than before, resulting in a significant narrowing of the gap between the two, the London talks broke down in late-August over the linking of a temporary test ban with an agreement to cease production of nuclear materials. With the close of talks in London, the dialogue returned to the United Nations, where it had begun in 1957. There, each side blamed the other for the failure to reach a test-ban agreement at London. Despite the ultimate failure of the discussions in London, the talks succeeded in breaking down several barriers, paving the way for more substantive negotiations in 1958.[30]

III

As Harold Stassen strove to make a test ban possible, AEC Chairman Lewis L. Strauss worked feverishly to make a test ban appear less desirable to Eisenhower. Largely a result of Strauss's monopolization of scientific advice, Eisenhower authorized only limited concessions for the London negotiations toward his goal of ceasing tests. Monopolizing the scientific advice that the president received, Strauss associated test-ban advocates with a communist-inspired propaganda campaign, prevented the president from receiving their evidence of health hazards resulting from testing, and convinced Eisenhower not to hear contrary opinions on testing even when he specifically requested them.

Although he proved to be up to the challenge, Strauss faced an increasingly difficult task in 1957 of controlling the information that reached Eisenhower. Private and public appeals to cease testing gradually grew in early 1957 following the heightened awareness of the issue during the election campaign the previous fall. Strauss received and answered most of the thousand plus letters expressing concern over testing addressed to the president.[31] A few, however, reached Eisenhower personally. In late January 1957 Dr. Albert Schweitzer, the famed musician, philosopher, physician, theologian, and winner of the Nobel Peace Prize in 1952, privately pleaded for a test ban in a letter sent to Eisenhower through Norman Cousins. Cousins, a test-ban advocate, editor of the *Saturday Review*, and later biographer of Schweitzer, began regular correspondence with Eisenhower on the test-ban issue. While news of the letter eventually leaked from Paris, Schweitzer withheld extensive public comment until late April, when he released a formal appeal through the Nobel Prize Committee for worldwide public opinion to demand a test ban. Schweitzer's appeal, which focused on the health hazards of radioactive fallout from testing, was broadcast on radio in over fifty countries, but not the United States.[32]

Ironically, it was the AEC's campaign to refute Schweitzer's claims, just as it was Nixon's attack on Stevenson's test-ban proposal the previous year, that brought more public attention to the issue than the original appeal itself. A broader segment of the public, exposed to the often bitter debate among scientists over the health hazards of testing, became concerned with the arguments of Schweitzer and other test-ban advocates. At the end of April, a Gallup Poll found that a majority of Americans believed that there was real danger in testing. In the same poll, 63 percent favored reaching a test-ban agreement with the Soviet Union. The previous October, only 24 percent had favored a test ban. Since then, debates within the United Nations, congressional hearings, and Schweitzer's appeal drew greater attention to the test issue. The polls suggest that the increased public debate over testing led to an important shift in public opinion; by the spring of 1957 a majority of the public had become convinced of the health hazards of testing and supported the cessation of testing.[33]

A second public appeal, this one from within the United States, generated even greater attention from both the general public and government officials. Linus Pauling, a Nobel Prize– winning chemist from Cal Tech, announced his opposition to testing in mid-May and began a petition campaign among scientists, calling for an international agreement to halt all nuclear tests. Pauling forwarded his petition with over 2,000 signatures to the White House in early June, then embarked upon an international campaign, presenting in January 1958 a petition of over 9,000 signatures from scientists across the globe to United Nations Secretary-General Dag Hammarskjöld.[34]

Although Pauling would eventually win the Nobel Peace Prize in 1962 on the basis of his test-ban activities, he often made exaggerated and dubious claims about the potential health hazards of fallout. While scientists associated with the AEC refuted his scientific arguments, the FBI and Senate became interested in his communist affiliation. Pauling, a member of several peace organizations believed to be communist dominated, was no stranger to such accusations. Senator Joseph McCarthy pegged him as a "hidden communist," while the House Un-American Activities Committee accused him in 1951 of following a "pattern of loyalty to the communist cause." McCarthy's demise did not prevent the return of congressional interest in Pauling's communist ties.[35] Three days after Pauling submitted his petition to the White House, the Senate Internal Security Subcommittee subpoenaed Pauling to investigate if communist organizations were behind his petition.[36] A FBI source, however, reported that Pauling could be expected to use his appearance to further publicize the dangers of fallout and use every opportunity to embarrass the Subcommittee. The Subcommittee quickly reversed its decision to have Pauling appear for questioning.[37]

While the Senate backed off, FBI Director J. Edgar Hoover circulated within the Eisenhower administration an analysis of the fallout controversy with Pauling identified as the "focal point." The report outlined the efforts of communists on both the international level and within the United States to exploit the fallout controversy. According to Hoover, "an outstanding feature of this controversy concerns the numerous scientists with subversive affiliations who have become associated with it." Pauling was just one of the many "familiar" scientists associated with communist front activities in the past who were "creating fear, misunderstanding, and confusion in the minds of the public on this issue."[38]

Accusations of communist direction in the nuclear test-ban movement appeared in the popular media as well. *US News and World Report* published articles depicting the fallout scare as communist inspired and the supporters of the Pauling petition as insignificant scientists with insufficient knowledge of atomic affairs. One article asserted that "much of the clamor about the danger of fallout is inspired by Communists."[39] The strong attack on test-ban advocates prompted Lewis Strauss to write the magazine's editor, David Lawrence, to praise him for the effective article.[40] A second FBI report in July, however, concluded that communists played only a minor role in the test-ban debate. According to the FBI investigation, the Communist Party played a marginal role because the test-ban campaign was "developing into a broad movement with a universal response among scientists, religious leaders, and pacifists." Although the second report minimized the influence of the Communist Party, Strauss continued to imply that its influence was central.[41]

Two weeks after publishing its flawed depiction of the communist direction of the fallout scare, US News minimized the qualifications of those who signed the Pauling petition. In this case, its analysis identified a valid concern; many of the scientists who signed the petition lacked expertise in atomic energy.[42] Curiously, the US News article contained a remarkably similar analysis of those signing the petition that the AEC circulated within the administration two weeks before, suggesting that Strauss leaked the information to the popular magazine.[43] In fact, Strauss raised the same shortcoming to Eisenhower, suggesting that he use it to respond to any related questions if they arose in his next press conference. When a question did come up, Eisenhower's response closely followed Strauss's suggestions. Strauss then cleverly cited Eisenhower's public comments, which he had privately crafted, in replies on the behalf of Eisenhower to the thousands of letters from citizens concerned about testing. In such a shrewd manner, Strauss dominated the administration's response to public demands to cease testing.[44]

During a press conference on 5 June, a reporter from the Associated Press asked the president how his own advisors reacted to the findings of some geneticists that nuclear weapons tests would damage "hundreds of thousands and, perhaps, millions of yet unborn in terms of physical deformities and shortened life spans." Eisenhower responded, closely following Strauss's suggested reply, that this was a field where scientists disagreed. Noting that scientists seemed to be commenting outside of their field of expertise on this issue, Eisenhower suggested that "it looks almost like an organized affair."

When pressed to clarify his comments that implied communist organization, Eisenhower replied that although he said there seemed to be some organization behind it, "I didn't say a wicked organization." The president evasively continued that "there are as many of these people just as honest as they can be, there is no question about that." Eisenhower's typically ambiguous answer left open the inference that a significant number of scientists opposed to testing were less than "honest."[45]

When Saturday Review editor Norman Cousins wrote the president to protest this illation, Eisenhower asked Strauss to draft a response; Strauss more than willingly obliged. His draft reply to Cousins admitted that Eisenhower's initial press conference utterance was "fuzzy" about the communist influence on test-ban advocates. It insisted, however, that the president's later comments about scientists talking out of their fields amplified what he truly meant. The reply suggested that Eisenhower was referring to an analysis of those signing the Pauling petition similar to the recent article in *US News* (which was likely based on the AEC's own analysis). That article identified biologists as the most represented scientific field while those most knowledgeable on atomic issues, physicists, comprised only 17 percent of those signing Pauling's petition.[46] The *US News* analysis, however, did not acknowledge that biologists were likely to be better informed of the dangers to humans of fallout, and thus more concerned, than physicists.

The Strauss-drafted reply failed to satisfy Cousins, who became even more concerned after reports speculated that the president's 24 June meeting with the three physicists from Livermore convinced him of the necessity to continue testing. Eisenhower called upon Strauss only weeks after his initial reply to respond to another letter from Cousins. Cousins expressed his concern that "the impression has been created that only scientists connected with the AEC have had a chance to present their evidence to you." He suggested that the president should listen to a group of scientists from outside of the administration who held contrary views.[47] In a letter to Strauss, Eisenhower approved of the idea and instructed him to select two or three names of various scientists whom Cousins had suggested meet with him.[48] Strauss moved quickly to prevent such a meeting. Responding the following day, Strauss discredited Cousins as a leader in the fallout propaganda campaign and pegged the scientists he listed as "pamphleteers or speakers" who had supported Adlai Stevenson's test-ban proposal. Adding support to Strauss's claims, Cousins's list included three scientists from the FBI's analysis of communist affiliated test-ban advocates. Strauss's strongly worded response convinced Eisenhower to reverse his willingness to consider outside scientific advice and decline Cousins's offer.[49]

Significantly, Cousins and his supporters were not the only ones to express concerns about Teller, Lawrence, and Mills monopolizing Eisenhower's views on testing. The Los Alamos chapter of the Federation of American Scientists issued a press release indicating their regret that the views of the three Livermore scientists served as an "oblique attack on initial forms of the U.S. disarmament proposals" and served to undercut progress at London. For the Los Alamos scientists, the pursuit of a disarmament agreement was the more dominant concern than the pursuit of the elusive clean bomb and the development of peaceful uses of atomic energy. Strauss successfully shielded from Eisenhower the fact that some of the AEC's own scientists were sufficiently troubled that they challenged the organization's official view. Instead, he never mentioned the AEC dissenters, portraying the outsiders opposing the views of the Livermore scientists as communists and pacifists who lacked the expertise to comment intelligently on the issue.[50]

Strauss not only misled Eisenhower in his depiction of test-ban advocates, he also skewed the technical arguments that he presented to Eisenhower for continued testing. After meeting with the president, Strauss and his aide, navy Captain Jack Morse, wrote Lawrence, Mills, and Teller to congratulate them on their "performance." Morse assured Mills that "the situation called for over-selling rather than under-selling, particularly when a simple statement could not cover all the complexities involved." As Morse suggested, the scientists had been less than forthcoming to the president. They neglected to mention that there were severe difficulties in developing the clean bomb; the modifications necessary to reduce radiation required a three to fivefold increase in the weight of the weapon and reduced its yield in half. With its increased size and decreased yield, a clean nuclear bomb offered few advantages over the original fission bombs. Strauss and the scientists thus kept Eisenhower unaware of the serious technical shortcomings that undermined one of the administration's primary justifications for continued testing.[51]

Lewis Strauss's sharp control over scientific advice frustrated Eisenhower's inclination to discontinue testing. A staunch cold warrior, Strauss was absolutely convinced that the Soviets would violate any test ban and gain a strategic advantage over the United States. Convinced that a test cessation would imperil the nation, Strauss red-baited test-ban advocates, prevented the president from reading most of their entreaties, and convinced Eisenhower not to hear contrary opinions on testing even when he specifically requested them. Most importantly, Strauss presented powerful (and sometimes misleading) scientific judgments against a test ban at critical stages, curtailing the London negotiations just as Eisenhower was pushing for greater flexibility. Although increasingly frustrated with Strauss's inflexibility on testing, Eisenhower lacked the technical counsel that would allow him to confidently challenge Strauss's powerful objections. Eisenhower's goal of ceasing tests would remain unrealized as long as Strauss retained strict control over the scientific expertise reaching the president.

IV

Strauss's incessant requests for continued testing made Eisenhower increasingly aware of his dependence upon the scientific expertise that Strauss delivered. Although this situation began to trouble Eisenhower, he did nothing to alter it until a national crisis pressured him to act. Eisenhower's hesitancy to alter the system of science advising reflected his weariness with the growing relationship between science and the government. In the fall of 1956, the president observed that every scientific survey that the government generated seemed to result in recommendations to undertake additional government-sponsored programs. The following spring, he revealed his opposition to the growing government sponsorship of basic scientific research in a meeting with Republican legislative leaders. Eisenhower later asked Strauss and James Killian, his first science advisor, to separate clearly the support of basic research and applied research. After Strauss and Killian entered a lengthy discussion of the difficulties of distinguishing between basic and applied research, Eisenhower declared, "Well I throw up my hands—this is beyond me. You fellows will have to do it as you have been doing it."[52] This was a relationship that increasingly troubled the president, but one that he was unwilling to tackle privately or confront publicly until his farewell address warning about the rise of a "scientific-technological elite."[53]

During his presidency, Eisenhower slowly recognized that the scientists affiliated with the administration played a powerful role in his foreign policy decisions. In Eisenhower's view, the scientists' unrestrained quest for knowledge spurred their ceaseless requests for additional experiments. When he discussed a test ban with Stassen in April 1957, the president indicated that the strongest worldwide opposition to a test ban might actually come from American scientists who were "fascinated by the research they are enabled to carry out through this means."[54] Cognizant of the president's great hopes for the peaceful uses of atomic energy, Strauss consistently justified the necessity of additional weapons testing to develop these peaceful capabilities. Strauss argued that the inspiration to test for peaceful uses was so great that *any* test ban would make it impossible to hold his scientific forces together. Initially persuaded, Eisenhower rejected Strauss's arguments at the end of May, indicating that the administration must offer some "tangible concessions" to worldwide opposition to testing. He assured Strauss that he was confident the AEC could keep the weapons laboratories running during a *temporary* test ban.[55]

At times, the press corps recognized the implications of Eisenhower's predicament more clearly than he did. In late June, James Reston of the *New York Times* suggested that Eisenhower had uncritically accepted the expertise of Lawrence, Mills, and Teller. In Reston's view, the president faced a multitude of such highly scientific and technical issues. What he sorely needed was a special science advisor to sift out the various technical issues and provide him with a balanced and independent judgment. At Eisenhower's press conference a few weeks later, one of Reston's colleagues in the press corps asked the president if he had ever considered appointing a scientific advisor. Eisenhower indicated that he already had scientists in the AEC and Department of Defense providing him advice and it "hadn't occurred" to him to have one reporting directly to him. Upon reflection, he indicated, "now that you have mentioned it I will think about it."[56]

Although press queries did not prompt him to appoint immediately an independent science advisor, Eisenhower's private conversations reveal a growing concern with his reliance on the counsel of scientists tied to his administration. After learning that the president was instructing Dulles to show more flexibility in the London negotiations, Strauss quickly intervened. Strauss convinced the president that he could be flexible only in the length of a temporary test ban, not in the inseparable concept of linking any test ban with a cutoff in the production of nuclear materials. Strauss's insistence on this inseparable link resulted in the final impasse at London. Although Eisenhower once again acceded to Strauss's assertions, Under Secretary of State Christian Herter recorded that the president was "disturbed by the fact that the scientists today in this field seemed to be running the government rather than acting as servants for the government." Even though Strauss and his scientists continued to frustrate Eisenhower's goals, he remained fatefully tied to their narrow range of scientific advice.[57]

Ten days later, Eisenhower met with a small group of advisors to discuss Strauss's next test series. Dulles recorded that the scale of the tests initially "appalled" the president, who was increasingly frustrated with the gap between his personal objectives and his administration's actions.[58] Since he had repeatedly expressed in public his commitment to limiting tests, Eisenhower lamented that "talking disarmament and at the same time planning a four-month period of atomic testing" placed him in a more awkward situation than any he could think of.[59] Lacking the confidence to flatly dismiss Strauss's incessant requests, which were backed by the dire warnings and the technical expertise of the AEC's top atomic scientists, Eisenhower curtly told his advisors "that our statecraft was becoming too much a prisoner of our scientists." Emphasizing that he wanted to curtail the length of the testing period and the number of test shots, Eisenhower ordered Strauss to return later in the afternoon with a revised proposal.[60]

According to records of the meeting that afternoon, Eisenhower remained deeply troubled, but still conflicted about testing. The meeting also illustrates Eisenhower's willingness to challenge Strauss in some cases, but accede to his requests in others. Strauss strongly protested Eisenhower's two-year test suspension proposal, again arguing that top scientists would be lost if they could not conduct tests or experiments over such a long period of time. While this same argument swayed Eisenhower in April, by this time he was convinced that the "world situation" was more important than this consideration. He was now willing to accept the resulting "organizational setbacks" of losing some scientific talent, though he also thought that Strauss was being "unduly pessimistic." According to Strauss's record of the meeting, Eisenhower asserted that "we had enough of 'public policy making by scientists.'" Further, Eisenhower cautioned that the "paradoxical conduct" of professing a readiness to suspend testing while planning and executing such an extensive test series would bring accusations of bad faith. Eisenhower rejected Strauss's vigorous arguments to limit the most recent test proposal to twelve months and Dulles's recommendation to limit the length to eighteen months. Instead, Eisenhower moved beyond the counsel of his advisors and approved a proposal for a twenty-four-month suspension.[61]

Although Eisenhower, exasperated with his advisors' inflexibility, acted decisively against their counsel to narrow the divided negotiating positions of the nuclear powers, he approved Strauss's request to conduct another series before any agreement would go into effect. Eisenhower authorized, albeit reluctantly, the number of tests that Strauss requested under the condition that the AEC minimize the yield of weapons tested and the length of the test series. He assured Strauss that he could complete the tests before the Senate had time to ratify an agreement with the Soviet Union. Thus, Eisenhower by August of 1957 remained concerned about testing and the arms race, while increasingly aware and critical of the sometimes overwhelming influence of the scientific advice that he received.[62]

For almost five years, the Eisenhower administration had resisted altering the structure of presidential science advising to match the technical demands of the nuclear age. Instead, that function remained largely in the hands of Lewis Strauss, who jealously guarded his ability to filter the scientific opinions on atomic energy matters reaching the president. Recognizing Strauss's powerful influence, scientists feared that the administration was receiving only one side of technically complex issues. Administration officials twice rejected the ODM's Science Advisory Committee's suggestions to assign a scientist to the NSC staff and to appoint a presidential science advisor. Although Eisenhower increasingly expressed his frustration at the power and influence of the scientific opinions he received, he declined to follow suggestions from the press corps to expand his range of science advice. Despite the growing recognition among scientists, the press, and even Eisenhower himself that the administration needed to revise its system of science advice, it took a national crisis to spur Eisenhower to act.

V

The Soviet launch of *Sputnik* on 4 October initiated a national crisis that prompted Eisenhower to broaden his access to science advice to meet the challenges to his national security and civil defense policies.[63] The Soviet feat aroused popular fears stoked by partisan political attacks that the United States had lost its strategic superiority to the Soviet Union. Strauss's previous justifications for testing and Eisenhower's decision not to divulge the secrets gathered by the U-2 made Eisenhower even more vulnerable to pressures from the AEC and DOD to continue testing. Strauss's previous arguments that more tests were necessary to develop defensive weapons against Soviet missiles received renewed emphasis from the Soviet satellite. In fact, *Sputnik* accelerated fears of a surprise Soviet attack that Strauss originally fostered to justify continued testing despite Eisenhower's private belief, supported by CIA analysis, that a Soviet assault was unlikely. Thus, Eisenhower's private commitment to halt nuclear weapons experiments suffered from his own administration's public rhetoric to justify additional testing.[64] Because of the administration's previous arguments, it would be extremely challenging to negotiate a test-ban treaty that the public would accept and the Senate would ratify. Based upon these circumstances, *Sputnik* should have eliminated the remote chance that Eisenhower would pursue a test ban during the remainder of his presidency.

Ironically, the opposite occurred. As part of his effort to calm public anxieties after *Sputnik*, Eisenhower created a science advisory committee that included many members who shared his inclination to pursue a test ban. Their technical expertise provided Eisenhower the confidence to counter Strauss's powerful arguments against a test ban. Eisenhower in 1958, assured by his science advisors' powerful technical conclusions, finally acted upon his inclinations to pursue a test ban.

As part of his initial response to *Sputnik*, Eisenhower turned to SAC for recommendations on several scientific issues. Marginalized within the administration until I. I. Rabi in 1956 became its chairman, SAC used the atmosphere of crisis following the launch of *Sputnik* to accomplish its frustrated goal of elevating its importance within the administration.[65] The scientists recommended that Eisenhower appoint a personal advisor on scientific affairs with an office in the White House. Eisenhower concurred, appointing James R. Killian in November as his Special Assistant for Science and Technology. Along with Killian's position, Eisenhower established the Presidential Science Advisory Committee (PSAC) to advise him on the range of complex scientific matters he confronted. Elevated from the ODM and reorganized in the White House, the science advisors before long replaced Stassen as the strongest advocates for a test ban among Eisenhower's closest advisors. Most importantly, these test-ban advocates possessed the technical expertise that penetrated Strauss's filtering of scientific advice reaching the president.[66]

Eisenhower's different response in October 1957 to two very similar test-ban proposals reveals the decisive role of science advice in providing Eisenhower the confidence he lacked to pursue his inclinations. Eisenhower received separate but remarkably similar test-ban proposals from his beleaguered disarmament advisor and from a respected scientist unaffiliated with the AEC. Harold Stassen remained the sole advisor who shared Eisenhower's deepest convictions about slowing the arms race. Although Stassen retained his position until March 1958, he had lost the trust of Eisenhower and had become a pariah within the administration for his opposition to Nixon, his diplomatic blunder in London, and his controversial disarmament proposals. Stassen was aware of his tenuous position, yet he continued to propose disarmament measures antithetical to the rigid positions of the AEC and DOD. Stassen's discussions in London convinced him that it was a "historic moment" when the Soviets sincerely desired a "first step" agreement.[67]

During his remaining months in the administration, Stassen advanced disarmament initiatives that sought to separate the link between testing and fissionable material production. Stassen in October 1957 proposed a separate test ban to Dulles and Eisenhower. Perhaps based upon Bethe's analysis, Stassen argued that international monitors could police a separate test ban with as few as eight inspection stations within Soviet soil. For Stassen, this would "open up" the Soviet Union, providing valuable espionage information to the west. Dulles quickly dismissed the idea, sharply pointing out that Stassen's views were unanimously opposed by the rest of the president's disarmament advisors. Eisenhower agreed that they could not yet break the link between a cut-off and a test ban, but appeared intrigued by the advantages of positioning a limited amount of inspectors within Soviet territory. Despite his interest in Stassen's presentation, Eisenhower had succumbed to the widespread perception within the administration that Stassen's excessively optimistic proposals lacked a sound technical backing.[68]

Significantly, I. I. Rabi, chairman of the Science Advisory Committee whose members included Bethe, presented a similar proposal to Eisenhower three weeks later. Interested but skeptical of Stassen's presentation, Eisenhower immediately asked Strauss to study Rabi's proposal. The contrasting response to like proposals illustrates the decisive influence of science advice in shaping Eisenhower's approach to a test ban. Rabi and Stassen both shared Eisenhower's inclination to pursue a test ban. Stassen's excessive optimism, overweening ambition, and lack of technical expertise made his views easily dismissed within the administration. Conversely, Eisenhower, who had known Rabi since the late 1940s, retained great confidence in Rabi's calm counsel, aura of objectivity, and Nobel Prize-winning credentials. Eisenhower's confidence in Rabi soon spread to Killian and the members of PSAC. With sober advice and unassailable expertise on the complex issues, Eisenhower's newly appointed science advisors soon succeeded where Stassen had long stumbled; Eisenhower declared a test moratorium in 1958 and initiated negotiations toward a comprehensive test-ban agreement with the Soviet Union.[69]

PSAC, the Test Moratorium, and the Geneva System (October 1957–August 1958)

> Scientists like Teller . . . are trying to run the policy of the Government.
>
> —Eisenhower, 1 May 1958

> Scientists and advisors are in complete disagreement as to [the] course that should be pursued.
>
> —Eisenhower, 6 August 1958

Despite the malaise after *Sputnik*, increased tensions resulting from the deployment of U.S. forces to Lebanon, a second Taiwan Straits crisis, and Khrushchev's Berlin ultimatum, Eisenhower in 1958 showed considerable flexibility in moving closer to a test-ban accord. Although world opinion continued to oppose testing and the administration feared that it could no longer avoid a UN resolution against testing, American public opinion remained divided, giving Eisenhower considerable leeway to chart his own course. Eisenhower's nuclear testing policy in 1958, contrary to the most recent study of the issue, did not remain tied to the counsel of the AEC and DOD.[1] In fact, on three separate occasions Eisenhower overruled their opposition to move closer to a test-ban accord with the Soviet Union. Eisenhower directed an internal study of a test ban, proposed technical talks with the Soviet Union to determine the control measures necessary to monitor a ban, and agreed to a temporary test moratorium without inspection as the administration began negotiations on a test-ban agreement with the Soviet Union.

Eisenhower began to part with his commitment to reaching a consensus among his advisors on disarmament in 1956. Then, he overruled the internal opposition in providing policy objectives, though he did little to act upon them. By 1958, he was willing to act against their counsel. The rising pressure of world opinion is the most cited reason for Eisenhower's belated decisiveness, but two other reasons provided stronger explanations for Eisenhower's transformation.[2] First, Eisenhower gained the support of his most trusted foreign policy advisor in this period: John Foster Dulles. After Harold Stassen departed the administration, Dulles curiously became much more flexible in his views on disarmament negotiations.His transformation is an important, though merely reinforcing explanation for Eisenhower's greater willingness to pursue his inclinations toward a test ban. The second, and most important, explanation is that PSAC provided Eisenhower and Dulles confidence that a test ban that could be adequately policed and strategically advantageous.

The elevation of PSAC made Eisenhower acutely aware of the schism in the scientific community. Significantly, both sides in the internal debate over the pursuit of a test ban represented Eisenhower's own divided mind on negotiating with the Soviet Union. Eisenhower shared test-ban opponents' fears that the Soviet Union would attempt to cheat on any agreement. However, he also shared the test-ban advocates' hopes that a test-ban accord would be an important first step toward easing tensions, slowing the arms race, and negotiating a disarmament agreement. Sympathetic to the views of both sides, Eisenhower's approach to a test ban depended upon which group of scientists retained his greatest confidence. In 1958, the new advisors of PSAC gained the edge, providing the strongest explanation for Eisenhower's monumental actions toward a test ban.

I

Before the creation of PSAC, Eisenhower continued to underestimate the continuing debate amongst the sharply divided scientific community on the test-ban issue that the 1956 election campaign greatly accelerated. Eisenhower finally felt the tensions that divided atomic scientists firsthand when I. I. Rabi visited Eisenhower, with Strauss present, at the end of October 1957 to encourage the president to pursue a test ban. Rabi informed Eisenhower that Bethe's analysis of Soviet tests identified a flaw in Soviet weaponry that made its warhead susceptible to preinitiation; a U.S. missile exploded at a high altitude could cause the incoming Soviet missile to detonate harmlessly in the atmosphere.[3]

In Rabi and Bethe's view, an immediate worldwide test-ban agreement would prevent the Soviet Union from identifying this disadvantage in further tests. A ban would thus provide the United States an opportunity to develop clandestinely a defensive missile system that would protect the nation from a Soviet nuclear missile attack. Emphasizing the need to freeze the U.S. technical advantage, Rabi lectured Eisenhower that it was a "tragedy" that the administration had not pursued a test ban earlier to prevent the Soviet Union from developing a deliverable thermonuclear warhead.

While somewhat surprised, Eisenhower signaled his agreement, responding that he "had often said that if we are ahead of the Soviets in these matters, we should agree to stop in order to freeze our advantage."[4] Although Eisenhower indicated that he had always hoped to cease testing to freeze a U.S. advantage, he expressed concern that "making a complete, sudden reversal of our position" would require a skillful presentation and explanation to the nation's allies "and our own people."[5]

Sensing Eisenhower's strong interest in the matter, Strauss interjected that he questioned some of Rabi's assumptions and conclusions. As tension filled the Oval Office, Rabi told Eisenhower that it had been a "great mistake" for him to accept the views of Teller and Lawrence (in June 1957) that continued testing was absolutely necessary.[6] Eisenhower commented that he thought both were "eminent in their field" and asked if there was not mutual respect between the various groups of scientists. Rabi simply indicated that he had known them for over twenty years. Drawn to the idea, but concerned about British opposition and the differing technical assessments, Eisenhower wrote in his diary that he directed the AEC and Rabi's Science Advisory Committee, which remained under the ODM until PSAC was formed the following month, to "try to get (if possible) an agreement of scientific opinion in this whole matter to see what we should do about it."[7]

After Rabi departed, the troubled Eisenhower informed Strauss that he considered Rabi "a brilliant scientist and friend of long standing" to whom he was deeply devoted. Eisenhower was deeply interested in his views, but concerned about the contradictory scientific opinion on the matter. Strauss responded that Rabi and Teller had "opposed each other very sharply over many years." In fact, there was a deep animosity between Rabi and AEC scientists, such as Lawrence and Teller. The divisions began over the postwar international control over atomic energy, intensified during the debate over the development of the H-bomb, and reached a peak during the Oppenheimer case. Rabi had angrily confronted Lawrence before the latter was scheduled to testify against Oppenheimer and had refused to shake Teller's hand after his crushing testimony against Oppenheimer.[8] Strauss, mentioning only the H-bomb dispute, informed Eisenhower of the hostility between many atomic scientists. Eisenhower recorded in his diary the following day: "I learned that some of the mutual antagonisms among the scientists are so bitter as to make their working together almost an impossibility. I was told that Dr. Rabi and some of his group are so antagonistic to Drs. Lawrence and Teller that communication between them is practically nil."[9]

In addition to questioning Strauss about the division between scientists, Eisenhower again reminded Strauss, as he had done in 1956, that he had discussed with him on numerous occasions that he would halt testing if the nation could do so advantageously. Eisenhower then revealed that his thoughts on the role of scientists as advisors had not changed since 1953, which explains, in part, why the president had relied upon the views of Strauss for such a long time. He commented to Strauss that scientific judgments often require modification after others provide "mature, experienced judgment in these broader matters." Eisenhower cautioned that Rabi's recommendation might not have considered "national risks and international purposes."[10] In Eisenhower's view, scientists rarely possessed the ability to consider the political and strategic implications of their technical conclusions. Eisenhower relied on Strauss, who shared his mistrust of the Soviet Union, to evaluate the technical advice based upon those broader considerations.

One example clearly illustrates Eisenhower's mistrust of scientists' ability to provide sober counsel on the military and political implications of technical developments. Ironically, it was Edward Teller's judgment, not Rabi's, that soon raised Eisenhower's ire. In late-November 1957, the president wrote Strauss that one development "that troubles me greatly" was the "extent to which scientists have suddenly become military and political experts." Eisenhower was specifically referring to Edward Teller's remark on national television that the Soviet launch of *Sputnik* represented a greater defeat to the United States than Pearl Harbor.[11] With such provocative comments as this coming from one of the nation's most talented scientists, Eisenhower trusted Strauss, who was not a scientist but possessed a fair understanding of scientific issues, to evaluate the broader implications of complex technical developments.

Eisenhower suffered a severe stroke the month after the showdown between Rabi and Strauss. The president amazed his doctors and advisors when he recovered sufficiently to attend the NATO summit in December. Meanwhile, international pressures continued to build for a test ban. The United Nations General Assembly in November rejected a test-ban resolution, but the vote was hardly a ringing endorsement of the U.S. test policy (the vote was twenty-four in favor, thirty-four against, and thirty abstentions). Analysts in the State Department warned that a vote the following year might not support the administration without significant revisions in its test policy.[12] Henry Cabot Lodge cautioned Dulles that "no matter how many big votes we are able to cajole in support of our position, we have a position which fundamentally lacks appeal."[13]

The day after Christmas, Eisenhower again discussed his interest in a test ban with Dulles. Indicating that he remained inclined to cease testing, Eisenhower asked Dulles to look into the international implications of pursuing a test ban. Dulles feared that the British and French, despite domestic political opposition to testing, would privately oppose a test ban without greater U.S. assistance in developing their own nuclear arsenals.[14] This, however, required pushing an amendment to the Atomic Energy Act through Congress. Most importantly, Dulles remained hesitant to pursue a ban as long as Harold Stassen remained the primary disarmament advisor in the administration.[15] Fearful that Stassen would provide concessions that were contrary to U.S. interests and would alienate the nation's allies, Dulles believed that "we are not going to get anywhere on disarmament as long as he [Stassen] is there." On the other hand, if Stassen left the administration Dulles believed that there was a chance for an agreement.[16] After Stassen departed in February 1958, Dulles, confident in his ability to cautiously manage negotiations without alienating the allies or diminishing the nation's strategic position, became one of the strongest advocates for greater flexibility in disarmament. Until then, Dulles discretely probed European attitudes toward separating testing from the multiple components of the administration's comprehensive disarmament package.

An NSC meeting at the start of the New Year symbolized the political demise of Stassen and the ascendancy of Eisenhower's new science advisors. The previous month, Stassen, perhaps on the basis of Bethe's letter to him in June 1957 advocating a separate test ban, requested the views of Killian and PSAC on his latest disarmament proposal for the NSC. Despite the fact that PSAC already had a disarmament panel studying the matter, Killian curiously responded to Stassen that "it is my feeling that the competences [sic] and experience within our Committee probably are not such as to enable us to assist you effectively in this area."[17] In his memoirs, Killian contended that he initially avoided making recommendations on a test ban because he sought to avoid embroiling PSAC in such a controversial issue of political policy that extended beyond technological issues.[18] Perhaps an additional reason was that Killian did not want his new committee to support the besieged Stassen, who was on his way out of the administration.

Stassen, without PSAC's endorsement or assistance, presented his final disarmament proposal at an NSC meeting on 6 January. Stassen recommended three specific revisions to the disarmament policy that Eisenhower had approved in August 1957. Stassen's proposals included a separate test ban with eight to twelve control posts within the Soviet Union. International technicians would staff each control post, which would be equipped with seismic, acoustic, and electromagnetic detection devices. Stassen's other revisions were the establishment of inspection zones to prevent a surprise attack in Central Europe and another series of inspection zones in parts of the United States and the Soviet Union. According to Stassen, these steps were acceptable to the Soviet Union and they would serve as a first step toward establishing the inspection and control measures fundamental to future disarmament agreements.

Strauss expressed dismay that Stassen recommended a "retreat" from the administration's "sound position" that placed greater emphasis on inspection and the linkage between testing and comprehensive disarmament measures. The AEC chairman warned that a twenty-four-month test suspension would not prevent the stockpiling of warheads for ICBMs or IRBMs, but would hinder the development of small, "clean" tactical bombs and the development of peaceful applications of nuclear explosions. Most importantly, he disagreed with Stassen's analysis that eight to twelve inspection stations within the Soviet Union could effectively monitor a test ban, asserting that Teller and Lawrence believed that "several score" of stations would be required.

Dulles sharply dismissed Stassen's assessment that the British would support a separate test ban. He strongly questioned Stassen's qualifications "as an expert in the knowledge of what our NATO allies will or will not accept." In Dulles's view, the British "were categorically opposed to any proposal for a test suspension unless and until there was an amendment" to the Atomic Energy Act (AEA) of 1954. An amended act could allow the sharing of nuclear information, which would significantly reduce, if not eliminate, the need for further British testing. Although Dulles agreed that the inflexible administration position was hurting its image abroad, he believed that in the post-*Sputnik* atmosphere it was a "very wrong time" to make concessions that would indicate weakness. He felt that it was essential not to "panic" or appear to "give in to the Soviets under present conditions." In Dulles's view, a disarmament revision would eventually be necessary, but not until the hysteria died down and Congress amended the AEA.[19]

Eisenhower concurred with Dulles's assessment on the poor timing of Stassen's proposals, the need to consult with the nation's allies, and the necessity of amending the AEA to gain their support. The president cautioned that "we could contemplate the break-up of NATO if we ceased nuclear testing in agreement with the USSR before the terms of the Act [AEA] had been changed." Yet he also agreed, based upon his discussions at the NATO summit, that world public opinion demanded a revision of the administration's disarmament policy. In sum, Eisenhower expressed interest in a test ban, but considered the completion of the next U.S. test series scheduled for that spring and an amended AEA as prerequisites for advancing any new test-ban proposals.[20]

Killian, attending the meeting as a "backbencher," then interjected that PSAC had completed a preliminary study of the test issue and concluded that the administration should make no revisions to its test policy without a new technical appraisal conducted by the experts from all applicable agencies. Expressing his hope that they could "advance rapidly" in the development of detection devices, Eisenhower accepted PSAC's recommendations for representatives from the AEC, DOD, CIA, and PSAC to conduct studies on the technical feasibility of monitoring a test-ban agreement and the impact of a test cessation on the U.S. and Soviet nuclear arsenals. Eisenhower again reminded his advisors of the dangers and burdens of the spiraling arms race and the necessity to "keep the hope of disarmament before the world."[21]

Significantly, Eisenhower also indicated his "great concern" with the differences in the scientific opinion on the ability to detect tests. He pointed out that Teller's arguments on the difficulties of inspection, which recently appeared in an article in *Foreign Affairs,* differed substantially from Rabi's views. Eisenhower commented that "apparently Governor Stassen believed in the opinion of one group of scientists and Admiral Strauss follows the views of another group." The president did not indicate which side he was inclined to believe.[22]

Strauss, concerned that Eisenhower had gained frequent access to scientists who favored a test ban, made a note to remind himself to "clear up" the differences Eisenhower identified between Rabi and Teller on the test issue.[23] Over the course of the next two months, Strauss submitted his own proposal to prevent a test ban, continued to emphasize the necessity of additional tests, and moved to discredit Rabi's views in Eisenhower's mind. Three days after the NSC meeting, Strauss wrote Eisenhower with evidence that resolved the "conflicting views of American scientists" on the ability to detect tests. According to Strauss, U.S. monitoring devices failed to detect a Soviet test; the AEC only knew about the test after the Japanese alerted them that they had collected radioactive debris. For Strauss, this strengthened his belief "that Soviet concealment of certain tests would be completely feasible." Strauss did not acknowledge that only the current U.S. ground system failed to detect the Soviet test; the system that both Stassen and Rabi advocated, with a limited number of monitoring stations within Soviet soil, would have identified the Soviet detonation.[24]

Strauss reinforced these misleading points in a meeting with Eisenhower two weeks later. At that meeting, Strauss presented an alternate proposal for ceasing tests that was inflexibly tied to other disarmament measures and inherently more difficult to police than a separate test ban. Strauss's three-part proposal called for a three-year test moratorium, the cessation of production of all fissionable materials (rather than just those used for weapons purposes as Stassen proposed), and the cannibalization of existing weapons to provide fissionable material for power and other peaceful purposes.

When challenged by Eisenhower, Strauss insisted that this proposal "could be far more easily inspected" than previous proposals. The record of the meeting is unclear on which proposals Strauss was making a comparison. In fact, Strauss's recommendation possessed the same advantages of Eisenhower's Atoms for Peace program; it offered a rich propaganda reward with little likelihood (in Strauss's view) of Soviet acceptance. Strauss, cognizant of the Soviet refusal to accept an extensive foreign presence within their territory, was likely advancing a proposal he knew the Soviets would reject, thus preventing the administration from proposing a test ban that he feared the Soviets may accept.[25]

Strauss received important personal encouragement and technical support in his efforts to forestall a test ban from Edward Teller. In a private letter to Strauss, Teller expressed his concern that the demands for a test moratorium were becoming "exceedingly powerful." Fearful of the "disastrous consequences" of a moratorium, Teller urged Strauss to "recapture the initiative" with alternatives that would prevent a total cessation of testing. Significantly, Teller emphasized the difficulties of policing a limitation on production that Strauss had proposed to Eisenhower as simple to monitor. In Teller's view, a test limitation agreement that restricted the amount of radioactivity released in the atmosphere offered the best alternative to a complete test ban. For Teller, it was "more easily checked than any other agreement I can imagine" and would allow underground testing to continue unimpeded.[26]

Strauss, after attempting to preempt the tabling of a test-ban proposal acceptable to the Soviets and discrediting the technical assumptions of test-ban advocates, renewed his efforts to justify the necessity of continued testing. After Eisenhower became "appalled" at the number of shots Strauss requested for the next test series, named *HARDTACK*, Strauss provided him with a detailed explanation of the purpose of each shot.[27] Two weeks later, his assistant, Naval Captain Jack Morse, prepared a lengthy memorandum for Eisenhower on "The Case for Clean Nuclear Weapons."[28] Morse's assessment expanded upon the arguments in Edward Teller's article, "The Compelling Need for Nuclear Tests," that appeared in *Life* magazine that week. Strauss and Teller, utterly convinced of the righteousness of their cause, worked feverishly to convince the press, the public, and the president not to accept a test cessation.[29]

II

As Strauss and Teller plotted to ensure that the administration continued to test nuclear weapons, other factors began to push the administration decisively in the opposite direction. Since January, the CIA began to warn that the Soviet Union might declare a unilateral test moratorium at the conclusion of their test series in March.[30] Such an announcement, arriving just before the United States began its previously announced spring test series, would place the United States in extremely unfavorable light. This concern spurred John Foster Dulles to propose a "dramatic" statement before the Soviets issued theirs; Eisenhower would approve no more tests after the upcoming *HARDTACK* series for the remainder of his presidency.[31] This was a complete reversal for Dulles, who two months earlier had strongly criticized Stassen's belief that the time was not right for a new disarmament proposal due to the loss of confidence after *Sputnik*, the need to consult with the nation's allies, and the necessity of first amending the Atomic Energy Act.[32] In fact, Dulles's proposal went beyond anything that Stassen, who departed the administration on 15 February, had advocated. Freed from the fear that Stassen's overweening ambition would lead him to isolate the allies and accept terms favorable to the Soviet Union just to reach an agreement, Dulles confidently managed a more flexible approach to disarmament. For Dulles, it was critical for the United States to exert moral leadership to win the propaganda war with the Soviet Union.

Dulles presented his proposal during a vigorously debated meeting on 24 March. He acknowledged that the steps he proposed meant accepting a test cessation without either inspection or the cessation of fissionable material for weapons in which the administration had always insisted. Dulles recognized that the abandonment of its previous position would leave the impression that they were "giving in to the Soviet line." He warned, "it will be said that the administration is adopting the Stevenson/Stassen position." Finally, Dulles recognized that the administration would face public and Congressional criticism, but he was convinced that they "desperately" needed "some important gesture" since the United States was "losing the struggle for world opinion."

Defense Department officials (Secretary of Defense Neil McElroy, his deputy, Donald Quarles, and the Chairman of the Joint Chiefs of Staff, Nathan Twining) strongly opposed Dulles's proposal, but Lewis Strauss provided the most vehement opposition. Most importantly, Strauss's technical assumptions and conclusions went unchallenged because, curiously, presidential science advisor James Killian did not attend this meeting. Strauss stated that he recognized the need for a more flexible position, but he did not see "any reason for abandoning our tests." He stressed the necessity of continued testing for the development of clean weapons, tactical weapons, and an anti-ICBM system.

Strauss's stale argument that a test ban would lead to the loss of scientists from the weapons laboratories brought a particularly sharp response from Eisenhower. After McElroy restated Strauss's concerns, Eisenhower responded that he "thought scientists, like other people, have a strong interest in avoiding nuclear war." Tellingly, Strauss responded by reading a letter from Edward Teller who argued strongly for the need to continue testing.

Twice, Strauss deflected suggestions from Eisenhower and Cutler to limit testing to underground shots only. Instead, Strauss again presented his proposal for a cessation of fissionable material production. Dulles immediately rejected Strauss's proposal as insincere for "putting impossible conditions on disarmament." The secretary of state also cautioned that Strauss's program required significant consultations with the nation's allies.

Although Strauss built no support for his counterproposal, he and the Defense officials succeeded in blocking Dulles's initiative. After a grueling debate that ran over two hours, an unusually long meeting between Eisenhower and his advisors, Dulles decided to withdraw his proposal. Deeply frustrated, Eisenhower lectured that "it was simply intolerable to remain in a position wherein the United States, seeking peace, and giving loyal partnership to our allies, is unable to achieve an advantageous impact on world opinion." Eisenhower indicated that he would suspend testing if Congress amended the AEA and the Soviet Union accepted the inspection system that Bethe's interagency working group currently had under study.[33]

Eisenhower lacked the technical assurance and the time to consult with his closest allies, both of which he believed were necessary to declare immediately a test moratorium. As intelligence sources predicted, Khrushchev on 31 March declared a unilateral test moratorium; the Soviet Union would not test nuclear weapons unless other nations did so. Khrushchev shrewdly timed the release of his announcement to occur just *after* the Soviets conducted an extensive test series and just before the United States began its scheduled test series. In effect, the previously announced U.S. tests provided the Soviet Union an almost immediate excuse to resume testing while drawing a negative public response to the United States for rejecting the Soviet proposal.[34]

Four days before the Soviet announcement, Bethe's interagency panel completed its final report on the feasibility of monitoring a test cessation. Test-ban opponents within the AEC and Defense would later charge Bethe with allowing his inclination to seek a test ban to skew the panel's technical conclusions. In fact, representatives from the AEC, Defense, and the CIA served as panelists and unanimously approved its final report. Bethe's strongest ally on the panel was Herbert Scoville, Jr., the CIA's representative who also supported a test ban. Most of the AEC and Defense representatives were skeptical, if not hostile, to the idea of a test cessation yet concluded that the system they outlined could adequately monitor a test-ban agreement. The AEC's representatives were Harold Brown of Livermore, Carson Mark and Roderick Spence from Los Alamos, and army Brigadier General Alfred D. Starbird, the director of AEC's Division of Military Applications. Representatives from Defense included Herbert York, a physicist who had been the director of Livermore before becoming the director of the Defense's Advanced Research Projects Agency; Doyle Northrup of the Air Force Office of Atomic Energy (AFOAT-1), an air force surveillance organization that collected air samples to detect and assess Soviet nuclear tests; and Herbert Loper, assistant to the Secretary of Defense for atomic energy and the chairman of the Military Liaison Committee to the AEC.[35]

The panel limited its report to the technical feasibility of monitoring a nuclear test suspension; it did not recommend whether a test cessation would be in the nation's best interests. Privately, the panelists disagreed on whether a suspension would be a net military advantage or disadvantage. They agreed unanimously, however, that it was technically feasible to monitor a test suspension.[36]

Three days after the Soviets declared a unilateral test moratorium, Bethe appeared before the NSC to submit his interagency panel's assessment. Bethe, after summarizing the panel's conclusions, outlined a monitoring system that included the establishment of about thirty ground observation stations within the Soviet Union, backed up by inspection teams to investigate underground tests and limited aerial reconnaissance rights. Dulles expressed concern with the number of control posts required within the Soviet Union.[37] In his view, the Soviets would never accept the complete system that Bethe had proposed. Instead, Dulles suggested that they propose a much less intrusive system that would be acceptable to the Soviet Union but still deter them from attempting to evade an agreement. He believed that a system that guaranteed as much as a fifty-fifty chance of detection would be sufficient to deter the Soviets from attempting to evade an agreement.

The president directed several detailed questions to Bethe that revealed a keen awareness, likely provided by Strauss and Teller, of the difficulties of distinguishing underground tests from earthquakes. Though cognizant of these limitations, Eisenhower concurred with Dulles that a foolproof system was not necessary to deter Soviet evasion. Moreover, he challenged the Defense assessment that the administration should not pursue a test ban simply because it would be militarily disadvantageous. Eisenhower and Dulles agreed that the psychological erosion of the U.S. position in the free world, a result of continued testing despite the worldwide concerns about fallout, must be considered along with the military implications. Bethe's briefing concluded without producing any policy revisions. Nevertheless, Bethe provided Dulles and Eisenhower with essential technical conclusions that would inform their decisions in the weeks ahead.[38]

The following week, Dulles and Eisenhower's comments in separate press conferences provided important insights into their movement toward a decision to pursue a test ban. Dulles discussed the Bethe Panel's conclusions in general terms, stating that there was no foolproof detection system, but that his own belief was that a system with only a high probability of detection would effectively deter efforts to clandestinely test. Dulles also hinted that the United States may halt testing after the next test series, even without agreement on an inspection system with the

Soviet Union, if they had gained substantially all of the information they needed from that test series.[39] That same day, the White House released Eisenhower's letter to Khrushchev that again proposed holding technical studies of procedures to monitor a disarmament agreement (though without mentioning a ban on testing specifically).[40] In his own press conference the following day, Eisenhower also said that he would "very strongly" consider unilaterally suspending tests after the HARDTACK series if "the scientists" told him that "they had largely or almost completely found out the things they wanted to know."[41]

The comments drew Admiral Strauss's immediate concern, prompting him to try to shore up opposition to a test ban within the administration and the press corps. Strauss feared that Dulles and Eisenhower had coordinated their comments to suggest that a unilateral test ban might be forthcoming. Strauss warned Dulles that the AEC scientists would treat these comments "with consternation" and it would be difficult for the AEC chairman to keep his "ducks in a row."[42] Dulles tried to reassure Strauss, who was a lame duck within the administration since his term as AEC chairman expired at the end of June.[43] Dulles assured Strauss that the press conference remarks were not prearranged, but suggested that they were carefully worded to emphasize that Strauss would have to declare the HARDTACK test series a complete success before the administration would cease testing unilaterally. Dulles deemed this unlikely. Strauss made sure of that; as long as he remained the chairman, there would always be ample justifications for additional tests.[44]

After shoring up his position within the administration, Strauss contacted influential journalists James Reston of the New York Times and Walter Lippmann, the greatly respected columnist. In a letter to Reston and during a meeting with Lippmann, Strauss emphasized the technical difficulties of monitoring a test ban and the necessity of continued testing of weapons for defensive purposes.[45]

As Strauss worked feverishly to justify the necessity of continued testing, Killian and Bethe consulted with the other members of PSAC to consider what role they should play in the test-ban debate within the administration. The Bethe Panel's conclusions were moderate with several qualifications, reflecting a compromise of the competing viewpoints of the agencies represented. Eisenhower instructed Killian to have PSAC evaluate the report and present him with their separate recommendations on the feasibility of monitoring a test ban.

Although not a scientist, Killian was acquainted with many of the distinguished members of PSAC and was adept at examining the implications of highly technical matters. The son of a southern textile worker, Killian earned in 1926 a degree in engineering and business administration from MIT. For the next thirteen years, Killian closely followed a range of developments in science and technology as the editor of the *MIT Technology Review*. MIT president Karl T. Compton selected Killian in 1939 as his executive assistant. Killian swiftly rose within the administration, helped organize MIT's extensive role in wartime research, and became in 1948 MIT's president.[46] Following the war, he served on a variety of government projects and advisory boards, including the ODM's Science Advisory Committee. Most significantly, Killian chaired in 1954 and 1955 the Technological Capabilities Panel, which recommended that Eisenhower accelerate work on ballistic missiles and initiate programs that developed the U-2 spy plane and the Corona reconnaissance satellite. By 1957, Killian had earned a reputation as a gifted administrator and a discrete governmental advisor. The distinguished figures on PSAC were quite pleased with Killian's appointment as Eisenhower's first science advisor.[47]

The members of PSAC were an impressive collection of scientists, engineers, and administrators from the nation's top research institutions and leading technological firms. Many had worked on the Manhattan Project or other military research and development projects during the Second World War. Several continued to serve as government consultants following the war, though their activities rarely brought them into positions to advise the highest levels of government before the creation of PSAC. Of the eighteen original members, nine had served previously on the ODM's Science Advisory Committee.[48]

Joining Killian, Bethe, and Rabi as founding members of PSAC were physicists Robert Bacher and H. P. Robertson of Cal Tech. Chemist William O. Baker and physicist James B. Fisk both joined PSAC from Bell Telephone Laboratories, Fisk as the executive vice president and Baker as the vice president for research. Lloyd Berkner, also a physicist, was the president of Associated Universities. Physiologist Caryl P. Haskins was the president of the Carnegie Institution. Detlev Bronk, another physiologist, was the president of the Rockefeller Institute for Medical Research, president of the National Academy of Sciences, and the chairman of the board of the National Science Foundation. James H. Doolittle, the famed wartime aviator, was the vice president of Shell Oil Company and served on the president's advisory board on foreign intelligence activities. George B. Kistiakowsky, a Harvard chemist, played an instrumental role in the Manhattan Project as the leader of the explosives division at Los

Alamos. Physicist Edward M. Purcell, also of Harvard, had worked with Rabi at MIT's Radiation Laboratory during the war. Edwin H. Land, a physicist and president of Polaroid Corporation, served with Killian, Doolittle, and Fisk on Killian's Technological Capabilities Panel. Jerome Wiesner, an engineer, was the director of MIT's Research Laboratory of Electronics. Physicist Jerrold R. Zacharias, also of MIT, worked at MIT's Radiation Laboratory and at Los Alamos during the war. Herbert York, also a physicist, was formerly the director of Livermore and served as the chief scientist of the Defense Department's Advanced Research Projects Agency. The final original member, Paul A. Weiss, was a biologist with the Rockefeller Institute for Medical Science.[49]

Ramey Air Force Base in Puerto Rico provided a secure setting detached from the bureaucratic pressures of Washington for PSAC's focused deliberations on the test ban. Their intense discussions on the controversial and complex issues extended over the course of a three-day weekend. The scientists quickly concurred with the Bethe Panel's conclusions that a reliable test detection system appeared feasible. They then moved beyond technical considerations to examine matters of policy. In their assessment, a test ban following the *HARDTACK* series would provide the United States a major advantage by freezing its weapons superiority for several years.

They vigorously debated, however, whether it was the proper role of PSAC to provide such policy recommendations based upon their technical conclusions. Up to this point, Killian had hesitated to extend PSAC's advisory role from purely technical assessments to the realm of policy recommendations bearing on national security strategy.[50] According to Killian's memoirs, PSAC's role in policy formulation was such an important question that evoked such intense discussion that they decided, for the first and only time, to vote on an issue.[51] The committee's unanimous vote to submit its policy recommendation to the president plunged PSAC headfirst into the administration's test-ban debate.[52] Killian, Rabi, and PSAC's CIA representative Herbert Scoville, who served on the Bethe Panel, warned PSAC members that no amount of technical evidence would alter the rigid opposition to a test ban within the AEC and DOD.[53] Nevertheless, the committee's impressive technical credentials and unanimous conclusions provided an unprecedented challenge to the powerful views in the AEC and DOD that testing must continue.

The following week, Killian briefed PSAC's conclusions in separate meetings with Dulles, Eisenhower, and Strauss. Lewis Strauss provided an immediate indication of the opposition PSAC would encounter when

Killian presented him their conclusions and recommendations. Strauss was surprised, and likely troubled, that the entire committee held Bethe's views on the feasibility to monitor adequately a test ban. Moreover, Strauss bluntly disagreed that the United States was technically ahead, and thus he rejected PSAC's conclusions that a test ban would be advantageous. Strauss emphasized the necessity of additional testing to develop defensive weapons systems. According to his record of the meeting, Strauss believed that his presentation left Killian surprised, shaken, and uncertain of the correctness of PSAC's proposals.[54]

Contrary to Strauss's hopeful assessment, Killian exhibited no such attributes when he briefed Eisenhower two days later. Killian firmly stated PSAC's recommendation that a ban on testing after the *HARDTACK* series would freeze technical advantages that would otherwise be quickly lost with additional Soviet testing. He reiterated Bethe's conclusions that it was feasible to install an inspection system that would provide a reasonable degree of assurance against evasion. Further, Killian suggested that the limited inspection system could "serve as an opening wedge" for an inspection system for an agreement on disarmament.[55]

Perhaps recalling Strauss's strong reaction to his conclusions, Killian cautioned Eisenhower that this was a "controversial subject" and that top officials in the AEC and Defense did not share PSAC's views. Most significantly, Eisenhower commented that he "had never been too much impressed, or completely convinced by the views expressed by Drs. Teller, Lawrence and Mills that we must continue testing of nuclear weapons."[56] Eisenhower's comments certainly understated the influence of the AEC scientists on his own views, but it did signal the end of their monopoly of technical advice. According to Killian, Eisenhower began to refer to PSAC as "his" scientists.[57]

Like Eisenhower, Dulles responded favorably to PSAC's conclusions. According to a record of his meeting with Killian, Dulles expressed "great interest" in the scientists' conclusion that an inspected test-ban agreement at the conclusion of the *HARDTACK* series "would be greatly to the advantage of the United States." He did express concern that the allies would have to be consulted and that their approval remained contingent upon an amended Atomic Energy Act. Still convinced that the Soviet Union would never accept the extensive inspection system that the Bethe Panel proposed, Dulles again requested PSAC's assessment of how many control stations would be sufficient to provide an adequate deterrent against Soviet clandestine testing.[58]

Although Eisenhower and Dulles both favored pursuing a test ban, they realized that the AEC and Defense opposed a ban. They were also aware that it would be difficult to justify to the Democrats and the public who were still concerned that *Sputnik* had indicated that the Soviet Union had overtaken the United States in technical superiority. Eisenhower and Dulles decided to appoint a high-profile group of disarmament consultants that, following Stassen's departure, would lend credibility to the flexible course that Eisenhower and Dulles had already decided to pursue. Dulles privately described the panel to Sherman Adams as "largely scenery" and a "public relations job."[59]

The formation of this panel of consultants revealed the lessons Eisenhower had learned from the Gaither Committee. The Gaither Committee, assigned in 1957 to assess America's ability to defend itself against a surprise Soviet nuclear attack, expanded its mandate in size and scope. A few of its many members leaked parts of the report's conclusions on the inability of the United States to defend itself against such an attack, contributing to the climate of fear following the launch of *Sputnik*.[60] After this episode, Eisenhower commented that he had become "allergic" to outside consultants.[61]

Ironically, it was Robert Sprague, co-director of the Gaither Committee, who recommended that Eisenhower establish a panel of consultants on disarmament.[62] Revealing that he had learned his lesson from the Gaither committee, Eisenhower instructed Dulles to limit the disarmament advisors to four men that he knew he could trust to be discreet and support his views.[63] In fact, all four members had close ties to Eisenhower. Walter Bedell Smith, who was Eisenhower's chief of staff during the Second World War, served as the director of the CIA from 1950 to 1953 before Eisenhower appointed him as under secretary of state. Alfred Gruenther, a close friend of Cy Sulzberger of the *New York Times,* was a longtime friend of Eisenhower's who served as his military advisor and had become NATO commander before retiring. Robert A. Lovett and John J. McCloy were both part of a foreign policy elite known as "the establishment" that moved back and forth between the government, elite law firms, and powerful banks in the first two decades of the cold war. Lovett, who studied law at Harvard and worked for a powerful Wall Street investment company, served as Truman's Secretary of Defense while Eisenhower was NATO commander. John J. McCloy was an aide to Secretary of War Henry Stimson, Eisenhower's civilian counterpart in the postwar occupation of Germany, and a powerful investment banker with Chase National Bank. Significantly, Lovett and McCloy had also served on the Gaither Committee's advisory panel; their support of a test-ban agreement would defang critics from charging that the test ban ignored the warnings of the Gaither Committee. The support of these four advisors, combined with the technical backing of PSAC, provided Dulles and Eisenhower a powerful counter to the opposition of the AEC and Defense.

Dulles highlighted Bethe and Killian's briefings in two meetings with his personal disarmament consultants in April. Dulles first met with his advisors without representatives from the other concerned agencies attending. Dulles emphasized the mounting world pressure for progress on arms control and cautioned that the United States could even lose the Cold War if they failed to "take into account such imponderables as world opinion." He underscored that the French and British would oppose a test cessation without an amended Atomic Energy Act, but would be forced to by domestic political pressures to follow the U.S. policy. Commenting on the Bethe Panel report, Dulles again expressed the view that a system that provided a "50-50 chance of detection" would be sufficient to deter clandestine testing.[64]

Gruenther, who Lawrence and Teller had briefed the previous October,[65] inquired about the strong AEC opposition to a test cessation and the need for additional tests to develop an AICBM system. Dulles, signaling that he had clearly sided with PSAC against Strauss and the AEC scientists, commented that he "did not believe there was as much glitter in future testing possibilities as some thought." He emphasized Killian's opinion that there were "great difficulties" with this system. In Dulles's view, "scientists have a tendency to want to go on and on with tests, and that all scientific advances are not necessarily in our interest."[66]

Dulles then drafted Eisenhower's response to Khrushchev's 31 March test-ban proposal. The response called for a conference of technical experts to meet and consider inspection mechanisms for disarmament measures (without highlighting inspection for a test ban). Significantly, Dulles conducted the meeting, drafted the response, and gained Eisenhower's concurrence without consulting Strauss or anyone from Defense.[67]

Dulles, after receiving Killian's briefing on PSAC's test-ban recommendation, called again on his disarmament consultants to discuss the administration's next course of action. This time, he allowed other departments and agencies to present their views. During that meeting on 26 April, a lively debate broke out between test-ban opponents Lewis Strauss and Donald Quarles and test-ban advocate James Killian. Killian reiterated PSAC's conclusions that the United States was ahead of the

Soviet Union and that a test ban would freeze that advantage for several years.[68]

Strauss "differed emphatically" from PSAC's conclusions.After asserting the necessity of further tests to develop defensive weapons, Strauss skewered the "group of scientists" in PSAC for having a "long record" of impractical recommendations. In Strauss's view, the test ban was "a phony issue which had been whipped up by the Soviets with the assistance of some disingenuous people in our own country." Strauss was deeply distressed that they were contemplating "paying a terrible price for an intangible gain in world opinion." For him, the most pressing danger of fallout was not from testing, but from the detonation of U.S. defensive warheads to halt Soviet missiles above its own citizens or those of its allies. Strauss argued that "our *best* scientists, Lawrence, [and] Teller" believed that they needed five more years of testing to reduce fallout to 1 percent or less.[69]

Killian calmly countered that PSAC believed that it made no difference if anti-missile warheads were clean or not. The global fallout hazard was a result of nuclear detonations near the earth's surface that pulled irradiated ground debris into the stratosphere. Nuclear explosions against incoming missiles occurred at too high of an altitude to irradiate and transport ground debris.

Dulles, signaling his acceptance of Killian's position, emphasized that the United States risked losing allies such as Japan, Great Britain, and Germany if it did not make some effort toward disarmament. Disagreeing with Strauss, he asked if the "refinement" of nuclear weapons was worth the price of "moral isolation."[70] Dulles's consultants clearly sided with the secretary of state and Killian in dismissing Quarles and Strauss's objections. They agreed that a U.S. proposal for an inspected test-ban agreement following the *HARDTACK* series was the next logical course of action. Deciding to pursue a test ban, their only concerns were how the administration proposed a ban and what concessions they could expect to gain in return.

Deeply disappointed, Strauss lamented that Dulles had been completely in accord with him only sixty days ago in opposing a test ban. The meeting left Strauss bewildered "at the change in Secretary Dulles," and wishing he "knew who had been influential with him." In fact, Dulles had reassured Strauss only two weeks before. Since that time, the burden of world opinion and the weight of Killian's technical conclusions spurred Dulles to propose a course he had long opposed when Stassen was in charge of disarmament.[71]

Strauss's frustrations surely grew after Dulles drafted, and Eisenhower approved, a second proposal, this time specifically focused on a test cessation, to hold technical talks on an inspection system. Breaking standard procedure within the administration, Dulles and Eisenhower did not "clear" the proposal with Strauss or Defense officials before sending it to Khrushchev. Strauss's arguments against the pursuit of a test ban had grown stale, while Killian's technical conclusions convinced Eisenhower and Dulles of the correctness of their chosen course.[72]

In his letter to Khrushchev on 8 April, Eisenhower had not indicated a willingness to discuss a test ban separate from other disarmament measures. His letter on 28 April made that separation clear, proposing that technical experts meet to seek agreement on the control system necessary to monitor a test suspension.[73] The letter was vague on whether this marked a change in administration policy in the linkage of testing and other disarmament measures, causing considerable disagreement among historians about its purpose.[74] In fact, this ambiguity was purposeful to obscure the deep fissures within the administration and the western allies over this issue. It remains clear, however, that Eisenhower, Dulles, and PSAC had already decided to accept a temporary test-ban accord without prior agreement on other disarmament measures.[75]

III

Eisenhower's decision to propose technical talks toward a test-ban agreement represented a major setback to Strauss and clearly signaled that he, Lawrence, and Teller no longer held Eisenhower's complete confidence in atomic energy matters. The fact that the AEC's technical arguments no longer went unchallenged illustrates how the formation of PSAC fundamentally transformed the administration. Nevertheless, Strauss, whose term as AEC chairman expired at the end of June, still exerted a powerful influence, though now restrained by PSAC. Strauss vigorously sought to curb the administration's movement toward a test cessation. Despite his efforts, Strauss was only partially successful. He strongly influenced the selection of delegates to the technical discussions in Geneva, but failed in his efforts to convince Eisenhower to declare a test limitation rather than a test cessation.

Congressional hearings in the spring of 1958 drew increased skepticism to the AEC's public statements and underscored the deep divisions between scientists on the issues of detection and fallout. Senator Hubert H. Humphrey's (D-Minn.) subcommittee on disarmament held hearings from February into April on the administration's test policy. Early in the hearings, the AEC reported that seismic stations had not detected an underground test, conducted in Nevada in September 1957, beyond a distance of 250 miles, which greatly challenged arguments of test-ban advocates that tests deep within the Soviet Union were easily detected. The comments prompted columnist I . F. Stone to review *New York Times* coverage of the test from the previous September. According to those public reports, seismic stations recorded the tests as far away as Toronto and Rome. Stone, after checking the reports with the U.S. Coast and Geodetic Survey and learning that stations as far away as 2,320 miles had detected the Nevada test, provided the contradictory information to Humphrey. When confronted with the embarrassing data, Willard Libby, who was serving as the acting AEC chairman while Strauss was out of the country, issued an immediate correction and called the error "entirely inadvertent."[76] Although most appeared to accept Libby's explanation, Humphrey commented that the episode fostered the impression that "scientific facts are being used by someone to prove a political point, a dangerous concept to perpetuate in our efforts to work out an effective arms control agreement."[77]

The Humphrey subcommittee limited the testimony, with one exception, to AEC representatives and members of the Bethe Panel. The witnesses quickly revealed the divisions between such eminent scientists as Hans Bethe and Edward Teller. Bethe responsibly acknowledged the difficulties of detecting both underground and high-altitude tests. He differed sharply from Teller, however, in asserting that a test ban would be greatly advantageous to the United States.[78]

Teller's views were well known through his television appearances, including a debate on testing with Linus Pauling, and articles advocating additional testing.[79] In his testimony, Teller repeated his well-rehearsed arguments that testing was necessary to develop clean bombs and nuclear explosions for peaceful purposes. Teller was on more solid ground when he presciently cautioned about the difficulties of detecting underground tests.[80] Instead of fostering public understanding, the hearings reflected a bitterly divided scientific community. James Reston of the *New York Times* lamented that the scientific disputes denied the American people the objective analysis essential to reach an informed conclusion. Reston wrote that instead the public was "getting a subjective debate, crammed with contradictory information and studded with personal squabbles."[81]

Other commentators noted that Eisenhower had changed sides in the scientific dispute. Some of those who had identified Eisenhower's reliance upon Strauss and AEC scientists such as Teller began to realize from the administration's decisions that a significant change had taken place. *Time* reported on 28 April that Bethe had become Eisenhower's leading disarmament advisor.[82] *Newsweek* the same week reported that Killian, Bethe, and Rabi had supplanted Strauss, Lawrence, and Teller as Eisenhower's most trusted advisors on nuclear issues.[83]

This transformation perhaps troubled Lewis Strauss the most. One week after the extensive press comment on the matter, Strauss experienced Eisenhower's changing opinion of Teller firsthand. On 1 May, Eisenhower grudgingly approved Strauss's request for an additional shot in the *HARDTACK* series, but made a disparaging remark about "the scientists like Teller who are tying to run the policy of the Government." Strauss made a note to himself: "I must take an early opportunity to explain to the president what has developed in the long feud between the two scientific groups."[84]

Strauss's draft letter to Eisenhower identified a "profound schism" in the scientific community between groups represented by Rabi and Teller. According to Strauss, Rabi's group had "a compulsion which stems from some sort of a guilt complex about weapons and from the necessity of rationalizing the bad advice they have given the government in the past." Strauss then detailed Rabi's support for the international control of atomic energy in 1946, his opposition to accelerating the development of the H-bomb in 1949, and his recommendation in October 1957 for a test ban. In Strauss's view, if any of those recommendations had been accepted, "the result would have been calamitous." He strongly cautioned that Rabi's group "completely dominate[s] your [Eisenhower's] science advisory committee," and warned him that he was "now susceptible entirely to one faction." Strauss perhaps failed to recognize the irony in his comments; for the first four and a half years of his presidency Eisenhower was also entirely susceptible to one faction—Strauss's.[85]

Two weeks later, the *New York Times* reported that Lewis Strauss seemed "to be at odds these days with just about everyone who counts in official Washington—with his old foes, the Democrats on the Joint Committee on Atomic Energy [JCAE]; with a sizable and even more vocal segment of the scientific community; with Secretary of State Dulles, and thus by indirection, with the administration itself."[86] Earlier that week, one of Strauss's staunchest opponents, Senator Clinton Anderson (D-N.M.) of the JCAE referred to Strauss as "the modern apostle of McCarthyism."[87] Eisenhower himself realized that Strauss had become a liability. He lamented to Dulles that the amended Atomic Energy Act "would go through [Congress] better if Strauss were not so disliked."[88]

Despite Eisenhower's recognition that his AEC chairman had become a political liability, the president continued to have great respect for Strauss and listened, though now not uncritically, to his views. Strauss's meeting with Eisenhower on 14 May illustrated their continued friendship amidst the heightened internal debate over testing. According to Goodpaster's record of the meeting, Strauss presented Eisenhower a book on the Civil War and handed him some information about the president's cattle at his Gettysburg farm. Eisenhower then discussed possible administrative positions for Strauss to occupy once his term expired as AEC chairman. For the time being, they agreed that Strauss would coordinate the Atoms for Peace program, serving under Dulles. Such a position would keep Strauss within the "NSC family" and authorize him to participate in NSC and cabinet discussions on atomic energy matters. Most importantly for Strauss, the position would grant him continued access to information to help him wage his battle against the test ban behind the scenes.[89]

Eisenhower's signal of appreciation for Strauss's counsel during the meeting opened the way for the admiral to attack PSAC's technical assumptions. According to Strauss, the AEC's General Advisory Committee (GAC) studied the technical aspects of a test cessation and reached conclusions that were "completely at variance" with those of PSAC.[90] In fact, GAC's conclusions were much less dire than Strauss portrayed to the president. GAC acknowledged that the administration was "approaching a crisis" on the continuation of testing due to the international concerns about fallout. It recommended seeking a test limitation that would allow continued testing underground and, if possible, permit strictly limited atmospheric tests up to a certain fission yield.[91] Strauss's presentation to the president ignored these recommendations and instead restated his own familiar argument that the administration was not ahead of the Soviet Union and that continued testing was essential to develop weapons for defensive purposes. Strauss then drew upon Eisenhower's mistrust of the Soviet Union by rejecting Bethe's conclusions that the United States could adequately monitor a test cessation agreement.[92]

After misrepresenting the views of GAC to present his case for continued testing, Strauss did the same with American public opinion. He cited to the president a recent Gallup Poll, asserting that it indicated that a majority of Americans favored continued testing. Strauss neglected to mention that the poll asked Americans if they favored a *unilateral* test ban, not a test-ban agreement with the Soviet Union. A poll three months earlier found that a strong majority of those with an opinion on the matter favored a *multilateral* test-ban agreement with the Soviet Union. Moreover, Strauss did not mention that the poll in May found that by a nearly two-to-one ratio many Americans believed that continued testing would threaten the health of future generations. In this case, Strauss's misrepresentation of American public opinion likely had little effect on Eisenhower, who had already decided to pursue a test ban to address negative world opinion and to slow the arms race.[93]

Admiral Strauss's next battle involved the selection of scientists to serve as delegates to the upcoming meeting of scientists, officially entitled "The Geneva Conference of Experts to Study the Methods of Detecting Violations of a Possible Agreement on the Suspension of Nuclear Tests." Based upon Killian's recommendation, the administration decided to appoint three distinguished scientists as the primary U.S. representatives. Dulles was concerned, however, that the administration would not know the scientists' inclinations before the conference. Killian feared the opposite situation; he insisted that they avoid scientists "who had so committed themselves as to indicate that there is no chance to negotiate or be flexible."[94] Killian's clear reference to Teller eliminated Strauss's first choice from serving on the delegation. Instead, the AEC chairman focused on adding Lawrence and preventing those whom he considered the strongest test-ban advocates from serving as delegates, Rabi and Bethe.

Dulles believed that the three lead scientists on the delegation should represent "a balanced group" on the test issue.[95] He asked PSAC, AEC, CIA, and the DOD to nominate scientists for chairman and delegates.[96] CIA, Defense, and PSAC all nominated Rabi, while Bethe received nominations from CIA and PSAC.[97] Dulles suggested to Eisenhower that he appoint Fisk, Lawrence, and either Bethe or Rabi.[98] Eisenhower had previously vetoed Lawrence as the chairman, since "his position on testing was too well known," but allowed him to serve as one of the delegates.[99] Before making a final decision, Eisenhower telephoned Strauss to receive his views. Strauss advised the president that Rabi and Bethe "were not wholly reliable."[100] Eisenhower acceded to Strauss's objections and selected Cal Tech physicist Robert Bacher to join Lawrence and James Fisk, whom he selected as chairman.

The delegates and their advisors reflected Dulles's proposal for a balanced group. Bacher was a member of PSAC who had opposed Teller during the H-bomb controversy and had testified on Oppenheimer's behalf during the latter's loyalty-security hearing. Bacher was also known to support a test ban.[101] Ernest Lawrence, generally an ally of Teller, had championed the necessity of additional testing, representing the opposite perspective from Bacher. Fisk, who was regarded as a neutral on the test ban, served as Killian's deputy on PSAC and had also testified in Oppenheimer's defense. He had been the AEC's director of research following World War II before becoming an executive with Bell Laboratories. Fifteen consultants, representing the primary government agencies and a cross section of scientific opinion, provided additional counsel to the delegates. The science advisors included test-ban advocate Hans Bethe as well as test-ban opponent Harold Brown, who served as Teller's deputy at Livermore.[102]

On 18 June, Eisenhower discussed with PSAC preparations for the technical conference, which was scheduled to begin on 1 July in Geneva. The U.S. participants to the talks included three PSAC members: Bacher, Bethe, and Fisk. Bethe's comments, on the eve of the Geneva discussions, were clearly designed to undermine the arguments of Strauss and Teller that continued testing was essential to make additional improvements in clean weapons. Bethe informed the president that the tests of clean weapons in the ongoing *HARDTACK* series had not been successful. In his view, the test results showed that "we are close to the limit of what we can attain in 'cleanness' of weapons." For Bethe, the low yield and heavy weight of the clean H-bombs made them more impractical than pure fission A-bombs.[103] Fearful of undermining one of its major justifications for continued testing to the rest of the world, the administration quietly cancelled its scheduled clean bomb demonstration for international observers.[104]

As Bethe moved to convince the president that testing was no longer necessary, Lewis Strauss sought to prevent the conference from reaching a positive conclusion. On the eve of the conference, Strauss encouraged the delegate he hoped would most strongly represent his opposition to a test ban, Ernest Lawrence. Strauss sent Lawrence on 23 June 1958 a "parting thought" before his longtime ally departed for Geneva. He cautioned Lawrence that "no matter how eminent the Russian scientists are or how persuasive, never let yourself forget that they are the envoys of men who are cold blooded murderers. Deal with them with reserve."[105] Strauss had previously depended upon Lawrence in 1955 to provide a negative assessment of the feasibility of inspection when the prominent physicist chaired Stassen's nuclear inspection task force. The AEC chairman had also drafted a cautionary letter to Lawrence before the physicist began work for Stassen.[106] Strauss's letter in 1958 thus may simply reflect his consistent mode of operation rather than a specific concern, as one historian has suggested, about a softening in Lawrence's position on the test issue.[107] Much to Strauss's disappointment, Lawrence's role was quite limited at Geneva.[108] Before the discussions reached many of the substantive issues, Lawrence suffered an acute colitis attack that compelled him to return to California, where he soon after died of complications from the illness.

After a slow start, the two sides at Geneva reached an agreement on the broad framework of a feasible system to monitor a test cessation accord. The delegates agreed to a British compromise proposal of 170 control stations based worldwide. They rapidly agreed on the capabilities of most methods of test detection, but concluded that further investigation was necessary to detect tests underground and at high altitudes.[109]

Several critical issues, however, remained vague or unresolved. In part, this was intentional. Dulles instructed the scientists leading the U.S. delegation to limit the issues they were willing to discuss to purely technical matters, leaving problems they considered political for future negotiations. As the discussions became more detailed, it became increasingly difficult to distinguish the technical from the political. As a result, the delegates did not consider the crucial issue of how many on-site inspections to authorize or what procedures to follow to investigate seismic readings that were not clearly identified as earthquakes. Similarly, they did not decide the number of stations within each nation or determine the nationality of the inspectors staffing them. Each of these unresolved questions became contentious issues when the nuclear powers began negotiations later that fall toward a test-ban agreement.[110]

IV

As scientists in Geneva reached a general agreement on a viable test detection system, test-ban opponents within the United States worked feverishly to try to convince Eisenhower to limit, rather than cease, testing. The most intense debates occurred among the "Principals," a committee formed to consider periodically the test-ban issue comprised of top officials from State, Defense, PSAC, AEC, and CIA. At a series of meetings in August, the Principals debated what course the administration should pursue following the conclusion of the technical conference. As in most matters related to disarmament since 1953, Eisenhower's leading advisors failed to reach a consensus. Although this stalemate had frozen the administration's disarmament policy for several years, Eisenhower in 1958 was willing to act decisively to break this impasse.

The AEC and Department of Defense were the strongest opponents to a complete test cessation. Instead of halting all tests, John McCone, a southern California Republican businessman and Strauss's successor as AEC chairman, proposed a test limitation that would restrict atmospheric tests to a cumulative yield of below 1 megaton annually. McCone's proposal also allowed unlimited underground testing. The JCS held the most inflexible position, opposing any change that would limit testing separate from a comprehensive disarmament agreement. Deputy Secretary of Defense Quarles proposed a threshold ban, which would permit continued testing below the level that could be effectively monitored, which he understood to be 1-2kt above ground and 5kt underground.[111]

The CIA and the State Department were the strongest advocates of a test cessation, with PSAC offering important support. CIA Director Allen Dulles and Under Secretary of State Christian Herter opposed the AEC and Defense positions, advocating instead a comprehensive test ban. Representing PSAC, Killian's position was less clear as he tried to limit his comments to technical considerations. The implications of his assessments, however, suggested that he favored a comprehensive ban. The Principals also disagreed on whether the administration should make an exception to allow continued peaceful explosions and whether to separate a test ban from the cutoff of fissionable material production and other disarmament measures.[112] After meeting at least four times during a ten-day period without reaching a consensus, the advisors presented Eisenhower on 18 August their differing views for him to make a decision.

By this time, it was clear that the president had already made up his mind to pursue a comprehensive test ban. In early July, Eisenhower instructed the AEC to add any necessary tests to the HARDTACK series because of the "probability" that he would soon decide to cease testing.[113] Three weeks later, Killian briefed Eisenhower on the encouraging progress at Geneva. Eisenhower commented that if the scientists reached a full agreement on the technical issues that the "weight of the argument" for ceasing tests would be "very great." He instructed the Secretary of State to get the Principals together to form a "plan of action . . . as a matter of urgency."[114]

Although the progress in Geneva reinforced Eisenhower's inclination to negotiate a test ban, he was aware that several of his closest advisors did not share his view. Eisenhower cautioned his press advisors that even though the scientists in Geneva appeared to be on the cusp of reaching an agreement on an inspection system, the greatest obstacle to a test-ban agreement may lie within the administration, where "scientists and advisors are in complete disagreement as to [the] course that should be pursued." Despite his desire to reach a consensus before pursuing a chosen policy, the president signaled that he would break this impasse, suggesting that he and Dulles had "long ago come to [a] conclusion [about] what should be done."[115]

Fearing that Eisenhower had already decided to pursue a test ban, McCone on 8 August sought his predecessor's advice. Strauss encouraged McCone to vigorously oppose this course and find out if it were scientists on PSAC or State Department officials who had influenced Eisenhower's views.[116] The AEC's most influential scientist, Edward Teller, along with McCone and Los Alamos director Norris Bradbury had a final opportunity to convince Eisenhower to continue testing underground as a minimum. Teller's arguments, unlike the clean bomb briefing of June 1957, no longer shook Eisenhower's commitment to cease testing. Eisenhower replied to Teller's plea for continuing testing that even as powerful as nuclear weapons were, they were "not, in many ways, as powerful as is world opinion today in obliging the United States to follow certain lines of policy."[117] Eisenhower would permit limited underground testing if the other nuclear nations accepted it, but he refused to sabotage a possible agreement by insisting upon it.[118]

By the time Eisenhower on 18 August met with the Principals to make a decision, he had already fended off the AEC's separate entreaties to continue testing and instead signaled his intent to suspend testing. Two other factors suggest that he had already confidently made his decision. First, Eisenhower had previously directed that it was "unnecessary" to have the "experts" at the meeting, illustrating that he clearly understood the issues.[119] Secondly, Eisenhower on 18 August made his decision even though John Foster Dulles, who was the strongest advocate for a test suspension and negotiations toward an agreement to cease testing, was not present to defend this approach against the AEC and DOD's opposition.[120]

With Eisenhower's mind made up, the meeting included little debate. Quarles and McCone indicated that Defense and AEC disagreed with the assessment of the State Department, PSAC, and the CIA that a test suspension would be militarily advantageous. Eisenhower responded by recalling Rabi's conclusion that a test ban would be advantageous. Killian confirmed that this remained the assessment of PSAC. Frustrated at this continued disagreement on such a complex technical matter of national security, Eisenhower stressed that "disagreement as to the balance of advantage is an element in the whole argument."[121]

With no way to resolve this disagreement, Eisenhower's comments implied that he would decide in favor of the scientific counsel that he most trusted. Clearly, Eisenhower no longer uncritically accepted the technical views of the AEC. Instead, he trusted the analysis of his new science advisory body. Contrary to a recent interpretation, Eisenhower in 1958 was not inflexibly tied to the AEC and Defense positions on testing.[122] He decisions on 18 August rejected their counsel, which advised a test limitation rather than a suspension of all tests.

Eisenhower's symbolic final break with his prior reliance on the views of Strauss and the AEC scientists occurred two days later. McCone had become so disheartened with Eisenhower's judgment that he asked Strauss to don a "bullet-proof vest" and attempt to reverse Eisenhower's decision. According to Strauss's record of his meeting, Eisenhower indicated some reservations about his decision to suspend testing and commented that it was Dulles who had a "fixation on the subject." Strauss recalled that Dulles had proposed a test suspension in March before Strauss convinced him otherwise. Strauss then bluntly told Eisenhower that the course he had just approved represented "a surrender to the views of Stassen and Stevenson."[123]

Eisenhower responded sharply that Strauss's position offered "no prospect except an arms race into the indefinite future," while the policy he just approved was at least a step in the direction of disarmament. Strauss belittled Eisenhower's hopes for disarmament with the Soviet Union, arguing that there was no prospect of living in peace with Communism. For Strauss, Communism was like sin in that there was no room for compromise. He lectured Eisenhower that "the arms race between good and evil had been going on for centuries" and there would never be an end. As he departed the president's office, Strauss feared that he had nearly reached a "permanent fundamental disagreement" with Eisenhower.[124]

Finally breaking with Strauss, Eisenhower, supported by the counsel of PSAC, sided with Dulles in declaring a suspension of all tests and proposing negotiations toward a permanent test cessation agreement. The experts in Geneva on 21 August released their final report, declaring that they had reached agreement on a technically feasible system to monitor a test suspension. The following day, Eisenhower urged the nuclear powers to proceed promptly with negotiations toward a test-ban agreement based upon the control system agreed at Geneva. Most importantly, Eisenhower declared that the United States would cease all weapons testing for a period of one year. The start of the moratorium would coincide with the opening of negotiations (suggested as 31 October 1958).[125]

Eisenhower's statement was purposefully vague in that it did not highlight any major changes in U.S. policy. This ambiguity, typical for Eisenhower, was likely deliberate to maintain the administration's flexibility and to provide it time to gain the concurrence of allies.[126] Yet, it has led one historian to conclude that Eisenhower's decision to suspend tests for one year and propose negotiations toward a permanent test cessation did not mark a major change in the administration's policy.[127] Although the public statement continues to vaguely link a permanent test cessation to progress in disarmament, it is clear from private policy deliberations that Eisenhower had decided to separate testing from the other issues. Thus, the announcement itself does not reflect the major transformation in Eisenhower's approach to a test ban that underlay his modest public proposal.

Eisenhower's decision is monumental for several reasons. It illustrates Eisenhower's determination to no longer permit the divisions among his central advisors to block his efforts to slow the arms race. In times other than crises, Eisenhower dreaded making decisions without a consensus and he was troubled that on the test-ban issue "half our own people are against us [Eisenhower and Dulles]."[128] Eisenhower perhaps also feared that domestic critics would cite the opposition of the AEC and Defense to bolster their arguments arising since *Sputnik* that the administration was allowing the Soviet Union to surpass the United States in technical superiority. Thus, Eisenhower acknowledged that he and Dulles were sticking their "necks out on a limb" by pursuing a test ban.[129]

Powerful reasons prompted Eisenhower to depart from his preferred style of presidential leadership and accept the domestic political consequences of a controversial issue. Mounting world opinion partially explains Eisenhower's actions. The report from the UN radiation committee, though not entirely alarming, provided a few concerning passages that test-ban advocates cited to increase world pressures for a test cessation. The administration feared that they could no longer prevent the passage of a resolution demanding an end to nuclear testing in the UN General Assembly.[130]

The nation's allies also began to increase pressures for a ban after

Congress finally passed an amended Atomic Energy Act that allowed a greater sharing of nuclear information with them. This was particularly essential for the British, who faced exceptionally strong public opposition to testing, but privately opposed a test ban without the amendment. Thus, the AEA eliminated the British insistence on linking a test ban to the cutoff of fissionable material and ended their private opposition to a test ban in general.

The most important factor explaining Eisenhower's decision to declare a test moratorium and negotiate a test-ban agreement was his broadened range of scientific advice. Eisenhower was deeply frustrated that scientists remained divided and unable to present to him a definitive technical recommendation on an issue of such importance to national security. Presented with contradictory interpretations, Eisenhower in 1958 departed from his dependence on the views of Strauss and Teller and instead increasingly accepted the counsel of PSAC. His new scientific advisory body shared his long held inclination to pursue a test-ban agreement. Their technical expertise provided Eisenhower the confidence to dismiss the vehement opposition within the AEC and Defense. For Eisenhower, a test-cessation agreement provided some hope for easing tensions and slowing the arms race. Eisenhower made the first step toward a goal he would pursue as long as he remained confident in PSAC's technical conclusions that the United States could effectively monitor a test-ban accord.

Hard Decisions after
HARDTACK II: Stalemate at Geneva
(August 1958–December 1959)

> We should desert the scientists, and to some extent
> the Department of Defense in their insistence on
> obtaining a perfect system.
>> —Eisenhower, 19 March 1959

> The scientific people there [Geneva] have gotten us
> into a mess but Killian doesn't want to take respon-
> sibility.
>> —Herter, 8 August 1959

> We cannot run the risk of having the U.S. Senate
> reject the treaty because our scientists will not tes-
> tify that it provides for adequate controls for under-
> ground testing.
>> —Herter, 20 October 1959

Khrushchev's acceptance of Eisenhower's proposal for a temporary test moratorium in conjunction with the opening of negotiations toward a test-cessation agreement prompted the most intensive period of nuclear testing to date. The press dubbed the flurry of tests "Operation Deadline," because the tests increased in frequency as the start date of the moratorium neared. The tests dramatically increased the worldwide level of radioactivity in the months ahead, renewing fallout fears and exerting further pressures on the nuclear powers to reach an agreement at Geneva. While much of the world held great hopes that the nuclear powers would reach an agreement to end the contamination of the atmosphere and ease Cold War tensions, Communist China feared a superpower détente. Indeed, the initiation of the second Taiwan Straits crisis, which began the day after Eisenhower issued his test-ban proposal, may have been a Chinese attempt to forestall an agreement between the Soviet Union and the United States.[1] Although the crisis in Asia passed before the talks began, tensions between the Soviet Union and the United States remained high when the Soviets conducted a few tests after the 31 October deadline. Khrushchev in November raised tensions further when he challenged western access to Berlin and issued a six-month ultimatum to resolve the Berlin question. Thus, the Geneva negotiations opened inauspiciously amidst a torrent of testing and a series of Cold War crises.

For the next fourteen months, the torturous course of negotiations made little progress as the nuclear powers exchanged charges of negotiating in bad faith, presented several proposals and counterproposals, and convened two more technical conferences that attempted to resolve the incredibly complex and largely unknown factors related to the detection of nuclear tests in various environments. Complicating matters even further, the administration suffered from bitter bureaucratic infighting over its objectives for the negotiations and the tactics employed to achieve them. As a result, the Eisenhower administration's objectives vacillated between pursuing a ban on all nuclear weapons tests and seeking a cessation agreement limited to those in the atmosphere.

The policy decisions involved a series of complex technical issues based upon theoretical principles that had not been scientifically proven. For test-ban opponents, the administration could not afford to risk the nation's security by agreeing to terms that left open the possibility that the Soviet Union could clandestinely develop advancements in its nuclear weapons arsenal. For advocates of an agreement to cease testing, the administration could not foreclose an opportunity to slow the spiraling arms race, inhibit the proliferation of nuclear weapons, and ease Cold War tensions simply on the basis of some unproven theoretical principles.

The complex technical issues naturally made the nature of the science advice for Eisenhower a central component of his approach to the test-ban negotiations. The counsel of James Killian played a pivotal role in providing Eisenhower the confidence in 1958 to pursue his inclinations for a test ban. When the initial assessment of the feasibility of detecting underground tests proved overoptimistic, Killian withdrew his support of a comprehensive ban. Without the support of his science advisor, Eisenhower abandoned, albeit temporarily, his goal of banning all nuclear tests. Illustrating the centrality of science advice, Eisenhower resumed his support of a comprehensive ban when George Kistiakowsky, who strongly advocated a ban on all tests, replaced Killian in July 1959 as the president's science advisor. Thus the counsel of Eisenhower's science advisors, contrary to some interpretations that emphasize the centrality of the AEC and DOD, was the dominant factor shaping his approach to the test-ban talks at Geneva.[2]

I

James J. Wadsworth, the deputy U.S. ambassador to the United Nations who had replaced Stassen as the administration's primary representative to disarmament discussions, headed the U.S. delegation to the Geneva Conference (officially entitled "The Geneva Conference on the Discontinuance of Nuclear Weapons Tests"). Wadsworth's position at the UN made him acutely aware of the negative implications of the U.S. testing program on world opinion. The administration faced increasing difficulties preventing the passage of UN resolutions that challenged its test program. Wadsworth clearly understood the importance of the Geneva talks for the United States to halt its eroding position among allied and neutral nations.[3]

Before Wadsworth departed for Geneva, Edward Teller attempted to puncture his desire for reaching an agreement. Deeply troubled by Eisenhower's test moratorium announcement, Teller had pledged to Strauss that he would gladly "continue in helping this battle" against any test-ban agreement.[4] Teller sought, unsuccessfully, to convince Wadsworth that an agreement with the Soviet Union would injure the United States. Teller, accompanied by AEC Commissioner Willard Libby and Strauss's former assistant Jack Morse, emphasized to Wadsworth the loopholes in the Geneva system, especially the difficulties of detecting tests underground and at high altitudes. For underground tests, Teller expressed his greatest concern with the possibility of "decoupling" or muffling the detected size of the explosion by one-third to one-tenth of its actual power. Teller also presented his familiar appeal of the necessity of continued testing to develop peaceful uses of nuclear explosions for such purposes of creating harbors and accessing oil reserves. Despite Teller's dire warnings, there is no indication from the record of the meeting that his familiar arguments had any influence on Wadsworth's hopes for reaching an agreement.[5]

Although Teller apparently failed to reduce Wadsworth's enthusiasm, the conference suffered from an inauspicious beginning. The Soviet Union in September presented a proposal for a UN resolution ceasing all tests without any form of inspection. The Eisenhower administration responded by criticizing the Soviet Union for not indicating yet whether it would accept Eisenhower's temporary test moratorium proposal scheduled to commence on 31 October, the day that the conference in Geneva was to begin.

The conference opened with both sides deadlocked on the agenda; the

Soviet Union insisted upon immediately agreeing to sign a treaty, while the United States and Great Britain demanded acceptance of the terms of the control system first. Meanwhile, the United States detected Soviet nuclear tests on 1 and 3 November, violating the 31 October deadline of Eisenhower's proposed moratorium. Eisenhower released a cautiously worded statement on 7 November that the Soviet testing beyond his deadline "relieved the United States from any obligation under its offer to suspend nuclear weapons tests." Although removing the administration's "obligation," Eisenhower declared that the United States would still refrain from testing and would "persevere in the negotiations at Geneva to reach sound agreement for [the] controlled suspension of nuclear testing."[6] The Soviet test on 3 November was their last during the Eisenhower presidency.[7] Although the deadline crisis passed, both sides continued to argue over the agenda for an additional five weeks.[8] Thereafter, the unresolved "political" questions that the technical experts declined to consider that summer immediately deadlocked the negotiations.

The delegates remained divided on the number of control posts in each country, the number and nationality of the technicians occupying them, and the procedures for determining which and how many unidentified seismic events would receive on-site inspections. The Soviet Union demanded that Soviet technicians comprise 28 of the 30 personnel staffing the control posts within their territory. The United States and Great Britain proposed a mixed team based upon equal representation from the West, the Soviet Union, and from neutral nations. On the procedures of on-site inspection, the Soviet Union demanded the right to veto any requests to inspect seismic events within its territory. For Eisenhower, who always emphasized that adequate inspection was fundamental to any arms control agreement, the Soviet proposals fell far short of the minimum standard of inspection.[9]

One idea to break the impasse came from Senator Albert Gore (D-Tenn.), who attended the first few weeks of the conference as a representative of the JCAE. Since the Democrats increased their majority in the Senate during the 1958 congressional elections, Gore's attitude toward the test talks would play a critical role in the ratification of any treaty that arose from the negotiations at Geneva.[10] Gore wanted to bring former commissioner Thomas Murray, whom to Strauss's chagrin was serving as a consultant to the JCAE, to Geneva as his personal advisor. When the State Department indicated that it might not pay for Murray's conference expenses, Gore declared that if he had to he would "sell a mule" to allow Murray to accompany him. Dulles expressed considerable concern that Murray would advocate during the proceedings the continued testing of low-yield weapons. Although some within the administration, such as McCone, favored this view, Eisenhower's objective was to ban all tests.[11] Dulles eventually allowed the former commissioner to attend after Murray assured him that he would not "speak out" when he disagreed and would express his views only privately to Senator Gore.[12]

Gore's impression of the first few weeks of the difficult talks convinced him that it would take years to negotiate and implement a comprehensive test-ban accord. Instead of a comprehensive agreement, he recommended that the administration declare a unilateral U.S. ban limited to tests in the atmosphere for a period of three years, while continuing studies of the means to detect tests underground and at high altitudes. In Gore's view, this would allow the United States to seize the propaganda initiative from the Soviet Union and quell worldwide concerns over radioactive fallout from testing. At the same time, it would allow the United States to continue to test underground to develop warheads for air defense weapons.[13]

Gore on 17 November discussed his proposal with Eisenhower. The president expressed interest in Gore's ideas and asked him to provide his thoughts in writing so his advisors could closely study his proposal.[14] Eisenhower, before receiving the consolidated views of the other advisors, privately discussed Gore's proposal with Dulles. They were both concerned that banning only atmospheric testing would signal a reversal of their public assurances that there were no significant health hazards from testing. Dulles indicated, however, that Gore's unilateral proposal was "not far removed" from the fallback position of tabling a multilateral ban on the most easily detectable tests if the talks broke down.[15]

When PSAC considered the Gore proposal, Bethe and Rabi reached a similar conclusion on the political implications of pursuing a ban limited to atmospheric tests. They wondered how the administration could make such a proposal "without national embarrassment and a severe propaganda setback." Most PSAC scientists discounted the health hazards of fallout and were privately critical of Pauling and other scientists who advocated a test ban for this reason. For Rabi and Bethe, the greatest advantage of a test ban was that it offered hope as a first step toward disarmament. For them, the Gore proposal would not serve this purpose because it did not "open up" the Soviet Union to a limited inspection system and it allowed continued testing underground and at high altitudes.[16] In their view, the Gore proposal was "strictly a propaganda step" since it would do little to slow the arms race or prevent the proliferation of nuclear weapons to other nations. Nevertheless, they agreed with Dulles that the proposal merited consideration as a fallback position if the negotiations failed.[17]

Gore's proposal within a month of the opening of the Geneva talks to limit a ban to atmospheric testing signaled the challenges that confronted Eisenhower's goal of reaching a comprehensive test-ban agreement. Eisenhower, rejecting Gore's proposal to settle for less than a comprehensive test ban, remained hopeful that despite the slow start and numerous points of contention, the Geneva talks would produce an accord that did more than merely score propaganda points. For the time being, Eisenhower remained committed to pursuing a ban on all nuclear tests.

II

Scientists assessing the data from additional underground experiments conducted in the final test series of 1958 made a troubling discovery that threatened to break up the Geneva talks and bolstered the views of those opposing a comprehensive test ban within the administration. The AEC, eager to complete several more tests before Eisenhower's moratorium went into effect at the end of October, included several underground shots as part of the *HARDTACK II* test series completed during September and October 1958 in Nevada. Scientists analyzing the data from those tests determined that the "Geneva system," which had been based upon the data culled from a single underground shot in 1957, possessed insufficient capabilities to detect underground tests and distinguish them from earthquakes. Consequently, the new data revealed that the nuclear powers would have to accept a much more intrusive inspection system than the scientists from the nuclear powers agreed upon during the summer of 1958 to provide the same degree of assurance against evasion.

At the Geneva test-ban talks, the U.S. presentation of the new seismic detection data opened the administration to charges that it was negotiating in bad faith. According to Wadsworth, it "spread a pall over the negotiations from which they never completely recovered."[18] Within the administration, the implications of the data from the underground tests renewed the debate over its objectives for the Geneva discussions. The findings lent credence to the dire warnings of test-ban opponents, such as Edward Teller, that it was not possible to monitor adequately an agreement that banned underground tests. Conversely, it discredited the technical assessments of those advocating a ban on all tests such as Hans Bethe, whose judgment Eisenhower had accepted in spite of the warnings of Strauss. Thus, the new data greatly dampened the atmosphere of the negotiations at Geneva, discredited test-ban advocates within the United States, and challenged Eisenhower's own commitment to seek a comprehensive test ban. A review of the administration's response to the troubling technical data reveals that Killian's counsel to abandon temporarily the effort to reach a comprehensive test-ban agreement was central to Eisenhower's approach to the Geneva talks.

Before discussing the implications of the new data with Eisenhower, scientists from PSAC and the AEC called upon leading seismologists to help them interpret the data from the underground tests. It became clear after seismologists confirmed the initial findings that negotiators in Geneva would have to agree on a revised monitoring system to meet Eisenhower's tenet of adequate inspection. The new data suggested that the Geneva system, originally believed to detect adequately underground tests down to 5kt, might only be effective detecting tests 20kt and larger. Additional on-site inspections and control posts could improve the system's effectiveness down to 5kt, but this would require either ten times as many inspections (a total of 200–1000 a year) or a network of 500 control stations (up from the original 180 stations). Administration officials unanimously agreed that the Soviet Union would never agree to that many inspections or control posts within its territory.

Hans Bethe, whose technical assessments strongly influenced the Geneva system, assured Killian that scientists, with additional study, could find less intrusive means to restore the control system to its originally intended capability. After seismologists in December 1958 confirmed the initial assessment of the *HARDTACK II* series, Killian established two panels to examine means to improve the capabilities of the Geneva system to detect tests conducted underground and at high altitudes. Lloyd V. Berkner chaired the Panel on Seismic Improvement, known as the Berkner Panel. Berkner, a member of PSAC, was a physicist and president of Associated Universities Incorporated, which operated Brookhaven National Laboratory. Physicist Wolfgang Panofsky, already well known within the administration as the promoter of the Stanford linear accelerator, chaired the Panel on High Altitude Detection, known as the Panofsky Panel. The panels met periodically over the next three months and expected to issue their final reports in March.[19]

Eisenhower, confronted with the troubling results of the *HARDTACK*

II series, remained committed to banning all tests that the nation could feasibly detect. At the first meeting with his principal advisors after learning of the new seismic data, Eisenhower on 12 January revealed the evolution of his approach to a test ban. He reminded his advisors that he was inclined to pursue a test ban two years earlier to freeze the U.S. technical superiority and press the Soviet Union on inspection, but had "given way" due to the "resistance on the part of Defense and AEC." Eisenhower stated that he had reversed course the previous year and began negotiations after Rabi assured him that the United States still maintained an advantage. Eisenhower lamented the fact that he had not pursued his inclination two years earlier when the U.S. advantage was even greater.[20]

Although confronted with a narrowing advantage and disheartening seismic data, Eisenhower remained committed to the pursuit of the broadest ban possible. He identified two possible courses of action. First, the administration could pursue a threshold ban, which would allow tests to continue below the adequate level of inspection based upon the revised seismic data. Second, they could continue to pursue a ban on all tests if the Soviets accepted many more control posts within its territory and agreed to submit to more on-site inspection.[21] Significantly, Eisenhower did not mention a third alternative favored by the AEC and Defense—a ban solely on tests in the atmosphere. Eisenhower, committed to pursuing the broadest ban feasible, was unwilling at this stage to retreat so far from his ultimate objective of a cessation of all testing.

As the administration awaited the findings of the Berkner and Panofsky Panels, it vigorously debated which of the three general courses of action to pursue. The debate naturally reflected the competing agency views of the administration's appropriate objective for the test cessation talks. For McCone and Defense officials, the decision was clear, the United States should abandon its pursuit of a comprehensive ban and resume underground testing. In their view, the administration should ban only atmospheric tests. This would eliminate the worldwide concern over the hazards of fallout from atmospheric testing, while permitting the administration to continue to develop and refine its nuclear arsenal through underground testing. In their view, it also offered the possibility of breaking the impasse at Geneva. An atmospheric ban would require few, if any, control posts within the Soviet Union, eliminating many of the issues that had deadlocked negotiations thus far.

For Eisenhower, top officials within the State Department, and members of PSAC, the administration should seek to modify the Geneva system to allow the broadest ban possible under proven methods of detection. For them, the administration should at least seek a minimum number of inspection posts within the Soviet Union to "open up" the Iron Curtain and build the confidence necessary for subsequent disarmament agreements. In their view, this would ease tensions, slow the arms race, and hinder proliferation. The question of how broad of a ban the administration could pursue rested on the assessment of how great of a risk it would be willing to accept on the level of detection. With much unknown and considerable disagreement within the scientific community over such complex issues, Killian's technical counsel was central to Eisenhower's ultimate decision.

In the immediate term, the administration had to decide whether to present the revised technical conclusions to the Soviet negotiators at Geneva. Killian had not even formally notified Eisenhower of the troubling new information until the panel of seismologists confirmed the initial assessment of the *HARDTACK II* data. Informed in early January 1959, Eisenhower decided to notify the Soviet delegation of the new conclusions immediately, but realized that the introduction of the increased requirements for inspection could result in the loss of confidence in U.S. motives and charges that the administration was negotiating in "bad faith."[22]

Eisenhower and Dulles, determined to avoid that perception and illustrate instead the administration's commitment to making progress in the negotiations, decided to remove the link between a test ban and progress on other disarmament issues. They had considered this approach, which the AEC and Defense strongly opposed, for the previous year. Several factors delayed their final decision; Dulles did not want to appear weak after *Sputnik*, the British and French insisted upon retaining the link until Congress amended the AEA, and Dulles feared that appearing to retreat on a major issue early in the Geneva negotiations would only embolden the Soviet Union to press for additional concessions.

The timing seemed appropriate to announce the change in January, as Eisenhower's disarmament advisors agreed that the new seismic data put them "in a bad spot." Eisenhower agreed and directed the policy change after commenting that he had favored dropping the link "for some time."[23] Eisenhower hoped that this symbol of flexibility would draw away criticism from the new data and highlight as the most contentious issue the Soviet intransigence on maintaining a veto over inspection.[24]

As Eisenhower awaited further analysis of the new seismic data, his administration embarked upon a vigorous debate over its objectives at

Geneva. For test-ban opponents, the new seismic data presented an opportunity to reverse, or at least modify, Eisenhower's decision to seek a comprehensive test ban. Lewis Strauss, whom Eisenhower in October 1958 nominated as his Secretary of Commerce, remained powerfully engaged in the test-ban debate. Edward Teller and Jack Morse, Strauss's former assistant, kept Strauss informed of the course of negotiations in Geneva. In early December 1958, they briefed Strauss on the implications of the seismic data from the *HARDTACK II* tests. According to Strauss's record of the meeting, Teller strongly criticized the scientists who developed the Geneva system at the Conference of Experts the previous summer for ignoring his warnings about the ability to detect underground tests.[25] Strauss later told Teller that he welcomed the administration's release of the new seismic data because it "completely vindicates you."[26]

For Teller, the "prime movers" of the effort to convince Eisenhower to pursue a test ban were Rabi, Bethe, and Bacher. Echoing Strauss's assessment of Rabi and Bethe earlier in the year, Teller commented that they were "the same individuals who bitterly opposed the H-bomb program and that their advice, whether sincere or innocent, has been invariably wrong." Deeply distraught, Teller contemplated issuing a public warning against the administration's pursuit of a test ban even though Strauss cautioned him that it might cost him his position as the director of Livermore. Strauss, perhaps mindful that Teller's position at Livermore increased his credibility as a test-ban opponent, suggested that Teller work quietly within government channels and attempt to influence Goodpaster and Nixon.[27]

While Strauss continued to influence the internal debate from behind the scenes, his successor as AEC chairman, John McCone, advanced Strauss's views on behalf of the AEC in administration discussions on the test ban. Although McCone differed remarkably from Strauss in temperament, they pursued similar policies as chairman; both strongly opposed Eisenhower's efforts to reach a comprehensive test-ban agreement. They both amassed tremendous wealth before joining the Eisenhower administration. McCone was a conservative Republican and a highly successful California businessman. He profited tremendously from shipbuilding during World War II and was the president of the Bechtel-McCone Corporation from 1937 to 1945. Following the war, McCone served in the Department of Defense as a deputy to Secretary Forrestal, before becoming under secretary of the air force. In addition to providing McCone valuable experience in government, these positions also brought McCone into contact with Eisenhower. McCone helped Eisenhower acquire air force officers for his NATO staff and supported his efforts to incorporate nuclear weapons into NATO's defense plans. Unlike Strauss, who had initially supported Ohio Senator Robert Taft for the Republican nomination for president in 1952, McCone supported Eisenhower from the start of the campaign.[28]

McCone differed most strikingly from Strauss in style and temperament. Where Strauss was secretive and preferred to consult with a few trusted advisors, McCone sought alternative views from multiple sources. McCone was also more tolerant of differences of opinion, which Strauss often viewed with suspicion. While McCone often backed down on an issue when he realized that he was outnumbered, Strauss refused to retreat from his strongly held positions and developed a deep personal animosity toward those whose views differed from his own. Importantly, McCone, who was much more congenial than the vindictive Strauss, was able to maintain a positive relationship with the members of the JCAE.[29]

Although the Senate overwhelmingly approved McCone's nomination as chairman, McCone's criticism of the political participation of scientists during the 1956 campaign caused some tense, though brief, moments in his confirmation hearings before the JCAE. McCone, who was a trustee of Cal Tech, rebuked ten scientists from the institute in 1956 who had signed a statement supporting Stevenson's test-ban proposal. McCone wrote to them that he considered it "improper" for a group of Cal Tech scientists to sign the public statement, which he considered "misleading," that advocated a test ban. The senators on the JCAE did not press the matter, permitting McCone to sidestep carefully the episode and simply affirm his commitment to allow individuals the freedom to express their opinions.[30]

As chairman, McCone was acutely aware of the deep schism in the scientific community. Although he attempted to defuse the personal rivalries in the eyes of the public, he privately took advantage of the divisions to impugn the technical credibility of test-ban advocates whose views clashed with his own. Most importantly, he followed Strauss in accepting and promoting within the administration the views of powerful test-ban opponents within the AEC.

In McCone's view, the new seismic data created such uncertainties over detection capabilities that any treaty signed at Geneva would face an embarrassing rejection from the Senate. McCone cautioned Dulles that the detection issue would awaken old personal conflicts among the scientists that would embarrass the administration. Emphasizing the "deep and serious splits among the scientists, who were lining up in a way that they did during the great debate over the development of the H-bomb," McCone warned Dulles that the bitter arguments among scientists during the ratification would be "extremely damaging" to the country.[31]

Privately, McCone encouraged one scientist in particular, Edward Teller, to express freely his opinions against a test ban. After promoting Teller's lobbying, McCone cautioned Christian Herter, the under secretary of state, that Teller had "such sway on the Hill" that he could persuade a substantial number of Senators to oppose the administration's test-ban efforts. On the other hand, he warned, "Bethe has created a very bad impression up there" because the administration accepted the Geneva system of inspection, since proven inadequate, that was based largely upon Bethe's technical conclusions.[32]

After attacking Bethe's scientific expertise, McCone questioned Bethe's loyalty to the administration by identifying him as the source of an embarrassing leak. Charles Murphy of *Fortune* magazine, who had collaborated with Strauss in a 1953 article that attacked Oppenheimer's opposition to the H-bomb, wrote another provocative piece for the March 1959 issue of *Fortune*. Murphy's cautionary article depicted the administration's pursuit of a test ban as one of its "most embarrassing predicaments." He strongly criticized the administration's "near miss" of opening negotiations toward an agreement based upon Bethe's technical assumptions, which he portrayed as terribly flawed. After directing his strongest criticism at Bethe, Murphy praised McCone's proposal for an atmospheric test ban as the most "sensible way to wind up an awkward diplomatic venture."[33]

Ironically, McCone identified Bethe as the source of the leak for the article that strongly criticized the prominent physicist. In fact, Bethe was infuriated at the "slant" of the article and frustrated that the editors provided him advance copies of the essay without giving him time to suggest revisions.[34] Nevertheless, McCone identified Bethe as the source of the leak of NSC discussions to Eisenhower, whose famous temper appeared after violations of his presidential order against disclosing the details of his private counsel. Furious at another leak, Eisenhower immediately instructed Killian to rebuke Bethe strongly.[35]

Eisenhower's decision, based on the Bethe Panel's recommendations, to declare a test moratorium and negotiate a test-ban treaty deeply troubled McCone, who had failed to convince Eisenhower to seek a test limitation rather than a cessation. Morse informed Strauss in December 1958 that McCone was "deeply depressed" and he feared that McCone had "given up the fight" to shape the administration's test policy.[36] Although McCone was dejected, he was not defeated. Morse's analysis was likely based upon a simple stylistic comparison between Strauss, who would never retreat, and McCone, who realized that it was sometimes best to take a tactical pause if his views were in a clear minority or he began to fall out of favor.

The new seismic data provided McCone the technical basis to challenge Eisenhower's commitment to a comprehensive ban. The *HARDTACK II* data bolstered McCone's argument to omit underground detonations, which were more difficult to detect, from any test-ban agreement. McCone in January 1959 advocated the immediate tabling of an atmospheric test-ban agreement.[37] Eager to resume underground testing, he argued that efforts to improve the effectiveness of the Geneva system were dangerously "theoretical."[38] Moreover, McCone strongly criticized those who suggested that the administration could accept a control system that provided sufficient detection capabilities to deter Soviet efforts to test clandestinely.[39] Sharing Strauss's mistrust of the Soviet Union, McCone remained convinced that the Soviet Union would cheat in any detection system that was not foolproof.

The views within the Defense Department largely supported McCone's proposal for an atmospheric test ban. Deputy Secretary Donald Quarles represented Defense in most of the upper-level meetings on the test issue. Quarles remained consistent in his position that the administration should agree to ban only those tests that it could adequately detect. Although his position differed semantically from McCone's insistence upon a foolproof detection system, their views remained quite close in practice. It quickly became clear that Quarles's conception of what constituted "adequate" inspection differed little from McCone's insistence upon a foolproof system. As a result, the Defense position on testing remained close to the views of McCone and the AEC.[40]

Dulles and his successor as the Secretary of State, Christian A. Herter, often opposed the AEC and DOD positions on the Geneva talks. For Dulles, propaganda considerations largely dictated his approach to the test-ban issue. Yet by 1959, Dulles's reconsideration of the administration's national security strategy, his concerns with the consequences of a nuclear war, and his acceptance of the health hazards of atmospheric testing may have raised hopes that results, rather than a mere propaganda victory, would arise from the test-ban talks. Dulles, the primary spokesperson for the administration's "massive retaliation" strategy, had privately concluded in 1958 that the strategy had become "inflexible" since the Soviet Union had acquired such a powerful nuclear arsenal.[41] In fact, the person most closely identified with confidently pursuing a policy of nuclear brinkmanship had become deeply troubled by the potential consequences of nuclear war. Dulles in 1958 privately requested information from Leo A. Hoegh, director of the Office of Civil Defense, so that he and his wife could improve and adequately supply the fallout shelter in their residence.[42]

By early 1959, Dulles had also changed his view on the hazards of fallout from testing. Previously, Dulles had discounted the actual health hazards, but realized that the administration had to alter its test policy to account for the reality of public opposition to testing. In March 1959, Dulles signaled for the first time his acceptance on the view that atmospheric tests were "injurious to life."[43]

Although these factors provided important reinforcing considerations, Dulles remained primarily concerned with the propaganda aspects of the negotiations. His greatest concern about the new seismic data was that the Soviet Union would use it to break off the negotiations before the United States and Great Britain could expose the Soviet intransigence on inspection to the world. Dulles, fearing a Soviet break if the administration changed the objectives of the conference along with the technical data, opposed McCone's recommendation to offer immediately a ban on atmospheric tests.[44] Instead, he favored dropping the link between testing and other disarmament measures to illustrate the administration's flexibility.[45]

Although Dulles may have been privately hopeful of a positive outcome at Geneva, he remained deeply pessimistic that the nuclear powers could reach an agreement on a complete cessation of testing. Dulles believed that the Soviet Union would never allow the level of inspection necessary to monitor a comprehensive ban, which included mobile inspection teams, from operating within its closed society. He also recognized the tremendous pressures from domestic test-ban opponents (within the AEC, Defense, and Congress) not to accept anything less than a foolproof system, which the new seismic data suggested might be technically infeasible for a comprehensive ban.[46]

Dulles, based upon his assessment of Soviet attitudes and the strength of test-ban opponents within the United States, acknowledged that the administration might eventually have to propose an atmospheric test ban. He rejected, however, McCone's calls for tabling immediately such a limited proposal. Dulles, ever conscious of world opinion, first wanted to draw out negotiations further to expose the Soviet intransigence on control. Convinced that the Soviet Union would never agree to the level of inspection provisions acceptable to the domestic test-ban opponents, Dulles advocated pushing negotiations to the breaking point over the issues of inspections, staffing, and the veto. Once the negotiations clearly illuminated the Soviet inflexibility on the matters of control, Dulles recommended breaking off the negotiations and proposing an atmospheric test ban.[47]

Dulles's bout with cancer prematurely ended his reassessment of strategy, nuclear war, fallout, and the test ban. Dulles believed that he had survived abdominal cancer until doctors in February 1959, operating on a hernia, discovered several malignant growths. Given only a few months to live, Dulles retained his position until mid-April. Although hospitalized for much of this time, Dulles remained remarkably engaged and influential in administration policies until his death in May.[48]

Although Dulles continued to monitor the developments in Geneva and Eisenhower still sought his counsel, the president had to rely increasingly upon acting secretary Christian Herter to develop and implement the administration's negotiating position at Geneva. Herter, a former congressman and governor of Massachusetts, was a prominent East Coast Republican who was Stassen's choice to replace Nixon as vice president on the 1956 Republican ticket. Herter, who did not encourage Stassen's efforts against Nixon, fared better within the administration after that episode than did Stassen. Appointed in 1957 as under secretary of state, Herter became familiar with the administration's ongoing policies, but he lacked Dulles's comprehensive knowledge and broad experience. Not surprisingly, Eisenhower never developed the trust and confidence in Herter that he had shared with Dulles. Nevertheless, Herter played a significant, if never decisive, role in the administration's test-ban debate. As the secretary of state, Herter had the responsibility to supervise the test-ban negotiations and provide instructions to the delegation in Geneva.[49]

For the first half of 1959, Herter respectfully advanced Dulles's views at interdepartmental meetings. Privately, Herter's attitude toward the test ban was initially closer to McCone's than to Dulles's position. Dulles's pessimism originated from his assessment of the Soviet unwillingness to accept adequate inspection rather than any concerns with the technical limitations of detection.[50] Herter, however, accepted Teller and McCone's dire warnings about the possibility of decoupling underground nuclear tests, despite Killian's initial skepticism about the cost and effort involved.[51]

By late-March, Herter and Dulles supported the same policy position, which deferred the pursuit of a comprehensive test ban, though they did so for different reasons. They both supported the majority view among Eisenhower's advisors that the administration should protest the Soviet intransigence on the veto and propose an interim atmospheric test ban. This proposal also called for a period of joint research on developing the means to extend eventually the atmospheric ban to tests underground and at high altitudes.[52]

III

With the shift in the State Department's support from a comprehensive test ban to a limited accord on atmospheric tests, James Killian became Eisenhower's sole advisor on the matter who continued to share his commitment to ban all tests. Yet Killian, whose counsel Eisenhower accepted to pursue the negotiations in the first place, was perhaps the individual most personally troubled by the technical implications of the new seismic data from the *HARDTACK II* test series. Killian eventually concluded, albeit reluctantly, that the uncertainties raised by the new data meant that the administration should suspend its effort to negotiate a comprehensive test-ban treaty.

As Eisenhower's first science advisor, Killian had initially hesitated to offer counsel that departed from the realm of technical assessments and encroached upon matters of policy. His first major policy recommendation, which he based upon inconclusive technical data that proved to be dangerously flawed, resulted in criticism at home and embarrassment abroad. Killian initially sought to reassure the president that the scientists could restore the effectiveness of the Geneva system to ban all tests after additional study and a few modifications. When it became clear that these later assessments were also tentative and theoretical, he withdrew his support for a comprehensive ban and advocated an accord limited to atmospheric testing. Already troubled that he had strongly advocated in 1958 the pursuit of a comprehensive test ban based upon a single experiment, Killian in 1959 was unwilling to continue to advance that controversial position in the absence of conclusive data on detection.

Killian's abandonment of his support for a comprehensive test ban evolved slowly and reluctantly. In January, when he was still confident that the Berkner Panel would discover relatively simple means to improve seismic detection, Killian focused his efforts on preventing the administration from abandoning the Geneva system and accepting McCone's proposal for an atmospheric test ban. In his view, banning atmospheric tests only would signal an admission "that the fallout hazard was real"[53] and that such tests were "hazardous to [the] world population."[54] He cautioned that this admission would be a reversal of a position that the administration had painfully defended for years.

Killian remained suspicious of McCone's advocacy of an atmospheric test ban, concerned that he merely proposed it to allow the AEC to conduct further tests, even if limited to those underground. Killian strongly questioned the necessity and even the usefulness of underground tests. He firmly stated to Eisenhower's advisors that there was "a serious difference of opinion in the scientific community" on the practicality of underground tests because of the increased costs and the yield limitations.[55] The issue even divided the AEC; while scientists at Livermore were strong advocates of underground testing, Los Alamos scientists questioned the usefulness of tests in that environment.[56]

Eisenhower, who had originally sought a comprehensive ban, also firmly rejected McCone's proposals and continued to hope for an agreement on the broadest test ban possible. Nevertheless, the technical data from the *HARDTACK II* series did prompt Eisenhower to revise his initial objective of a ban on all tests. After learning of the new data, Eisenhower's first inclination was to pursue a threshold ban, which would end all tests except those conducted underground that fell below an adequate level of detection.[57] Eisenhower instructed Herter that they "should be working toward acceptance of a test ban, which may not be so good as we want, but would test whether both sides are acting in good faith." He insisted that they could no longer be rigid on control just because they had been rigid in the past. In his view, they must not forsake an opportunity to get a meaningful agreement. Eisenhower sought a system that banned all but "small tests" underground, insisting only that the Soviet Union abandon its insistence on the right to veto inspections of unidentified seismic events.[58]

The president pursued this course, realizing that a ban on some underground tests, which was not foolproof, faced considerable opposition within the administration and Congress. Referring to the test-ban opponents such as Teller, Eisenhower asserted that "we should desert the scientists, and to some extent the Department of Defense in their insistence on obtaining a perfect system." Herter, aware that Teller's views held a powerful sway over several senators, cautioned Eisenhower that they could anticipate difficulties securing senate ratification of any treaty incorporating a threshold ban.[59] Despite Herter's warnings, Eisenhower was willing to challenge the powerful opposition and pursue the broadest ban possible.

Although initially hopeful that modifications could restore the detection capabilities of the Geneva system or confirm the feasibility of a threshold agreement, the disappointing report of the Berkner Panel on underground test detection convinced Killian and, ultimately, Eisenhower to suspend their support for continuing negotiations toward a comprehensive ban. The panel's final report, issued in mid-March, assessed the data from the underground shots in the *HARDTACK II* test series. The report validated the limitations of the Geneva system. Although scientists at the Conference of Experts in 1958 agreed that the original Geneva system provided adequate detection for tests down to 5kt, the Berkner Panel's analysis of the *HARDTACK II* data revealed that the system was only effective detecting tests down to 20kt. The panel concluded that immediate modifications could improve the Geneva system to detect seismic events above 10kt. The panelists believed that within three years additional research could develop improvements that would restore the system to the original effective threshold of 5kt.[60]

Most significantly, the Berkner Panel confirmed McCone's warnings that it was theoretically possible to decouple, or muffle the magnitude of underground detonations, which raised serious questions about the ability to monitor effectively a ban on underground tests. The panelists assessed what became known as the "Latter hole" theory, named for Dr. Albert Latter of the RAND Corporation who worked closely with Edward Teller on the concept. Latter, who served as a consultant to the Berkner Panel, theorized that nuclear devices detonated in large spherical cavities deep underground would emit a much smaller seismic signal, masking the true size of the test. According to Latter and Teller, it was theoretically possible to reduce the seismic signal from a given yield by a factor of ten or more, possibly as high as a factor of one thousand, by detonating a nuclear device in a hole drilled deep into the earth's surface.

The Berkner Panel's assessment of the Latter hole theory acknowledged that the ability to decouple underground explosions remained theoretical; no known tests had thus far been conducted under those conditions. Moreover, the cost and engineering problems of drilling a hole deep in the earth's surface would be prohibitive and the risks of another nation detecting the preparations for the tests (such as excavating tons of earth) would be high. Nevertheless, the panel concluded that decoupling represented a potential loophole that the administration could not ignore. Since the Latter hole theory made it extremely difficult to determine the size of a weapon detonated underground, the Berkner Panel seriously questioned the desirability of pursuing any test ban based upon a specific yield threshold. Instead, it recommended that, for the time being, the administration only agree to an atmospheric ban.[61]

Killian in February tempered Eisenhower's hopes for a broader agreement, cautioning him that initial discussions of the Berker Panel suggested that the theoretical possibility of decoupling "invalidate[d] the threshold concept."[62] After the Berkner Panel submitted its final report, Killian advised Eisenhower that it was "impossible" without further tests "to give any firm estimate of the capability of the Geneva system for [detecting] underground tests."[63]

The implications of Killian's counsel was clear; Killian advised Eisenhower to suspend, pending the development of improved methods of underground test detection, his hope for even a threshold ban. Instead of seeking a broader ban that included large tests below ground, Killian advised Eisenhower to accept a ban limited to atmospheric tests. Eisenhower eventually accepted Killian's recommendation, based upon the Berkner Panel's conclusions, that the administration could not agree to any ban on underground tests without further research and development. Previously, Eisenhower had resisted the pressures from the AEC and Defense to agree only to a ban that permitted continued underground testing. Ultimately, Eisenhower yielded to the weight of his scientific counsel, rather than the pressures from the AEC and Defense, in abandoning his inclination for a threshold ban.[64]

Killian's retreat from the comprehensive ban and his reluctant support of McCone's test-ban proposal occurred toward the end of his service as the president's science advisor. Perhaps embarrassed by the detection issue, fatigued by the criticism, and concerned with the failing health of his wife, Killian in April submitted his resignation to Eisenhower. Killian remained onboard until mid-July, exerting a central influence on the president's approach to the test-ban talks.[65]

For Eisenhower, the conclusions of the Berkner Panel that temporarily dashed his hopes for achieving a comprehensive test-ban agreement arrived as his assessment of the hazards of atmospheric testing underwent a monumental change. Up to this point, Eisenhower, who had been aware of the possible health risks since 1947, had not believed that radioactive fallout from testing alone posed a sufficient health hazard to compel a cessation of atmospheric tests. Although he rejected the dire warnings of test-ban advocates such as Linus Pauling, he acknowledged that the administration had to respond to the worldwide concerns about testing, even though he considered them unfounded.[66]

In early March 1959, Eisenhower's attitude on the hazards of testing underwent a pivotal transformation. Ironically, AEC Commissioner Willard Libby convinced Eisenhower to abandon atmospheric tests for the remainder of his presidency. For the previous five years, Libby had led the AEC's public relations campaign minimizing the health hazards of fallout against the dire warnings of Pauling. At a meeting on 6 March, Libby briefed Eisenhower and the Cabinet that the amount of radioactive strontium-90 in Minnesota wheat was nearing dangerous levels (Minnesota's location made it susceptible to fallout from both U.S. and Soviet tests from the unprecedented testing in 1958).[67] Moreover, a recent study concluded radioactive strontium-90 spent one year, instead of ten as originally believed, deteriorating in the stratosphere before returning to the earth. With less time decaying in the stratosphere, the strontium was much more hazardous when it fell to the earth.[68]

Libby's information had an immediate impact on Eisenhower, convincing him not to authorize any additional atmospheric tests for the remainder of his presidency. Two days after receiving Libby's briefing, Eisenhower informed his advisors that he had changed his personal assessment of the testing hazards. He acknowledged, "all available evidence indicates that nuclear testing is bad."[69] Eisenhower revealed that he had "come to the conclusion that testing in the atmosphere was something we wouldn't do in any event."[70]

For Eisenhower, this was a monumental change with important implications for his approach to the test-ban negotiations. Eisenhower had already overruled the vehement opposition of test advocates to declare a moratorium on testing, partially to quell what he then considered to be an unreasonable worldwide anxiety over atmospheric testing. Now personally convinced of the fallout hazards, Eisenhower deepened his resolve to fend off the persistent requests from the AEC and Defense to resume testing.

Just as the Berkner Panel rejected the feasibility of pursuing a threshold ban, British Prime Minister Harold Macmillan suggested another option to consider as an alternative to McCone's atmospheric ban proposal. Macmillan became convinced after meeting with Khrushchev that the Soviets feared most that the West would use an extensive mobile inspection system for espionage operations.[71] In an effort to mollify Khrushchev's fears of intrusive inspection, Macmillan, without consulting the Eisenhower administration, proposed establishing an annual quota of allowable on-site inspections. Khrushchev seemed receptive toward this idea, as long as the number of annual inspections was low, as a means of breaking the impasse at Geneva.[72]

Macmillan's quota proposal received a strongly negative response from the Eisenhower administration. Eisenhower initially dismissed Macmillan's proposal, characterizing it as "silly" and "infeasible."[73] He presciently feared that accepting a quota in principle would lead to a freeze in the negotiations over a specific annual figure before the sides reached an agreement on the veto and control post staffing issues. The president also rejected the quota proposal because it based the method of control upon an arbitrary and static political agreement rather than the scientific evidence of seismic events, the number of which varied each year. Finally, Eisenhower worried that accepting a quota in principle would then pressure the West to accept a number of annual inspections below "an acceptable level of deterrence."[74] Macmillan, who faced an election amidst strong domestic political pressures to break the impasse at Geneva, scheduled a visit with Eisenhower for late-March to consult on the test-ban issue and the Berlin crisis.

Eisenhower and Killian, disappointed that the Berkner Panel's conclusions narrowed the administration's options at Geneva, were still determined to reach an agreement that would prevent the further contamination of the atmosphere and still provide some means of opening up the Soviet Union. For Eisenhower, the most important thing was to reach an agreement on a minimal level of inspection to build the mutual confidence necessary for broader arms control agreements. As Eisenhower instructed Herter, "anything we and the Soviets can do to build confidence in each other's word is a step forward."[75] Three days later, Eisenhower opined to Macmillan and Dulles that an agreement "limited to atmospheric tests, and including as few as three or four control posts, would be better than no agreement at all."[76]

Eisenhower and Macmillan, along with some of their advisors, discussed the Geneva talks extensively in conversations held between 20 and 22 March. The negotiations at Geneva, which remained locked in a stalemate over the veto and control issues, had recessed for Easter and were set to resume on 13 April. Both leaders believed that they needed to reconsider their approach to the talks and coordinate their policies for the resumption of the negotiations. In the conversations, Macmillan discussed his visit with Khrushchev to explain why the British Prime Minister believed that a ban tied to a fixed quota of annual inspections offered the best hope for an agreement. Eisenhower remained uncon-vinced of Macmillan's quota proposal and explained why his own views had shifted from supporting a threshold treaty to a ban limited to at-mospheric tests. Although the leaders failed to reach an agreement, their conversation pointed toward proposing a phased agreement that initially banned only atmospheric tests, but also included studies to improve the methods of detection. In this manner, they left open the possibility of extending the control system to underground and high-altitude tests.[77]

Eisenhower and Macmillan agreed to continue to consult in the weeks ahead to prepare their position for the resumption of talks following the Easter recess. After an exchange of letters with Macmillan, Eisenhower on 13 April, the day that the negotiations resumed at Geneva, sent a letter to Khrushchev based upon the framework developed during Macmillan's visit to Washington.[78] Critical of the Soviet refusal to accept adequate controls, Eisenhower proposed a phased agreement, first ban-ning tests in the atmosphere up to 50 kilometers. Eisenhower suggested that they could extend the agreement to tests below ground and at higher altitudes after both sides at Geneva resolved the outstanding political and technical issues.[79]

Eisenhower's April proposal marked the greatest retreat in his efforts the previous six months to pursue a comprehensive test-ban agreement. The complexity of underground detection, rather than any weakening in Eisenhower's desire for reaching an agreement, caused Eisenhower to shift toward McCone's position. Confronted with an intricate technical matter, Eisenhower relied heavily on Killian's counsel. Killian, however, decided to base his advice much more conservatively on the unproven theoretical possibilities of decoupling underground tests rather than the potential improvements in detection. As a result, Eisenhower suspended his effort to ban testing underground.

IV

McCone's triumph in April of moving the administration to table a lim-ited test-ban treaty that would permit underground testing to continue proved short lived. Khrushchev issued a counterproposal ten days after receiving Eisenhower's interim atmospheric ban proposal. The Soviet leader's counterproposal for a test ban based upon a quota system re-vived the possibility of pursuing a comprehensive test ban within the administration. Dismissing Eisenhower's framework as misleading to the world since it allowed certain tests to continue, Khrushchev proposed a comprehensive test ban with on-site inspections limited to an annual quota. Khrushchev did not specify how many annual inspections he would be willing to accept, suggesting only that the number "should not be great." Khrushchev's framework was essentially the same as the framework Macmillan had suggested in March to the Eisenhower administration.[80]

Although Eisenhower and his primary advisors unanimously rejected the quota proposal in March as providing insufficient inspection, Eisenhower in May authorized Ambassador Wadsworth in Geneva to explore the degree to which the Soviet Union would allow mobile inspections in its territory. Within the administration, Eisenhower directed PSAC to determine the minimum number of annual inspections the United States could accept. Killian reported in June that 100 inspections per year would provide a high probability of deterring a Soviet effort to test clandestinely and would be a good figure to begin negotiations. In his view, 25 or less would provide an unacceptable deterrent.[81]

The Eisenhower administration had tabled the atmospheric test-ban proposal in an effort to break the deadlocked talks at Geneva. Rather than breaking the stalemate over the veto and control post staffing, Khrushchev's counterproposal of a quota system simply dropped another contentious issue, the number of annual on-site inspections, into the laps of the beleaguered negotiators at Geneva. Delegates remained deadlocked over the quota figure and the issues of staffing, inspection, control, and a reconsideration of the *HARDTACK II* seismic data through the summer and into the fall.

Eisenhower's willingness to consider Khrushchev's quota proposal reopened the debate within the administration whether it should accept a comprehensive test ban if the Soviet Union agreed to a reasonable figure of on-site inspections. Herter reported to Eisenhower that McCone had made it clear that, due to the uncertainties of underground detection, the United States could not accept anything but an atmospheric test ban. According to a record of that conversation, Eisenhower "reacted sharply" at the "the continuing reservations of the AEC." Eisenhower lectured Herter that "it was not up to Mr. McCone to dictate to the president how the U.S. will be secure." For Eisenhower, McCone's insistence upon a foolproof detection system was unrealistic. Eisenhower was willing to accept a system that provided sufficient detection to deter attempts to evade the agreement. After Herter mentioned that Teller was pressing for the resumption of testing, Eisenhower instructed Herter to "reprimand the AEC in his name" for continuing to challenge his policy decisions.[82]

Three days later, Eisenhower met with the principals to consider whether, in light of the new seismic data, the administration should be prepared to accept a comprehensive test ban if the Soviet Union relented on the veto issue and accepted an adequate number of annual on-site inspections. McCone, citing the *HARDTACK II* data and Teller's concern with the possibility of decoupling tests, responded that the most that the administration could offer would be a phased approach similar to Eisenhower's proposal to Khrushchev the previous month. McCone admitted that world opinion placed them "out of the business" of atmospheric testing, but emphasized the necessity to continue testing underground.[83]

Eisenhower rejected McCone's rigid position. In Eisenhower's view, they could not retreat to an atmospheric test ban if the Soviet Union relented on the veto and other issues. Although he acknowledged that he had received "conflicting advice from the scientists" as to whether or not continued testing would work to the nation's advantage, Eisenhower indicated that he did not accept McCone's assessment of the necessity of additional testing.[84] In his view, they should seek a "reasonable and decent" agreement even if "not necessarily perfect." Eisenhower acknowledged that he was "not of course personally in a position to decide what is scientifically reasonable."[85]

Eisenhower later directed Killian to study what minimum level of inspection the administration should accept that would provide an adequate deterrent against efforts to test clandestinely. Although he had retreated in April to an interim atmospheric ban, Eisenhower decided to probe the Soviet response further to determine if a broader test-ban agreement remained possible. Although he remained hopeful that Khrushchev's formula would produce results, he acknowledged that a long list of unresolved issues indicated that "the negotiations clearly had a long way to go."[86]

As Soviet delegates at Geneva remained fixed in their positions on staffing and their rejection of the new seismic data, Eisenhower vacillated on the test issue through the month of June. On separate occasions, Eisenhower expressed doubts that the Soviet Union would relent on the other issues or accept a reasonable number of on-site inspections. On 8 June, he acknowledged that he was becoming "pessimistic" about the test negotiations in Geneva because they seemed "to be getting nowhere."[87] Leery of the theoretical possibilities of evasion, Eisenhower commented that he had "come to the conclusion that it would be much worth our while to abandon [our] effort to control underground tests."[88]

course outlined in July. The British, who had just recently received a briefing from Killian on the Bacher Panel conclusions, desired more time to study its conclusions on the limitations of detecting underground tests. Most importantly, they did not want to table a limited test ban, which they feared would break up the negotiations in Geneva, before the anticipated October elections in Great Britain. Within the administration, the State Department sought a recess in the talks while James Wadsworth, head of the U.S. delegation at Geneva, returned to New York. Wadsworth was scheduled to serve as the acting U.S. Representative to the United Nations while Henry Cabot Lodge accompanied Nikita Khrushchev on his visit across America.

A recess in the Geneva negotiations had important implications for extending Eisenhower's test moratorium, scheduled to expire on 31 October. The proposed recess, which extended from 26 August to 27 October, allowed little time to reach a test-ban agreement before the moratorium expired. Under Secretary of State C. Douglas Dillon feared that the Soviet delegates would oppose the request for a recess because they believed that the administration would end the moratorium and resume testing if there was no progress in the negotiations by the end of October. Thus, Dillon recommended that Eisenhower extend the test moratorium to the end of the year to allow the talks at Geneva to resume without being overshadowed by an immediate end to the moratorium.[106] Eisenhower approved Dillon's recommendation without hesitation. Dillon revealed the president's decision to extend the moratorium in a 13 August meeting with the principals, provoking a "wild reaction" from Thomas Gates, the Deputy Secretary of Defense, and McCone who deplored another delay in the resumption of testing.[107]

Test advocates received another setback when the Panel on Nuclear Requirements (known as the McRae Panel after its chairman, James McRae) concluded that there was no immediate urgency to resume testing. Eisenhower on 16 July had directed that PSAC, which he referred to as "his scientists" to distinguish them from those such as Teller who advised the AEC and DOD, form a panel to study the necessity of resuming tests.[108] Although the McRae Panel's report acknowledged that tests could help refine and improve weapons currently in the nuclear arsenal, it determined that the development and fielding of those weapons was not "clearly contingent on the outcome" of the tests that the AEC and DOD proposed for early 1960. Thus, the panel concluded that "there is not a strong technical requirement for the conduct of any single proposed test in the immediate future." Finally, the panel suggested that the

AEC could accomplish most of its objectives for developing and refining weapons in the future through underground testing.[109]

Test advocates, such as Teller and the Joint Chiefs of Staff, immediately protested the conclusions of the McRae Panel. In a heated conversation with Kistiakowsky, Teller castigated the panel for minimizing the necessity of resuming tests.[110] The Joint Chiefs of Staff considered "the resumption of nuclear testing so vital to the security of the United States" that they felt compelled to submit a critical response to the report's conclusions. In their view, the "overall long-range effects of a test cessation will be to the distinct disadvantage of the United States."[111] Despite the vehement protests of Teller, the AEC, and the DOD, Eisenhower accepted the McRae Panel's conclusions that there was no urgent necessity to resume testing.

Rebuffed in their efforts to resume testing, Teller and the Defense Department posed greater challenges to the ratification of a comprehensive test-ban treaty. Kistiakowsky feared that the powerful combination would derail any possible agreement to ban underground tests. He remarked in his diary that "it was quite obvious that Teller has done a good job in the Pentagon" arousing fears of the Soviet Union clandestinely developing improvements to their nuclear arsenal.[112] Kistiakowsky acknowledged that even in the remote chance that the Soviets agreed to an acceptable quota of inspections, the administration would be in a "hopeless political situation" because Teller's senate testimony would emphasize the possibility of evading the detection system.[113] Thus Kistiakowsky recognized that it may be politically impossible to ratify a treaty "in the face of the theoretical possibility of the Latter hole."[114] Despite his progress swinging Eisenhower's views in his favor, Kistiakowsky realized the difficulties that lay ahead.

On the eve of Khrushchev's visit, Kistiakowsky's efforts and the McRae Panel conclusions had at least temporarily halted the rush toward tabling a limited test-ban treaty and resuming testing. Khrushchev's visit began with a blustery address at the United Nations that proposed the abolition of all weapons, nuclear and conventional, without any means of inspection. He followed this clearly unacceptable proposal with a plea to the United States to accept a test ban, which he termed "eminently ripe for solution."[115]

In conversations with Henry Cabot Lodge, Khrushchev's escort on his travels within the United States, the Soviet premier suggested that he had not closely followed the talks in Geneva. Khrushchev told Lodge that he believed the West insisted upon unnecessary inspection provisions because it sought to plant intelligence operatives in Soviet soil. Despite his claims of not following the talks, Khrushchev later revealed some familiarity with the remaining issues and offered some hope for progress with a suggestion to Lodge that they could reach a compromise on the staffing issue.[116]

Unfortunately, Khrushchev and Eisenhower never discussed the test-ban issue in any great detail. The president did not intend to undertake any substantive discussions on the test-ban talks until Khrushchev agreed to remove all time limits on resolving the Berlin issue. The two leaders did not reach an understanding on that matter until late in Khrushchev's visit, limiting any progress on the test-ban negotiations.[117]

Although the delay reaching an understanding on Berlin left little time for any substantive discussions on the test ban during Khrushchev's visit to the United States, the discussions at Gettysburg and Camp David may have convinced Eisenhower to redouble the administration's efforts thereafter to reach an agreement at Geneva. Eisenhower wrote to Macmillan that the Soviet premier talked at great length about the costs of armaments and of his anxiety about the prospects of general war.[118] Two weeks after Khrushchev's visit, Eisenhower commented to Herter that Khrushchev "really seems to want to talk about disarmament in concrete terms, and that he fully understands the need for effective inspection."[119] Llewellyn Thompson, the U.S. Ambassador to the Soviet Union, concurred with Eisenhower's assessment of Khrushchev's objectives and provided powerful support for Kistiakowsky's encouragement of a comprehensive ban. Thompson briefed Eisenhower that Khrushchev would likely reject an atmospheric ban because only a comprehensive ban would accomplish his primary purpose in pursuing a test ban, which was to prevent Communist China and West Germany from acquiring nuclear weapons. Although Eisenhower did not commit to seeking a comprehensive ban to Thompson, he did indicate that their "real effort should go into making some meaningful move toward disarmament."[120]

Following Khrushchev's visit, the administration resumed the debate of its objectives for the Geneva talks, which were scheduled to resume at the end of October.[121] For the AEC and DOD, the course outlined in late July remained valid; the administration should abandon its efforts to ban underground testing and immediately table a phased ban on atmospheric tests. For others, the recess provided an opportunity to reconsider the administration's policy in light of the McRae Panel's conclusions and the progress made, though limited, during Khrushchev's visit. The lengthy recess proved especially fortuitous for Kistiakowsky, who gained confidence in confronting test-ban opponents and in presenting his own policy recommendations.

Significantly, Kistiakowsky used the time to convince Herter and Dillon that abandoning a comprehensive ban without first exhibiting greater flexibility on the quota issue would place the United States in an extremely unfavorable position before the world. More concerned with propaganda than reaching an agreement, Herter and Dillon agreed that the United States could not back away from a comprehensive test ban without placing the blame on the Soviet Union for refusing to reassess the challenges of detecting underground tests.

The State Department, influenced by Kistiakowsky's arguments, outlined in early October a new strategy for the negotiations at Geneva. Western delegates would spend the next several weeks presenting technical data aimed at placing the onus for the failure to reach a comprehensive test-ban agreement on the Soviet Union. After establishing this case, the delegates would table a phased test-ban agreement.

The delegates would present a limited amount of technical data that would reveal that the Soviet refusal to reconsider the original Geneva system prevented the conclusion of a properly safeguarded and comprehensive agreement. The delegates would also emphasize the Soviet intransigence on the veto and control post staffing issues. Although the delegates would not state a specific figure for a quota of on-site inspections, they would ensure that the weight of evidence revealed that the number must be quite large (in the order of 200 to 375 annual inspections). The strategy assumed that the Soviet Union would reject such an intrusive number of inspections.

The delegates would then present a limited treaty similar to the one originally outlined in the July policy deliberations; the phased treaty would initially ban tests in the atmosphere and in outer space while joint research determined the means to extend the ban to underground tests. Dillon assured the DOD and AEC that they would table the phased treaty by the end of the year to free the administration's hand to resume testing.[122]

Eisenhower approved the outlined course of negotiations, which in many ways reconciled the divided objectives within his administration. For test-ban advocates, the tactics kept open the possibility of pursuing a comprehensive ban if the Soviet Union agreed to reconsider the system for detecting underground tests and accept a large number of on-site inspections. Although many remained hopeful of a positive Soviet response, few within the administration considered this likely. For the AEC and DOD, certain of a few additional weeks of Soviet intransigence, the tactics seemed certain to table the limited proposal that they had long advocated to pave the way for the resumption of underground testing.

VII

The administration's new negotiation tactics assumed that the Soviet delegates would continue to oppose reopening technical talks. Surprisingly, and to the great consternation of test-ban opponents, the Soviet Union agreed soon after the talks in Geneva resumed to send technical experts to consider the new data on underground detection from the *HARDTACK II* test series.[123] Since experts had already met the previous summer to discuss the difficulties of detecting high-altitude tests, the Geneva delegates referred to the discussions on underground testing as Technical Working Group II. The Eisenhower administration's significant difficulties convincing scientists to serve as delegates to the technical talks reveal how unexpected the Soviet acceptance was and how skeptical some scientists remained about the administration's commitment to negotiate a comprehensive test-ban agreement.

Administration officials realized that they could not appoint any scientists easily identified as test-ban opponents without being charged that they were negotiating in bad faith, but they had difficulty convincing prominent scientists of the opposite view to head the delegation. Herter insisted that they not select Harold Brown, Teller's deputy at Livermore, or anyone from the "Teller outlook" to head the delegation.[124] Rabi, who was Eisenhower's first choice, declined due to health reasons.[125] Killian and Bacher both declined to head the U.S. delegation to the scientific discussions. Killian feared that his initial support of the flawed original Geneva system would open him up to personal attacks, leading to a "catastrophic" outcome in the talks.[126] Bacher also refused because he considered the talks merely a "holding operation" while the administration continued to debate internally whether it would accept a comprehensive test ban.[127] Kistiakowsky, attempting to force a decision on the administration's objectives that he had slowly been moving in his desired direction, encouraged Bacher to emphasize to Herter that the lack of a decided policy would make it impossible to get any "independent" scientists to participate in the technical talks.[128] After Killian, Bacher, and Rabi declined, Herter eventually convinced James Fisk, who led in 1958 the scientific delegation during the original Conference of Experts, to head the delegation.

Herter and McCone briefed Eisenhower on the difficulties of convincing scientists to participate in the technical talks. According to McCone, many scientists believed that the administration sought to use the technical talks as a means of disengaging from the Geneva talks and abandoning the goal of suspending underground tests. Eisenhower responded that his objective for the talks was not to prepare for disengagement, but to make progress toward an agreement that he genuinely desired. The president acknowledged that they would have to give the limitations of underground detection "due consideration," but was unwilling to abandon the effort to ban some underground tests.[129]

From 25 November until 19 December, scientists participating in Technical Working Group II debated the implications of the *HARDTACK II* data and the possibilities of decoupling tests in a Latter hole. Unlike the technical talks on high-altitude detection that summer, where both delegations were cooperative and they reached an agreement on the substantive issues, the discussions on underground detection concluded with little agreement and much bitterness. Fisk wrote Herter that he considered the talks not "a failure, but it certainly wasn't a success." In his view, the Soviet Union "obviously instructed" its delegates to accept anything that made the original Geneva system look effective and "belittle, refute, or ignore" any data which suggested that a more intrusive inspection system was necessary.[130] Most disturbing to some U.S. scientists, the Soviet delegation ended the discussions by attacking the competency and the objectivity of the American scientists. The bitterness between the international delegations of scientists seemed to doom the hopes of some scientists that their own community could succeed where diplomats had failed in finding a solution to ease Cold War tensions.[131]

The tangled course of the test-ban debate within the Eisenhower administration reached its most complicated stage between August 1958 and December 1959. In this period, diplomats presented proposals and counterproposals, scientists raised and challenged new theories, and bureaucrats continued their infighting that included leaks and direct appeals to the public. Not surprisingly, negotiators at Geneva made little progress toward a test-ban agreement. The test ban, so appealing initially as a relatively easy first step to break the impasse on previous efforts at arms control, proved to be more complex than anyone imagined.

The range of technical issues related to nuclear weapons and seismic detection placed an even greater premium on scientific expertise than ever. Yet, many of the issues that scientists grappled with remained largely theoretical. The formation of several panels to assess the technical matters involved in the nuclear weapons testing failed to produce a consensus within the scientific community other than the need for additional study of the issues at hand. In the absence of conclusive data, many of the nation's scientists allowed their political inclinations to fill the voids created by the absence of experimental data.

In this technically complex environment, the different counsel of Killian and Kistiakowsky shaped Eisenhower's approach to the test-ban issue. Eisenhower followed Killian's advice in suspending his pursuit of a comprehensive test ban. Much less concerned with the theoretical possibilities of evading a detection system, Kistiakowsky worked feverishly to reverse Killian's counsel. After several months, Kistiakowsky expressed tremendous satisfaction that his "boring from within" had "finally borne some fruit" in convincing Eisenhower to return to the pursuit of a comprehensive test ban.[132]

For Kistiakowsky, who had worked so hard to keep the possibility of pursuing a comprehensive test ban alive within the administration, the failed technical talks at the close of 1959 were especially disheartening. Instead of breaking the deadlock on the negotiations and reaching an understanding on underground inspection, the discussions served to increase the frustrations of test-ban advocates and bolster the arguments of those within the administration who favored the resumption of testing. As Eisenhower neared his final year in office, the failure of the technical talks and the looming deadline of his test moratorium demanded decisions on what course he would pursue at the Geneva negotiations and whether or not he would authorize the resumption of testing.

The Threshold Ban, the Paris Summit, and the Farewell Address (December 1959–January 1961)

A useful purpose is served simply by keeping on talking.

—Eisenhower, 18 May 1960

It is hell trying to operate in a political year when no one wants to take responsibility for anything.

—Herter, 28 June 1960

Although disappointed and frustrated that the scientists meeting at Geneva failed to agree on the necessity of seismic improvement, Eisenhower refused to accede to the pressures from the AEC and DOD to abandon his quest for a test ban and to resume testing. During his last year in office, Eisenhower made one final effort to reach an agreement with the Soviet Union. He remained hopeful that a test-ban accord would ease tensions and provide an important first step toward slowing the arms race and the building of mutual confidence necessary for subsequent disarmament measures. After an intensive internal debate and extensive consultations with the British, Eisenhower and Macmillan exchanged a series of proposals and counterproposals with Khrushchev that appeared to narrow the gap between the positions of the nuclear powers.

Although several issues remained unresolved and domestic critics mounted a spirited campaign against a test-ban agreement, the scheduled summit meeting in Paris in May 1960 provided an opportunity for the heads of state to discuss the salient political questions that had deadlocked the talks at Geneva. The Soviet downing of a U-2 on the eve of the summit, however, unleashed a chain of events that culminated with Khrushchev walking out on the Paris summit. The disastrous outcome of the summit raised tensions between the superpowers and ended perhaps the last chance for making significant progress in the test-ban negotiations during Eisenhower's presidency.

The upcoming presidential election dominated Eisenhower's approach to nuclear testing for the remainder of his term in office. On one hand, Eisenhower during the summer of 1960, recognizing that he had perhaps dangerously extended the unmonitored moratorium on weapons testing for an extended time with no immediate prospect for reaching an agreement, began to sympathize with those advocating a resumption of testing. On the other, he refused to authorize tests because he wanted to provide his successor a final opportunity to reach an agreement at Geneva, and he believed that a test resumption would likely break up the negotiations.

To provide his successor flexibility, Eisenhower pursued a static policy at Geneva that ensured that the test-ban talks would continue, but offered little prospect of making progress. Eisenhower avoided making concessions that could have broken the impasse, fearing that the concessions would anger hard-liners and provoke criticism from Democrats at home. At the same time, he rejected the calls of some test advocates to issue an ultimatum on resolving the outstanding issues, which would also risk breaking up the Geneva talks.

Congressional opposition during an election year also inhibited Eisenhower's actions. The administration sought the congressional authorization necessary to allow Soviet officials to inspect "outdated" U.S. nuclear devices for use in a joint research program to improve the methods of detection. Democratic political attacks on the mythical missile gap and the inadequacies of the Republican defense policies made congressional leaders from both parties hesitant to provide any information to the Soviets on U.S. designs, no matter how outdated.

Despite their focused efforts, the administration never found a solution to the dilemma of conducting nuclear experiments for seismic improvement while convincing the Soviet Union that the tests did not also provide the United States any advantageous information for improving their nuclear arsenal. With both sides awaiting the results of the presidential election and then the arrival of a new administration, delegates at Geneva during the fall of 1960 agreed to lengthy recesses in the test-ban negotiations. Not surprisingly, the delegates made little progress on the several remaining unresolved issues.

Eisenhower departed the presidency without reaching an accord on banning nuclear weapons tests. His farewell address reflects his disappointment in the failure to reach a test-ban agreement. Although the outcome was the result, in part, of his own lack of flexibility, Eisenhower's cautionary warnings in his most famous presidential address also revealed his assessment of the powerful forces that he believed frustrated his efforts.

I

The failure of Technical Working Group II in December to agree upon revisions to the Geneva system prompted a debate within the administration over its pursuit of a comprehensive test ban and another extension of the test moratorium, which expired on 31 December 1959. The Soviet rejection of suggested improvements to the detection capabilities of the Geneva system convinced Kistiakowsky that it was a political impossibility to ratify a comprehensive test-ban agreement. His support of a threshold ban, which did not prohibit underground tests that produced inconclusive seismic signals, ironically aligned him with John McCone, his strongest enemy within the administration's test-ban debate. Eisenhower continued to accept the judgment of his trusted science advisor. He remained committed to reaching an accord that banned all tests that Kistiakowsky convinced him could be adequately detected and politically accepted. Eisenhower increasingly stated that his aim was to reach an agreement that brought international inspectors into the Soviet Union, "opening up" the country to outside monitoring. Confronted with opposition from the Defense Department, McCone, and another appeal from Lewis Strauss, Eisenhower refused to consider the resumption of weapons tests and remained hopeful, despite the most recent setback at Geneva, that negotiators could conclude a test-ban agreement before he left office.

As the 31 December expiration of his test moratorium neared, Eisenhower remained privately adamant about his refusal to authorize a resumption of tests, but in his public statements maintained his flexibility to do so. Eisenhower's first inclination was to make no statement at all about whether he would extend the moratorium or order a resumption of testing. Privately, Eisenhower emphasized that there would be no further testing or consideration of the matter without his formal approval.[1] After his advisors convinced him that he must publicly address the issue, Eisenhower suggested an ambiguous statement that announced the formal expiration of the voluntary moratorium on 31 December 1959, but pledged not to resume testing without prior notification.[2] In this manner, Eisenhower hoped to use the continued pause in testing as leverage for Soviet concessions at Geneva.

Eisenhower's private rejection of renewed testing did little to halt the mounting internal pressures in early 1960 for a test resumption. McCone expressed concern over the low morale within the AEC's weapons laboratories resulting from the lengthy test moratorium. Eisenhower acknowledged that he was aware of the problem, which was an argument Strauss had advanced for several years, but simply stated that other policy considerations took priority.[3] The president also declined McCone's request in February to meet with British officials to discuss the resumption of underground tests below the threshold under consideration. Eisenhower responded that he would not authorize such tests, but that he would not publicly reveal his intentions. Eisenhower feared that indications of preparations to resume testing at any level would erode the chances of reaching an agreement on the broadest ban possible with the Soviet Union.[4]

As it became clear that the technical experts meeting at the end of 1959 would fail to reach an agreement on the means of improving the detection capabilities of the Geneva system, Kistiakowsky reluctantly reached a disappointing conclusion. He recognized that the Senate would never ratify a comprehensive test-ban agreement based upon the flawed Geneva system of detection. With the failure of Technical Working Group II to agree upon improvements, Kistiakowsky acknowledged that the ratification of a comprehensive test ban was politically impossible. Kistiakowsky in December 1959 remarked in his diary that he had become "convinced that a comprehensive treaty would not be ratified by the Senate since AEC, DOD, and Teller will all testify in opposition."[5] Kistiakowsky considered Teller "almost hysterical on the subject of nuclear tests and is against arms limitations of any kind. He envisages the future as an ever-intensifying arms race, but refuses to consider what its ultimate outcome will be." Kistiakowsky agreed in January 1960 with Trevor Gardner, a former assistant for research and development to the secretary of the air force, that Teller was "the most dangerous scientist" in America because of his influence over powerful senators such as W. Stuart Symington (D-Mo.), Truman's first secretary of the air force and a candidate for the Democratic nomination for President in 1956 and 1960.[6] As the election year wore on, Kistiakowsky became increasingly concerned that his opponents within the scientific community commanded a stronger influence over the leading presidential candidates.

Three days before the formal conclusion of the technical discussions in Geneva, Kistiakowsky met with McCone to consider the administration's policy toward the test-ban negotiations. Surprisingly, McCone and Kistiakowsky, who typically represented opposing views in the administration's test-ban debate, reached a general agreement on a recommended policy to present to Eisenhower. According to Kistiakowsky, the meeting began inauspiciously, as McCone accused the PSAC scientists of "getting us into the mess we are in now, politically." McCone was referring to PSAC's conclusion after its 1958 meeting in Puerto Rico that a comprehensive test ban could be adequately monitored. Kistiakowsky reminded McCone that PSAC's findings merely confirmed the conclusions of Bethe's interagency panel, which included representatives from the AEC.[7]

After this tense exchange, the two rivals reached agreement on a proposal that would ban tests in the atmosphere, in outer space, and underground down to a threshold commensurate with the level of on-site inspection that the Soviet Union agreed upon.[8] In Kistiakowsky's view, this would "toss the hot potato back to the Soviets" by lowering the threshold based upon the number of inspections that they were willing to accept. This threshold proposal differed from one previously considered and rejected as too complex. Negotiators made little progress on the former proposal because both sides disagreed over how to calculate the yield of tests from the seismic signals. Kistiakowsky's new proposal avoided this contentious procedure by simply establishing the threshold based upon seismic signal rather than calculated yield.

Significantly, the two rivals within the internal test-ban debate agreed to accept the possibility of evasion by decoupling and testing in outer space. McCone accepted, for the first time, Kistiakowsky's argument that the risk of detecting the preparations for decoupled underground tests was sufficient to deter an effort to test clandestinely. He also accepted Kistiakowsky's conclusion that tests in outer space were too difficult and expensive to be useful. Finally, they agreed to include in their proposal a provision for a joint research program to determine improvements in seismic detection that would increasingly lower the threshold. In this manner, the compromise proposal initially banned only those tests above a threshold easily detectable as McCone demanded, and offered Kistiakowsky the possibility in the future of extending the ban to additional tests as the scientists improved the means of detection.[9]

Kistiakowsky considered the agreement with McCone a tremendous personal triumph, offering a chance to break the "incredible morass of indecision" that reigned over the administration's test-ban policy the last several months of 1959. He also believed that the proposal marked a "major liberalization" in McCone's attitude toward a test ban.[10] Yet, their agreement over tactics did not represent concurrence over ends. For Kistiakowsky, the proposal offered the hope of evolving into a comprehensive ban as technology improved. For McCone, skeptical of the ability of scientists to improve methods of detection, the proposal allowed the AEC to resume testing below the threshold.

The principals discussed the unlikely collaborators' threshold proposal on 28 December when they met to decide how to advise Eisenhower on the administration's approach to the test negotiations. Herter favored the threshold proposal since it still provided a basis for demanding a modest number of on-site inspections within the Soviet Union. In his view, it was better to ban large underground tests rather than abandon the objective of banning underground tests entirely. Although Gates, who Eisenhower recently elevated to Secretary of Defense, and Twining favored immediately tabling an atmospheric test ban to permit a resumption of testing underground, the other principals reached a general agreement on pursuing a threshold ban if it proved technically feasible. Herter asked Fisk, who had just returned from the failed technical talks at Geneva, to determine the feasibility of a threshold proposal with representatives from other agencies. Fisk expected to complete his study in one week.[11]

The following day, the principals presented their recommendations to Eisenhower, who was vacationing in Augusta. Eisenhower, after receiving a briefing on the technical conference from Fisk, was deeply troubled by the Soviet attack on the American scientists' integrity and competence. Kistiakowsky recorded in his diary that the president was clearly "tired and impatient" with the course of negotiations.[12]

Despite Eisenhower's frustrations, he remained determined to reach an agreement on the most extensive ban possible. The president identified a three-phased approach to the negotiations. First, the administration would continue to press the Soviet delegates to accept the limitations of underground detection and work toward a comprehensive ban by expanding the detection system. Second, the administration would propose a threshold ban if Fisk's study concluded that a ban based on seismic magnitude would be feasible to negotiate and monitor. Third, the administration would revert to a ban only on tests in the atmosphere.[13] In Eisenhower's view, their "real aim" was to open the Soviet Union to some degree of inspection, even if that meant only a few inspection stations.[14] Despite his frustrations with the tortuous course of negotiations, Eisenhower remained committed to reaching an agreement that banned all tests that an inspection system could adequately detect. For him, this would establish confidence in the inspection mechanisms necessary for the disarmament measures that he deeply desired.

Eisenhower's commitment to reaching the broadest test ban possible faced pressures from several corners. Senator Gore urged him in late December to reconsider the proposal he suggested a year earlier for a unilateral ban on atmospheric tests.[15] Lewis Strauss, who was no longer a member of the administration after the Senate in June 1959 rejected his nomination as Secretary of Commerce, also continued his efforts to convince Eisenhower not to reach a test-ban agreement.[16] Before a January 1960 meeting with Eisenhower, Strauss carefully reviewed the classified portion of Bethe's April 1958 congressional testimony on the ability to detect underground tests.[17] When he met with the president, Strauss emphasized that Bethe's confidence in the ability to detect underground tests had misled him. Deeply disturbed at the administration's willingness to negotiate at Geneva, Strauss urged Eisenhower to abandon his effort to ban any tests underground, suggesting that the administration release a simple statement that underground tests could go "virtually undetected."[18] Although Eisenhower maintained a friendship with Strauss that continued beyond his presidency, the former AEC chairman's views on nuclear testing no longer went unchallenged. Despite Strauss's efforts, Eisenhower remained committed to Kistiakowsky's counsel to seek a threshold ban.

From within the administration, Eisenhower faced an effort from the DOD to omit underwater tests from the threshold proposal two days before presenting it to the Soviet delegation. Herter, who was initially inclined to agree with Defense's wishes, conferred with Kistiakowsky and Goodpaster before agreeing to the deletion. Kistiakowsky confirmed that a monitoring system could detect tests in the oceans.[19] Goodpaster emphasized to Herter that Defense was "fighting a lost cause" because Eisenhower already approved the proposal. Nevertheless, Goodpaster raised the issue with the president. According to Goodpaster, Eisenhower was "very clear and very strong" that he wanted to ban all tests that the scientists agreed that a monitoring system could detect.[20] The late-hour appeal from Defense failed to shake Eisenhower's commitment to seeking the most extensive ban possible. Once again, the president overruled Defense and instead sided with his science advisor.

Unlike the internal opposition, which criticized the threshold ban as too broad, the British opposed the administration's proposal for being too limited. The principals recognized that the British government, for this reason, was violently opposed to the threshold ban.[21] British officials believed that the Soviets would accept nothing less than a comprehensive test ban. Domestic opinion in Great Britain also strongly favored a ban on all nuclear weapons tests.

Some British officials feared that the United States would resume underground testing below the established threshold. The administration indirectly learned that David Ormsby Gore, the British Minister of

State, suggested that the British would break with the United States if the Eisenhower administration did not also agree to ban voluntarily tests below the threshold of detection. He suggested that the British would even support a UN resolution condemning any U.S. resumption of testing below the threshold.[22]

These threats failed to alter Eisenhower's approach and provoked a bitter response from McCone. The AEC chairman angrily replied that the British had no need to test because they had been "living off of us" in terms of weapons information since Congress in 1958 amended the Atomic Energy Act.[23] McCone threatened to leak the British threat to the JCAE, whom he was certain would quickly end the bilateral agreement with the British if they did not support the administration's threshold proposal.[24] Eisenhower expressed "considerable displeasure" at the British stand, but was non-committal on his reaction. He simply responded to McCone that if they reached an agreement on the threshold proposal that "we will do whatever we decide to do."[25] Eisenhower's ambiguous comment shrewdly suggested to McCone that he would authorize tests below the threshold, yet Eisenhower had told Herter the day before that he had no intention of authorizing any tests. Aware of McCone's powerful allies in Congress, Eisenhower was likely deliberately ambiguous to prevent McCone from turning the issue into a public debate.

For McCone, the greatest appeal of the threshold ban was that it would permit the AEC to resume testing, albeit on a strictly limited basis. As a result, he strongly opposed modifying the proposal in any way that would further inhibit the AEC's ability to test below the threshold. McCone issued a dire warning on the implications if the administration bowed to British pressure and accepted a moratorium on tests below the detectable threshold. According to McCone, he told Herter that such a ban "would be met with serious opposition in the Senate. I said that it would be violently opposed by scientists as well as the military, and that I, myself, would be forced to oppose it even though doing so would require me to leave my post as part of the Eisenhower administration."[26] After strong pressure from the United States, the British moderated their opposition to the threshold proposal. Selwyn Lloyd assured Herter that they would support the administration's policy as far as they possibly could. For the time being, McCone did not have to face up to his ultimatum.

On 11 February, Eisenhower opened his press conference with a brief statement outlining the administration's threshold proposal. The compromise program included a ban on all tests in the atmosphere and in the oceans. It called for an end to all tests underground and in outer space that an international control agency could effectively monitor. Combining this proposal with a coordinated program of research and development, Eisenhower underscored that this was merely a first step toward a comprehensive ban.[27]

The same day, Wadsworth presented the compromise program to the Soviet delegation at Geneva. Wadsworth suggested establishing the initial threshold at 4.75 on the Richter scale, but emphasized that the delegates could lower the threshold to include smaller tests if the Soviet Union accepted additional control posts and more on-site inspections. Several outstanding issues, such as of the number of on-site inspections, the criteria for selecting which events to inspect, and the staffing of the control posts, remained unresolved. Although the threshold proposal offered no solutions to those complex issues, it had the potential to break the deadlock on underground detection, which had caused the sharpest disagreement among the delegates at Geneva. An agreement on the limits of underground detection would offer some hope for progress on the control issues.

II

As the administration awaited the Soviet response to the threshold proposal, McCone once again probed Eisenhower's willingness to resume testing. At a meeting with the president on 11 March, McCone described his recent visit to the AEC's weapons laboratories. McCone detailed the dramatic improvements that he expected to gain from the resumption of tests. He then stressed that although the labs had not yet lost any of their top scientists since the moratorium began, morale was quite low over the uncertainty of future testing. According to McCone, the scientists at the weapons labs continuously pressed him on when they could resume testing. Eisenhower again demurred, stating that the test resumption was a "political decision," thus the administration's policy and must remain "open" and could not be hurried.[28] This time, McCone seemed to sense what Eisenhower had told others in the administration. Soon after, McCone informed Herter and Kistiakowsky on separate occasions that he believed Eisenhower had no intention of resuming weapons tests of any kind for the remainder of his presidency.[29]

Eisenhower's refusal to authorize the resumption of testing reflected his broader concerns about slowing the arms race and taking steps that could lead toward lasting disarmament agreements. After reviewing the

State Department's latest disarmament policy review, Eisenhower emphasized the importance of getting some sort of inspection system operating within the Soviet Union. In his view, this would build the confidence necessary to establish more intrusive inspection systems. He opposed simply tabling an atmospheric test ban because it did not require inspection posts within Soviet territory.[30]

The following month, Eisenhower revealed the depth of his concerns with the nature of nuclear warfare and the necessity of slowing the arms race in a meeting with McCone and Dillon. Eisenhower first criticized a press release that suggested that the administration had abandoned the goal of reaching a comprehensive test-ban agreement at Geneva.[31] According to McCone's record of the conversation, Eisenhower "seemed entirely preoccupied by the horror of nuclear war" and the fact that the nations that developed nuclear weapons had been unable to reduce tensions between them, which made the development and the expansion of their nuclear arsenals a necessity. Eisenhower insisted that they must "find a way to arrest the development of weapons of mass destruction." McCone recorded that this objective was "paramount" in Eisenhower's mind and that the failure to reach it could result in an "ultimate catastrophe to civilization." According to McCone, the president continuously returned to the necessity of "bringing this situation under control and urged that everything possible be done" to reach an agreement on the cessation of tests.[32]

McCone's record of his conversation with the president supports Eisenhower's later description of his hopes for a test ban. In his memoirs, Eisenhower wrote that by early 1960 "an effective ban on nuclear testing had become an essential preliminary to—even though not a definite part of—attaining any worthwhile disarmament agreement. Consequently, I ordered that we continue our efforts to achieve this first step."[33] With broader purposes in mind, Eisenhower continued to seek a test-ban agreement and reject requests for the resumption of testing.

On 19 March, Khrushchev's conditional response to Eisenhower's threshold proposal underscored the latter's commitment to do "everything possible" to reach an agreement. Khrushchev accepted the threshold concept and acknowledged the difficulties of detecting small underground tests, but insisted that the monitored ban on tests above 4.75 be accompanied by an unmonitored ban on tests below that threshold. His counterproposal still did not make clear how large of a quota of on-site inspections the Soviet Union would be willing to accept. Many other issues related to control remained unresolved, such as the criteria for determining which seismic events were subject to inspection and the composition of the personnel staffing the control posts. Despite these shortcomings, many administration officials considered the counterproposal a significant breakthrough that required a constructive response.[34]

Khrushchev's reply prompted an urgent telephone call and a hastily arranged visit from British Prime Minister Harold Macmillan. During their telephone conversation on 21 March, Macmillan pressed Eisenhower to accept Khrushchev's proposal for a temporary moratorium on all tests: "You would then go down as the man in history who put an end to all this." Although Eisenhower indicated that he was "very sympathetic" with Macmillan's goal of ending all tests, he cautioned that his administration needed additional time to study the "fuzzy" Soviet proposal. Eisenhower's greatest concern was that the temporary moratorium on tests below the threshold would not be subject to control. Even if he decided to accept this risk, he was skeptical about the legality of an outgoing president committing the nation to a temporary moratorium beyond his term in office. Furthermore, Eisenhower noted that there was little time for the Senate to consider it as part of a treaty; the Senate recessed in late June for the 1960 election campaigns.[35] Alternatively, he could sign an Executive Order committing the nation to a test moratorium, but that might only be binding for ten months because his term expired in January 1961. Macmillan, deeply committed to reaching a test-ban agreement, arranged to visit Eisenhower at Camp David a week later to convince him to find a way around those legal obstacles and accept the risk involved in Khrushchev's counterproposal.

Over the course of the next week, the State Department resolved the legal issues, Kistiakowsky provided a hopeful assessment of improving the means of detection within the next two years, and Eisenhower dismissed the vigorous opposition of the AEC and DOD. By the time that Macmillan arrived at Camp David, he no longer had to convince Eisenhower to respond constructively to the Soviet proposal. Two days after his initial telephone conversation with Macmillan, Eisenhower had essentially made up his mind to accept an unmonitored moratorium on underground tests below the threshold for a period of up to two years. Meeting with Herter and Dillon, Eisenhower identified the Soviet acknowledgment of the difficulties of detecting small underground tests as significant progress. In his view, this provided hope for making progress in the stalled test-ban negotiations. He emphasized, however, that he would not accept a long-term ban on tests below the threshold for any longer than two years and he wanted to make sure that his agreement did not bind his successor.[36]

The following morning, Eisenhower met again with Herter, who briefed him on the discussions between the principals the previous two days.[37] According to Herter, McCone was "violently opposed" to accepting a temporary moratorium below the threshold. Eisenhower responded that he too was uneasy with that aspect of the proposal, but had decided that he was willing to accept a short-term risk to reach an agreement with the Soviet Union. He simply stated that McCone would have to accept his policy determination.[38]

Forewarned of McCone's opposition, Eisenhower met with the principals two hours later to discuss the administration's response. Eisenhower began the meeting by assuring the principals that he would do nothing that he believed would damage the nation's vital interests and would not accept a prolonged test suspension that a monitoring system could not enforce.[39] On the other hand, he emphasized that he considered it in the nation's vital interests to reach a test cessation agreement with adequate safeguards.[40] Eisenhower stressed the importance of making "some progress somewhere in the disarmament area."[41] He then revealed his decision. Eisenhower would accept a temporary moratorium for up to two years while a joint research program studied the means to improve the capabilities of the monitoring system to detect tests below the initial threshold.

McCone immediately objected to the president's decision, deeming it "a mistake" and a "surrender of our basic policy" since it accepted a ban on tests beyond the detection capabilities of the control system. According to Kistiakowsky's record of the meeting, Eisenhower became visibly angry and responded to McCone "in a sharp voice" that reaching a test-ban agreement with the Soviet Union was "in the interests of the country, as otherwise all hope of relaxing the cold war would be gone."[42] Eisenhower was so irritated at McCone's objections that he privately suggested that he was ready to accept McCone's resignation[43] and initially excluded him from the scheduled test-ban discussions with the British officials at Camp David.[44]

At Camp David, Eisenhower and Macmillan were pleasantly surprised that they agreed on most aspects of a counterproposal to Khrushchev. Eisenhower was concerned that they would be "hoodwinked" into extending the unmonitored test moratorium indefinitely while fruitless negotiations dragged on. The president informed Macmillan that, despite the opposition within his administration to any moratorium beyond easily detectable tests, he had decided to accept one of limited duration. Eisenhower stressed, however, that he would not accept a moratorium for longer than two years, which was significantly shorter than

Khrushchev's proposal for a four- to five-year moratorium while the nuclear powers studied means to improve the detection capabilities below the threshold. Macmillan indicated his general approval, though he later suggested a willingness to accept a temporary moratorium for a period of three years.[45]

The following day, Kistiakowsky briefed Eisenhower, Macmillan, and their advisors on the anticipated outcome of the coordinated research program. In heavily qualified language, Kistiakowsky suggested that if all went well scientists could restore the detection system to what they believed was its original capability—a 90 percent chance of detecting all tests above 5kt. Eisenhower considered this an acceptable level of progress, commenting that he did not expect a 100 percent certainty of detection. Although Kistiakowsky cautioned again about being too optimistic of the chances of finding a solution to the detection problems within two years, Eisenhower accepted the fact that they "would never have a perfect control system."[46] While Eisenhower and Macmillan accepted the risks of an imperfect detection system, they did not discuss the quota of on-site inspections. Eisenhower accepted Herter's recommendations that on-site inspection was a political issue that would have to be decided by the heads of state at the Paris summit.[47]

At the conclusion of their discussions, Eisenhower and Macmillan agreed to issue a joint declaration that outlined their response to Khrushchev's proposal. Identifying their ultimate objective as the cessation of all tests, they declared their willingness to accept a voluntary moratorium on tests below the threshold for an unspecified "agreed duration" while a coordinated research program studied the means to detect such tests. Significantly, the declaration identified several unresolved matters, including the quota of on-site inspections and control post staffing, urging the negotiators to reach a rapid agreement on these issues.[48]

Kistiakowsky took enormous satisfaction from the agreement between Eisenhower and Macmillan. He reflected that day on the evolution of the test-ban debate within the administration since he had replaced Killian as Eisenhower's science advisor. At that time, Killian had convinced Eisenhower to abandon his pursuit of a comprehensive test ban. Kistiakowsky identified the McRae Panel's conclusions that there was no immediate need to resume testing as having a tremendous influence on Eisenhower's renewed commitment. Kistiakowsky suggested that his own views convinced Eisenhower to accept an imperfect monitoring system, producing a gradual change in Eisenhower's attitude for "the good of the country."[49]

McCone and Strauss's alarm at the course of the test-ban debate within the administration surpassed Kistiakowsky's sense of accomplishment. During a lengthy conversation on 31 March, McCone and Strauss shared their bitterness with the administration's direction on the test-ban issue. McCone compared his isolation within the administration and negative press comments to the troubles that Strauss had experienced. Strauss, in a rare admission of his own failings, assured McCone that he would handle the situation "with better grace" than Strauss did because McCone was a more "even tempered" man. McCone replied that he had lost his effectiveness within the administration, having "objected right up to the Boss [Eisenhower] to the point where perhaps I will tell him tomorrow that this effort is no longer worth my time." Strauss encouraged McCone not to "hang up his suit" but to continue to fight against the test ban from within the administration as the "balance wheel" in the debate.[50]

Although critical of the State Department and the press, McCone held the greatest contempt for scientists. McCone charged State Department officials with planting articles with leading journalists and minimizing to Congress the implications of the Soviet proposal. McCone suggested that he would inform congressional leaders of the real implications and "blow the whole thing out of the water." Most of all, McCone was "disgusted with the scientists" for flooding him with telegrams that urged him to reverse his opposition to Khrushchev's counterproposal. According to McCone, "Bethe was responsible for all of our troubles and for getting us into the deplorable situation in Geneva." Strauss agreed, remarking that "a few of the scientists who have been wrong from the beginning were the prime movers" in building support for a test ban within the administration.[51] With their counsel rejected by Eisenhower, McCone and Strauss lamented that the president's scientific advice greatly dictated his approach to a test ban.

After McCone and Strauss failed to convince the president privately, they supported the efforts of test-ban opponents within Congress to derail the administration's efforts to reach a test-ban agreement. Between 19 and 22 April, the JCAE held hearings that emphasized the risks of accepting a proposal that included an unsupervised ban on underground tests below the threshold of detection. The hearings highlighted the differences between Teller and Bethe.[52] Teller contended that the means to evade a monitoring system would remain easier and cheaper than the means of improving detection.[53] Bethe countered that the means of improving detection were more realistic than the outlandish theories of evasion. Significantly, the JCAE narrowly restricted the testimony to detection issues, preventing test-ban advocates such as Bethe from commenting on the political and military advantages that they believed outweighed the risks of temporarily accepting an imperfect detection system.[54]

The hearings provided a resounding victory for test-ban opponents. Press reports became much more critical of the administration's appraisal of the risks involved and were much more pessimistic of the likelihood that the Senate would ratify a treaty based upon the threshold principle. Many test-ban advocates within the administration feared that the JCAE hearings were part of a broader campaign by their opponents to doom the chances of ratifying a test-ban agreement. According to Kistiakowsky, Herbert York was "very much afraid that McCone and his friends are maneuvering public opinion, including the Senate, so that the President will have a very difficult time getting a treaty ratified."[55] From Geneva, Wadsworth became "convinced more than ever" through conversations with *Washington Post* journalist Marquis Childs that there was a "deliberate planned campaign to sabotage the treaty."[56] State Department officials acknowledged the powerful influence of the hearings in its position papers for the upcoming Paris Summit, commenting that the hearings reinforced the "skepticism and even hostility" toward a test suspension in the Senate and the press.[57]

The hearings temporarily dampened the optimism of the prospects of reaching an agreement that developed after Macmillan's visit. Consequently, the hearings increased the challenges of reaching an agreement with Khrushchev; Eisenhower would now have to convince the Soviet leader that he could get an agreement ratified.[58] Fortunately for test-ban advocates, other factors soon suggested that Eisenhower retained flexibility to pursue his chosen course on the test ban. Two leading Democrats, Senators Humphrey and Gore, declared their support for the threshold treaty despite the concerns raised during the Democratic-led JCAE hearings. Humphrey, a firm test-ban advocate and the chairman of the Senate disarmament subcommittee, possessed considerable influence over the possible ratification debates over any treaty resulting from the Geneva negotiations. Gore's support was especially significant given his previous position to accept only an atmospheric ban and his role as a Senate delegate to the Geneva talks.[59] The support of these two influential Democratic senators, along with Eisenhower's high public approval ratings, suggested that Eisenhower possessed sufficient flexibility at the Paris summit to reach a test-ban agreement that the Senate would ratify.[60]

Developments abroad also indicated improved prospects for making progress in Paris. Soviet delegates at Geneva in early May accepted some of the important aspects of Eisenhower and Macmillan's 29 March proposal. They agreed to engage in a seismic research program that included a strictly limited number of underground nuclear tests to confirm detection capabilities. The Soviets also indicated their willingness to accept a moratorium based upon unilateral declarations rather than incorporating it into a treaty. Significantly, this Soviet concession resolved the problem of obtaining Senate ratification during the election year and provided the flexibility Eisenhower sought for his successor. Although these measures represented important progress, several issues remained unresolved. The Soviets still insisted upon a moratorium below the threshold for a period of four to five years. They also offered no hint of yielding on the issues of staffing and the quota of annual on-site inspections. Despite the challenges that remained, the prospects for making progress on a test-ban agreement appeared brighter than ever on the eve of the Paris summit.[61]

III

Khrushchev's reaction at the Paris summit to the downing of a U-2 spy plane over the Soviet Union destroyed any chances of making progress there on the test-ban issue. Eisenhower had clearly hoped to move closer toward a test-ban agreement at the Paris summit. Whether or not Eisenhower was willing to make further concessions toward this goal remains unclear. For some historians, such as Robert Divine and Stephen Ambrose, Eisenhower was determined to make progress on the test-ban issue at the Paris summit and was willing to make some concessions toward an agreement.[62] Others conclude that Eisenhower remained unwilling to compromise on the control issues that continued to deadlock the negotiations at Geneva.[63] Eisenhower, perhaps sensitive to charges that his authorization of the ill-fated U-2 flight was responsible for the breakup of the summit, wrote in his memoirs that he believed the summit would have been a failure even without the U-2 incident. In his view, the Soviet Union's unwillingness to accept adequate inspection and their mistrust of the West made it unlikely that they could have reached an agreement in Paris.[64]

Interpretations remained divided, in part, because there is little evidence that indicates Eisenhower's attitude toward the resolution of the salient issues to be discussed at the Paris summit. Although Eisenhower emphasized his hopes for making progress and stressed the necessity of reaching an agreement to slow the arms race, he did not indicate how much, if at all, he would be willing to modify his position on the most substantive issues: the duration of the moratorium on tests below the threshold and the annual quota of on-site inspections. The scant evidence that exists suggests that he would not have agreed to extend the moratorium for longer than two years, but that he would have been willing to negotiate the number of annual inspections. Although the test-ban talks between Eisenhower, Khrushchev, and Macmillan never materialized at Paris, subsequent negotiations at Geneva revealed that the two sides remained deeply divided on both issues. Short of an extraordinary development of mutual confidence at the Paris summit, the likelihood of significant progress on the test-ban issue appears small.

Perhaps counting on Soviet concessions, Eisenhower revealed his hopes for making progress in Paris in press conferences and in conversations with Republican senators and allied leaders. Eisenhower's public comments on this matter were typically vague. During a press conference in late March, he defended the framework that he had worked out with Macmillan. Responding to a critical question about his willingness to accept a temporary ban without a fully functioning detection system, Eisenhower commented, "You have to do something if you are going to get a system established that is going to be mutually acceptable as to its accuracy and reliability; well, then, you have to make some concessions as to stopping this whole business."[65]

Harold Macmillan recorded in his diary during his Camp David visit in March that Eisenhower was "*really* keen" on reaching a test-ban agreement. According to Macmillan, although Eisenhower had not suggested a willingness in public to be even more flexible on the remaining issues, the president privately assured the British prime minister that "he would accept further concessions in the course of negotiation" to reach an agreement."[66] Eisenhower's desire for an agreement and his initial negotiating positions are clear. What remains unclear is how much farther, if at all, he was willing to negotiate to reach an agreement. Although Macmillan suggested that Eisenhower was willing to make greater concessions, nothing else in the record, beyond his stated hopes for reaching an agreement, suggests he was willing to do so.

Eisenhower met with Republican senators four days after Khrushchev announced that the Soviet Union shot down a U-2 and captured the pilot alive. Despite this provocative and embarrassing episode, Eisenhower remained hopeful for a successful summit. Although he cautioned that the senators should not expect "great or far-reaching" agreements from the summit, he remained "hopeful that some useful progress could be made." Eisenhower listed one area of discussion at the summit as "the elimination of nuclear tests," believing that they would reach agreement on some of the unresolved issues.[67]

Although Eisenhower's comments only mention hopes and broad principles, position papers prepared for the summit suggest more precisely the range of options that the administration was considering. An examination of this evidence suggests that Eisenhower was ill prepared to offer additional concessions at the Paris summit. Khrushchev proposed a four- to five-year ban on tests below the threshold while the joint research program attempted to improve the means of underground detection. Although administration officials believed that the British would accept a three-year ban, there was no support from any of Eisenhower's central advisors for accepting a temporary ban for longer than two years.[68] Eisenhower, concerned about tying the hands of his successor and sensitive to mounting criticism that he had already accepted an unmonitored test ban since November 1958, never suggested a willingness to agree to a moratorium for longer than two years. Revealing remarkable consistency on this matter, State Department position papers and records of meetings with British officials before the summit indicate no flexibility on the duration of the moratorium.[69]

On the quota of annual on-site inspections, the administration's policy was to accept no fewer than twenty unless the Soviet Union accepted additional control posts, allowed the repositioning of those already agreed upon, or both.[70] At the time of the summit, Soviet delegates had thus far refused to provide a specific number as a baseline for discussions. Khrushchev's private conversation with Macmillan in late February and his public comments only suggested that the number should not be large. Subsequent negotiations revealed that Soviet officials considered three an appropriate figure.[71] Eisenhower had repeatedly emphasized that a central purpose of reaching a test-ban agreement was to open up the Soviet Union to a small degree of inspection from the West. In his view, this would establish the confidence necessary for disarmament agreements. Although this purpose suggests greater flexibility in negotiating the number of inspections, Eisenhower also continuously emphasized the necessity of adequate inspection. On this matter, Eisenhower relied upon the judgment of Kistiakowsky, who considered twenty annual on-site inspections as adequate. Although Eisenhower may have been inclined to accept fewer, it is unlikely that he would have done so without first consulting with his trusted science advisor. Curiously, Kistiakowsky did not attend the Paris summit, suggesting that Eisenhower did not expect to reach an agreement or had already privately made up his mind how far he was willing to go to achieve one.[72] In the end, the gap between Eisenhower's insistence on adequate inspection and Khrushchev's hesitance to accept a mobile international presence on Soviet soil may have been simply too great for Eisenhower, Macmillan, and Khrushchev to bridge at the Paris summit.

IV

The world will never know if the U-2 incident foreclosed an opportunity for Eisenhower and Khrushchev to build upon the understanding that they had developed during Khrushchev's visit to the United States the previous fall. It is clear, however, that the increased hostilities after the failed Paris summit severely diminished the prospects for reaching an agreement before the conclusion of Eisenhower's presidency. At the end of May, Soviet delegates at Geneva reneged on their previous agreement to participate in a coordinated seismic research program. With the Soviet Union returning to their initial insistence that the original Geneva system remained the only basis for negotiations, the test-ban talks took several steps back. Eisenhower wrote in his memoirs that this gesture essentially terminated the "dreary exercise" of the torturous negotiations. Although he suggested that his administration's extensive efforts over the years resulted in considerable progress, he acknowledged that by the end of May the negotiations had "reached a blind alley."[73] Eisenhower's later recollection accurately portrays the ultimate course of the negotiations, but it betrays the hopes that he held for progress in the talks for a few months after the summit.

Although he retained hopes for progress at Geneva in the immediate aftermath of the summit, he acknowledged a few months later that the failed summit likely doomed the prospects for reaching a test-ban agreement with the Soviet Union before he left office. Kistiakowsky later recalled that Eisenhower revealed his frustration and disappointment that the U-2 incident had "ruined all of his efforts" to make progress on ending the cold war. According to Kistiakowsky, Eisenhower sadly commented that he "saw nothing worthwhile" left for him to do until the end of his presidency.[74] As the talks fruitlessly wore on during his final months in office, Eisenhower became pessimistic about the outcome of the negotiations and somewhat troubled by the implications of the de facto test moratorium. Nevertheless, Eisenhower vigorously fended off requests from McCone and Defense to resume testing and to begin a seismic research program unilaterally, steps that would likely result in the break up of the stalled negotiations at Geneva.

At home, the impending fall presidential election heavily influenced Eisenhower's approach in 1960 to the test talks. Eisenhower, mindful that Stevenson's challenge on the test ban limited his flexibility during and immediately after the 1956 campaign, was determined to prevent the issue from again becoming part of the political debate in the race for the presidency. He was also committed to keeping the talks going at Geneva to provide his successor the flexibility to either make his own effort to reach an agreement or authorize the resumption of testing. Determined to allow the next president to chart his own course, Eisenhower did not want to do anything that would risk breaking up the talks.

Not surprisingly, the test-ban talks dragged on without significant progress, interrupted only by two lengthy recesses. The discussions remained deadlocked as delegates attempted, unsuccessfully, to coordinate a seismic research plan that was technically and politically acceptable to the first three nuclear powers.[75] By the fall of 1960, the principals no longer met to consider the test ban and the administration offered no new policy initiatives. After Kennedy won the presidential election, the talks recessed again from December 1960 until February 1961 to await instructions from the new administration.

For McCone, the failure of the Paris summit clinched his arguments that further negotiations were futile and that the resumption of testing was essential. McCone, using the increase in hostilities to push for an immediate resumption of testing, on 18 May argued that there was no prospect of reaching an agreement with adequate inspection. In his view, the moratorium was adversely affecting the nation's vital interests of maintaining its superiority in nuclear weapons; the administration should break off the talks and resume underground testing.[76]

Eisenhower, who believed that the Soviet Union wanted to make progress on the test issue until the U-2 incident raised hostilities, was less skeptical of Soviet intentions at Geneva. Although he agreed with McCone that the Soviets possessed an almost "pathological fear" of inspection, Eisenhower believed that they also sought progress on disarmament. In his view, simply continuing a dialogue of discussions served a useful purpose.[77] Although Eisenhower acknowledged that they could not continue the talks indefinitely if they failed to make any progress, he refused to determine at what time or what stage the United States should place a time limit on the duration of the talks.[78] Despite his disappointment at the outcome of the summit, Eisenhower initially refused to abandon his hopes for a test ban.

Asked at an August press conference to provide his assessment of the chances of achieving a test-ban agreement before the end of this term, Eisenhower acknowledged that the history of negotiations to that time suggested that the prospects were not good. He remained hopeful, however, insisting nothing would gratify him more than reaching an agreement that would "bring a bit more peace of mind to all our people" and would do so by making sure that the United States could adequately police the agreement.[79] Although not optimistic of the outcome, Eisenhower hesitated to foreclose any opportunity to reach an agreement that would ease tensions and provide a first step toward greater arms control measures.

Privately, Eisenhower increasingly expressed frustration with lack of progress in resolving the numerous remaining issues at Geneva. He pressed for a solution in July on the coordinated research program, insisting, "something must be done to get negotiations with the Soviets off dead center."[80] When the issue remained unresolved the following month, Eisenhower cautioned, "if we do not do something to keep the negotiations going along, then we are saying in effect that we give up."[81]

For McCone, giving up and resuming nuclear weapons tests was the appropriate course. He periodically prodded Eisenhower for authorization to restart their testing program. Although Eisenhower privately acknowledged that the administration was under no obligation to continue the voluntary moratorium and could resume testing at any time, he firmly informed McCone that he had "no intention" of authorizing them to do so.[82] Publicly, Eisenhower declared at a 10 August press conference that he would not authorize any atmospheric tests for the remainder of his presidency, stating, "as long as I am here . . . I will not allow anything to be exploded in the atmosphere that would add to the apprehensions of people about their health."[83]

In fact, Eisenhower had much earlier made his decision not to authorize any atmospheric tests. The previous year, he had privately acknowledged for the first time that testing posed unacceptable health risks. Eisenhower's concerns with the hazards of radioactive fallout from atmospheric testing grew the following spring. On 30 March 1960, Kistiakowsky informed Eisenhower that the concentration of radioactive strontium in wheat samples from nine states was nearing dangerous levels. According to Kistiakowsky, Eisenhower was "obviously unhappy about the past assurances from the AEC that there was no problem from fallout."[84] For Eisenhower, the data confirmed his inclination not to resume testing in the atmosphere.[85]

The following month, Eisenhower confronted McCone about the comforting past assurances by Libby and other AEC officials. Eisenhower told McCone that he was "increasingly alarmed over atmospheric testing" and its consequences "on the human body." In his view, the AEC scientists had been "overly optimistic" and "too rosy" in minimizing the dangers from fallout." After Eisenhower appointed a science advisor, the AEC's calming assessment of the hazards of fallout no longer went unchallenged within the administration. Sensing the futility of arguing against Kistiakowsky's technical expertise, McCone concurred and insisted that he would not recommend a resumption of testing in the atmosphere.[86]

Eisenhower's public announcement in August thus merely confirmed a decision that he had made and was accepted within the administration, albeit reluctantly by some, before the Paris summit. As a result, those that advocated the resumption of testing began to limit their proposals to tests conducted underground. McCone, hoping to keep open the possibility of resuming underground testing, stressed that tests below the earth's surface produced no dangers from fallout.[87] Despite McCone's extensive efforts, Eisenhower rebuffed his recommendations to resume underground testing.[88]

Eisenhower's approach in his final months in office to the Geneva discussions reflected the unresolved conflict between his lingering hopes for progress and his fear of breaking up the talks. On one hand, Eisenhower remained hopeful for a test-ban agreement and considered making positive proposals toward the remaining issues. On the other, he strictly limited his range of options by refusing to offer any concessions to the Soviet Union that would appear too soft to Democratic critics. Conversely, he also avoided any hard line actions that risked breaking up the test talks. In his view, concluding the negotiations without reaching an agreement would hurt Nixon's electoral chances. Confronted with these conflicting considerations, Eisenhower maintained a rigid position.

The problems associated with the implementation of a coordinated seismic research program illustrated Eisenhower's dilemma. Such a program required the detonation of nuclear explosions to confirm improvements in the capability to detect underground weapons tests. The Soviet Union, which insisted that improvements were unnecessary, feared that the United States would gain beneficial information from these experiments and use it to make advances in their nuclear arsenal.

Using primitive nuclear devices and opening them to inspection by the Soviet Union would solve this problem, but it created another. The Atomic Energy Act mandated congressional approval before sharing any atomic weapons information. McCone convinced Eisenhower that members of Congress, who feared appearing weak on communism during an election year, would not authorize the Soviets to inspect even outdated weapons. Eisenhower regrettably agreed, commenting, "Congress so loves to keep secrets which the enemy has had for so long."[89] Eisenhower, who was already facing stiff attacks from Democrats on his defense policies and the mythical missile gap, accepted McCone's assessment and deferred until January the effort to gain congressional approval.[90]

Deeply troubled by the delays in the resumption of testing, McCone proposed a solution to break this impasse. He advocated issuing the Soviet Union an ultimatum to accept the terms of a coordinated research program or else the United States would conduct the seismic improvement tests unilaterally. Eisenhower refused to issue any ultimatum or conduct experiments separately, at least until after the election, fearing that either would prompt the Soviets to walk out of the talks at Geneva and resume weapons testing.[91] For Eisenhower, this would greatly diminish Nixon's position in the election. Although frustrated with the lack of progress, Eisenhower in the second half of 1960 was unwilling to accept the international and domestic political consequences of changing course.[92]

The challenges of pursuing Eisenhower's hope for progress while delaying decisions and actions that would lead in that direction fell upon Herter and Wadsworth. Since their primary objective was keeping the talks going until the next administration arrived, they both became deeply pessimistic about the prospects of making progress at the negotiating table.[93] The delegates at Geneva remained deadlocked over the issues that were unresolved at the time of the Paris summit, such as the duration of the temporary moratorium, the quota of on-site inspections, and the staffing of control posts. Significantly, the U.S. delegation sought agreement on the seismic research program before tabling proposals on other matters.

Deadlocked on seismic research, the delegates made little progress on the remaining unresolved issues. The Soviet Union proposed an annual quota of three on-site inspections, but Eisenhower considered this "inadequate to provide effective inspection."[94] The U.S. delegation did not provide a formal counteroffer, under instructions not to issue a reply until the Soviets responded to the latest proposal for seismic research. The remaining sessions in 1960 proceeded in this manner, without substantive discussions or even a clear delineation of each side's position on the numerous remaining issues.[95]

As McCone's frustrations mounted with the impasse in negotiations, the ever-extending test moratorium, and the deadlock over seismic research, he became increasingly isolated within the administration. He increasingly expressed his "violent disagreement" with the administration's approach to the test issue to the point that Herter and Kistiakowsky found it even difficult to discuss the matter with him.[96] The beleaguered AEC chairman, recognizing the toll that his position on the test ban took on his status within the administration, confided to a sympathetic Lewis Strauss that his "stock" had fallen with Eisenhower and that they no longer had a strong rapport.[97]

The deadlocked test-ban talks also wore heavily upon Eisenhower's science advisor, though for decidedly different reasons. Kistiakowsky, who played such a pivotal role in convincing Eisenhower to pursue the broadest test ban possible, reacted to the impasse at Geneva with growing frustration and pessimism. Initially, Kistiakowsky's greatest fear was that the failed Paris summit would lead to saber rattling moves such as calls to resume testing.[98] McCone proved that this fear was well founded, but Kistiakowsky did not need to convince Eisenhower to reject McCone's belligerent proposals.

Although successful in advocating the continuation of the talks at Geneva, Kistiakowsky grew increasingly pessimistic about the prospects for a positive outcome.[99] By August, Kistiakowsky considered the effort to ban tests "a hopeless mess." He too felt that the Soviet Union had "boxed in" the United States, achieving a prolonged test moratorium without inspection while the test-ban talks continued without progress.[100]

With Eisenhower hesitant to present any positive proposals at Geneva during the campaign, Kistiakowsky's accomplishments were negative in character. He prevented the unilateral commencement of a seismic research program, blocked the Department of Defense from using the seismic improvement detonations for assessing weapons effects, and delayed "peaceful" detonations of nuclear devices under Project Plowshare. Each of those actions could have broken up the test-ban negotiations and led to a Soviet resumption of nuclear weapons testing.

Critical of the impasse at Geneva, McCone pressed Eisenhower to begin the seismic research experiments, known as Project Vela, uni-laterally. The first experiment, code-named *LOLLIPOP*, would be an underground shot to determine the ability to detect tests in a Latter hole. Although the nuclear device did not contain any new designs that would violate the proposed terms of the coordinated research program, Defense's effort to assess weapons effects from the experiment violated the spirit of the proposed agreement. Defense contractors built a missile silo in a connected tunnel to assess its ability to withstand seismic shock. Kistiakowsky, fearing that the Soviets would likely regard the effort to determine "weapons effects" as a breach of the moratorium and resume weapons testing, immediately notified Herter of the possibly disastrous implications of the Defense's plans.[101] Had Eisenhower approved the plan to proceed with Project Vela, Kistiakowsky's efforts limiting its scope would have likely mitigated the negative effects of proceeding with seismic research unilaterally.

Kistiakowsky's other significant restraining action sought to moth-ball one of Edward Teller's pet programs, Project Plowshare. Plowshare involved a series of nuclear explosions designed to develop the "peace-ful" applications of atomic energy. Kistiakowsky considered the projects provocative and economically suspect. Aware that the Soviet Union was deeply skeptical of peaceful explosions, Kistiakowsky feared that allow-ing them to continue would risk ending the negotiations and prompt a Soviet resumption of weapons testing.

PSAC members strongly supported Kistiakowsky's views when they met with Eisenhower in July to discuss their concerns with the Geneva talks, seismic research, and Project Plowshare. The scientists encour-aged Eisenhower to continue to seek a threshold ban. Although they ac-knowledged that no detection system would be perfect, they emphasized that available detection methods provided a sufficient deterrent against efforts to test clandestinely. Thus in their view, the seismic research pro-gram, which had deadlocked the test-ban talks at Geneva, was not "suf-ficiently critical" to control the outcome of the negotiations. They con-tinued to favor a test-ban agreement; in their assessment, it was militar-ily advantageous to the United States and could serve as an important first step in arms control and toward "opening up" the Soviet Union. Especially critical of the planned assessment of weapons effects as part of the *LOLLIPOP* shot, PSAC members stressed that the possible data acquired from a unilateral research program was not worth the risk of breaking up the negotiations at Geneva.[102]

The scientists also criticized Teller's proposals to conduct peaceful nuclear blasts under Project Plowshare. In their view, such tests were uneconomical and unnecessarily provocative. Since advanced weapons technologies were involved in even the "peaceful" devices, PSAC reluctantly conceded the argument of Soviet officials that such tests would also provide information on weapons designs, which would be a violation of the moratorium. Although Eisenhower was very interested in the peaceful applications of atomic energy, such as releasing trapped oil reserves or digging canals, he assured the PSAC members that he would proceed cautiously and would not approve such tests if they prejudiced the ongoing test-ban talks. Although Eisenhower expressed little hope for a positive outcome at Geneva, he informed PSAC that he intended to continue negotiating.[103]

PSAC's support for the test ban and skepticism over the necessity of seismic research and Project Plowshare prompted a strong response from McCone. After receiving a copy of PSAC's briefing paper, McCone expressed to Kistiakowsky and Herter his "violent disagreement" with its conclusions.[104] McCone, on the losing side in the battle within the administration over the scientific assessments related to the test-ban issue, became spiteful in his actions toward scientists favoring a ban. One incident involved the awarding of the Enrico Fermi Award, a presidential award presented annually to a prominent scientist for a lifetime of exceptional achievement in the development, use, or production of energy. When the AEC's General Advisory Committee (GAC) unanimously recommended presenting the award to Hans Bethe, McCone purposely delayed forwarding the recommendation to Eisenhower.

McCone shared his plans with Strauss, who encouraged his efforts. Strauss told McCone that Bethe "had probably done more than anyone else to hamstring the defense of the United States, perhaps in good faith, first in opposing the hydrogen bomb and secondly in advising a moratorium on testing."[105] After McCone researched Bethe's record, he agreed with Strauss, telling him that it would make him "sick to see the award given to Bethe." With Strauss's encouragement and support, McCone refused to forward the GAC's nomination to Eisenhower. As a result, no scientist won the annual award in 1960. Bethe received the Fermi award in 1961.[106]

McCone's actions highlighted the continuing divisions within the scientific community. Policy decisions involving personalities were not limited to test-ban opponents. PSAC's presentation in July to Eisenhower sought to halt Edward Teller's Plowshare projects, which was the subject of his briefing in April to the Cabinet. Most concerning to Kistiakowsky, Teller remained the nation's foremost advocate for the resumption of testing. Kistiakowsky learned at the PSAC meeting in July that Nixon had asked Killian to become his science advisor if he won the presidential election. Kistiakowsky pleaded with Killian to accept the offer. Kistiakowsky was convinced that if Killian turned down Nixon, the Republican nominee would turn to Teller, who already exerted a strong influence on him. Kistiakowsky stressed that Killian would "perform a real national service" if he prevented Teller from becoming the president's science advisor.[107] On another occasion, Kistiakowsky convinced Republican Party officials not to ask Teller to present a speech on science at the GOP national convention. After offering some alternatives, Kistiakowsky reflected on what good he had done "for the country."[108]

Kistiakowsky also feared Teller's influence on the Democratic candidates. After Eisenhower commented that he believed Stuart Symington and Lyndon Johnson would both resume testing if elected president, Kistiakowsky noted in his diary that PSAC had "failed to reach the really important people—the candidates for the presidency—and let Teller sell them a bill of goods."[109] Kistiakowsky's comments suggest that he may have instructed PSAC members to reach out to the Democratic candidates. Although Kistiakowsky avoided public comment and refused to participate in any campaign events, he exerted an influential role over the political process from behind the scenes.

Back in March, Eisenhower's initial concern with the upcoming presidential election was that it would inhibit his ability to negotiate a test-ban agreement at Paris. His concerns about the legality of agreeing to a temporary moratorium that extended beyond his term received a comforting response from Senator John F. Kennedy. Kennedy wrote Eisenhower in March expressing his concern that the campaign might jeopardize the test-ban negotiations. He pledged that if elected president, he would "undertake to carry out in good faith any moratorium extending beyond your term of office which you now decide to be in the best interests of the nation."[110]

Other leading candidates followed Kennedy's pledge, providing Eisenhower the flexibility to agree to a temporary moratorium that extended beyond his term in office. Since Eisenhower insisted on first agreeing upon the procedures involved in a seismic research program, the negotiations never advanced far enough to consider the duration of the moratorium. Despite his desire to provide his successor flexibility, Eisenhower expressed his "deep concern" about how they would use it. He believed that Symington and Kennedy lacked the judgment required for such responsibilities, though he acknowledged that Kennedy was "a man of some intelligence."[111] Yet after Kennedy won his party's nomination for president, Eisenhower became increasingly critical of the Democratic nominee, whom he considered "incompetent" compared to Nixon.[112]

Nixon during the second half of 1960 became regularly involved in the administration's consideration of the test-ban issue for the first time in the Eisenhower presidency. Like Eisenhower, Nixon favored avoiding any ultimatums or presenting any substantive proposal that risked breaking up the talks until after the election. Although Nixon avoided stating his position on the resumption of testing, he carefully judged his competitors' attitudes on the issue. In his view, Symington and Johnson were inclined to resume testing, while Kennedy, "being in the hands of certain liberals, will say that we should not resume testing."[113] Nixon's private comments strongly suggested that he was inclined to resume testing.

Publicly, Nixon and Kennedy's campaign positions were quite similar, supporting Eisenhower's efforts to prevent the matter from becoming a divisive campaign issue. Even Thomas Murray's open letter to both candidates urging them to declare their commitment to the resumption of underground testing failed to prompt the candidates to take a firmer position on the issue.[114] Both pledged to make a final effort toward reaching a test-ban agreement that provided adequate safeguards. Each emphasized, however, that they would strongly consider resuming underground tests if negotiators did not make progress.[115]

Neither candidate specified how long he considered it appropriate to hold out for progress. Kennedy pledged to make "one last effort" to reach an agreement on a treaty, but established no time limit on his effort.[116] Nixon indicated that he would resume testing once he became convinced that the Soviet Union would not accept adequate inspection. He later refined this to suggest that he would order the United States to proceed unilaterally with the seismic research program by 1 February 1961 if the Soviets had not agreed to participate. The Republican nominee pledged to resume the testing of underground weapons if they had not reached an agreement "in a reasonable period" after 1 February. Nixon did not indicate what length of time he considered reasonable.[117]

Both candidates thus supported Eisenhower's approach to the test ban in the second half of 1960. At Geneva, the delegates did not table any significant new proposals and both sides avoided any provocative actions that risked breaking up the conference. Thus, the discussions carried on fruitlessly, interrupted only by a five-week recess in the late summer and a two-month recess from December to February to await Kennedy's "last effort" to reach an agreement.

As the months that the United States abided by the unmonitored moratorium swept by, Eisenhower periodically expressed private concerns about the implications of the lengthy moratorium for the nation's nuclear arsenal. In his memoirs, Eisenhower maintained that he began to recognize that the voluntary suspension placed the United States in a disadvantageous position. He suggested that he "may have acted unwisely in suspending nuclear testing" for such an extended time. In his view, "prudence demanded a resumption of testing." He asserted that he would have immediately resumed testing if it were not an election year. According to Eisenhower, he emphasized in a transition meeting with President-elect Kennedy his "conviction that our nation should resume needed tests without delay."[118]

In fact, Eisenhower twice in the summer of 1960 considered approving clandestine underground tests. In June, he asked McCone if they could secretly conduct underground tests in Nevada. McCone responded that they could conduct one or two tests in secrecy, but could not conduct an entire series, which was necessary to make significant improvements in weapons designs, without the public learning about it.[119]

Eisenhower dropped the idea in June, but raised it again two months later. Frustrated that the negotiations had dragged on so long without resolution, Eisenhower suggested to McCone that the president might authorize small clandestine shots. Goodpaster, who rarely noted the advice that he offered to the president in his memoranda of meetings, recorded that he urged Eisenhower not to consider approving such tests because the administration could never keep them secret. McCone agreed that the scientists involved would probably leak the information to the press. Eisenhower then suggested that they could use large-scale high-explosives detonations, then introduce a nuclear component clandestinely. After Goodpaster again urged him not to consider this, Eisenhower dropped the matter.[120] In the end, Eisenhower's suggestive comments about authorizing clandestine testing is likely more illustrative of the speculative ruminations that he was prone to, such as his consideration of preventive war, rather than his serious consideration of the matter. By this stage in his presidency, he relied heavily on his science advisors, rather than his AEC chairman, for counsel on such complex matters.

Eisenhower's final meetings with PSAC revealed his dependence on scientific advice and the scientists' dedication to continue to advise Eisenhower in his retirement. Eisenhower told the scientists that before the arrival of Killian and Kistiakowsky, and the creation of PSAC, he was "floundering, bewildered by conflicting claims of the departments, by the predictions of the different scientists." He praised PSAC for providing the expertise that did "much to hearten the people who have to make the hard decisions."[121] Though unstated, Eisenhower certainly considered himself foremost among those making the decisions. Eisenhower acknowledged that he had increasingly depended upon scientific advice for a growing number of subjects of national policy. In reply, the scientists offered to provide Eisenhower their advice on any matters that Eisenhower wanted to examine or comment upon during his retirement.[122] It was an offer that Eisenhower remembered and accepted. Eisenhower in 1963 refused to comment publicly on the Limited Test Ban Treaty until he discussed its provisions with his scientists.[123]

V

Eisenhower's farewell address is most remembered for its warning to the American people against the unwarranted influence of the "military-industrial complex." Although the cautionary words from the old warhorse elicited few comments immediately following the speech, they received increased acclaim in the late 1960s, ironically from the left, as part of the opposition to the war in Vietnam and the critique of the national security state.[124] Since then, even Hollywood has enshrined Eisenhower's warning, as Oliver Stone framed his conspiratorial film *JFK* with the farewell address of the martyred president's predecessor.[125] Despite the heightened interest in what has perhaps become Eisenhower's most famous remarks as president, debate continues about the source of the term "military-industrial complex," Eisenhower's reasons for including it in his final address, and the warning's contemporary relevance.[126]

A second warning in Eisenhower's farewell address, since overshadowed by the first, is seldom quoted and even less understood.[127] Eisenhower cautioned Americans that the influence of government-sponsored scientific research risked making public policy the "captive of a scientific-technological elite." This second warning, combined with an eloquent expression of his disappointment over the lack of progress on disarmament, suggests Eisenhower's frustration with the forces that opposed his efforts to conclude a test-ban agreement.

An early speech draft in Eisenhower's handwriting identifies him as the initial author of the section on disarmament.[128] In his final address,

Eisenhower emphasized the imperative of achieving disarmament "with mutual honor and confidence." For Eisenhower, confidence grew from adequate inspection, a fundamental component of his approach and a contentious issue that challenged his efforts to achieve a test-ban agreement. Stressing his desire for peace, Eisenhower recalled his experience of having "witnessed the horror and the lingering sadness of war." The victorious commander of allied forces during the Second World War feared that another global conflict "could utterly destroy this civilization which has been so slowly and painfully built over the thousands of years." Because he considered the avoidance of war so necessary, Eisenhower felt compelled to "confess" that he relinquished his "official responsibilities in this field with a profound sense of disappointment." He regrettably wished that he could say "that a lasting peace is in sight."[129]

After warning against the rise of a military-industrial complex, Eisenhower cautioned Americans against becoming "captive of a scientific-technological elite." According to Eisenhower, the technological revolution largely responsible for the "sweeping changes" in the relationship between the military and industry also altered the relationship between science and government. The complex issues and high costs of research had replaced the "solitary inventor" with "task forces of scientists in laboratories and testing fields."[130] Since the costs of research often required funding and direction from the federal government, Eisenhower feared that "a government contract becomes virtually a substitute for intellectual curiosity."[131] He cautioned, "the prospect of domination of the nation's scholars by Federal employment, project allocations, and the power of money is ever present—and is gravely to be regarded." Eisenhower strongly encouraged Americans to continue to respect independent scientific research and discovery, but warned them that they must also be alert to the "danger that public policy could itself become the captive of a scientific-technological elite."[132]

The meaning of Eisenhower's cautionary words created immediate concern among many scientists. According to Kistiakowsky, several of his colleagues telephoned him the following day to determine if Eisenhower was "turning against science." Kistiakowsky, who played no role in the drafting of the speech, informed Eisenhower of the concerns among scientists the day following his farewell address. Eisenhower responded to his science advisor that he was unhesitatingly for basic academic research, but feared the growing influence of applied research for military purposes. According to Kistiakowsky, Eisenhower asked him to make this point clear to the scientific community.[133]

Kistiakowsky wrote a letter to the editor of *Science* magazine to ex-

plain Eisenhower's remarks in his final address. According to Kistiakowsky's published letter, Eisenhower wanted to emphasize that the
part of science engaged in military applications "must never be allowed
to dominate all of science or curtail basic research."[134] In Eisenhower's
press conference the day following his farewell address, the departing
president indicated that he was troubled that advertisements for Atlas or
Titan missiles filled the pages of popular magazines. In his view, this led
to "an almost insidious penetration of our own minds" that American
science was only involved in developing armaments.[135] Kistiakowsky's
explanation similarly emphasized that Eisenhower sought to focus attention on science as a cultural endeavor and "a source of advancing
welfare to the people" rather than simply the development of bigger and
better missiles. Finally, Kistiakowsky stressed that Eisenhower wanted
to ensure that universities did not allow the true scientific endeavors of
"free intellectual inquiry and the acquisition of new scientific knowledge"
to become subsumed by massive military research and development contracts. Eisenhower feared that massive government contracts could create a powerful and dangerous special interest group within industry and
academia.[136]

After reading Kistiakowsky's comments for *Science*, Eisenhower wrote
to his former science advisor, "I would just like to say that your letter
expressed my views exactly and I am grateful to you for giving them this
wide dissemination among your fellows in the scientific world."[137] After
his brief response in his final press conference, Eisenhower did not comment again publicly on his caution against the rise of a scientific-technological elite. His memoirs briefly commented on the military-industrial
complex, but he did not mention his second warning.[138] In the following
years, Eisenhower declined Herbert York's several requests to explain
more fully what he had meant in his warning, commenting only that
he had not meant anything more detailed than what he had said at the
time.[139]

Kistiakowsky's brief explanation, Eisenhower's silence on the matter,
and the absence of archival evidence on the genesis of the second warning leaves its origins and purpose unclear. With most analyses focused
on Eisenhower's concerns about the relationship between the military
and industry, assessments of the origins and the purpose of his lesser-
known warning have been limited to a few interested observers within
the scientific community. Spurgeon Keeny, a member of Kistiakowsky's
staff responsible for disarmament issues, believed that Eisenhower was
most concerned about scientists like Edward Teller.[140] For Herbert York,
Eisenhower was troubled by the "self-righteous extremists" who felt that

the nation's survival was dependent upon the pursuit of expensive and complicated technologies that only they understood. Although York did not suggest any examples, his comments provided an apt description of Teller.[141]

There is nothing in the historical record that definitively links Eisenhower's farewell address warning to Teller or any other individual scientist. There is a substantial amount of evidence, however, that illustrates Eisenhower's previous frustrations with Teller and other powerful scientists who opposed his efforts to reach a test-ban agreement. As this study has emphasized, Eisenhower on numerous occasions privately criticized "scientists," often singling out Teller, for departing the realm of science and publicly advancing their views on policy,[142] for making "it look like a crime to ban tests,"[143] and for insisting upon a foolproof detection system as part of any test-ban agreement.[144]

For the first part of his presidency, Eisenhower permitted himself to become the captive of a scientific-technological elite within his administration. With Strauss nearly monopolizing the scientific advice reaching him, Eisenhower did not initially pursue his inclination to seek a test-ban agreement. Instead, he accepted Teller's assessment of the necessity of further weapons tests and Libby's dismissal of the health hazards of atmospheric testing. After scientists such as Bethe, Kistiakowsky, and Rabi gained direct access to the president, Eisenhower overruled the firm opposition of the AEC and Defense to cease testing for the remainder of his presidency and open negotiations toward a permanent test-ban agreement with the Soviet Union.

In the end, Eisenhower was no longer the captive of Strauss and Teller's views, but he never entirely broke free of their influence. While he rejected their dire appraisals of the necessity to resume testing, he sympathized, in part, with their mistrust of the Soviet Union. Their public and private assertions of the difficulty of detecting tests limited Eisenhower's domestic political flexibility and, more importantly, sometimes raised doubts in his own mind about the safety of his desired course. Deeply desiring progress on disarmament, Eisenhower insisted throughout his presidency and stressed in his farewell address that the nuclear powers must disarm with "confidence." The complex issues related to the detection of testing, which baffled the nation's top scientists, undermined Eisenhower's confidence in his pursuit of a test ban as the first step toward his ultimate goal. Eisenhower, disappointed at his inability to reach a test-ban agreement, suggested in his farewell address his bitterness with the forces that he allowed to frustrate his efforts.

Epilogue: The Resumption of Testing and the Limited Test-Ban Treaty (1961-1963)

> The test ban as an isolated issue, separate from a more comprehensive disarmament agreement, in my opinion, is no longer a desirable goal to pursue.
> —Bethe, September 1962

> As the country has had reason to note in recent weeks during the debate on the nuclear test-ban treaty, scientists do not always unite themselves in their recommendations to the makers of policy . . . the big issues so often go beyond the possibilities of exact scientific determination.
> —Kennedy, October 1963

The test-ban debate among leading advisors within the Eisenhower administration extended beyond Eisenhower's presidency. It simply changed venues after Eisenhower departed the White House. Eisenhower's principal advisors on nuclear matters continued their public and private battles over the nation's nuclear testing policy as the new administration resumed negotiations with the Soviet Union and the United Kingdom.

By the time of John F. Kennedy's inauguration as the nation's thirty-fifth president, the voluntary test moratorium, declared by his predecessor, was entering its twenty-seventh month. As a presidential candidate, Kennedy had declared that, if elected, he would make "one last effort" to reach a test-ban agreement with the Soviet Union before he authorized a resumption of testing. Although he refused to establish a deadline, he suggested that the time would be brief.[1]

Yet Kennedy entered office with no plan for resolving the deadlocked talks at Geneva. He declined to discuss the test-ban negotiations in the transition meetings with the outgoing administration.[2] Kennedy, with no firm strategy or new proposal to offer, requested a delay in the resumption of negotiations, originally scheduled for 7 February, until 21 March to allow his new administration adequate time to consider its approach to the talks.[3] Once the discussions at Geneva resumed, the Kennedy administration was baffled that the Soviet Union responded to the U.S. concessions by retreating from the previous Soviet positions, backing further away from a test-ban agreement.

The Soviet resumption of nuclear testing in September 1961, soon followed by underground tests in the United States, appeared to foreclose any chances of an agreement between the nuclear powers to ban permanently nuclear weapons tests. Yet several factors kept the desire for a test-ban accord alive within the Kennedy administration. The resumption of testing increased international pressures to conclude a permanent ban on testing. Detection capabilities continued to improve, while fears of nuclear proliferation, especially to Communist China, increased.[4] Finally, a narrowly averted nuclear catastrophe during the Cuban missile crisis provided the strongest impetus for the leaders of both nations to take concrete measures to ease tensions and to slow the arms race. These efforts eventually culminated in the Limited Test-Ban Treaty, signed in July 1963 in Moscow. The treaty prohibited tests in the atmosphere, under water and in outer space, while permitting continued testing underground. The Kennedy administration thus achieved, in part, what Eisenhower had tried but failed to accomplish during his presidency.

This epilogue briefly reviews the course of negotiations toward a ban on nuclear testing during the Kennedy administration, concluding with the agreement reached in Moscow. It then assesses the activities and positions of the central participants in the test-ban debate during Eisenhower's presidency between 1961 and the ratification of the accord in 1963. Senate hearings and the public debate over the ratification of the treaty provided settings for Eisenhower's former advisors to clash once again in their efforts to convince Eisenhower, the Senate, and the American people of their opposing views on nuclear testing.

I

Although the negotiators had made some progress in the test-ban talks at Geneva during the Eisenhower presidency, Kennedy quickly realized that a number of important issues stood in the way of an agreement. While the number of on-site inspections remained the most easily understood difference between the nuclear powers, several other issues remained unresolved. The negotiators at Geneva remained deadlocked over the duration of a temporary moratorium on underground tests below the 4.75 threshold, the nationality of personnel operating the control stations, the composition of the control commission, and the procedures for determining which unidentified seismic events were subject to on-site inspection.

Although significant challenges remained in the negotiations with Soviet officials, Kennedy faced fewer internal obstacles complicating his pursuit of a test ban than Eisenhower. While the AEC and DOD opposed Eisenhower's efforts to seek a test-ban accord, Kennedy's civilian heads of those agencies supported his decisions. Kennedy selected an AEC chairman who, unlike Lewis Strauss and John McCone, possessed impressive scientific credentials: Glenn Seaborg. A Nobel Prize–winning chemist, who took an extended leave of absence from Berkeley, where he was chancellor and the associate director of the Lawrence Radiation Laboratory, Seaborg replaced McCone as the chairman of the AEC. Seaborg had headed the Manhattan Project's work on extracting plutonium from uranium at Chicago's Met Lab, served on the AEC's General Advisory Committee (GAC) under Truman, had been a longtime associate of Ernest Lawrence, and became in 1959 a member of PSAC. Unlike Lewis Strauss and John McCone, who both vigorously opposed Eisenhower's pursuit of a test-ban agreement, Seaborg ultimately supported Kennedy's efforts.[5]

Kennedy, like his predecessor, received a great deal of encouragement and support from his science advisor and PSAC. The young president selected MIT physicist Jerome Wiesner, a strong test-ban advocate and a member of PSAC who had served as Kennedy's de facto science advisor during his presidential campaign, to serve as his special assistant for science and technology.[6] Secretary of State Dean Rusk, who as director of the Rockefeller Foundation in 1955 had contacted Eisenhower to help fund a study of the harmful effects of radioactive fallout, and the leading officials within the State Department also favored a test-ban agreement.

Within the Department of Defense, Secretary Robert McNamara, previously a Ford executive, supported Kennedy's efforts to negotiate a ban. Kennedy's greatest internal challenges thus came from the Joint Chiefs of Staff. Although the chiefs opposed any limits on testing under Eisenhower, they were much more outspoken, publicly and privately, in their opposition to the relatively inexperienced Kennedy than they were to the great general who preceded him.

Kennedy sought to provide greater direction over the nation's efforts at disarmament by appointing a special assistant, as Eisenhower had done with Harold Stassen, to focus his administration's efforts. Kennedy selected for this assignment John J. McCloy, an eminent Republican and World War II executive under Secretary of War Stimson. Kennedy directed McCloy, who had served as one of Dulles's private disarmament advisors, to consider whether the United States should continue the test-ban negotiations at Geneva.[7] As part of his assessment, McCloy reviewed the report of a panel headed by James Fisk that evaluated whether a test-ban agreement remained in the nation's best interests.[8] McCloy, drawing upon the conclusions of the Fisk Report, advised Kennedy that the potential benefits of easing Cold War tensions, slowing proliferation, and improving world opinion by reaching a test-ban agreement outweighed the risks of extending the unmonitored test ban further while the United States exhausted every reasonable step to obtain a satisfactory agreement.[9]

Kennedy concurred with McCloy's assessment and directed a reevaluation of the U.S. position at the Geneva talks. After several more weeks of consultations, Kennedy in April and May authorized a few minor revisions to the U.S. negotiating position. U.S. and British delegates at Geneva presented a draft treaty in April that extended the duration of the moratorium on underground tests below the 4.75 threshold to three years, up from the maximum two-year period that Eisenhower had proposed. The following month, western negotiators proposed a new formula that would determine the annual number of on-site inspections. Instead of twenty fixed annual inspections, the new formula would produce a range of twelve to twenty inspections based on a ratio of the number of unidentified seismic events each year.[10]

The Soviet negotiators offered little in return, leaving the Geneva talks deadlocked as Cold War tensions increased after crises in Cuba and Berlin and the tense talks in June 1961 between Kennedy and Khrushchev at Vienna. At Vienna, Khrushchev insisted that the Soviet Union would not accept more than three annual inspections. Any more, he declared, would be tantamount to espionage. Most importantly, Khrushchev signaled a significant reversal of the Soviet position by linking a test-ban monitoring system to a broader disarmament agreement. Ironically, this shifted the Soviet position to the one held by the Eisenhower administration until 1958.[11] When Kennedy returned to the United States, he briefed congressional leaders that he determined that Khrushchev, due to pressure from the Chinese or other reasons, had lost interest in a test ban. For Kennedy, the main question was then how to disengage from the talks at Geneva.[12]

Kennedy in August received a blunt clue about the reasons for Khrushchev's unwillingness to bargain at Vienna. The Soviet Union announced in late August its plans to break the voluntary moratorium between the first three nuclear powers (France began testing nuclear weapons in February 1960) that had held since early November 1958. Seeking to reap a propaganda victory, Kennedy and Macmillan responded by proposing an immediate atmospheric test ban without any requirements for inspections or control stations within the Soviet Union.[13] Kennedy, waiting less than two days for a Soviet reply, announced on 5 September the resumption of U.S. testing, albeit limited to underground shots.[14] The president's actions earned him a personal note of praise from Lewis Strauss for having the "courage" to resume testing.[15]

As testing resumed, the talks at Geneva dragged on with little progress before finally recessing in late January 1962. International pressures led the three negotiating nuclear powers to reopen talks in mid-March as part of the Eighteen Nation Disarmament Conference, also at Geneva.

At its meetings in mid-March, the principals, expanded by Kennedy to include the chairman of the JCS and the director of the newly created Arms Control and Disarmament Agency (ACDA), debated the administration's negotiating position for Geneva.[16] The Kennedy administration prepared for the resumption of talks by reviewing whether improvements in seismic detection justified reducing or eliminating the seismic threshold, the number of on-site inspections, or both. They had to balance these technical gains in detection, however, with the possibility that the recent Soviet tests had provided the Soviet Union with significant technological improvements to their nuclear arsenal. A panel led by Hans Bethe assessed Soviet tests from the fall of 1961 and concluded in mid-January 1962 that the Soviet Union had made impressive gains and had significantly narrowed the U.S. advantage over the Soviet Union in weapons technology.[17] Kennedy accepted the possibility of Soviet gains and, based upon the assessment of improved methods of seismic detection, decided to make two concessions. The president proposed to eliminate the threshold under which tests would not immediately be a part of the test-ban agreement and to accept a reduced number, though unspecified how few, of annual on-site inspections.[18]

Soon after, however, criticism at home that the concessions went too far and pressure from abroad to eliminate the requirement for on-site inspections undercut support for Kennedy's new position. Khrushchev declared publicly, as he had done privately the year before in Vienna, that an international control system with control posts within the Soviet Union was not necessary to verify a ban on underground tests. The

Soviet leader's announcement repudiated the Geneva system, which had served as the basis of negotiations since 1958, and withdrew his previous offer of three on-site inspections. Ambassador Arthur Dean, chairman of the U.S. delegation to the Geneva talks, then appeared to agree with Khrushchev when he publicly suggested that the seismic improvements eliminated the need for control posts within the Soviet Union.[19] Kennedy moved quickly to distance himself from Dean's comments, which alarmed critics within Congress and may have prevented Khrushchev from later convincing hardliners within the Soviet Union to accept a greater number of on-site inspections.[20]

The talks at Geneva remained deadlocked as the Kennedy administration continued to debate the implications of the improvements in seismic detection for their position at Geneva. Extensive deliberations in July and August 1962 resulted in two draft treaties, a comprehensive and a limited ban, that the U.S. and British delegations submitted on 27 August at Geneva.[21] The draft comprehensive ban suggested additional reductions, though unclear how many, in the numbers of monitoring stations and on-site inspections within the Soviet Union. Although the draft treaty left the specific figure blank, Kennedy authorized Dean to offer a quota of eight to ten on-site inspections. The draft treaty also eliminated the requirement for an equal number of national and international technicians to operate the monitoring stations. In the new proposal, host nationals would operate the stations with only a few international technicians to observe them. The proposed limited ban would prohibit all tests but those underground, eliminating the requirements, and all of the related contentious issues, for international monitoring stations within the United States or the Soviet Union.[22]

The Soviet delegation promptly rejected both proposals without qualification, leaving the talks stalled until the Cuban missile crises prompted the nuclear powers to take steps to ease tensions and slow the arms race. For Kennedy and Khrushchev, a test-ban treaty, despite the torturous course of negotiations the previous four years, appeared to be an achievable step.[23] Both sides made concessions, but a gap still separated them on the number of on-site inspections required to verify a comprehensive test ban. Khrushchev, who had withdrawn a previous offer of three inspections and insisted that none were necessary, proposed again a control system with two to three annual inspections. Kennedy, who faced opposition in the Senate to a ban with no more than eight on-site inspections, later authorized as few as six. In exchange, he insisted that the Soviets accept the relocation of some of the previously agreed upon monitoring stations and agree to the U.S. criteria for determining which unidentified seismic events would be inspected and how those inspections would be conducted. Khrushchev, possibly under the belief that the United States would accept two to four inspections, refused to budge from his offer of two to three inspections.[24]

With strong encouragement from British Prime Minister Macmillan, Kennedy, who was increasingly concerned about the possible proliferation of nuclear weapons to China and other nations, continued to seek a formula acceptable to the negotiating powers.[25] Kennedy and Macmillan in April 1963 sent a joint message to Khrushchev offering to each send a personal representative to Moscow to discuss matters directly with the Soviet leader. Khrushchev on 7 June privately agreed to receive the representatives, paving the way for a pivotal speech by Kennedy.[26]

Kennedy's commencement address at American University in June 1963, often noted as one of his greatest speeches, presented a strategy for peace with a comprehensive test ban as its immediate step.[27] Kennedy also declared a voluntary moratorium, pending a binding treaty, on aboveground tests for as long as the other nuclear powers refrained from testing in the atmosphere. Finally, the president announced that Khrushchev had accepted his offer to hold private talks in Moscow toward a test-ban agreement.[28]

The Soviet Union responded favorably to Kennedy's address, providing extensive coverage of it in the national press. Although both sides expressed hopes for reaching an agreement following the speech, neither signaled a willingness to modify their positions on the inspection requirements for a comprehensive ban. The domestic political situation in the United States prevented the Kennedy administration from simply proposing to split the difference with the Soviet Union and suggesting a ban on all tests based upon five inspections. The Kennedy administration's previous offer of eight on-site inspections for a comprehensive ban continued to receive bitter criticism from Teller, the Joint Chiefs of Staff, and some members of the Senate, such as Senator Henry M. Jackson (D-Wash.). This powerful opposition threatened the ability of the administration to secure the ratification of a comprehensive treaty with eight inspections. Thus, the administration appeared to have little room to maneuver closer to the Soviet offer of two to three inspections.[29]

The prospects appeared much brighter for an agreement on a limited ban to result from the discussions in Moscow. Khrushchev signaled a willingness to accept a separate ban on atmospheric testing, retreating from the position he had held the previous two years that linked a test ban to a broader agreement on disarmament. A limited ban, which permitted continued testing underground, eliminated the requirement for control stations and inspections within Soviet soil that had stalled the test-ban negotiations for nearly five years. By permitting continued testing underground, however, it at best delayed, rather than prevented, the proliferation of nuclear weapons to nations that signed and abided by the treaty.

Kennedy appointed W. Averell Harriman, a wartime ambassador to the Soviet Union who was the under secretary of state for political affairs in the Kennedy administration, to serve as the president's personal representative at the test-ban talks in Moscow. Kennedy insisted in a letter to Khrushchev that a comprehensive ban remained his primary objective.[30] He authorized Harriman to discuss the inspection requirements for a comprehensive ban in general, but not to discuss the specific number of acceptable annual inspections without further instructions. Kennedy considered it "unlikely" that Harriman could reach an agreement "at this time" on a comprehensive ban since Khrushchev had recently publicly shifted his position, again rejecting the presence of an international inspection system within Soviet soil. Therefore, the president instructed Harriman to focus his efforts on negotiating an atmospheric test-ban accord based upon the U.S.–U.K. draft treaty proposed in August 1962 as a first step toward a comprehensive ban.[31]

Harriman arrived in Moscow with U.S. and U.K. negotiating teams on 15 July to begin talks with leading Soviet officials. Significantly, the meetings took place in Moscow during heightened tensions between the Soviet Union and China. In fact, Kennedy authorized Harriman to pursue the possibility of joint U.S.–USSR actions to prevent China from developing its own nuclear weapons. For Kennedy, a nuclear test-ban agreement would justify such a strike. Although Khrushchev apparently revealed no interest in joint actions, the test-ban talks certainly accomplished the Kennedy administration's objective of widening the Sino-Soviet split.[32]

Although Khrushchev rebuffed Kennedy's exploration of joint actions against China, the Soviet leader quickly revealed his interest in reaching a test-ban accord. Khrushchev, who played an active role in the test talks, emphasized on the first day of the discussions that the Soviet Union would accept no inspections on its soil as part of a comprehensive agreement, but was very interested in reaching an agreement on a partial ban.[33] By the third day of the talks, a comprehensive ban had virtually disappeared from the agenda and Frank Press, a PSAC member and Cal Tech seismologist appointed to advise the U.S. delegation on seismic detection, departed Moscow early as the detailed talks focused on a limited ban.[34]

Representatives at Moscow worked out the details of a treaty banning tests in the atmosphere in eleven days of private and informal negotiations that involved concessions on both sides. The United States withdrew its demand to exclude from the treaty a ban on nuclear explosions outside of its own territory for peaceful purposes, which Teller had championed for years. In exchange, the Soviet Union accepted an article that permitted a country to withdraw from the treaty if its national interests were threatened, a provision the Kennedy administration felt was necessary for Senate ratification.[35]

The three principal delegates from the United States, the United Kingdom, and the Soviet Union initialed the completed treaty on 25 July. The following evening, President Kennedy's televised address to the nation opened his administration's campaign to ensure that public opinion strongly favored the Senate's ratification of the treaty initialed in Moscow.[36] The Kennedy administration, as part of its campaign, turned to Eisenhower to seek his endorsement for a treaty that reflected a goal of his presidency that he had failed to achieve. Eisenhower, seeking counsel on the highly technical questions, quickly discovered that his former advisors remained sharply divided over the testing issue, though equally eager to convince him of their views.

II

Leading participants in the test-ban debate within the Eisenhower administration reacted to Kennedy's nuclear test policies with varying degrees encouragement, alarm, and contempt. While a few retained advisory roles within the government, albeit at reduced levels of influence, others increasingly presented their views on testing to the American public. After the signing of the Limited Test-Ban Treaty, Eisenhower's former advisors again presented him with their arguments on testing in an effort to shape his public position on ratification.

For I. I. Rabi, a test-ban agreement remained a desirable national objective, one that he could best work toward from within the channels of government. Rabi, who was one of Eisenhower's most trusted science advisors, certainly felt his influence diminish within the Kennedy administration. Although his term as a PSAC member expired, Rabi continued to advise the panel of scientists as a consultant and became a member of the General Advisory Committee (GAC) of the newly formed Arms

Control and Disarmament Agency (ACDA).[37] From that position, Rabi continued to support the new administration's efforts to reach a test-ban agreement through his discreet counsel.[38]

David Inglis, concerned about congressional criticism of the test-ban talks, asked Rabi in March 1963 to sign a statement along with other prominent scientists endorsing the Kennedy administration's pursuit of a comprehensive test-ban agreement. Rabi replied that as a private consultant to the government he could not sign a petition that publicly encouraged the administration to redouble its efforts to reach a test-ban agreement. Rabi instructed Inglis that since he was a consultant, he must conduct all of his battles in support of a test ban "behind the scenes."[39] Yet Rabi, perhaps frustrated at the decline in his personal influence on government policy, also became disillusioned with the relative unimportance of the ACDA's advisory committee. In his view, the GAC had little influence on policy making because it primarily received briefings from officials within the administration rather than providing the administration advice from the outside.[40]

In time, Rabi reversed his position on avoiding a public role in policy debates as the ratification debate within the Senate over the Limited Test-Ban Treaty heated up. To offset the opposition of Teller, and perhaps underscore the fact that Teller had never won a Noble Prize, Rabi drafted and circulated a statement signed by thirty-four other Nobel laureates, including AEC chairman Seaborg, that supported the ratification of the treaty. Rabi, who also played a prominent role convincing PSAC to issue a public endorsement of the treaty, timed the public release of the statement to coincide with Teller's Senate testimony against ratification.[41] He then sent a copy of the petition and a personal letter to each senator, urging them to vote for ratification. Rabi kept a close tally of the replies that indicated each senator's position on the treaty.[42]

Hans Bethe, whose technical assessments in 1958 were so critical to convince Eisenhower to propose negotiations toward a test-ban agreement, temporarily withdrew his support of a test ban separate from a comprehensive disarmament agreement. Bethe chaired a panel that analyzed data from the 1961 Soviet nuclear tests. His panel concluded that the tests had allowed the Soviet Union to narrow the gap in weapons technology between the United States and the Soviet Union.[43] Based upon this analysis, Bethe believed that there were sound military and technical reasons for the resumption of testing.[44] The test ban had appealed to Bethe in the late 1950s to freeze the U.S. superiority in weapons technology and to establish an international inspection system within the

Soviet Union that would serve as a first step toward future disarmament agreements. With the U.S. lead narrowed and the Soviet rejection of any inspection stations within its soil, Bethe in a September 1962 essay in the *Bulletin of the Atomic Scientists* revealed that he no longer considered a separate test ban "a desirable goal to pursue."[45]

Bethe's subsequent analysis of Soviet nuclear tests in 1962, however, convinced him that his panel had overestimated in 1961 Soviet technological gains achieved with the resumption of testing. His panel concluded in October 1962 that the United States continued to hold a substantial technological lead in nuclear weaponry.[46] Bethe, who was not asked to testify during the treaty's ratification hearings, wrote to Senator J. William Fulbright (D.-Ark.), the chairman of the Senate Committee on Foreign Relations, to criticize Teller's alarming testimony on the necessity of atmospheric testing for the development of an anti-ballistic missile system. Bethe contended that Teller, though an expert on weaponry, knew relatively little about missile defense technology, while those that did considered underground testing sufficient to develop warheads for such a system.[47] Although Bethe believed that the resumption of testing and the Soviet rejection of inspection made a test ban less desirable than during the Eisenhower presidency, he ultimately announced his unequivocal support for the ratification of the Limited Test-Ban Treaty.[48]

For George Kistiakowsky, who had worked so vigorously to keep the possibility of a comprehensive test ban alive within the Eisenhower administration, the change in administrations required a shift in his tactics for promoting a test ban. Kistiakowsky, replaced by Jerome Wiesner as the president's science advisor, continued to advise the government as a member of PSAC through 1963 and as a member of the GAC of the ACDA. Kistiakowsky criticized both bodies as having a relatively insignificant influence on the Kennedy administration's consideration of the test-ban issue.[49]

Kistiakowsky, disillusioned with his decreased influence within the government, engaged in personal diplomacy with Soviet scientists in an effort to break the impasse on inspections. At a London Pugwash Conference, an annual international meeting of scientists concerned with world affairs that began in 1957, Kistiakowsky and other American and British scientists met privately on 16 March 1963 with some Soviet scientists to discuss improvements in seismic detection.[50] According to Kistiakowsky, Lev Artsimovich, a leading Soviet physicist who claimed to have direct access to Khrushchev, asked the American scientists to convey to the Kennedy administration that Khrushchev would be willing to accept as many as five annual on-site inspections.[51] Kistiakowsky, hopeful that a compromise on on-site inspection would lead to a comprehensive ban, relayed the message to Carl Kaysen, deputy to Kennedy's national security advisor McGeorge Bundy, but did not raise the issue higher. Eisenhower's former science advisor was later disappointed that the Kennedy administration apparently did not pursue such a compromise on inspection.[52] Although disappointed at the failure to reach an agreement on a comprehensive ban, Kistiakowsky worked feverishly to convince Eisenhower and others to support the ratification of the limited ban.[53]

Until the ratification debate heated up, Kistiakowsky, as well as Killian and Rabi, corresponded minimally with Eisenhower. Kistiakowsky continued to shun partisan politics, rejecting Eisenhower's appeal in November 1961 to support Republican fund-raisers. His rejection of the former president's requests, though tactful, may have briefly soured relations between Eisenhower and Kistiakowsky.[54]

In contrast, Lewis Strauss was a staunch supporter of the Republican Party, Eisenhower College, and other political and philanthropic interests of the former president. Strauss also corresponded regularly with Eisenhower and was a frequent visitor to the former president's retirement home in Gettysburg. Thus, Strauss's ability to influence Eisenhower's thoughts about nuclear testing, which had waned while Kistiakowsky served as the president's science advisor, increased after Eisenhower departed the White House. Thereafter, Lewis Strauss and Edward Teller once again dominated the scientific counsel reaching Eisenhower, just as they had during the first term of Eisenhower's presidency. Unlike that earlier period, the former president realized that Strauss and Teller represented only one side of a sharply divided scientific community.

Strauss and Teller intensified their public campaigns against a test ban along with their continued efforts to influence members of Congress and leading officials from the Kennedy and Eisenhower administrations. Concerned that the Kennedy administration would make additional concessions to the Soviets when the test-ban talks resumed in 1961, Strauss contacted Kennedy's disarmament advisor, John McCloy, to offer any assistance he needed to make sure that the new administration did not continue the "folly of suspending tests."[55]

Although Strauss's efforts to convince officials within the administration to terminate the negotiations at Geneva failed, the former AEC chairman continued to cultivate successfully test-ban opponents within the Senate. Strauss sharply criticized the Kennedy administration's "calamitous course" of continuing negotiations to Democrat Stuart Symington of Missouri. Strauss convinced Symington to hold congressional hearings to question the wisdom of extending the test-ban talks and to have Strauss and Teller testify against a ban.[56]

Moving beyond government officials, Strauss and Teller sought to extend the reach of their arguments against a test ban by using the popular media. Strauss published an essay in *Reader's Digest*, a letter to editor of the *New York Times*, and an interview in *US News and World Report*.[57] Teller participated in a televised debate with Linus Pauling and submitted editorials to the *New York Times* warning of the importance of continuous atmospheric testing to the nation's security.[58] The "father of the H-bomb," in a series of essays published in the *Saturday Evening Post* and *Reader's Digest*, termed the test moratorium "idiotic" and even suggested that radioactive fallout from atmospheric testing "might be slightly beneficial" for humans.[59]

The editor of the *Saturday Evening Post*, aware that some readers may "violently" object to Teller's views, offered Eisenhower, the unnamed "idiot" who began the moratorium, an opportunity to comment on Teller's article. Eisenhower, without reading the proofs, replied that he considered Teller a "very good friend" and a brilliant scientist who was "completely dedicated to the security and welfare of the United States." Although Eisenhower acknowledged that he disagreed with a few points of Teller's previous arguments, he believed that Teller's views were very deserving of the public's close attention.[60] Eisenhower's reply likely reflected a combination of his lingering respect for Teller, his neglecting to read the proofs, his long-standing avoidance of publicly commenting on personalities, and his own concerns with the extension of the moratorium.

Publicly, Eisenhower had previously expressed concerns raised by Strauss and Teller in earlier correspondence about the duration of the unmonitored moratorium, which Eisenhower had initiated in November 1958. At a brief press conference before an appearance at a Republican fund-raiser in June 1961, Eisenhower, perhaps troubled that Kennedy and Khrushchev resolved none of the outstanding issues on the test ban during their Vienna meetings, insisted that the United States fix a date for making progress in the negotiations after which it should resume testing. He also suggested that the Soviet Union might already be testing clandestinely, a charge Teller and Strauss stated much more forcefully in their appeals to the public.[61]

Eisenhower's public comments followed his private conversations with Strauss at Gettysburg on the former president's mounting concerns with the extended moratorium. Strauss reassured Eisenhower that as president the previous year he had publicly cautioned against permitting the moratorium to continue indefinitely.[62] Eisenhower later contacted his top advisors to confirm his recollection of his attitude during the fall of 1960. Eisenhower recalled that he had become disillusioned with the length of the unmonitored moratorium and had planned to order the resumption of underground testing if Nixon had won the election.[63] Although none of Eisenhower's advisors had access to records of meetings and conversations, their memory of discussions and attitudes coincided with the former president's recollection.[64]

Strauss, perhaps sensing Eisenhower's frustration with the Kennedy administration's reluctance to end the deadlocked talks at Geneva, sought in July 1961 to present Eisenhower with additional evidence to justify an immediate resumption of testing. Just as Strauss emphasized in 1957 the necessity of continued testing to develop a "clean bomb," the former AEC chairman arranged for Eisenhower to receive a briefing in September on the neutron bomb, which developers believed would kill personnel through neutron radiation without destroying cities, as a primary reason to resume nuclear testing.[65] According to Strauss, the development of the neutron bomb had proceeded as far as possible without testing. Eisenhower responded that the new weapon had the potential to bridge the gap between a skirmish and a general war. He expressed concern that Kennedy's science advisors downgraded the project and that it had not received priority funding.[66]

Eisenhower, despite his growing private concerns and his rare public comments in June 1961, avoided public criticism of the Kennedy administration's policies. In fact, events likely overcame Strauss's original purpose for the briefing. By the time that Eisenhower received the details in September about the neutron bomb, the Soviet Union had resumed testing and Kennedy already announced that the United States would resume testing underground, which Eisenhower endorsed. Thus, Strauss no longer needed to use another theoretical device to convince Eisenhower to pressure the Kennedy administration to resume testing.

Strauss continued to belittle the scientists that he believed convinced Eisenhower to enter an unmonitored test moratorium and initiate lengthy and, in his view, perilous negotiations toward a test ban with the Soviet Union and Great Britain. Strauss, who was in the process of writing his memoirs, informed Eisenhower that he blamed the former president's decision to pursue the test suspension talks on the "bad scientific advice" of Killian and PSAC who had "misled" him. According to Strauss,

Eisenhower conceded, in retrospect, that it was a bad decision to allow the negotiations, which had dragged on for three years along with the unmonitored test moratorium, to continue for longer than a year. Eisenhower refused, however, to blame the scientists advising him, and instead accepted full personal responsibility for the decision.[67]

Strauss's frequent correspondence certainly heightened Eisenhower's concerns about the test moratorium, but the former president refused to blame his technical advisors and had not forgotten the importance of a wide range of scientific advice. He lamented to Killian in 1962 that they did not correspond regularly. Eisenhower confided to Killian the he would "feel a lot better about a lot of things" if he could occasionally have a long conversation with Killian and Kistiakowsky since their counsel meant so much to him during his presidency.[68]

Despite Strauss's efforts, Eisenhower, after urging in June 1961 that the United States fix a date to conclude the test-ban negotiations, made no further negative public comments on the Kennedy administration's pursuit of test ban. Conversely, Eisenhower publicly endorsed Kennedy's announcements in September 1961 to resume underground testing and in March 1962 to conduct atmospheric tests.[69] Kennedy made a conscious effort to keep the former president informed on the major issues involving national security, including the test-ban negotiations, through periodic briefings with administration officials.[70] In several cases, such as the aftermath of the failed Bay of Pigs invasion and during the Cuban missile crisis, Kennedy personally discussed the crises with Eisenhower.[71] These periodical consultations likely reinforced Eisenhower's inclination to either publicly support the actions or remain silent on the issues confronting his successor. Kennedy, by courting his predecessor, hoped to gain Eisenhower's public endorsement of the test-ban treaty.

III

The signing of the Limited Test-Ban Treaty in 1963 and the subsequent debate over its ratification brought Eisenhower into heightened contact with the individuals that dominated the clashes over the issue within his administration. As the prospects for reaching an agreement in Moscow appeared favorable, Kennedy sent Dean Rusk and John McCone, who had replaced Allen Dulles after the Bay of Pigs fiasco as the director of the CIA, to Gettysburg to brief the former president on the likely treaty provisions and perhaps seek his early endorsement. The first question that Eisenhower asked after Rusk outlined the agreement was if the lead-

ing U.S. scientists favored the treaty. McCone replied that Bethe, Kistiakowsky, Killian, Libby, and Rabi supported the treaty, while Teller and
some of the laboratory scientists opposed it.[72] Eisenhower rejected the
concern, as he did during his presidency, that the ban would adversely
affect the weapons laboratories. In his view, this was less of a concern
than before because the limited ban permitted continued testing underground. He cautioned, however, that the French and the Chinese would
resist signing the accord and that the Kennedy administration's greatest
problem would be that the limited ban might create "a state of euphoria"
inconsistent with the treaty's very limited impact on slowing the arms
race. Moreover, Eisenhower noted that the technological advantages to
the United States might be less certain in 1963 than they had been in
1958 when he was fully confident of his nation's superiority in nuclear weaponry. Despite these concerns, Eisenhower's comments suggested
that he was inclined to favor the treaty, though he indicated that he did
not intend to discuss the matter publicly.[73]

Although Eisenhower initially hoped to remain aloof from the ratification debate, requests from several quarters, including the Kennedy
administration, ultimately prompted him to address the matter publicly.
Leading world figures, former Eisenhower advisors, and members of the
press sought the former president's reaction to the signing of a treaty that
originated in his administration. British Prime Minister Harold Macmillan appealed to Eisenhower to endorse publicly the treaty, emphasizing,
"*your* opinion and *your* words may be decisive" to the ratification in
the U.S. Senate. Macmillan apologized for appealing to Eisenhower's
twenty-year long friendship to support the treaty, but stressed that he
felt "more deeply about this than about any great issue in my lifetime."[74]
Eisenhower's former disarmament advisor, Harold Stassen, also strongly
encouraged Eisenhower to support ratification publicly, insisting that the
former president's endorsement would carry great weight among Republican senators.[75] By the middle of August, Senator J. William Fulbright,
the chairman of the Senate Foreign Relations Committee, had formally
requested Eisenhower's comments as part of his committee's hearings on
the ratification of the treaty.[76]

Despite the pressures from test-ban opponents and advocates to comment on the treaty, Eisenhower delayed discussing his thoughts on the
treaty in public until he returned from a trip to Europe, where he was to
appear in a documentary about the invasion of Normandy. The former
wartime commander informed reporters that he would like to hear the
views of some scientists and the military before he commented publicly

hower repeated concerns he had expressed previously with his former advisors; the treaty might not halt the Chinese nuclear program and risked providing the world with a false sense of reduced tensions. Although Eisenhower endorsed the ratification of the treaty, he was careful not to refute too strongly the opinions of Strauss and Teller, who he disagreed with on several points but still greatly respected. The former president simply acknowledged that there were "great differences of opinion" on a number of matters, including concerns about clandestine testing in space, the potential loss of laboratory personnel, and the ability to conduct all necessary tests underground.[88]

Yet, Eisenhower did not consider those issues as sufficient reasons to reject the treaty, and he clearly chose Kistiakowsky's analysis over Strauss and Teller's of the continued U.S. superiority in nuclear weapons technology. Significantly, Eisenhower's public comments mirrored Kistiakowsky's private assessment that the Soviet Union possessed a lead only in weapons of the highest yield, which the United States did not consider militarily necessary.

Contrary to the hopes of Strauss and Teller, Eisenhower concluded that the Senate should ratify the treaty. His endorsement included one qualification, which Strauss and Teller had emphasized in their private conversations with the former president. Eisenhower wanted it to be made clear that the treaty did not prohibit the United States from using nuclear weapons to counter Chinese or Soviet aggression against one of America's allies.[89] Eisenhower later accepted the assessments of legal experts and the assurances of congressional leaders and that the treaty did not preclude the United States from using its nuclear arsenal in such a manner.[90]

Although Strauss and Teller failed, due in part to Kistiakowsky's counterarguments, to convince Eisenhower to oppose the treaty, they took satisfaction in knowing that they were most responsible for the reservation that Eisenhower issued along with his endorsement. Strauss thanked Teller for helping him with the "rear-guard action which you will be able to look back upon . . . with a consciousness of responsibility not shirked."[91] Teller replied by congratulating Strauss for being personally responsible for Eisenhower's reservation. The eminent physicist agreed with Strauss that the prospects of ratification were unfortunately favorable; their best hope was to work for a formal reservation rather than a rejection.[92]

Eisenhower submitted his endorsement amidst Senate hearings on the treaty. Among those who testified in favor of ratification were Kistiakowsky, Seaborg, and York. Strauss and Teller both testified against ratification. Strauss made clear his total opposition to the treaty, asserting that it was not in the best interest of the United States and that instead of signaling peace it could be "the first step on the path to disaster." Teller's testimony was also dire, cautioning that the treaty would give "away the future safety of our country and increase the dangers of war."[93]

Teller's scientific credentials and apocalyptic warnings against ratification concerned many test-ban advocates within the scientific community. Rabi's petition of Nobel laureates sought to defang Teller's damning testimony. Even PSAC, which strove to keep its counsel to the president private, departed from traditional practice to counter Teller publicly. Members and consultants of PSAC held a special meeting to discuss how to counter Teller's testimony against the treaty.[94] Several PSAC members and consultants, including Kistiakowsky, Fisk, Killian, and Rabi, signed a statement that strongly encouraged the ratification of the treaty. According to PSAC's endorsement, the treaty provided relief from the spread of radioactive fallout, slowed the proliferation of nuclear weapons, and posed "no danger to our military security."[95]

McGeorge Bundy forwarded the statement to Senator Hubert Humphrey (D.-Minn.), a longtime test-ban advocate and a member of the Senate Foreign Relations Committee, for possible use in the Senate debate over the treaty. According to Bundy, the members of PSAC wrote the statement to refute Teller's testimony and to provide evidence that Teller was "not speaking for the scientific community but rather against the position taken by the overwhelming majority of informed scientists."[96]

Despite the warnings of Strauss and Teller, the Senate on 24 September ratified the Limited Test-Ban Treaty without qualification by a vote of eighty to nineteen.[97]

The ratification of the treaty did not provide Eisenhower any special gratification for the ultimate accomplishment of one of his deeply cherished goals. Although Eisenhower acknowledged the hazards of radioactive fallout from testing during the close of his presidency, his concern with this aspect of testing receded.[98] Still, Eisenhower shared Kennedy's hopes that the treaty would widen the rift between the Soviet Union and China.[99] The former president was under no illusion, however, that the treaty heralded "the coming of the millennium" or the end of the Cold War.[100] As president, Eisenhower had pursued an agreement that prohibited the broadest range of adequately detected tests. He repeatedly stated that a main purpose of his quest for an agreement was to open up the Soviet Union to a modest international inspection system. For Eisenhower, building mutual confidence was essential before the nuclear powers could achieve his ultimate objective, a lasting disarmament agreement.[101] Thus, by Eisenhower's own criteria, the Limited Test-Ban Treaty, which did not include any international inspection stations within the Soviet Union, fell short of his hopes for using a ban on testing to slow the arms race and to serve as a first step toward building the confidence necessary for a safeguarded nuclear disarmament agreement.[102]

The ratification debate over the Limited Test-Ban Treaty only temporarily brought Eisenhower into greater contact with his former science advisors who had encouraged him to seek a test-ban agreement during his presidency. He corresponded with them infrequently thereafter. The escalating conflict in Vietnam, however, prompted Killian, Kistiakowsky, and Rabi in 1968 to turn to Eisenhower one final time to address a great concern of the time. The three former advisors sent a joint telegram to Eisenhower expressing their alarm at reports that President Lyndon B. Johnson was considering the use of tactical nuclear weapons to relieve the embattled Marines at Khe Sanh in Vietnam. They feared that the use of nuclear weapons in Vietnam would erode the nation's international position, destroy progress toward a nuclear non-proliferation treaty, and possibly lead to a general nuclear war. Killian, Kistiakowsky, and Rabi urged Eisenhower to contact the Johnson administration and strongly discourage them from considering the use of nuclear weapons.[103] According to Killian, Eisenhower discussed the matter personally with Johnson, who then directed Secretary of Defense Robert McNamara to telephone each of Eisenhower's former science advisors to assure them that no responsible member of the Johnson administration was seriously considering the use of nuclear weapons in Vietnam.[104] The victorious commander of allied troops in Europe during the Second World War, once largely skeptical of the advice of scientists on military matters, had learned in the nuclear age to respect and value the opinions of his trusted science advisors.

Conclusion

> An effective ban on nuclear testing had become an
> essential preliminary to—even though not a definite
> part of—attaining any worthwhile disarmament
> agreement. Consequently, I ordered that we continue
> our efforts to achieve this first step. I was unwilling
> to give up.
>
> —Eisenhower, *Waging Peace*, 1965

After a thirty-five year military career and eight years in the White House, seventy-year-old Dwight D. Eisenhower finally decided to retire. To escape the northern winters at his Gettysburg farm, Eisenhower vacationed near Palm Springs, California. One of his California neighbors in 1961 asked the former president to endorse a plan to build a community fallout shelter within the country club to which the Eisenhower's were members. Eisenhower soberly commented on the suggestion to a friend that he was "not sure" that he "would really want to be living if this country of ours should ever be subjected to a nuclear bath."[1] Eisenhower's thoughts on warfare in the nuclear age and his understanding of the harmful effects of radioactive fallout underwent monumental transformations during his eight-year presidency. Deeply troubled by the consequences of both, Eisenhower sought as president to reach an agreement to ban nuclear testing as a means to ease tensions, slow the arms race, build confidence for future disarmament negotiations, and end the contamination of the atmosphere resulting from nuclear weapons tests.

In analyzing the secret test-ban debate within the Eisenhower administration in greater detail than previous studies, this study also contributes to the broader body of historical literature on Eisenhower's leadership and his approach to arms control. Historians continue to disagree whether Eisenhower's determination to sign a nuclear test-ban treaty with the Soviet Union and the United Kingdom matched his memoir's assertion that he was "unwilling to give up." Some revisionists generally agree with Eisenhower that he genuinely desired an agreement during his second term in office.[2] One recent study, however, maintains that the Eisenhower administration never seriously pursued an accord to ban nuclear testing.[3] Contrary to that argument, this study concludes that Eisenhower, despite his delayed and tentative actions, strongly desired a nuclear test-ban agreement. In fact, Eisenhower was inclined to ban nuclear testing as early as 1954. Previous examinations of the test-ban issue during the Eisenhower administration have not identified the depth of the president's interest in a ban at this early stage or assessed the multiple factors that inhibited his actions throughout his presidency.

Studies of the test-ban debate often criticize Eisenhower for a lack of leadership on the issue. They typically fall short of explaining why the president failed to achieve a goal that some argue he genuinely desired. Eisenhower's leadership on the test ban was at times hesitant and indecisive. That was a result of an amalgam of causes—the deceitful and manipulative acts of Lewis Strauss and other test-ban opponents within the administration, the president's leadership style, and his understandable confusion with the complex technical problems that dominated the test-ban debate.

One major theme of this study of the test-ban debate is the relationship between Eisenhower and Lewis Strauss. Several reasons explain why Eisenhower vested so much power in Strauss. Eisenhower entered office generally skeptical of scientists, considering them, despite his personal liking of Rabi, dangerously prone to releasing classified information and unqualified to offer advice on the political, diplomatic, and strategic implications of their inventions. As a result, Eisenhower perilously, and unwisely, depended upon Strauss to translate technical issues into policy advice.

Eisenhower also shared the AEC chairman's mistrust of the Soviet Union, though not to Strauss's level of paranoia. They both possessed a penchant for secrecy and an interest in developing the peaceful uses of atomic energy. Their similar worldview, Strauss's talented cultivation of the president's trust and friendship, and the absence of an organizational structure that provided the president scientific expertise beyond Strauss's closely held circle of atomic scientists left Strauss in a uniquely influential position.

The vindictive and self-righteous Strauss, who was utterly convinced that the nation's survival depended upon improving its nuclear arsenal through constant testing, was a highly skilled bureaucrat. He largely prevented contrary advice from reaching Eisenhower, and imposed his own views, supported by AEC scientists such as Willard Libby and Edward

Teller: that continued nuclear weapons testing was essential, that it did not pose any health hazards, and that it could not be effectively monitored in any international agreement. The shrewd AEC chairman used his position to deceive the president, skillfully marginalizing test-ban advocates and virtually dominating the nation's policies on atomic energy for the first four and a half years of Eisenhower's presidency.

Strauss's apocalyptic assessments clashed with Eisenhower's inclination to ban testing. The president became increasingly frustrated as his private hopes and public pronouncements in favor of disarmament contradicted his administration's extensive test program. After I. I. Rabi in 1956 presented some rare scientific advice from beyond Strauss's range of control, Eisenhower began to moderate Strauss's demands for additional testing and to move closer toward test-ban negotiations.

Eisenhower slowly began to break free of Strauss's dominant influence amidst the 1956 presidential election campaign. Despite the fact that Adlai Stevenson had made a ban on nuclear testing a central theme of his campaign, Eisenhower privately directed his advisors to develop a proposal to ban testing. This study details the largely unexamined efforts of the administration to ridicule publicly Stevenson's proposal and conceal from the public Eisenhower's own sincere desire to seek a test-ban agreement. Ironically, Stevenson's campaign position allowed Strauss and other test-ban opponents within the administration to reopen the administration's secret debate and publicly issue some privately rejected justifications for continued testing. The substantial 1956 efforts to counter Stevenson limited Eisenhower's ability to reverse course immediately following his reelection. Nevertheless, the president moved increasingly away from Strauss's advice during his second term. Eisenhower, despite his break with Strauss over the test issue, continued to respect Strauss's views and to value their growing friendship that extended beyond his presidency.

A second major theme of this study is Eisenhower's leadership. Eisenhower blamed his leadership style for authorizing, against his inclinations, one more U-2 flight before the Paris summit. He later regretted that he had not followed his instincts, dejectedly revealing that he "had not felt that he could oppose the combined opinion of all his associates."[4] The internal test-ban debate provided an analogous situation in 1954 when Eisenhower's closest advisors unanimously concluded that a ban on testing would not be in the nation's best interests. Eisenhower, lacking confidence in his technical assumptions, trusted the counsel of his advisors rather than his instincts.

Eisenhower exercised firm leadership in times of international crises, but often sought a consensus among his closest advisors on less pressing matters. For Eisenhower, nuclear testing was a central anxiety, but testing never became a crisis issue that demanded quick and decisive actions from the president. The course of the test-ban debate within the Eisenhower administration reveals that the president, confronted with the opposition of Strauss and others on an issue of such tremendous technical complexity, often deferred to the counsel of his subordinates during the first half of his presidency.

A third major theme of this study, closely connected to the first and second, is Eisenhower's relationship with scientists and the centrality of scientific counsel to understanding his approach to the test-ban issue. Before the Soviet launch of *Sputnik*, Eisenhower complained that his statecraft was becoming a prisoner of the AEC's scientists; their incessant demands for additional nuclear weapons tests undermined his efforts at arms control. Eisenhower gained the confidence to overrule Strauss and other test-ban opponents within his administration when the technical conclusions of scientists beyond Strauss's tightly controlled orbit supported the president's inclinations.

For Eisenhower, the inventions of scientists transformed the strategic environment in ways that reached beyond his intellectual ability. Matters had become too recondite for him to master. Earlier, as a military planner between the world wars, Eisenhower possessed sufficient education and understanding of the salient issues to prepare with confidence America's industrial base for mobilization. In his view, the nation's industrial might played a central role in the ultimate defeat of Japan and Germany during the Second World War.[5] As president in the still rather new nuclear age, Eisenhower inherited a different strategic environment. Scientists had created weapons beyond his comprehension, challenging his ability to master matters of the gravest significance to his national security strategy. Moreover, the advice he received from scientists, initially strictly limited to those affiliated with the nation's nuclear weapons laboratories, confirmed his suspicions that scientists' unyielding quest for knowledge would prompt them to continue to develop greater means of destruction without considering the social implications of their discoveries.

As part of his response to *Sputnik*, Eisenhower appointed a personal advisor for science and technology and created an advisory panel of prominent scientists and administrators who operated outside of Strauss's realm of control. Significantly, the members of PSAC concluded that a test ban would be advantageous to the United States and they encouraged Eisenhower to pursue negotiations toward a permanent ban.

Largely as a result of PSAC's assessments, Eisenhower did not invariably side with the AEC and DOD, contrary to one recent interpretation, on the test-ban issue during this period.[6]

The combined weight of the expert counsel of eminent scientists and science-administrators such as Bethe, Killian, Kistiakowsky, and Rabi convinced Eisenhower that a test ban could be adequately policed and strategically advantageous. PSAC's views provided Eisenhower the confidence in his technical judgments that he previously lacked to pursue his inclinations and overrule his dissenting advisors. Eisenhower, assured by his new body of science advisors, declared a voluntary test moratorium in 1958 and opened negotiations with the Soviet Union and the United Kingdom toward an agreement ending all nuclear weapons tests. For the remainder of his presidency, he resisted pressures from AEC and Defense officials to terminate the talks at Geneva and to resume testing.

Many of those favoring a test-cessation accord, including Eisenhower, initially perceived a ban as a relatively simple step in which an agreement could break the deadlock over inspection provisions that had blocked previous efforts at disarmament. Eisenhower and other advocates hoped that an agreement to ban tests, monitored by an international control system, would instill the confidence necessary for the nuclear powers to reach a meaningful disarmament agreement. The complex issues related to testing and detection, however, proved much more difficult to resolve than even the nation's top scientists had imagined. As a result, scientific assessments, based upon incomplete data and untested theories, became highly contested terrain between the negotiating powers and among scientists within the United States. Additional underground tests during the *HARDTACK II* series in 1958 revealed that the Geneva system would not be as effective as originally believed. The troubling new data prompted James Killian, an administrator rather than a scientist, to advise Eisenhower to suspend his efforts to reach a comprehensive test-ban agreement.

A change in science advisors encouraged Eisenhower to pursue once again a ban on all nuclear weapons tests. George Kistiakowsky inherited from Killian what he later described as a policy in "shambles." Kistiakowsky quickly discovered that the scientific disagreements over the effectiveness of seismic detection caused a "rather shocking story of indecision in high places" over the administration's approach to the test-ban negotiations at Geneva.[7] Kistiakowsky, a distinguished chemist, was committed to a comprehensive ban, skeptical of decoupling, and had much greater faith in the ability of scientists to improve the means of seismic detection than the administrator that preceded him as the president's top science advisor. Kistiakowsky convinced Eisenhower to once again overrule the vehement protests of leading AEC and Defense officials and pursue a comprehensive ban.

Although Eisenhower's new science advisors convinced him to negotiate a test-ban agreement, the president continued to share Strauss and Teller's fears of Soviet duplicity and their hopes for developing the peaceful uses of atomic energy. As a result, Eisenhower never broke completely free of the influence of the most prominent and powerful test-ban opponents and was unwilling to accept an agreement that did not include an international detection system sufficient to deter Soviet clandestine testing. Assessments of what constituted adequate inspection thus also became hotly contested scientific disputes waged in congressional hearings, the popular press, and at the bargaining table in Geneva. Test-ban opponents drew upon Eisenhower's mistrust of the Soviet Union to undercut his willingness to compromise on the unresolved issues at Geneva, such as the number of annual on-site inspections of unidentified seismic events.

The question of missed opportunities often arises in considering efforts at arms control and disarmament between the nuclear powers. For many, the 1960 Paris summit offered the best opportunity during the Eisenhower presidency for reaching a test-ban agreement.[8] Eisenhower and Khrushchev, during the Soviet leader's visit to the United States the previous year, developed a shared understanding of the necessity of reducing tensions and easing the financial burdens of the arms race. Nevertheless, many complex and contentious issues related to inspection and control remained unresolved, casting great doubt on British Prime Minister Macmillan's assessment that "all the omens were good" for concluding a test-ban agreement at the Paris summit.[9]

Although Khrushchev and Eisenhower may have shared Macmillan's hopes for reaching an agreement, neither appeared on the eve of the summit prepared to offer additional concessions. Eisenhower indicated little willingness to compromise on inspection and did not even ask Kistiakowsky to accompany him to Paris for the anticipated discussions on the test ban. Khrushchev faced the growing resistance of hardliners at home to his proposed military cuts. Although optimistic immediately following his visit to the United States, Khrushchev had since tempered his hopes for progress at the Paris summit.[10] It is thus highly unlikely that the nuclear powers would have reached an agreement on a treaty at Paris if the U-2 incident had not destroyed the summit. It is clear, however, that the failed summit marked a strong setback in relations between the two nations and likely ended any chance for making progress at Geneva while Eisenhower remained in office.

Although Eisenhower failed to achieve his goal of concluding a test-ban accord during his presidency, he merits praise for halting testing for over two years and for paving the way for his successor to reach an agreement, albeit limited in scope. Eisenhower, convinced only late in his presidency of the dire warnings of some test-ban advocates that atmospheric testing posed unacceptable health hazards to humans, never wavered publicly or privately in his determination not to test in the atmosphere for the remainder of his presidency. Belatedly acknowledging the perils of radioactive fallout, Eisenhower dismissed the vehement protests of several of his advisors and refused to resume testing, sparing the world the contamination of additional atmospheric testing.

The lengthy negotiations at Geneva, which Eisenhower hoped would prove to the world his nation's willingness to negotiate in good faith and its seriousness in the pursuit of peace, suffered humiliating setbacks as hopes for an agreement preceded knowledge of the related technical issues. He wrote in his memoirs that he found "no compelling reason to regret" the test moratorium or his efforts to negotiate a test-ban agreement.[11] Privately, Eisenhower expressed misgivings that he had permitted the moratorium to extend indefinitely as the test-ban talks at Geneva dragged on for over two years without an agreement. Although Eisenhower in 1961 succumbed to the fears of Strauss that the moratorium had permitted the Soviet Union to catch up with or even surpass the United States in nuclear technology, the United States in fact maintained its technological edge and a massive numerical superiority in its nuclear arsenal.

Eisenhower's test moratorium and the 1963 treaty that followed provided decidedly mixed results according to his own criteria. Although the moratorium decreased the levels of radioactivity from testing and eased tensions, it only briefly slowed the arms race between the superpowers and did nothing to inhibit the nuclear programs of France and China. The Limited Test-Ban Treaty also did little to slow proliferation and permitted underground testing, which continued at an accelerated pace. Technological advances developed through underground testing created even more dangerous nuclear arsenals than existed before Eisenhower's moratorium. Thus, the limited treaty concluded by the Kennedy administration failed to serve many of the purposes for which Eisenhower originally pursued a test ban.

Most importantly, the 1963 treaty did not accomplish Eisenhower's fundamental reason for seeking a test-ban agreement. For Eisenhower, the "real aim" of the test ban was to open up the Soviet Union to some degree of international inspection, even if just a few monitoring stations, to build the confidence necessary for his ultimate objective, a safeguarded disarmament agreement.[12] For the Soviet Union, accepting the presence of international inspectors within its territory first required the development of confidence in the motives of the United States. For the United States, confidence only came after the acceptance of a functioning inspection system. Negotiators, despite over four years of effort, failed to resolve this dispute over sequencing. As a result, the treaty in 1963 only banned those tests that did not require international monitoring stations within the territories of the nuclear powers, eliminating the aspect of the test ban that appealed most to Eisenhower. Disagreements over inspection and control issues continued to frustrate arms control negotiations for decades to come.

Eisenhower deserves credit, however, for his willingness in the face of tremendous opposition to initiate negotiations with the Soviet Union. Eisenhower insisted that the opportunity to ease tensions and slow the arms race was worth taking some risks in an unmonitored test moratorium and in negotiations toward a permanent ban.[13] Eisenhower's overall popularity and prestige remained tremendously high, despite the setback of *Sputnik* and the criticism that followed. Therefore, Eisenhower likely possessed the ability to persuade the American people and the Senate that there were greater risks worth accepting in exchange for a complete ban on testing had he first convinced himself. Yet Eisenhower's mistrust of the Soviet Union, heightened by the dire warnings of Strauss and Teller, imposed limits on the degree of risk that he was willing to accept for a comprehensive test-ban treaty. Nevertheless, his proposal in 1959 for a partial ban ultimately led to the first significant arms control accord between nuclear powers.

In the end, the advantages of the Limited Test-Ban Treaty were largely confined to halting the spread of radioactive fallout from atmospheric testing. The United States no longer faced, as Eisenhower feared, being "crucified on a cross of atoms" by world opinion for continuing its atmospheric testing program. Eisenhower, however, received little comfort from this accomplishment. Taking a broader view, Eisenhower realized that the greater perils of the nuclear arms race and the potential for a catastrophic nuclear war were unabated.

Reference Matter

Notes

For complete authors' names, titles, and publication data on the works cited in short form in the Notes, see the Sources, pages 337–49. The following abbreviations are used:

AES		*The Papers of Adlai E. Stevenson*
BAS		*Bulletin of the Atomic Scientists*
C-K		Compton-Killian Papers
DDEL		Dwight D. Eisenhower Library, Abilene, Kansas
	AWF	Ann Whitman File
	DS	Dwight D. Eisenhower Diary Series
	OFA	Office Files—Administration Series
	OFI	Office Files—International Series
	D-H	Dulles-Herter Series
	NS	Name Series
	CH	Christian A. Herter Papers
	CCS	Chronological Correspondence Series
	TC	Memoranda of Telephone Conversations
	CMS	Correspondence and Memoranda Series
	JFD	John Foster Dulles Papers
	WHMS	White House Memoranda Series
	TC	Telephone Conversations Series
	CS	Chronological Series
	GCMS	General Correspondence and Memoranda Series
	DPCSS	Draft Presidential Correspondence and Speeches Series
	McC	John A. McCone Papers
	NSCS	National Security Council Staff Papers
	OSAD	Office of the Special Assistant for Disarmament

OSANSA   Office of the Special Assistant for National Security Affairs
  NSC   NSC Series
  SAS   Special Assistant Series
OSAT   Office of the Special Assistant for Science and Technology
OSS   Office of the Staff Secretary
  SA   Subject Series, Alphabetical Subseries
US PSAC U.S. President's Science Advisory Committee
WHCF   White House Central Files
  CF   Confidential File
  OF   Official File
DDRS   *Declassified Documents Reference System*
DOE/NTA DOE Nuclear Testing Archive, Las Vegas, Nevada
FRUS   *Foreign Relations of the United States*
GBK   George B. Kistiakowsky Papers
HAB   Hans A. Bethe Papers
IIR   I. I. Rabi Papers
JFKL   John F. Kennedy Presidential Library, Boston, Massachusetts
JRK   James R. Killian Papers
JRO   J. Robert Oppenheimer Papers
LLS   Lewis L. Strauss Papers
NAII   National Archives II, College Park, Maryland
  RG   Record Group
NAUK   National Archives of the United Kingdom, Kew, United Kingdom
  FO   Records created and inherited by the Foreign Office (FO)
  PREM   Records of the Prime Minister's Office
NYT   *New York Times*
PDDE   *The Papers of Dwight D. Eisenhower*
PPP   *Public Papers of the Presidents of the United States*
WP   *Washington Post and Times Herald*

Introduction

EPIGRAPH: "Farewell Radio and Television Address to the American People," 17 Jan. 1961, *PPP, Eisenhower, (1960–1961),* 1035–40.

1. Stephen E. Ambrose, *Eisenhower,* vol. 2, *The President* (New York: Simon and Schuster, 1984), 563–64.

2. Martha Smith, "The Nuclear Testing Policies of the Eisenhower Administration, 1953–1960" (Ph. D. diss., University of Toronto, 1997), 8. She qualifies her argument in a later essay, acknowledging that Eisenhower became more co-operative on the test-ban issue in the final year of his presidency, Martha Smith-Norris, "The Eisenhower Administration and the Nuclear Test Ban Talks, 1958–1960: Another Challenge to 'Revisionism,'" *Diplomatic History* 27 (Sep. 2003): 503–41.

3. Writing shortly after the Kennedy administration in 1963 signed the Limited Test Ban Treaty with the Soviet Union, Harold Jacobson and Eric Stein criti-

cized Eisenhower for his indecision and his unwillingness to resolve the bitter differences within his administration over the pursuit of a test ban. In their view, Eisenhower did not consider the test ban as strategically advantageous, was unconvinced of the health hazards of atmospheric testing, and did not believe that a test ban could contribute to a slowing of the arms race. Jacobson and Stein also criticized the performance of scientists as negotiators for failing to prepare adequately for technical discussions and for their inability to comprehend the political implications of their scientific conclusions. Their analysis, which begins in 1957, is based upon popular accounts and interviews with participants. See Harold Karan Jacobson and Eric Stein, *Diplomats, Scientists, and Politicians: The United States and the Nuclear Test Ban Negotiations* (Ann Arbor: University of Michigan Press, 1966), 471–73, 486–90.

4. Robert A. Divine, *Blowing on the Wind: The Nuclear Test Ban Debate, 1954–1960* (New York: Oxford University Press, 1978), 314, 321–22.

5. Richard G. Hewlett and Jack M. Holl, *Atoms for Peace and War 1953–1961: Eisenhower and the Atomic Energy Commission* (Berkeley: University of California Press, 1989), 546, 561–65.

6. Smith, "The Nuclear Testing Policies of the Eisenhower Administration, 1953–1960." Smith-Norris, "The Eisenhower Administration and the Nuclear Test Ban Talks, 1958–1960."

7. Smith-Norris, "The Eisenhower Administration and the Nuclear Test Ban Talks, 1958–1960," 506.

8. "Address to the American People," Jan. 17, 1961, *PPP, Eisenhower, 1961*, 1035–40.

9. This study explores these complex issues to illustrate Eisenhower's thinking on nuclear weapons because of its important implications for understanding his motives for pursuing the test ban. It does not, however, purport to examine comprehensively each of Eisenhower's efforts at arms control or attempt to analyze the torturous course of proposals and counterproposals during the disarmament discussions in the 1950s. Neither does this study assess in great detail Eisenhower's overall approach to national security or his consideration of the use of nuclear weapons in several crises throughout his presidency.

10. The rich scholarly literature on the Eisenhower presidency does not include a single monograph that fully examines Eisenhower's efforts at disarmament and arms control throughout his presidency. The best account remains by Charles A. Appleby Jr., "Eisenhower and Arms Control, 1953–1961: A Balance of Risks," Ph.D. Dissertation, Johns Hopkins University, 1987. Others provide useful overviews. See David S. Patterson, "President Eisenhower and Arms Control," *Peace and Change* 11, no. 3–4 (1986): 3–24; and Thomas F. Soapes, "A Cold Warrior Seeks Peace: Eisenhower's Strategy for Nuclear Disarmament," *Diplomatic History* 4 (Winter 1980): 57–71. See also Robert R. Bowie and Richard H. Immerman, *Waging Peace: How Eisenhower Forged an Enduring Cold War Strategy* (New York: Oxford University Press, 1998).

11. For an earlier version of this study that focuses in this period, see Benjamin P. Greene, "Eisenhower, Science and the Test Ban Debate, 1953–1956,"

Journal of Strategic Studies 25 (Dec. 2003): 156–85. See also the journal's website at http://www.tandf.co.uk.

12. For Divine, Eisenhower's lack of leadership in permitting a difference of opinion within his administration to paralyze the test-ban negotiations at Geneva was most responsible for its failed outcome. See Divine, *Blowing on the Wind*, 314. Smith-Norris, "The Eisenhower Administration and the Nuclear Test Ban Talks, 1958–1960," 537–41.

13. For an overview of the extensive literature on the Eisenhower presidency, see Stephen G. Rabe, "Eisenhower Revisionism," *Diplomatic History* 17 (Winter 1993): 97–115. The most prominent examples of Eisenhower revisionism include: Ambrose, *Eisenhower*, vol. 2; Robert Divine, *Eisenhower and the Cold War* (New York: Oxford University Press, 1981); and Fred I. Greenstein, *The Hidden-Hand Presidency: Eisenhower as Leader* (New York: Basic Books, 1982).

14. H. W. Brands reaches a similar conclusion on Eisenhower's style of decision-making. See Brands, "The Age of Vulnerability: Eisenhower and the National Insecurity State," *American Historical Review* 94 (Oct. 1989): 963–89.

15. Smith, "The Nuclear Testing Policies of the Eisenhower Administration, 1953–1960," 514–20; Smith-Norris, "The Eisenhower Administration and the Nuclear Test Ban Talks, 1958–1960," 503–4. Other examples of "post-revisionist" interpretations include H. W. Brands and Jeremy Suri, "America's Search for a Technological Solution to the Arms Race: The Surprise Attack Conference of 1958 and a Challenge for 'Eisenhower Revisionists,'" *Diplomatic History* 21 (Summer 1997): 417–51.

16. For example, Smith-Norris emphasizes that the AEC and DOD fought a successful "rearguard action" within the administration to prevent an agreement on a test ban. See Smith-Norris, "The Eisenhower Administration and the Nuclear Test Ban Talks, 1958–1960," 503–4, 537–41.

17. Memorandum of Meeting, 8 Aug. 1957, DDEL, OSANSA, NSC, Subject Sub, Box 1, Atomic Wpns and Classified Intell—Misc [1] [1955–57].

18. For example, Herbert York initially opposed a test ban, but later became a firm advocate. Conversely, James R. Killian, Jr., who played a central role in convincing Eisenhower to pursue a comprehensive test ban, later supported only an atmospheric ban.

19. The substantial scholarly literature on the Eisenhower administration does not include a thorough examination of Eisenhower's attitude toward science. Most of the previous studies focus narrowly on a particular issue, a specific period, or both. My study covers the entire Eisenhower presidency, but is largely limited to the issues surrounding the test ban and the organization of presidential science advising. It does not attempt to assess several other important scientific issues that Eisenhower confronted, such as the development of missiles, space exploration, and science education. For an account of the evolution of scientific advice and an overview of the technical issues that Eisenhower confronted, see Gregg Herken, *Cardinal Choices: Presidential Science Advising from the Atomic Bomb to SDI*, rev. ed. (Stanford: Stanford University Press, 2000). Richard Damms emphasizes the importance of the Technological Capabilities

Panel of 1954–1955 for revising the scientific advisory system. See Richard V. Damms, "James Killian, the Technological Capabilities Panel, and the Emergence of President Eisenhower's 'Scientific-Technological Elite,'" *Diplomatic History* 24 (Winter 2000): 57–78. Philip Taubman, *Secret Empire: Eisenhower, the CIA, and the Hidden Story of America's Space Espionage* (New York: Simon & Schuster, 2003). Robert Divine, *The Sputnik Challenge: Eisenhower's Response to the Soviet Satellite* (New York: Oxford University Press, 1993). See also the memoirs and diary of Eisenhower's science advisors. James R. Killian, Jr., *Sputnik, Scientists, and Eisenhower: A Memoir of the First Special Assistant to the President for Science and Technology* (Cambridge: MIT Press, 1977); and George B. Kistiakowsky, *A Scientist in the White House: The Private Diary of President Eisenhower's Special Assistant for Science and Technology* (Cambridge: Harvard University Press, 1976).

20. George H. Gallup, ed. *The Gallup International Public Opinion Polls: Great Britain, 1937–1975* (New York: Random House, 1976), 409, 411–12, 450, 463, 482–83, 518, 552–53.

21. Eisenhower lamented in 1958 that British opposition to a test ban prevented an agreement in 1957. Because the British had just completed their first H-bomb test in May 1957, Prime Minister Harold Macmillan privately opposed a test ban, fearing that an early agreement linked to a cutoff in the production of weapons materials would prevent the British from producing their own deterrent. See Memorandum of Conference with the President, 24 Mar. 1958, DDEL, AWF, DS, Staff Notes (1) Mar. 1958. Macmillan to Eisenhower, 3 June 1957, *DDRS*, <http://www.DDRS.psrmedia.com>, 1996–37, (12 Jan. 2001); Charles Appleby supports Eisenhower's assertion, arguing that "in the final analysis" British reluctance to support a test ban swayed Eisenhower from pursuing a separate test-ban agreement in 1957; see Charles A. Appleby, Jr., "Eisenhower and Arms Control, 1953–1961: A Balance of Risks," 240.

22. George H. Gallup, ed., *The Gallup Poll: Public Opinion, 1935–1971* (New York: Random House, 1976) 2: 1229, 1452, 1487–88, 1541, 1552–53, 1643.

Chapter 1

EPIGRAPH: Dwight D. Eisenhower, *Crusade in Europe* (Garden City, N.J.: Doubleday, 1948), 455–56.

1. For Eisenhower's comments in his memoirs, see Eisenhower, *Crusade in Europe*, 443. Eisenhower revised his account of the exchange with Stimson fifteen years later for the first volume of his presidential memoirs. In this later version, Eisenhower even more forcefully stated his horror at the development of the A-bomb and his argument to Stimson that the United States should not use it on Japan. See Eisenhower, *The White House Years: Mandate for Change, 1953–1956* (Garden City, N.J.: Doubleday, 1963), 312–13. For another recollection of this episode that reveals that Eisenhower's memory was clearly influenced by the postwar myth that estimates of casualties of an invasion of Japan would

cost one million lives, see Eisenhower to John J. McCloy, June 18, 1965, DDEL, DDE Post-Presidential Papers, Secretary's Series, Box 14, McA.

2. For an analysis that raises serious doubts that Eisenhower raised his opposition to dropping the bomb to Stimson, see Barton J. Bernstein, "Ike and Hiroshima: Did He Oppose It?" *Journal of Strategic Studies* 10 (Sep. 1987): 377–90. The only other primary account that corroborates the conversation, without mentioning Eisenhower's opposition to the use of the bomb, is the memoir of Eisenhower's son, John S. D. Eisenhower. See John S. D. Eisenhower, *Strictly Personal* (Garden City, N.J.: Doubleday, 1974), 97.

3. Truman originally planned three tests, one air burst followed by two underwater tests. He cancelled the third after the JCS advised him that they expected to receive little additional information from it. See W. A. Shurcliff, *Bombs at Bikini: The Official Report of Operation Crossroads* (New York: W. H. Wise and Co., 1947), 205–6. Eisenhower's role as Army chief of staff involved mediating a dispute between the navy and the army air corps over the positioning of ships to be used as targets. For the rival services, the tests had lasting implications in the postwar debate over budgets and service responsibilities. The navy favored dispersed targets, fearing that a devastating test would bolster the arguments of air power advocates that atomic weapons made the navy obsolete. Conversely, air power advocates favored positioning the targets closer together. See Lloyd J. Graybar, "The 1946 Atomic Bomb Tests: Atomic Diplomacy or Bureaucratic Infighting?" *Journal of American History* 72 (Mar. 1986): 888–907.

4. Eisenhower, Broadcast on Bikini Atom Bomb Test, NBC, 29 June 1946, *Eisenhower Speaks: Dwight D. Eisenhower in His Messages and Speeches* ed. Rudolph L. Treuenfels (New York: Farrar, Strauss & Company, 1948): 115–16. Eisenhower later told reporters that he planned his schedule with the intent to observe the tests just to satisfy his own curiosity. A decision to delay the tests created a conflict in Eisenhower's busy schedule, preventing him from observing one of the tests. See *NYT,* 30 Apr. 1946. Eisenhower's curiosity over atomic tests continued into his presidency. Although he frequently expressed a desire to observe one of the tests, he always declined because he believed that doing so would be seen as a belligerent act.

5. Eisenhower to Zimmerman, 6 May 1947, *PDDE,* 8:1686 n. 2.

6. Zimmerman to Eisenhower, 6 May 1947, ibid. Conant, who was instrumental in the development of the atomic bomb, had become a vigorous defender of the decision to use the bomb on Japan. See Barton J. Bernstein, "Seizing the Contested Terrain of Early Nuclear History: Stimson, Conant, and Their Allies Explain the Decision to Use the Atomic Bomb," *Diplomatic History* 17 (Winter 1993): 35–72. Although Conant played an important role in the wartime quest for the bomb and was a staunch defender of its use on Japan, he favored the international control of atomic energy and famously declared that the H-bomb would be built "over my dead body." See James Hershberg, *James B. Conant: Harvard to Hiroshima and the Making of the Nuclear Age* (New York: Alfred A. Knopf, 1993).

7. Only in the final years of his presidency did Eisenhower acknowledge that

the warnings Warren initially raised in private and later publicly propagated by politicians and scientists alike were correct; atmospheric detonations generated sufficiently alarming health hazards to abandon testing in the atmosphere. Eisenhower, assured by AEC scientists that the health hazards were minimal, dismissed such warnings for several years, but eventually accepted the view that testing posed sufficient hazards to refrain from testing. Eisenhower rejected pressures from within his administration in deciding not to test in the atmosphere for the final two years of his presidency.

8. Stephen Ambrose argues that Eisenhower sincerely favored the international control of atomic energy. In his view, Eisenhower recognized that attempting to maintain an atomic monopoly would only raise tensions and usher in an atomic arms race. Ambrose acknowledges that Eisenhower insisted on stringent inspection standards that he did not expect the Soviet Union to accept. According to Ambrose, Eisenhower's views had little influence on the Truman administration's decisions. See Stephen E. Ambrose, *Eisenhower,* vol. 1, *Solider, General of the Army, President-Elect, 1890–1952* (New York: Simon and Schuster, 1983), 444–46. Ira Chernus views Eisenhower's support for the Baruch plan more skeptically. He suggests that Eisenhower offered so many objections that his strongly qualified support for the Baruch plan "may actually be read as a veiled rejection." See Ira Chernus, *General Eisenhower: Ideology and Discourse* (East Lansing: Michigan University Press, 2002), 124.

9. Richard G. Hewlett and Oscar E. Anderson, Jr., *A History of the United States Atomic Energy Commission,* vol. 1, *The New World, 1939–1946* (University Park: Pennsylvania State University Press, 1962), 575–76.

10. For analyses of the failed effort to place atomic energy under international control, see Barton J. Bernstein, "The Quest for Security: American Foreign Policy and International Control of Atomic Energy, 1942–1946" *Journal of American History* 60 (Mar. 1974): 1003–44. See also McGeorge Bundy, *Danger and Survival: Choices About the Bomb in the First Fifty Years* (New York: Random House, 1988), 130–96.

11. *PDDE,* 7: 1128 n. 2–3. Eisenhower already developed a strong relationship with Baruch when they worked on plans in 1930 and 1933 for industrial mobilization during wartime. For a study that emphasizes Baruch's influence on Eisenhower, see Andrew P. N. Erdmann, "'War No Longer Has Any Logic Whatever': Dwight D. Eisenhower and the Thermonuclear Revolution," in *Cold War Statesmen Confront the Bomb: Nuclear Diplomacy since 1945* ed. John Lewis Gaddis and others (New York: Oxford University Press, 1999): 91–96.

12. For a discussion of the meeting on 15 April, see *PDDE,* 7: 1077–78 n. 1.

13. U.S., Congress, House, Subcommittee of the Committee on Appropriations, *Hearings on the Military Establishment Appropriations Bill for 1947,* 79: II, 1123–24.

14. Eisenhower's emphasis. Eisenhower to Baruch, 14 June 1946, *FRUS, 1946,* 1: 854–56. See also *PDDE,* 7: 1125–28. Although Eisenhower did not send his formal views until the day that Baruch presented the U.S. proposal to the United Nations, Baruch was already well aware of Eisenhower's thoughts on

the issue through his meetings and correspondence with Eisenhower the previous two months. In addition to their meeting on 15 April, see Record of Telephone Conversation, Eisenhower and Baruch, 8 Apr. 1946, DDEL, DDE Pre-Presidential Papers, Box 10, Baruch (4); see also Eisenhower to Baruch, 1 June 1946, *PDDE*, 7: 1092–94.

15. 6 Dec. 1946, *PDDE*, 8: 1394 n. 5.

16. Eisenhower wrote that the JCS should be *"for* disarmament," but emphasized that "verification is essential." Eisenhower's emphasis; see *PDDE*, 8: 1394 n. 3. According to Ira Chernus, Eisenhower, despite his frequent public comments emphasizing the threat of atomic warfare and his commitment to disarmament, showed little real commitment to disarmament in his actions. See Chernus, *General Eisenhower: Ideology and Discourse*, 123–27.

17. 15 Jan. 1947, *PDDE*, 8: 1484–85 n. 4. See also a slightly modified version in Rusk to Petersen, 16 Jan. 1947, *FRUS, 1947*, 1: 362.

18. Eisenhower to the Director of Plans and Operations (Norstad), 5 Feb. 1947, DDEL, DDE Pre-Presidential Papers, Box 140, Disarmament.

19. Eisenhower to George Whitney, 26 Mar. 1952, *PDDE*, 13: 1124–26.

20. Eisenhower, *Crusade in Europe*, 455–56.

21. Ambrose, *Eisenhower*, 1: 444.

22. The Joint Strategic Survey Committee, an inter-service group that provided analysis to the service chiefs and the joint staff, prepared the report. See *PDDE*, 7: 576–77 n. 2.

23. Eisenhower to the Joint Chiefs of Staff, 3 Dec. 1945, *PDDE*, 7: 575–79. Eisenhower later broadened the scope of their analysis to account for the possibility of an atomic arms race and to consider the impact of atomic weapons on the size, composition, and missions of the military. See Eisenhower to the Joint Chiefs of Staff, 17 Dec. 1945, *PDDE*, 7: 639–42.

24. Eisenhower to the Joint Chiefs of Staff, 16 Jan. 1946, *PDDE*, 7: 760–62.

25. Frederick Dunn to Eisenhower, 7 Mar. 1946, DDEL, DDE Pre-Presidential Papers, Box 127, Atomic Weapons and Energy, (1).

26. Bernard Brodie, "Implications for Military Strategy," in *The Absolute Weapon: Atomic Power and World Order*, ed. Bernard Brodie (New York: Harcourt, Brace and Company, 1946), 76.

27. For Eisenhower's notes, see manuscript, "The Absolute Weapon," DDEL, DDE Pre-Presidential Papers, Box 127, Atomic Weapons and Energy (2). LTC James Stack to the Secretary of War and others, 25 Mar. 1946, DDEL, DDE Pre-Presidential Papers, Box 127, Atomic Weapons and Energy, (1).

28. Eisenhower to Dorothy Thompson, 25 June 1946, *PDDE*, 7: 1149–51.

29. Eisenhower to Robert P. Patterson (Secretary of War), 17 Mar. 1947, *PDDE*, 8: 1606. Although Eisenhower approved planning for the unrestricted use of atomic weapons, the nation's atomic arsenal contained less than fifty assembled weapons until 1948. See David Alan Rosenberg, "The U.S. Nuclear Stockpile, 1945–1950," *BAS* (May 1982): 25–30. Eisenhower in March 1946 had already approved a strategic planning outline that assumed that the United States would use atomic weapons in a future conflict. See *PDDE*, 7: 850 n. 4, 6.

30. Eisenhower to the Joint Chiefs of Staff, 12 Mar. 1947, *PDDE*, 8: 1581–

85. See also Eisenhower to the Joint Chiefs of Staff, 22 Dec. 1947, *PDDE*, 9: 2155–58.

31. Stephen T. Ross, *American War Plans, 1945–1950* (London: Frank Cass, 1996), 62.

32. For an analysis of debates over the role of strategic bombing in this era, see Gian P. Gentile, *How Effective is Strategic Bombing? Lessons Learned From World War II to Kosovo* (New York: New York University Press, 2001), 131–66.

33. Eisenhower to Louis A. Johnson (Secretary of Defense) 14 July 1949, *PDDE*, 10: 698–704. Eisenhower was then serving informally as the chairman of the Joint Chiefs of Staff, a position that gave him "maximum exposure and minimum influence." See Ambrose, *Eisenhower*, 1: 487. During this period, the JCS was embroiled in a controversy over the Strategic Air Command's claims about its ability to bring victory in a general war through a strategic air offensive using atomic weapons. Eisenhower's comments suggest that he agreed with the conclusions of the Harmon Committee, a joint ad hoc committee formed by the JCS to evaluate the impact of such a strike on the Soviet war effort. See Report by the Ad Hoc Committee, 12 May 1949, "Evaluation of Effect on Soviet War Effort Resulting from the Strategic Air Offensive," in Steven T. Ross and David Alan Rosenberg, eds., *America's Plans For War Against The Soviet Union, 1945–1950*, vol. 11, *The Limits of Nuclear Strategy* (New York: Garland Publishing, 1989), 6–8, 41.

34. Ambrose suggests that Eisenhower considered it mad and immoral to rely solely upon atomic weapons for the defense of Europe. See Ambrose, *Eisenhower*, 1: 508. For others, Eisenhower was less concerned with the morality of using atomic weapons than he was skeptical of their capabilities to halt a Soviet drive in Europe. For Erdmann, Eisenhower sought to combine atomic weapons with greater allied conventional forces in NATO to hold the Soviet Union while the European allies mobilized additional conventional forces and the United States mobilized its industry. See Erdmann, 95–96.

35. Erdmann, "War No Longer Has Any Logic Whatever," 96.

36. *NYT*, 24 Sep. 1949.

37. *NYT*, 12 Mar. 1950; 30 Mar. 1950. Eisenhower was likely aware of the massive increase in military spending envisioned in NSC-68.

38. *NYT*, 10 Feb. 1950. Eisenhower asserted that every invention "has been capable of two uses, good and evil. It is up to the moral fiber of mankind to decide to which use an invention is put."

39. Secretary of Defense Forrestal formed a panel to consider what information the government should release to the public on the capabilities of, and the defense against, atomic, biological, and chemical weapons. Others joining Eisenhower on the panel included John Foster Dulles and James Conant, who served as its chairman. See Eisenhower to Karl Compton, 27 Oct. 1949, *PDDE*, 10: 799–800. Eisenhower early in his presidency received a different report from a panel of experts, this one chaired by J. Robert Oppenheimer, that considered the release of information on thermonuclear weapons. Chapter 2 discusses his response to the latter panel's conclusions.

40. *NYT*, 12 Mar. 1950.

41. *NYT*, 3 Oct. 1950.

42. Dwight D. Eisenhower to Edgar N. Eisenhower, 2 Aug. 1950, *PDDE*, 11: 1256–58.

43. Conant to Eisenhower, 16 Oct. 1947; Eisenhower to Conant, 20 Oct. 1947; Conant, "The Atomic Age: A Preview 1947 Edition" (paper presented to the National War College, Carlisle Barracks, PA, October, 1947) all in DDEL, DDE Pre-Presidential Papers, Box 27, Conant (2).

44. Eisenhower to Conant, 26 Sep. 1950, *PDDE*, 11: 1341–42.

45. Eisenhower to Karl Compton, 27 Oct. 1949, *PDDE*, 10: 799–800. See also Conant to Eisenhower, 16 Oct. 1947; Conant, "The Atomic Age: A Preview 1947 Edition" both in DDEL, DDE Pre-Presidential Papers, Box 27, Conant (2).

46. For a discussion of the Oppenheimer loyalty-security case, see Chapter 3.

47. J. Robert Oppenheimer was GAC's chairman from December 1946 until August 1952. Rabi replaced Oppenheimer, serving as the chairman until July 1956.

48. Eisenhower appointed Conant as the U.S. High Commissioner to Germany until 1955 and the Ambassador to Germany from 1955–1957. Killian chaired the Technological Capabilities Panel that advised Eisenhower to accelerate the development of ICBMs and the U-2 spy plane and later became Eisenhower's first science advisor. Stassen headed Eisenhower's foreign aid program and became Eisenhower's special assistant for disarmament.

49. John S. Rigden, *Rabi: Scientist and Citizen* (New York: Basic Books Inc., 1987), 238.

50. "Ike's Campus Trouble," *Newsweek* (8 Aug. 1949): 8.

51. Eisenhower to John Krout, 17 Aug. 1949, *PDDE*, 10: 727.

52. Under the directorship of J. Robert Oppenheimer, the Institute for Advanced Study included such prominent figures as Albert Einstein.

53. Eisenhower, *At Ease* (Garden City, N.J.: Doubleday, 1967), 347–48.

54. Columbia University, Oral History Project, Butler Library, New York, Columbia University Sesquibicentennial Project, I. I. Rabi, 1026–28. See also Travis Beal Jacobs, *Eisenhower at Columbia* (New Brunswick, N.J.: Transaction Publishers, 2001), 242–43.

55. Eisenhower to Acheson and others, 2 Dec. 1948, *PDDE*, 10: 338–40.

56. Hewlett and Holl, *Atoms for Peace and War 1953–1961*, 1–16.

57. The evolution of Eisenhower's thinking on the use of nuclear weapons falls beyond the scope of this study. For analyses of the transformation of Eisenhower's thinking toward warfare in the thermonuclear age, see Erdmann, "War No Longer Has Any Logic Whatever," 87–119. See also Campbell Craig, *Destroying the Village: Eisenhower and Thermonuclear War* (New York: Columbia University Press, 1998).

Chapter 2

EPIGRAPHS: Report of the Scientific Panel, "Recommendations on the Immediate Use of Atomic Weapons," 16 June 1945, *The Manhattan Project: A Doc-*

umentary Introduction to the Atomic Age, Michael B. Stoff et. al., eds. (New York: McGraw-Hill, 1991), 149–50; *PPP, Eisenhower, 1953*, 1–8.

1. Eisenhower's left hand covered two bibles, the second bible was the one used by George Washington at the first presidential inauguration, "Eisenhower Takes Oath on Two Bibles," *NYT*, 21 Jan. 1953.

2. *PPP, Eisenhower, 1953*, 1–8. In another illuminating speech on Sep. 23, 1953, Eisenhower emphasized the importance of the United Nations since "every new invention of the scientist seems to make it more nearly possible for man to insure his own elimination from this globe." See *PPP, Eisenhower, 1953*: 605.

3. "Armaments and American Policy: Report by the Panel of Consultants of the Department of State to the Secretary of State," Jan. 1953, *FRUS, 1952–54*, 2:1055–96.

4. Memo of Discussion at the 132d Meeting of the NSC, 18 Feb. 1953, ibid., 1106–9.

5. Memo of Discussion at the 134th Meeting of the NSC, 25 Feb. 1953, ibid., 1110–14.

6. Hewlett and Holl trace the origins of Eisenhower's interest in the peaceful uses of atomic energy to the period before his presidency; see Hewlett and Holl, *Atoms for Peace and War 1953–1961*, 1–16.

7. "Armaments and American Policy: Report by the Panel of Consultants of the Department of State to the Secretary of State," Jan. 1953, *FRUS, 1952–54*, 2: 1055–96.

8. As discussed in Chapter 1, Eisenhower, as a member of the ad hoc Conant Committee, had reached a similar conclusion on releasing additional atomic weapons information to the public following the Soviet detonation of their first A-bomb. See Eisenhower to Karl Compton, 27 Oct. 1949, *PDDE*, 10: 799–800.

9. Memorandum of Discussion at the 134th Meeting of the NSC, 25 Feb. 1953, *FRUS, 1952–54*, 2: 1110–1114.

10. Strauss's family lived comfortably, with the assistance of a domestic servant, until his father's company suffered from decreased sales during a recession. Strauss, then 16 years old, assisted in the recovery of the business as a traveling shoe salesperson instead of attending college. Richard Pfau, *No Sacrifice Too Great: The Life of Lewis L. Strauss* (Charlottesville: University Press of Virginia Press, 1984), 1–10.

11. Pfau, *No Sacrifice Too Great*, 1–63; Lewis L. Strauss, *Men and Decisions* (Garden City, N.J.: Doubleday, 1962).

12. Pfau, *No Sacrifice Too Great*, 83–142.

13. Ibid., 105–7, 132.

14. *New York Times* publisher Arthur Hays Sulzberger, a member of Columbia's board of trustees, wrote Eisenhower in 1950 to inform him that he intended to nominate Strauss to fill a vacancy on the board. Eisenhower responded that he had met Strauss only briefly and could not "claim him as a friend," but that he had no objection to Sulzberger's nomination. For reasons that remain unclear, the trustees did not ask Strauss to fill the vacancy on the board. Instead, Strauss received an honorary degree from Columbia in 1954. See Eisenhower to Sulzberger, 28 June 1950, *PDDE*, 11: 1180–81.

15. Pfau, *No Sacrifice Too Great,* 136–37.

16. Ambrose, *Eisenhower*, vol. 1: 291–92.

17. Eisenhower considered the Senate's rejection in 1959 of his nomination of Strauss as Secretary of Commerce, "one of the most depressing official disappointments I experienced during my eight years in the White House." See Eisenhower, *Waging Peace*, 392–96. The Strauss's, whom Eisenhower characterized in his memoirs as "two of the ablest, most personable, and dedicated persons," hosted Eisenhower's farewell luncheon following Kennedy's inauguration. See ibid., 618.

18. Strauss to Ernest O. Lawrence, 23 June 1958, LLS, AEC, Box 59, Lawrence.

19. For the text of Oppenheimer's remarks, see DDEL, WHCF, OF, OF108A, (1).

20. J. Robert Oppenheimer, "Atomic Weapons and American Policy," *Foreign Affairs* 31 (July 1953): 525–35.

21. Strauss's memo of telephone conversation with Eisenhower suggests that it was Eisenhower's idea to counter Oppenheimer, see Strauss Memo, 22 July 1953, LLS, AEC, Box 66, MFR 1953.

22. "The Hidden Struggle for the H-Bomb: The Story of Dr. Oppenheimer's Persistent Campaign to Reverse U.S. Military Strategy," *Fortune* 48 (May 1953). For a discussion of Oppenheimer's views and Strauss's efforts to counter them, see Kai Bird and Martin J. Sherwin, *American Prometheus: The Triumph and Tragedy of J. Robert Oppenheimer* (New York: Knopf, 2005), 462–70. See also Priscilla J. McMillan, *The Ruin of J. Robert Oppenheimer and the Birth of the Modern Arms Race* (New York: Viking, 2005), 160–64. Charles J. V. Murphy, "The Atom and the Balance of Power," *Fortune* 48 (Aug. 1953): 97, 202.

23. Strauss memorandum, 15 Oct. 1953, LLS, AEC, Box 66, MFR; Bush most likely did not know that the week before Eisenhower directed that all statements concerning atomic weapons had to be cleared by Strauss, see Memorandum, 12 Oct. 1953, DDEL, AWF, OFA, Radford (2);

24. The University of Chicago Metallurgical Laboratory is often referred as the "Met Lab." "Political and Social Problems" (Franck Report), 11 June 1945, *The Manhattan Project: A Documentary Introduction to the Atomic Age*, Michael B. Stoff et. al., eds. (New York: McGraw-Hill, 1991), 140–47.

25. For an analysis of the views of these four prominent scientists on atomic energy following the war, see Barton J. Bernstein, "Four Physicists and the Bomb: The Early Years, 1945–1950," *Historical Studies in the Physical and Biological Sciences* 18, no. 2 (1988): 231–63.

26. Report of the Scientific Panel, "Recommendations on the Immediate Use of Atomic Weapons," 16 June 1945, ibid., 149–50. This document and the Franck Report are in the Manhattan Engineer District Records, National Archives II, College Park, Md.

27. Barton J. Bernstein, "Seizing the Contested Terrain of Early Nuclear History: Stimson, Conant, and the Their Allies Explain the Decision to Use the Atomic Bomb," *Diplomatic History* 17 (Winter 1993): 58.

28. Peter Goodchild, *Edward Teller: The Real Dr. Strangelove* (Cambridge: Harvard University Press, 2004).

29. Herken, *Brotherhood*, 64–67; 117–18.

30. Panel of Consultants, "The Timing of The Thermonuclear Test," *FRUS, 1952–54*, 2: 994–1008; for the NSC consideration of the proposal, see Minutes of the Special NSC Committee, 9 Oct. 1952, *FRUS, 1952–54*, 2: 1033–37; Barton J. Bernstein concludes in his study of this episode that "because of the domestic political consensus and the views of the Truman administration itself, there was no likelihood that this 1952 proposal could have won acceptance in the United States." See Bernstein, "Crossing the Rubicon: A Missed Opportunity to Stop the H-Bomb?" *International Security*, 14 (Fall 1989): 132–160.

31. Hewlett and Holl, *Atoms for Peace and War 1953–1961*, 47–50, 57; Pfau, *No Sacrifice Too Great*, 137–38; Gregg Herken, *Brotherhood of the Bomb: The Tangled Lives and Loyalties of Robert Oppenheimer, Ernest Lawrence, and Edward Teller* (New York: Holt, 2002), 263.

32. Bethe to Rabinowitch, 9 June 1953, HAB, Box 12, F14 (R); and Bethe to Rabinowitch, July 20, 1953, HAB, Box 10, F9 (BAS).

33. SAC attempted to detach itself from the ODM and place itself under the NSC during the summer of 1952, but Truman rejected their request; see Herken, *Cardinal Choices*, 54–65. California Institute of Technology (Cal Tech) physicist Lee DuBridge served as the chairman of SAC until Rabi replaced him in 1956. Others joining Killian, Oppenheimer, Rabi, Conant, and DuBridge on the committee were two other physicists from Cal Tech, Robert Bacher and Charles Lauritsen; physicist and president of the National Academy of Sciences Detlev Bronk; electrical engineer Oliver Buckely and physicist James Fisk of Bell Laboratories, physicist Hugh Dryden; physician Robert Loeb of Columbia; metallurgist Bruce Old of Arthur Little, Inc.; chemist Charles Thomas of the Monsanto Chemical Corporation; physicist Alan T. Waterman of the National Science Foundation; chemical engineer Walter Whitman of MIT; and physicist Jerrold R. Zacharias of MIT. Conant and Oppenheimer both resigned from the committee soon after Eisenhower took office, Conant in 1953 and Oppenheimer in 1954. Rabi and Killian stayed on, playing central roles in the 1957 elevation of presidential science advising. For an assessment of the limited influence of SAC/ODM in this period, see Richard V. Damms, "James Killian, the Technological Capabilities Panel, and the Emergence of President Eisenhower's 'Scientific-Technological Elite,'" *Diplomatic History* 24 (Winter 2000): 57–78.

34. Lee A DuBridge to Members of SAC, 20 May 1953, IIR, Box 43, ODM 1951–56.

35. Flemming to Eisenhower, 12 May 1954, DDEL, AWF, OFA, Flemming 1953–1955 (3); Eisenhower to Dulles, 14 May 1954, DDEL, AWF, DS (microfilm) 4:361; Dulles to Eisenhower, 17 May 1954, DDEL, JFD, CS, Box 7, JFD Chron May 1954 [3]. Flemming to Eisenhower, 21 June 1953, DDEL, AWF, D-H, Box 4, JFD.

36. Strauss, Memorandum for Files, 16 Sep. 1953, LLS, AEC, Box 66, MFR.

37. S. S. Schweber, *In the Shadow of the Bomb: Bethe, Oppenheimer, and*

the Moral Responsibility of the Scientist (Princeton: Princeton University Press, 2000).

38. Bethe to Gordon Dean, 9 Sep. 1952, DOE/NTA, Accession # NV0073974.

39. Bethe's original letter to Strauss, dated 30 Dec. 1954, is not part of the Strauss papers at the Hoover Library or part of Bethe's papers at Cornell. From Strauss's reply, Bethe's original letter likely proposed establishing a similar committee of U.S. scientists not affiliated with the U.S. weapons program to assess the debris from U.S. tests, perhaps with the idea that those scientists could develop a pool of expertise that could then assist in the analysis of Soviet tests. Strauss to Bethe, 5 Jan. 1954 and 13 Jan. 1954, both in LLS, AEC, Box 9, Bethe, 1950–59. Allen Dulles to Strauss, 12 Jan. 1954, LLS, AEC, Box 9, Bethe, 1950–59.

40. J. Edgar Hoover to Strauss, 4 Feb. 1954, LLS, AEC, Box 9, Bethe, 1950–59.

41. John Rigden, *Rabi: Scientist and Citizen* (New York: Basic Books, 1987), 238–39.

42. Bernstein, "Crossing the Rubicon," 135–37.

43. Rabinowitch to Rabi, 21 Oct. 1953 and Ruth Adams to Rabi, 30 Nov. 1953 both in IIR, Box 17, BAS.

44. For a discussion of Strauss's efforts to inform Eisenhower about his suspicions of Oppenheimer before their private meeting, see Hewlett and Holl, *Atoms for Peace and War 1953–1961,* 51–52; Herken, *Brotherhood,* 263; and Pfau, *No Sacrifice Too Great,* 139–40.

45. Piers Brendon, *Ike: His Life and Times* (New York: Harper & Row, 1986), 255.

46. Robert R. Bowie and Richard H. Immerman, *Waging Peace: How Eisenhower Shaped an Enduring Cold War Strategy* (New York: Oxford University Press, 1998). Campbell Craig emphasizes the differences in the strategic thoughts of Dulles and Eisenhower, characterizing the latter's strategy as "nuclear evasion." In Craig's analysis, Eisenhower dwelled on the horrific consequences of nuclear war to restrain the more aggressive approaches of his advisors. See Craig, *Destroying the Village: Eisenhower and Thermonuclear War* (New York: Columbia University Press, 1998).

47. For an analysis of the formulation and acceptance of NSC-68, see Ernest R. May, ed., *American Cold War Strategy: Interpreting NSC 68* (Boston: St. Martin's Press, 1993). For a study of the New Look that begins with an analysis of the Eisenhower administration's assessment of the Truman administration's national security strategy, see Bowie and Immerman, *Waging Peace.* For comments on the other components of the New Look, see Walter LaFeber, *America, Russia, and the Cold War, 1945–2000* 9th ed. (New York: McGraw Hill, 2002). For Eisenhower's early recognition of the limits of massive retaliation, see Eisenhower to Dulles, 15 Apr. 1952, *PDDE* 13: 1178–81.

48. For an analysis of Eisenhower's limitations on atomic threats, see Andrew P. N. Erdman, "'War No Longer Has Any Logic Whatever': Dwight D. Eisenhower and the Thermonuclear Revolution," in *Cold War Statesmen Confront the Bomb: Nuclear Diplomacy since 1945,* eds. John L. Gaddis et. al. (New York:

Oxford University Press, 1999). As Gordon Chang notes, the administration's continual threats against Communist China served to spur their own development of atomic weapons, see Gordon Chang, *Friends and Enemies: The United States, China, and the Soviet Union, 1948–1972* (Stanford: Stanford University Press, 1990), 139–142.

49. Eisenhower, *Crusade in Europe*, 443.

50. Memorandum of Discussion at the 131st Meeting of the NSC, 11 Feb. 1953, *FRUS, 1952–54*, 15: 769–72; Memorandum of Discussion at the 143rd Meeting of the NSC, 6 May 1953, ibid., 975–79.

51. Memorandum of Discussion at a Special Meeting of the NSC, 31 Mar. 1953, ibid., 825–27.

52. Memorandum of Discussion at the 144th Meeting of the NSC, 13 May 1953, ibid., 1012–17.

53. One could argue that these are examples of the speculative ruminations that Eisenhower was prone to offer. The consistency of his advocacy of tactical atomic weapons in Korea, however, suggests that he was doing more than simply thinking aloud or attempting to foster debate about all available options.

54. Ambrose, *Eisenhower*, 2: 184, 688 n. 95.

55. The quote reappears in the textbook of a usually careful analyst, Walter LaFeber, *The American Age: U.S. Foreign Policy at Home and Abroad* 2nd ed. (New York: Norton, 1994), 550. A recent example of a biographer repeating this passage is Tom Wicker, *Eisenhower* (New York: Times Books, 2002), 34. Wicker does responsibly mention in a footnote that Eisenhower's remembered words do not comport with other evidences of his views at the time. Although it appears that Ambrose uncritically accepted Eisenhower's recollection of this episode, he has shrewdly identified a previous effort of Eisenhower to recast his past. Ambrose reveals that Eisenhower's remembrance of his 1945 efforts to warn Roosevelt about the Soviets are at odds with his very optimistic attitude in 1945 toward maintaining good relations with the Soviet Union. See Eisenhower, *At Ease*, 264, 267–268; Ambrose, *Eisenhower*, 1: 402–4.

56. Eisenhower, *Mandate*, 178–81. Although Eisenhower did not approve NSC 162/2, which codified the New Look, until October 1953, the ideas therein were present earlier in the year when the administration issued its veiled threats.

57. James Shepley, "How Dulles Averted War," *Life* (16 Jan. 1956): 70–72.

58. For skeptical views of the effectiveness of Eisenhower's threats, see Rosemary J. Foot, "Nuclear Coercion and the Ending of the Korean Conflict," *International Security* 13 (Winter 1988/1989): 92–112; Sean L. Malloy, "A 'Paper Tiger?' Nuclear Weapons, Atomic Diplomacy, and the Korean War," *The New England Journal of History* 60 (Fall 2003-Spring 2004): 227–52; and Edward C. Keefer, "President Dwight D. Eisenhower and the End of the Korean War," *Diplomatic History* 10 (Summer 1986): 267–89. For contrary views that support Dulles's claim, see Michael Schaller, "U.S. Policy in the Korean War," *International Security* 11 (Winter 1986–1987): 162–66; Daniel Calingaert, "Nuclear Weapons and the Korean War," *Journal of Strategic Studies* 11 (June 1988): 177–202. For contingency planning on the use of A-bombs in the expansion of the war see Conrad C. Crane, "To Avert Impending Disaster: American Military

Plans to Use Atomic Weapons During the Korea War," *Journal of Strategic Studies* 23 (June 2000): 72–88 and *American Airpower Strategy in Korea, 1950–1953* (Lawrence: University Press of Kansas, 2000).

59. Eisenhower, *Mandate*, 178–181. Memo of Discussion at the 156th Meeting of the NSC, 23 July 1953, *FRUS, 1952–54*, 15: 1420–1423.

60. Eisenhower Press Conference, 16 Mar. 1955, *PPP, Eisenhower, 1955*, 332.

61. Eisenhower Press Conference, 23 Mar. 1955, ibid., 358. See Eisenhower's comments in his memoirs that he hoped his press conference comments would "have some effect in persuading the Chinese Communists of the strength of our determination." Eisenhower also reveals in his memoirs that he told his Press Secretary, Jim Hagerty, that if that question came up, he would "just confuse them." Eisenhower, *Mandate for Change*, 477–78.

62. Ambrose, *Eisenhower*, 2: 244–45.

63. Eisenhower, *Mandate for Change*, 483.

64. Ambrose agreed with Robert Divine's earlier analysis that Eisenhower's approach maintained his flexibility. According to Divine, "the beauty of Eisenhower's policy is that to this day no one can be sure whether or not he would have responded militarily to an invasion of the offshore islands, and whether he would have used nuclear weapons." Divine, *Eisenhower and the Cold War* (New York: Oxford University Press, 1981), 61–66.

65. Gordon Chang's analysis of this episode, using additional declassified documents, concludes that, though Eisenhower's public remarks were ambiguous, there was no ambiguity in Eisenhower's own mind about whether or not he would use nuclear weapons; he was willing and prepared to use them to defend Taiwan if deterrence failed. Moreover, the ambiguity served to embolden the Communist Chinese rather than give them sober pause. See Chang, *Friends and Enemies*, 116–142.

66. For Eisenhower's comments on the Bonus March, see Eisenhower, *At Ease*, 215–18. For a valuable discussion on the use of memoirs and other remembrances as sources, see Bernstein, "Ike and Hiroshima," 384–85 and Bernstein, "Reconsidering the 'Atomic General': Leslie R. Groves," *Journal of Military History* 67 (July 2003): 883–920.

67. An earlier version of this section appeared as part of an essay in the *Journal of Strategic Studies* (http://www.tandf.co.uk.). Greene, "Eisenhower, Science and the Test Ban Debate, 1953–1956."

68. Hewlett and Holl, *Atoms for Peace and War 1953–1961*, 1–17, 54–59.

69. Eisenhower to Churchill, 19 Mar. 1954, NAUK, PREM 11/1074.

70. Memorandum of Discussion at the 146th Meeting of the NSC, 27 May 1953, *FRUS, 1952–54*, 2: 1169–74.

71. Memorandum of Discussion at the 134th Meeting of the NSC, 25 Feb. 1953, ibid., 1110–14.

72. Memorandum of Discussion at the 146th Meeting of the NSC, 27 May 1953, ibid., 1169–74. For an analysis of the administration's recognition of the importance and the power of ideas and words, see Ira Chernus, "Operation Candor: Fear, Faith, and Flexibility," *Diplomatic History* 29 (Nov. 2005): 779–809.

73. Herken, *Brotherhood*, 263; Hewlett and Holl, *Atoms for Peace and War 1953–1961*, 54–55, 59; Dean to Eisenhower, 17 June 1953, DDEL, AWF, OFA (microfilm), 3:935.

74. The best examination of the Soviet nuclear development is David Holloway, *Stalin and the Bomb: The Soviet Union and Atomic Energy 1939–1956* (New Haven, Yale University Press, 1994), 303–9.

75. Eisenhower to Jackson, 24 Aug. 1953, DDEL, AWF, OFA, Candor (1) (microfilm), 8:584.

76. Cutler to Strauss, 10 Sep. 1953, DDEL, AWF, OFA, Atoms for Peace (microfilm), 4:720.

77. Eisenhower to Dulles, 8 Sep. 1953, DDEL, JFD, WHMS, (microfilm), 1:076.

78. Cutler to Strauss, 10 Sep. 1953, DDEL, AWF, OFA, Atoms for Peace, (microfilm), 4:720.

79. Eisenhower to C. D. Jackson, 31 Dec 53, DDEL, AWF, OFA (Jackson). For interpretations of Eisenhower's consideration of preventive war, see Russell D. Buhite and W. Christopher Hamel, "War for Peace: The Question of an American Preventive War against the Soviet Union, 1945–1955," *Diplomatic History* 14 (Summer 1990): 379–84; Bundy, *Danger and Survival*, 250–55; Bowie and Immerman, *Waging Peace*, 164–65, 203–5; Ira Chernus, *Eisenhower's Atoms for Peace* (College Station: Texas A&M Press, 2002), 60–65; Craig, *Destroying the Village*, 44–49.

80. Cutler to Strauss and Jackson, 10 Sep. 1953, DDEL, AWF, OFA, Atoms for Peace (microfilm), 4:717.

81. Eisenhower Diary Entry, 10 Dec. 1953, DDEL, AWF, DS (microfilm), 5:491.

82. Strauss, *Men and Decisions*, 357; Strauss to Eisenhower, 17 Sep. 1953, DDEL, AWF, OFA, Atoms for Peace (microfilm), 4:718.

83. Jackson to Dulles, 25 Sep. 1953, DDEL, JFD, WHMS, General Foreign Policy Subseries (4) (microfilm), 5:429. See also Jackson to Eisenhower, 2 Oct. 1953, DDEL, AWF, OFA, Candor (1), (microfilm) 8:607.

84. Hewlett and Holl, *Atoms for Peace and War 1953–1961*, 66, 602 n. 83. Ambrose, *Eisenhower*, 2:131–35.

85. Ambrose, *Eisenhower*, 2:147–51. For an analysis of the arms control component of Atoms for Peace, see Henry Sokolski, "The Arms Control Connection," in Joseph F. Pilat et. al., eds., *Atoms for Peace: An Analysis after 30 Years* (Boulder: Westview Press, 1985). Alternate views include McGeorge Bundy, *Danger and Survival: Choices about the Bomb in the First Fifty Years* (New York: Random House, 1988), 328–34; Bundy argues that Atoms for Peace was essentially an internally developed gimmick. Ira Chernus contends that there was no sincere disarmament component of Atoms for Peace. Instead, its main purpose was to gain the support of the European allies for the New Look. See Chernus, *Eisenhower's Atoms for Peace*.

86. Memorandum of Conference, 4 Dec. 1953, *FRUS, 1952–54*, 5:1750–54.

87. Eisenhower to Swede Hazlett, 24 Dec. 1953, DDEL, AWF, DS, (microfilm), 2:647.

88. Eisenhower diary entry 10 Dec. 1953, DDEL, AWF, DS, (microfilm), 5:491.

89. Dwight D. Eisenhower to Milton Eisenhower, 11 Dec. 1953, DDEL, AWF, DS (microfilm), 2:720.

90. Eisenhower Press Conference, 16 Dec. 1953, *PPP: Eisenhower, 1953,* 831–40.

91. Eisenhower to Swede Hazlett, 24 Dec. 1953, DDEL, AWF, DS (microfilm), 2:647.

92. Eisenhower diary entry 10 Dec. 1953, DDEL, AWF, DS (microfilm), 5:491.

93. Teller to Strauss, 11 Dec. 1953, LLS, AEC, Box 111, Teller 1948–53.

94. Telegram, Hans Bethe to Federation of American Scientists, 9 Dec. 1953, HAB, Box 10, F31 (Federation of Atomic Scientists).

95. Strauss's emphasis, Strauss, *Men and Decisions,* 336–37. For a view skeptical that this conversation took place as Strauss described it his memoirs, see Chernus, *Eisenhower's Atoms for Peace,* 40. For a recent use of this quote to illustrate Eisenhower's early commitment to arms control, see Bowie and Immerman, *Waging Peace,* 223.

Chapter 3

EPIGRAPHS: Eisenhower Press Conference, 24 Mar. 1954, *PPP, Eisenhower, 1954:* 342, 346; Joseph and Stewart Alsop, "Do We Need Scientists?" *New York Herald-Tribune,* 1 Oct. 1954.

1. Divine, 12–13; *NYT,* 29 Mar. 1954, 1 Apr. 1954, and 3 Apr. 1954.

2. Churchill to Eisenhower, 29 Mar. 1954, DDEL, AWF, DS (microfilm), 3:621.

3. *NYT,* 31 Mar. 1954.

4. United States, Department of State, *Documents on Disarmament, 1954–59* (Washington: G.P.O, 1960), 1:409, 411.

5. Eisenhower Press Conference, 24 Mar. 1954, *PPP, Eisenhower, 1954:* 342, 346.

6. Strauss failed to mention that officials identified the wind shift before the shot, but proceeded with the test anyway, nor did he mention that the evacuation of exposed islanders occurred two days after the blast. See Smith, "The Nuclear Testing Policies of the Eisenhower Administration, 1953–1960," 45–49, 68–77. Divine, *Blowing on the Wind,* 9–13.

7. James C. Hagerty, *The Diary of James C. Hagerty: Eisenhower in Mid-Course, 1954–55,* ed. Robert H. Ferrell (Bloomington: Indiana University Press, 1983), 36–37.

8. Divine, *Blowing on the Wind,* 25–27.

9. Gallup, *The Gallup Poll: Public Opinion, 1935–1971,* 2: 1229, 1322.

10. Telegram, Compton to Eisenhower, 30 Mar. 1954, DDEL, WHCF, OF, Box 525, OF108-A (2).

11. Argonne was a cooperative venture of several Midwestern universi-

ties funded by the AEC. Inglis to Bowie, 14 May 1954, NAII, RG59, Dec File, 600.0012, 1950–1954, Box 2564; Inglis to Strauss, 17 May 1954, LLS, AEC, Box 44, Inglis; Inglis to W. B. Smith, 18 Apr. 1954, NAII, RG59, Dec File, 600.0012, 1950–54, Box 2564; Inglis to G Smith, 23 June 1954, NAII, RG59, Rec Rel A/E Matters, Lot 57D688, 3008B, Box 348, Inglis to Gerald Morgan, 25 June 1954, LLS, AEC, Box 44, Inglis.

12. David R. Inglis, "H-Bomb Control," *Nation* 179 (24 July 1954): 67–70. Inglis, "Ban H-Bomb Tests and Favor the Defense," *BAS* 10 (Nov. 1954): 353–56.

13. The three-member Personnel Security Board declared Oppenheimer a security risk and recommended that his clearance not be renewed. The AEC, finding Oppenheimer guilty not of disloyalty but of fundamental defects in his character, voted to uphold this board's decision by a vote of 4–1. Bird and Sherwin, *American Prometheus*, 462–550.

14. *NYT*, 1 July 1954.

15. *NYT*, 4 July 1954.

16. Herken, *Brotherhood*, 297–99.

17. Eisenhower quoted on 10 Apr. 1954 in *The Diary of James C. Hagerty*, 43.

18. Conant had returned to Washington to testify on Oppenheimer's behalf, a move strongly discouraged by John Foster Dulles. See James Hershberg, *James B. Conant: Harvard to Hiroshima and the Making of the Nuclear Age* (New York: Alfred A. Knopf, 1993), 676–82. As Stephen Ambrose points out, this is another case where Eisenhower's memoirs conflict with the historical record. In his memoirs, Eisenhower contends that he gave no weight to Oppenheimer's opposition to the H-bomb in deciding to proceed with the loyalty-security case. See Eisenhower, *Mandate*, 312. His unsent letter to Conant suggests otherwise. See Eisenhower to Conant, 26 Apr. 1954, DDEL, AWF, OFA, Box 10 Conant (1). See also Ambrose, *Eisenhower*, 2:167.

19. Ambrose, *Eisenhower*, 2:170.

20. Bethe sent the telegram in his capacity as the president of the American Physical Society, 19 Apr. 1954 in HAB, Box 12, F5 (Oppenheimer Case).

21. Strauss to Bethe, 3 July 1954, HAB, Box 9, F53 (AEC - 3).

22. Joseph and Stewart Alsop, "We Accuse," *Harper's* (Oct. 1954): 25–45.

23. Quoted in *Time* (8 Nov. 1954): 25–27.

24. Vannevar Bush, "If We Alienate Our Scientists," *NYT*, 13 June 1954. *NYT*, 19 Oct. 1954.

25. For a discussion of Oppenheimer's relative absence from public life following the hearing, see Bird and Sherwin, 551–78.

26. Oppenheimer, 5 Jan. 1955, NAII, RG59, 600.0012/1–1155.

27. *NYT*, 31 May 1955.

28. Oppenheimer, Memorandum to File, 5 Jan. 1955, NAII, RG59, 600.0012/1–1155.

29. Oppenheimer to Dulles, 11 Jan. 1955, NAII, RG 59 Dec File, 600.0012, 1950–54, 1–1155, Box 2565.

30. Strauss, 17 Jan. 1955, LLS, AEC, Box 26A, JF Dulles.

31. Smith to Key, 17 Jan. 1955, NAII, RG59, 600.0012/1–1155; Key to Oppenheimer, 4 Feb. 1955, ibid.

32. Oppenheimer, Memorandum to File, 5 Jan. 1955, ibid. The Soviet launch of *Sputnik* led to a failed effort by some members of Congress to return Oppenheimer's advisory role.

33. See Memorandum of Conversation, Dulles and British Ambassador to the United States, Sir Roger M. Makins, 5 Nov. 1954, DDEL, OSAD, Box 5, Moratorium 1955 (1); Memorandum of Conversation, Dulles and French Premier Mendes-France, 20 Nov. 1954, NAII, RG 59, Rec Rel A/E Matters, Lot 57D688, Box 348; State Department Position Paper, 18 Feb. 1955, DDEL, OSAD, Box 5, Moratorium 1955 (1).

34. Studies by Roger Dingman and Martha Smith-Norris assess the impact of the *BRAVO* test on Japanese-American relations in great detail. See Roger Dingman, "Alliance in Crisis: The Lucky Dragon Incident and Japanese-American Relations" in *The Great Powers in East Asia, 1953–1960,* eds. Warren Cohen and Akira Iriye (New York: Columbia University Press, 1990), 187–214; Martha Smith-Norris, "Only as Dust in the Face of the Wind: An Analysis of the *BRAVO* Nuclear Incident in the Pacific, 1954," *Journal of American-East Asian Relations* 6 (Spring 1997): 1–34. See also Smith, "The Nuclear Testing Policies of the Eisenhower Administration, 1953–1960," 93–129, 215–41.

35. *The Diary of James C. Hagerty,* 40–42.

36. Frank Wisner to Strauss, 29 Apr. 1954, LLS, AEC, Box 28, Fortunate Dragon.

37. Strauss to Helms, 6 Oct. 1966, LLS, AEC, Box 5, CIA. Helms responded four days later that the CIA would "pursue it," see Helms to Strauss, 10 Oct. 1966, ibid. There is no further evidence of a reopened investigation in the Strauss papers at the Hoover Library.

38. The FBI concluded that Dalton Trumbo, one of the "Hollywood Ten" cited in 1947 for contempt by the HUAC was the source of one series of "chain letters." See J. Edgar Hoover to Cutler, 29 Apr. 1954, DDEL, OSANSA, FBI Series, Box 1 C (1).

39. For OCB suggestions for an atomic reactor in Hiroshima see 24 Mar. 1954, *DDRS,* 2000–1504.

40. Telegram from Dulles to the U.S. Embassy in Tokyo, 7 Apr. 1954 cited in Smith, 51.

41. Dingman, 187–214; Smith-Norris, "Only as Dust in the Face of the Wind," 1–34, and Smith, "The Nuclear Testing Policies of the Eisenhower Administration, 1953–1960," 93–129, 215–41. The United States never seriously considered Edward Teller's proposal to conduct the largest tests in Alaska rather than the Pacific proving ground; see Herken, *Brotherhood,* 303.

42. Quoted in Divine, *Blowing on the Wind,* 20.

43. For more on the fate of the Marshallese and the debate in the UN Trusteeship Council, see Smith, "The Nuclear Testing Policies of the Eisenhower Administration, 1953–1960," 68–77, 215–21.

44. *NYT,* 19 Apr. 1954.

45. Telephone Conversation, Dulles and Stassen, 28 Dec. 1955, DDEL, JFD, TC, Box 4, Sep-Dec '55 [1].

46. *NYT*, 25 Dec. 1955.

47. Strauss to Dulles, 27 Dec. 1955, LLS, AEC, Box 26A, Dulles, JF. Although Dulles denied the original request, Strauss eventually prevailed, visiting the Pope himself on 17 Apr. 1956. See Strauss Memorandum for Files, 17 Apr. 1956, LLS, AEC, Box 83, Pope Pius XII.

48. For more on the origins and purpose of the OCB, see Bowie and Immerman, 93–95. OCB Progress Report, 1 Dec. 1954, DDEL, NSCS, OCB Central Files, Box 8, OCB 000.9 A/E File 2 (6).

49. Bethe to Citizens for Reason, 13 Apr. 1955, HAB, Box 10, Folder 9, C(3); Motoharu Kimura to Bethe, 3 Oct. 1954, HAB, Box 11, Folder 5, K[3].

50. Divine, *Blowing on the Wind* , 37. Strauss Memorandum of Conversation, 7 Feb. 1955, LLS, AEC, Box 66, MFR.

51. Strauss to Eisenhower, 9 Feb. 1954, DDEL, AWF, OFA (microfilm) 4:332. Smith blames Strauss for the delay, contending that the main reason for its eventual release was to "beat the British to the punch," see Smith, "The Nuclear Testing Policies of the Eisenhower Administration, 1953–1960," 135–41.

52. For evidence that Strauss wanted to release the report in 1954, but was blocked by Dulles, see Gerald Smith, 26 Oct. 1954, NAII, RG 59, Lot 68D349, Subj Files of S/AE, 1950–66; Strauss Memorandum for Record, 10 Dec. 1954, LLS, AEC, Box 66, MFR 1954; Strauss to Eisenhower, 10 Dec. 1954, DDEL, AWF, OFA, (microfilm) 3:743.

53. Ralph Lapp also charged the administration with keeping "secret the facts about fallout—a life-and-death importance to millions of Americans." See Ralph Lapp, "Fallout and Candor," *BAS* 11 (May 1955): 170, 200.

54. The AEC report itself is in NAII, RG 59, Lot 68D349, Box 4, Fallout Studies 1956. The most thorough analysis of this episode is Hewlett and Holl, *Atoms for Peace and War 1953–1961*, 279–87.

55. Quoted in Divine, *Blowing on the Wind,* 44–46.

56. Ibid. Smith, "The Nuclear Testing Policies of the Eisenhower Administration, 1953–1960," 154–158.

57. Ibid.

58. *NYT*, 8 Apr. 1955.

59. *NYT*, 9 Apr. 1955. Hewlett and Holl, *Atoms for Peace and War 1953–1961*, 278–84.

60. *NYT*, 8 and 9 Apr. 1955. Hewlett and Holl, *Atoms for Peace and War 1953–1961*, 278–84.

61. Rusk to Eisenhower, 23 Feb. 1955, DDEL, WHCF, OF, Box 525, OF 108-A (2). Ironically, Rusk visited Eisenhower at Gettysburg eight years later in an effort to gain the former president's endorsement for the ratification of the Limited Test Ban Treaty.

62. Staats to Hirsch, 15 Apr. 1955, DDEL, NSCS, OCB Central Files, Box 9, OCB 000.9 (File 3) 1; OCB Progress Report, 20 June 1955, *DDRS*, (Sep. 22, 2000) 1984–176.

63. *NYT*, 8 Apr. 1955. As Hewlett and Holl point out, Warren continued to

refute the exaggerated claims about radiation hazards, but even he became leery of the military necessity for further atmospheric tests. See Hewlett and Holl, *Atoms for Peace and War 1953–1961*, 377, 454–55, 472–73. Divine, *Blowing on the Wind*, 63–65.

64. Divine, *Blowing on the Wind*, 321–22.

Chapter 4

EPIGRAPH: Memorandum of Discussion at the 195th Meeting of the NSC, 6 May 1954, *FRUS, 1952–54*, 2: 1423–29.

1. An earlier version of this section appeared as part of an essay in the *Journal of Strategic Studies* (http://www.tandf.co.uk.). Greene, "Eisenhower, Science and the Test Ban Debate, 1953–1956."

2. Writing before the declassification of the pertinent documents, Robert Divine mentions the secret 1954 deliberations on a test ban in a single paragraph, see Divine, *Blowing on the Wind*, 24–25. According to Hewlett and Holl, Eisenhower was "genuinely disappointed" that a nuclear test ban appeared unenforceable at the time, see Hewlett and Holl, *Atoms for Peace and War 1953–1961*, 222–225, 274–76. Challenging Hewlett and Holl's interpretation, Martha Smith argues that "there is little evidence" to support their conclusion that Eisenhower favored a test ban. In her view, Dulles reversed his initial position in support of a ban because he sensed that Eisenhower opposed a test ban and Dulles did not want to conflict with him. Smith bases her analysis on the circumstantial evidence that Eisenhower committed his administration to the "New Look" and its emphasis on maintaining nuclear superiority during the same period. She ignores the substantial evidence that Eisenhower was also favorably inclined to a test ban without attempting to reconcile these seemingly contradictory goals. See Smith, "The Nuclear Testing Policies of the Eisenhower Administration, 1953–1960," 93–129.

3. Memo of telephone conversation, Dulles and Strauss, 29 Mar. 1954, DDEL, JFD, TC, microfilm, (2:234).

4. Hewlett and Holl, 274–75. Dulles handwritten note to Eisenhower, 6 Apr. 1954, LLS, AEC, box26D, Eisenhower. Unaware that Eisenhower had already directed a study of the matter, Henry Cabot Lodge, Jr., the U.S. Representative at the United Nations, suggested that the United States should consider limiting detectable tests on large weapons to ease pressures building in the United Nations for adopting Nehru's proposal. See Lodge to Department of State, 12 Apr. 1954, *FRUS, 1952–54*, 2: 1383. Dulles replied that he had already discussed a test ban with Eisenhower and the British. Dulles commented, "this is an area where we have a chance to get a big propaganda advantage—and perhaps results." See Dulles to Lodge, 20 Apr. 1954, ibid., 1387.

5. Dulles memo of conversation, 12 Apr. 1954, DDEL, JFD, WHMS, Box 1, Meetings with the President, 1954 (4); Department of State, Memorandum of Conversation, 12 Apr. 1954, NAII, RG59, Executive Secretariat, Conference Files 1949–1963, Box 46, CF 287.

6. Dulles Memo of conference with Eisenhower, 19 Apr. 1954, DDEL, JFD, WHMS, CS, Box 1, Meetings with the President, 1954 (3).

7. Dulles to Wilson, Strauss, and Department of State, 2 May 1954, *FRUS, 1952–54,* 2:1418.

8. Meeting of the NSC, 6 May 1954, *FRUS, 1952–54,* 2: 1423–29.

9. Meeting of the Cambridge-New York Group of the Science Advisory Committee, 10 Mar. 1954, C-K, Box 195, Science Advisory Committee, 1954. Damms, "James Killian, the Technological Capabilities Panel, and the Emergence of President Eisenhower's 'Scientific-Technological Elite,'" 62–64.

10. Memorandum of Phone Message, I. I. Rabi, 8 Apr. 1954, LLS, AEC, Box 92, Rabi. Rabi to Strauss, 14 June 1954, IIR, Box 7, Strauss.

11. Flemming to Eisenhower, 12 May 1954, DDEL, AWF, OFA, Flemming 1953–55 (3).

12. Eisenhower to Dulles, 14 May 1954, DDEL, AWF, DS (microfilm) 4:361; Dulles to Eisenhower, 17 May 1954, DDEL, JFD, CS, Box 7, JFD Chron May 1954 [3].

13. Hewlett and Holl, *Atoms for Peace and War 1953–1961,* 274–76. Bradbury to Strauss, 11 June 1954, LLS, AEC, Box 26, DDE.

14. Dulles, memo of conversation with Eisenhower, 11 May 1954, DDEL, JFD, WHMS, CS, Box 1, Meetings with President, 1954 (3); Memo, Dulles to Eisenhower, May 17, 1954, DDEL, AWF, D-H, Box 3, JFD, May 1954 (2). For a State Department memoranda that indicates that Eisenhower was favorably inclined to pursue a test ban, see Gerald C. Smith (Special Assistant to the Secretary of State for Atomic Energy Affairs), Memorandum for the File, 25 May 1954, NAII, RG59, Rec Rel A/E Matters, Lot 57D688, Box 348 and Smith, Memorandum for the File, 15 June 1954, ibid.

15. Hewlett and Holl, *Atoms for Peace and War 1953–1961,* 222–25; Merchant to Bowie, 25 May 1954, *FRUS, 1952–54,* 2: 1448; Dulles to Anderson, Strauss, and Allen Dulles, 26 May 1954, *FRUS, 1952–54,* 2: 1448–49.

16. Memo of Discussion at the 199th Meeting of the NSC, 27 May 1954, in *FRUS, 1952–54,* 2: 1452–56; for impact of Eisenhower's comments see also Rowland Hughes to Eisenhower, 1 June 1954, DDEL, AWF, DS (microfilm), 4:727.

17. Memo of Discussion at the 203rd Meeting of the NSC, 23 June 1954, *FRUS, 1952–54,* 2: 1467–72.

18. Memo of meeting, 25 June 1954, *FRUS, 1952–54,* 6 (*Western Europe and Canada*): 1085–86; Dulles memo of conversation with Eisenhower, 11 May 1954, DDEL, JFD, WHMS, CS, Box 1, Meetings with President, 1954 (3); Hewlett and Holl, *Atoms for Peace and War 1953–1961,* 276.

19. Dulles to NSC, 23 June 1954, *FRUS, 1952–54,* 2: 1463–67; Memo of Discussion at the 203d Meeting of the NSC, 23 June 1954, *FRUS, 1952–54,* 2: 1467–72.

20. Hewlett and Holl, *Atoms for Peace and War 1953–1961,* 203, 243.

21. Murray to Eisenhower, 4 Jan. 1954, DDEL, AWF, OFA, (microfilm) 3:911; Eisenhower to Strauss, 4 Jan. 1954, DDEL, AWF, DS, (microfilm) 3:538;

Strauss to Murray, undated, DDEL, AWF, OFA, (microfilm) 3:900; Alberta (last name unknown) to Sherman Adams, undated, ibid. Smith 116–17.

22. Murray to Eisenhower, 5 Feb. 1954, DDEL, AWF, OFA (microfilm) 3:885.

23. Strauss draft, 10 Feb. 1954, DDEL, AWF, OFA (microfilm) 3:882; Eisenhower's reply is unchanged from Strauss's draft, Eisenhower to Murray, 11 Feb. 1954, DDEL, AWF, DS, Box 5; 2/54 (1). Hewlett and Holl, *Atoms for Peace and War 1953–1961*, 223.

24. Record of Telephone Conversation, 18 Oct. 1956, DDEL, JFD, TC, WH (microfilm), 9:806.

25. Memorandum of Telephone Conversation, Dulles and Strauss, 9 Dec. 1954, DDEL, JFD, TC (microfilm) 3:088. Strauss's account of the conversation is in LLS, AEC, Box 66, MFR 1954.

26. Memorandum of Conversation, Dulles and Murray, 14 Dec. 1954, NAII, RG 59, Rec Rel A/E Matters, Lot 57D688, 3008B, Box 348, 18.14, NM, 54–5.

27. Memorandum of Telephone Conversation Dulles and McCardle, 22 Dec. 1954, DDEL, JFD, TC, Box 3, Nov-Dec '54 [2].

28. Murray to Eisenhower, 14 Mar. 1955, DDEL, NSCS, Exec Sec Subj File Series, Box 6, #20 Moratorium on Tests [1].

29. Eisenhower to Cutler, 15 Mar. 1955, DDEL, AWF, OFA, Cutler (microfilm), 9:351.

30. Fisk was also a member of SAC and the AEC's GAC. Discussion at the 241st Meeting of the NSC, 17 Mar. 1955, *DDRS*, 1996–229.

31. According to Richard Damms, Killian sought to use the committee to convince Eisenhower of the necessity of expanding his range of science advice beyond Strauss. In Damms's view, Killian also sought to improve the relationship between government and science after the divisive Oppenheimer case. See Damms, "James Killian, the Technological Capabilities Panel, and the Emergence of President Eisenhower's 'Scientific-Technological Elite,'" 57–78.

32. Beckler to Flemming, 24 Mar. 1955, DDEL, AWF, OFA, Flemming (2).

33. Lawrence sought in 1939 Strauss's help in raising funds for his hundred-million volt cyclotron. Although Strauss provided only minor assistance, the two developed a lasting friendship forged in battle over the H-bomb decision and other atomic energy issues. Pfau, *No Sacrifice Too Great*, 54–55. Strauss, *Men and Decisions*, 165–66, 241–42.

34. Strauss, Memorandum of Conversation, 21 Mar. 1955, LLS, AEC, Box 66, MFR; Goodpaster, Memorandum of Conversation, 21 Mar. 1955, DDEL, AWF, Ann Whitman Diary Series, Box 4, ACW Diary March 1955 [3].

35. 25 Mar. 1955, DDEL, NSCS, Exec Sec Subj File Series, Box 6, #20 Moratorium on Tests [2].

36. Memo of Discussion at the 161st Meeting of the NSC, 9 Sep. 1953, *FRUS, 1952–54*, 2:1210–12.

37. Memo of Discussion at the 236th Meeting of the NSC, 10 Feb. 1955, *FRUS, 1955–57*, 20 (*Regulation of Armaments; Atomic Energy*): 20–35. Herken, *Brotherhood*, 311–12.

38. Memorandum of Conversation, Dulles and Eisenhower, 18 May 1955,

DDEL, JFD, WHMS, Box 3, Mtgs w/ Pres 1955 [4]. Memorandum of Conversation, Dulles and Stassen, 20 May 1955, DDEL, JFD, CS, Box 11, JFD Chron May 1955 [2].

39. Notes of Meeting, 15 June 1955, *FRUS, 1955–57*, 20:118–20.

40. Stassen to Lawrence, 13 July 1955, NAII, RG59, S/AE, Disarm, 12A.90.

41. Lawrence sought in 1939 Strauss's help in raising funds for his hundred-million volt cyclotron. Although Strauss provided only minor assistance, the two developed a lasting friendship forged in battle over the H-bomb decision and other atomic energy issues. Pfau, *No Sacrifice Too Great*, 54–55. Lewis L. Strauss, *Men and Decisions* (Garden City, N.J.: Doubleday, 1962), 165–66, 241–42.

42. Herken, *Brotherhood*, 304–10. Other Livermore scientists serving with Lawrence and Teller included Harold Brown, Mark Mills, and Herbert York.

43. Ibid.; Herken, *Cardinal Choices*, 94; Strauss, unsent letter to Lawrence, 14 Oct. 1955, LLS, AEC, Box 59, Lawrence.

44. Toner to Stassen, 29 Nov. 1955, NAII, RG59, Sp A/E, Disarm, Box 127; Herken, *Brotherhood*, 304–306.

45. Wadsworth to Lodge, 11 May 1954, *FRUS, 1955–57*, 20: 78–81. For Stassen's analysis of the Soviet proposal, see his Progress Report, 26 May 1955, *FRUS, 1955–57*, 20: 93–97. Press opinion at the time applauded the Soviet proposal as an important step, but cautioned against possible pitfalls, warning that the Soviet position on several important issues remained unclear. For example, see C. L. Sulzberger, "Foreign Affairs: A New, Gradual Approach to Peace," *NYT*, 12 May 1955; see also "Soviet Disarmament Plan," *BAS* (June 1955), 231. Although Martha Smith contends that the Eisenhower administration's failure to respond to this signal of Soviet flexibility represents a "missed opportunity" to reach an agreement on disarmament, the contentious negotiations on a test-ban control mechanism that followed revealed how far apart the United States and Soviet positions remained. See Smith, "The Nuclear Testing Policies of the Eisenhower Administration, 1953–1960,"165–214. David Holloway identifies this proposal as "a major shift in Soviet policy, and looked like an attempt to move beyond the rhetoric of disarmament to a position from which agreements might be reached." Yet he cautions that it remains impossible to know how flexible and serious the Soviets were since they never became the subject of serious negotiations. The scope of Holloway's study, however, concludes before considering the Geneva test-ban negotiations between 1958 and 1963. The agonizing course of those negotiations reveals that the United States and the Soviet Union remained deeply divided on several related issues, such as the composition and procedures of personnel occupying control posts. See Holloway, *Stalin and the Bomb*, 340–42. Wadsworth to Lodge, 11 May 1954, *FRUS, 1955–57*, 20: 78–81. For Stassen's analysis of the Soviet proposal, see his Progress Report, 26 May 1955, *FRUS, 1955–57*, 20: 93–97.

46. Eisenhower to Alfred Gruenther, 25 July 1955, DDEL, AWF, DS.

47. Patterson, "President Eisenhower and Arms Control," *Peace and Change* 11, no. 3–4 (1986): 9–13. For a study of Open Skies, see W. W. Rostow, *Open Skies: Eisenhower's Proposal of July 21, 1955* (Austin: University of Texas Press, 1982). For a collection of essays examining the Geneva Summit, see Gunter

Bischof and Saki Dockrill, eds., *Cold War Respite: The Geneva Summit of 1955* (Baton Rouge: Louisiana State University Press, 2000).

48. *WP*, 29 Nov. 1955.

49. *WP*, 4 Dec. 1955.

50. *NYT*, 30 Nov. 1955.

51. Dulles to Stassen, 11 Dec. 1955, NAII, RG59, S/AE, Box 190.

52. Strauss to Dulles, 13 Dec. 1955, DDEL, OSS, Subj Series, Alphabet Sub, Box 4, AEC Acct Docs [7]. Strauss forwarded the same memo to Eisenhower the following day. See Strauss to Eisenhower, 14 Dec. 1955, DDEL, OSS, SA, Box 4, AEC (Acct Doc) (7).

53. Summary of Meeting, 12 Dec. 1955, LLS, AEC, Box 106, Stassen.

54. Nelson to Strauss, 21 Dec. 1955, LLS, AEC, Box 73, NSC; Notes of NSC Planning Board Meeting, 21 Dec. 1955, *FRUS, 1955–57*, 20: 247. Report on Disarmament, 22 Dec. 1955, *DDRS*: WH; 1986–249.

55. Bowie, Smith, and Wilcox to Dulles, 9 Jan. 1956, DDEL, OSAD, Box 5, Nuclear Weapons Tests (Jan.-May 1956) (1). Department of State to Stassen, 9 Jan. 1956, DDEL, DDE Post-Presid, Principle File, 1963, Box 65, Test Ban Treaty [4].

56. Memorandum of Conversation, Dulles and Eisenhower, 10 Jan. 1956, DDEL, JFD, WHMS, Box 4, Meetings with the President January 1956 to July 1956 (6).

57. Memorandum of Conversation with the President, 11 July 1960, DDEL, OSS, Subj Series, DoS Sub, Box 4, State Dept - 1960 [Jun-Jul] [3].

Chapter 5

EPIGRAPH: Dulles, Press Conference Comments, 24 Jan. 1956, *NYT*, 25 Jan. 1956.

1. The two prominent studies that explore the test-ban issue either focus on the administration's public opposition to Stevenson's proposal or explore the private consideration of a test-ban initiative during the campaign. Neither combines the two approaches to analyze the implications of this disjunction. Writing before many of the relevant classified documents became available to scholars, Divine's *Blowing on the Wind* focuses on Eisenhower's public reaction to Stevenson's proposal. Venturing beyond the public realm, Divine speculates, correctly as it turns out, that despite the administration's intense public opposition to Stevenson's proposal, Eisenhower was favorably inclined to pursue a test-ban agreement with the Soviet Union in 1956. See Divine, 84–112. With greater access to a wide range of documents, many that remain classified, Hewlett and Holl's *Atoms for Peace and War* confirms Divine's suspicions. Although they describe the administration's ongoing internal study of the test ban on the eve of the election and acknowledge that Stevenson was campaigning unaware of this secret study, Hewlett and Holl's revealing official history does not make an effort to contrast the private consideration with the public posturing or discuss the implications of the administration's deception about its position. They conclude that the campaign did not derail Eisenhower's commitment to seek a test ban

and "probably" did not delay the eventual test moratorium of 1958. See Hewlett and Holl, 351–74. Smith argues that Eisenhower, though indicating frustration with the static disarmament review at times, made no decisions to change to the administration's test policy during 1956. See Smith, "The Nuclear Testing Policies of the Eisenhower Administration, 1953–1960," 271–80.

2. Smith, "The Nuclear Testing Policies of the Eisenhower Administration, 1953–1960," 249.

3. Record of a Meeting at the White House, 1 Feb. 1956, NAUK, PREM 11/1676.

4. Extract from record of a meeting between the Secretary of State (Lloyd) and Mr. Dulles, 31 Jan. 1956, NAUK, PREM 11/1676. Gerald Smith, Memorandum of Conversation, 1 Feb. 1956, NAII, RG59, Lot 68D349, Box 11, Nuke Sharing-UK-Consultations-Eden Visit—1956.

5. Memorandum of Conversation, 31 Jan. 1956, *FRUS, 1955–57*, 27: 629–34.

6. Strauss, Memorandum for Files, 1 Feb. 1956, LLS, AEC, Box 26C, Eden.

7. Memorandum of Conversation, 6 June 1956, *FRUS, 1955–57*, 20: 400–02; Memorandum of Conversation, 24 July 1956, *DDRS*, 1995–124. Telegram, Aldrich to Dulles, 25 July 1956, DDEL, OSAD Box 5, Tests 1956 June-August (3). Smith to Murphy, 26 July 1956, DDEL, OSAD, Box 5, Tests 1956 June-August (3).

8. Telegram, Lodge to Department of State, Sep. 11, 1956, NAII, RG59, Rec Rel Disarm, 3009B, Box 24, File 2.22a Nuclear Wpns Tests; Gullion to Matteson, Oct. 25, 1956, NAII, RG59, Rec Rel Disarm, 3009B, Box 159, NK, Mattes, 10/56. For more on the growing international pressures and challenges in the United Nations, see Smith, "The Nuclear Testing Policies of the Eisenhower Administration, 1953–1960," 215–34.

9. Smith to Murphy, 26 July 1956, DDEL, OSAD, Box 5, Tests 1956 June-August (3).

10. Paul Foster to Strauss, 25 July 1956, DDEL, NSCS, OCB Cent Files, Box 10, OCB 000.9 A/E File 4, [10]. Divine, *Blowing on the Wind*, 85. Smith, "The Nuclear Testing Policies of the Eisenhower Administration, 1953–1960," 256.

11. Strauss to Eisenhower, 3 Mar. 1955, DDEL, AWF, OFA, (microfilm), 4:323.

12. Dulles's News Conference, 24 Jan. 1956, *NYT*, 25 Jan. 1956.

13. Anderson to Flemming, 18 Feb. 1956, DDEL, NSCS, Exec Sec Subj File Series, Box 18, Spec Asst [Anderson] - Memoranda, 1955–56 [4].

14. Adams to Waterman, 8 May 1956, DDEL, OSS, Minnich, Box 1, Misc-S.

15. "The Biological Effects of Atomic Radiations," DDEL, NSCS, OCB Cent Files, Box 10, OCB 000.9 A/E File 4, [9]. Divine, *Blowing on the Wind* 78–81. Hewlett and Holl, *Atoms for Peace and War*, 264–69, 328–31, 340–41. Smith, 263.

16. Divine, *Blowing on the Wind* 78–81. Hewlett and Holl, *Atoms for Peace and War,* 264–69, 328–31, 340–41.

17. Mar. 1, 56, DDEL, OSAD, Box 5, Tests '56 (A) (3). Divine, *Blowing*

on the Wind, 81–83. Ralph Lapp, "The Humanitarian H-bomb," *BAS* 12 (Sep. 1956): 264. Hewlett and Holl, *Atoms for Peace and War*, 347; Herken, *Brotherhood*, 308.

18. Televised speech 15 Oct. 1956, *AES*, 6: 281–86.

19. *NYT*, 17 Oct. 1956.

20. *Newsweek* 48 (29 Oct. 1956): 31.

21. Rabinowitch, "Science and the Affairs of Man," *BAS* 12 (June 1956): 186–88. Rabinowitch, "The Bomb Test Controversy," *BAS* 12 (Nov. 1956): 322. Inglis, "National Security with the Arms Race Limited," *BAS* 12 (June 1956): 196–201. Inglis, "Prospects for Stopping Nuclear Tests," *BAS* 13 (Jan. 1957): 19–20.

22. Divine, *Blowing on the Wind*, 104.

23. Oppenheimer to Stevenson, 14 Apr. 1956, JRO, Box 69, AES (2); Stevenson to Oppenheimer, 6 Aug. 1956, ibid. Hewlett and Holl, *Atoms for Peace and War*, 366–68, 376.

24. *NYT*, 17 Oct. 1956; Scientists endorsing Eisenhower's views with their AEC affiliations omitted included John Bugher, Director of the AEC's Division of Biology and Medicine, Gioacchino Failla, chairman of the AEC's advisory committee on biology and medicine, Warren C. Johnson, Chairman of the AEC's GAC, and GAC members T. Keith Glennan, Eger V. Murphree, and John C. Warner. Strauss to Eisenhower, Oct. 18, 1956, LLS, AEC, Box 26E, Eisenhower. Divine, *Blowing on the Wind*, 104–5.

25. Telegram, Warren to Strauss, 16 Oct. 1956, LLS, AEC, Box 14, Campaign 1956. *WP*, 4 Nov. 1956. Divine, *Blowing on the Wind*, 104–105. Herken, *Brotherhood*, 306–8.

26. Eisenhower to Strauss, 30 Aug. 1956, DDEL, AWF, DS, Aug. 1956 Misc (1).

27. Strauss, Memorandum for Files, 15 Oct. 1956, LLS, AEC, Box 14, Campaign 1956.

28. Rabi's comments on the dilemmas of government science advising are attached to Ruth Adams to Rabi, 30 Nov. 1953, IIR, Box 17, BAS.

29. Memorandum of Phone Message, 17 Oct. 1956, LLS, AEC, Box 111, Teller.

30. Strauss to Eisenhower, 18 Oct. 1956, LLS, AEC, DDE, Box 26E, Eisenhower; Herken, *Brotherhood*, 290–94, 309–10. Telegram, Lawrence to Strauss, Nov. 5, 1956, LLS, AEC, Monitoring of Soviet Tests. *NYT*, 6 Nov. 1956.

31. Divine, *Blowing on the Wind*, 106; Rabinowitch, "The Lessons of a Fateful Month," *BAS* 12 (Nov. 1956): 354.

32. An earlier version of the next two sections appeared as part of an essay in the *Journal of Strategic Studies* (http://www.tandf.co.uk.). See Greene, "Eisenhower, Science and the Test Ban Debate, 1953–1956."

33. Dulles, Memorandum of Conversation with Murray, 9 Jan. 1956, DDEL, JFD, GCMS, Box 1, Memo of Conv - Gen- L thru M [4].

34. Dulles, Memorandum of Conversation with Eisenhower, 10 Jan. 1956, DDEL, JFD, WHMS, Box 4, Meetings with the President January 1956 to July 1956 (6).

35. Eisenhower diary entry, 11 Jan. 1956, DDEL, AWF, DS (microfilm) 5:705.

36. Murray Press Release, 12 Apr. 1956, DDEL, OSAD, Box 4, Senate Disarmament Hearings.

37. Stevenson, Address Before the American Society of Newspaper Editors, 21 Apr. 1956, Washington, D.C., AES, 6: 110–20.

38. Divine, *Blowing on the Wind*, 69. Herken, *Brotherhood*, 305–310. The best examination of Stassen's torturous disarmament review is Charles A. Appleby Jr., "Eisenhower and Arms Control, 1953–1961: A Balance of Risks." Stassen to Eisenhower, 29 June 1956, *FRUS, 1955–57*, 20: 402–8; Memo of conference, 12 July 1956, DDEL, AWF, DS, July 1956 Misc (3). Stassen interrupted his disarmament review to take a leave of absence to support the "Dump Nixon" campaign to find a replacement for Nixon as Eisenhower's running mate. Naturally, this made Stassen a pariah within the administration. The implications of this on the test-ban debate are discussed in Chapter 6.

39. Stassen indicated that Radford and Wilson would be willing to consider limited the "size" of tests. It is unclear if they meant the size of specific yields, the number of tests, or both. For the views of Radford and Wilson, see Stassen to Eisenhower, 20 July 1956, *FRUS, 1955–57*, 20: 410–11; Stassen to Eisenhower, 20 July 1956, DDEL, AWF, OFA, Stassen 1956 (2) (microfilm), 28:168.

40. Stassen to Eisenhower, 20 July 1956, *FRUS,1955–57*, 20: 412; Strauss to Stassen, 26 July 1956, DDEL, OSS, Subject Series, Department of Defense Subseries, Box 3, Defense Classified (3).

41. Gerald Smith to Robert Murphy, 26 July 1956, DDEL, OSAD, Box 5, Tests 1956 (3); Hewlett and Holl, *Atoms for Peace and War*, 361; Dulles also talked with Radford about tests, asking if it was possible to rely upon nuclear weapons for defense without continuing to test them. Radford replied that it would be "dangerous" to do so, see Dulles and Radford, telephone conversation, 20 July 1956, DDEL, JFD, TC (microfilm), 5:180.

42. Murphy to Stassen, 31 Aug. 1956, *FRUS, 1955–57*, 20: 419–22.

43. Memorandum of Conversation, 5 Sep. 1956, NAII, RG59, Decimal File 600.0012, 1955–1959, Box 2267.

44. Eisenhower to Strauss, 30 Aug. 1956, DDEL, AWF, DS, August 1956 Misc (1). It remains unclear how Eisenhower learned of Rabi's views on testing in August 1956.

45. *NYT*, 6 Sep. 1956, 7 Sep. 1956.

46. Strauss, Memorandum for Files, 11 Sep. 1956, LLS, AEC, Box 26A, JF Dulles.

47. Dulles and Stassen, telephone conversation, 7 Sep. 1956, DDEL, JFD, TC (microfilm), 5:44; Dulles and Stassen, telephone conversation, 11 Sep. 1956, DDEL, JFD, TC (microfilm), 5:27.

48. Two slightly different versions of this conference exist. Goodpaster's account, based upon Sherman Adams's notes, sets no fixed date to report back and stresses the formation of a common position, Memo of conference, 11 Sep. 1956, DDEL, AWF, DS, Staff Memoranda Sep. 1956; Jackson's version establishes 15 October as the completion date and permits dissenting views attached to the rec-

ommendation, Memo of conference, 11 Sep. 1956, *FRUS,1955–57*, 20:423–27. Dulles's frustration with Stassen for ignoring his opinion on bringing up the test-ban issue is evident in his conversation the following day with Sherman Adams when Dulles recommended that Stassen should be removed from his position as the disarmament advisor, Memo of telephone conversation, Dulles and Adams, 12 Sep. 1956, DDEL, JFD, TC (microfilm), 9:845.

49. *AES*, 6: 110–120; *NYT*, 25 Apr. 1956; Eisenhower Press Conference, 25 Apr. 1956, *PPP, Eisenhower, 1956*, 434–35.

50. *NYT*, 6 Sep. 1956, 7 Sep. 1956; *The Christian Science Monitor*, 7 Sep. 1956; *WP*, 6 Sep. 1956.

51. RNC to Stassen, 10 Oct. 1956, NAII, RG59, Records Related to Disarmament, Box 28, File 2.227 Nuclear Wpns Tests, H-bomb Testing, 1956 Campaign Issue; the press often included the Republican's sharp criticism of Stevenson in the headlines, while the inconspicuous statement of Eisenhower's commitment to a negotiated test ban with inspection provisions remained within the article text, see *NYT*, 7 Sep. 1956, 4 Oct. 1956, 24 Oct. 1956.

52. *PPP, Eisenhower, 1956*, 786–87; *NYT*, 21 Sep. 1956. For Stevenson's speech at Minneapolis on 29 Sep. 1956, see *AES*, 6: 245–51.

53. *NYT*, 4 Oct. 1956.

54. Eisenhower press conference, 5 Oct. 1956 and "Statement by the President on the Testing of Nuclear Weapons," 6 Oct. 1956, both in *PPP, Eisenhower, 1956*, 858–67. Eisenhower's written statement, released before all applicable staff agencies reviewed it, included a critical concession to one of Stevenson's main arguments: "Tests of large weapons, by any nation, may be detected when they occur." This forced the administration to develop other arguments to distance Eisenhower's position from Stevenson's.

55. Hewlett and Holl, *Atoms for Peace and War*, 365–66; Divine, *Blowing on the Wind*, 91–92; *NYT*, 8 Oct. 1956; Eisenhower press conference, 11 Oct. 1956, *PPP, Eisenhower, 1956*, 880–82.

56. *NYT*, 13 Oct. 1956, 15 Oct. 1956; Televised speech, 15 Oct. 1956, *AES*, 6: 281–86; Ambrose, *Eisenhower*, 2: 349. The candidates also disagreed on the time required to restart testing. Stevenson insisted that it could be done in eight weeks, while the Eisenhower administration insisted that it would take a year.

57. Televised speech, 15 Oct. 1956, *AES*, 6: 281–86.

58. *NYT*, 17 Oct. 1956; Divine, *Blowing on the Wind*, 96; Ambrose, *Eisenhower*, 2: 349.

59. Dulles and Wilson, telephone conversation, 16 Oct. 1956, DDEL, JFD, TC (microfilm), 5:446; Dulles and Gerald Smith, telephone conversation, 16 Oct. 1956, DDEL, JFD, TC (microfilm), 5:452.

60. Adams to Dulles, 16 Oct. 1956, DDEL, JFD, WHMS, CS, White House Correspondence, General 1956 (1); Adams held a second round of meetings with representatives on 18 Oct. 1956, see Adams and Dulles, telephone conversation, DDEL, JFD, TC (microfilm), 9:805.

61. Stassen to Adams, 17 Oct. 1956, NAII, RG59, Records Related to Disarmament, 1942–1962, Box 142, Name File: Adams.

62. Robert Matteson to Stassen, 16 Oct. 1956, NAII, RG59, Records Re-

lated to Disarmament, Box 28, File 2.227 Nuclear Wpns Tests, H-bomb Testing, 1956 Campaign Issue.

63. Eisenhower speech in Portland, 18 Oct. 1956 and Eisenhower speech at the Hollywood Bowl, Oct. 19, 1956, both in *PPP, Eisenhower, 1956,* 959–77; *NYT,* 17–19 Oct. 1956.

64. Bulganin letter DDEL, AWF, OFI, USSR, Bulganin 1955–58 (2).

65. Dulles and Strauss, memo of telephone conversation, 19 Oct. 1956, DDEL, JFD, TC (microfilm), 5:426.

66. Strauss to Dulles, 20 Oct. 1956, DDEL, JFD, DPCSS, President's correspondence with Bulganin, 1955–56 (1) (microfilm), 6:724; Eisenhower to Bulganin, 21 Oct. 1956, DDEL, AWF, DS, Oct. 1956 Misc (2).

67. *Newsweek* (29 Oct. 1956): 29–31; *NYT,* 22–23, 26 Oct. 1956.

68. Dulles and Eisenhower, telephone conversation, 23 Oct. 1956, DDEL, AWF, DS, Oct 1956 Phone Calls and DDEL, JFD, TC (microfilm), 9:791.

69. "Memorandum on Disarmament Negotiations," *Department of State Bulletin,* 35 (5 Nov. 1956): 709–15. There are important differences between the public version and the original chronology that the Department of State prepared, see Hoover to Cutler, 20 Oct. 1956, DDEL, OSS, Subject Series, Alpha Subseries, Box 21, Nuclear Testing-Campaign Material, Oct.-Nov. 1956 (2).

70. Joseph Toner to Matteson, 1 Nov. 1956, NAII, RG59, Rec Rel Disarmament, Box 160, Matteson Nov. 1956; *NYT,* 27 Oct. 1956; *NYT,* 1 Nov. 1956.

71. *NYT,* 2 Nov. 1956; *NYT,* 3 Nov. 1956; *WP,* 2 Nov. 1956; *WP,* 4 Nov. 1956. Stevenson himself returned to the matter afterward in an article published in *Look.* In it, he claimed that the NSC had voted unanimously in mid-September to seek a test ban, only to have it rejected for obviously political reasons. Actually, Stevenson got it wrong; Eisenhower *approved* the formation of a test-ban initiative in the face of unanimous opposition. Further, it was Eisenhower's inner circle of disarmament advisors that discussed the matter, not the NSC. When asked to comment on this at a press conference, Eisenhower simply refused to confirm or deny the claim, citing his practice never to discuss NSC convictions. Stevenson, "Why I Raised the H-Bomb Question," *Look* 21 (5 Feb. 1957): 23–25; Eisenhower press conference, 23 Jan. 1957, *PPP, Eisenhower, 1957,* 74.

72. On the eve of the election, the Suez Crisis combined with the invasion of Hungary to focus attention on international affairs, where Eisenhower possessed tremendous experience and prestige. While Bulganin's note certainly hurt Stevenson on the test-ban issue, Eisenhower's margin of victory was so overwhelming that the test-ban issue itself did not influence the outcome. It did, however, make nuclear tests a consistent issue of public concern. See Divine, *Blowing on the Wind,* 109–12; *Newsweek* (12 Nov. 1956).

73. Greenstein, *The Hidden-Hand Presidency,* 5–9, 57–72.

Chapter 6

EPIGRAPHS: Memorandum of Conference, 24 June 1957, DDEL, AWF, DS, Staff Memo June 1957; Cutler, Memorandum of Conference, 9 Aug. 1957, *FRUS, 1955–57,* 20: 694–95.

1. The United States avoided another Indian proposal for a General Assembly vote on a test ban by referring the proposal to the United Nation's five-nation disarmament subcommittee. The nations on the subcommittee were Canada, France, Great Britain, the Soviet Union, and the United States.

2. Memorandum of Conference with the President, 21 Nov. 1956, DDEL, AWF, DS, Nov '56 Staff Memo (microfilm), 10:506; Annex to NSC Action No. 1553, 21 Nov. 1956, *FRUS, 1955–57*, 20: 444–46; Summary Minutes of the President's Special Committee on Disarmament Problems, 4 Dec. 1956, DDEL, OSAD, Box 4, DPC, Record of Actions (6).

3. For Strauss's request for approval for the May 1957 test series, *OPERATION PILGRIM,* see Strauss to Eisenhower, 21 Dec. 1956, DDEL, AWF, OFA (microfilm), 4:0045; Memorandum of Conversation, 26 Dec. 1956, *FRUS, 1955–57,* 20:447–48.

4. Memorandum of Conversation, 22 Mar. 1957, *FRUS, 1955–57,* 27: 736–43; *PPP: Eisenhower,1957,* 405;

5. Ambrose, *Eisenhower,* 2: 402. Cole believed that negative world opinion and the nation's weapons superiority necessitation a limitation on testing. See Cole to Eisenhower, 22 May 1957, DDEL, WHCF, OF, Box 526, OF 108-A (3). Eisenhower to Cole, 27 May 1957, DDEL, AWF, DS, Misc (1) May 1957.

6. Memorandum of Conversation, 23 May 1957, *FRUS, 1955–57,* 20: 532–38; Appleby, "Eisenhower and Arms Control," 200.

7. Memorandum of Conference, 25 May 1957, *FRUS, 1955–57,* 20: 551–55; Divine, *Blowing on the Wind,* 144; Hewlett and Holl, *Atoms for Peace and War,* 392–93; Strauss, Memorandum for Files, 25 May 1957, LLS, AEC, Box 26E, Eisenhower. For Lawrence's views on the effect of a test cessation on lab personnel see Donkin McKay, 22 May 1957, LLS, AEC, MFR, Jan-Jun 1957.

8. Minutes of Cabinet Meeting, 3 June 1957, DDEL, AWF, DS, Misc (2) June 1957; Ambrose, *Eisenhower,* 2: 398.

9. "Global Nuclear Stockpiles, 1945–2002," *BAS* 58 (Nov./Dec. 2002): 103–4.

10. H. W. Brands, Jr., *Cold Warriors: Eisenhower's Generation and American Foreign Policy* (New York: Columbia University Press, 1988), 138–62. According to one of Stassen's assistants, Robert E. Matteson, Stassen believed that his last chance for the Presidency in 1960 was to pull off in 1957 the first real meaningful arms control agreement in the nuclear age, quoted in Appleby, "Eisenhower and Arms Control," 179. As it turned out, Stassen sought the Republican presidential nomination for almost every election through 1992.

11. Dulles, Memorandum of Conversation With the President, 20 Dec. 1956, DDEL, JFD, WHMS, Meetings with the President, Aug-Dec 1956 (1).

12. Telephone Conversation, Dulles-Eisenhower, 21 Dec. 1956, DDEL, AWF, DS, Oct '56 Phone Calls; 21 Dec. 1956, DDEL, JFD, TC, WH (microfilm), 9:720.

13. Eisenhower to Whitney, 11 June 1957, *FRUS, 1955–57,* 20: 616–617. Along with the procedural *faux pas,* the NATO allies were particularly upset that Stassen's memorandum proposed opening most of Western Europe to Soviet

aerial inspection, see Hewlett and Holl, *Atoms for Peace and War,* 394–96; Telegram, Herter to Stassen, 30 May 1957, *FRUS, 1955–57,* 20:565.

14. Telephone conversation, Adams and Dulles, 10 June 1957, DDEL, JFD, TC, Box 12, White House, March-August 1957(2).

15. Macmillan to Eisenhower, 3 June 1957, *DDRS,* 1996–37, (12 January 2001); Draft Letter, Eisenhower to Macmillan, 4 June 1957, DDEL, AWF, OFI, Great Britain, Macmillan-President, May-Nov '57 (6); Telegram, Department of State to London Embassy, 4 June 1957, *FRUS, 1955–57,* 20:597–98; Upon Ambassador Whitney's recommendation, Eisenhower toned down his comments, replacing "astonished and chagrined" with "disappointed," see Editorial Note, *FRUS, 1955–57,* 20: 596–97.

16. Memorandum of Conversation, 4 June 1957, DDEL, JFD, WHMS (microfilm), 4:230.

17. Telephone Conversation, Dulles and Eisenhower, 11 June 1957, DDEL, JFD, TC, Box 12, White House, March-August 1957 (2); Dulles, Memorandum of Conversation, June 11, 1957, DDEL, JFD, WHMS, Box 6, Mtgs w/ Pres 1957 [5].

18. Smith to Dulles, 21 June 1957, DDEL, OSAD, Box 26, Basic Disarmament Documents 1957 [3]. Strauss to Dulles, 17 June 1957, LLS, AEC, Box 26A, Dulles, JF.

19. Bethe to Stassen, 11 June 1957, LLS, AEC, Box 9, Bethe.

20. Bethe to Strauss, 12 June 1957, ibid.

21. Telephone Conversation, Dulles and Strauss, 13 June 1957, DDEL, JFD, TC, Box 6, May-Jun '57 [2].

22. Strauss to Dulles, 17 June 1957, LLS, AEC, Box 26A, Dulles, JF.

23. Hewlett and Holl, *Atoms for Peace and War,* 398–402; Katherine Magraw, "Teller and the 'Clean Bomb' Episode," *BAS* 44 (May 1988): 32–37.

24. Herken, *Brotherhood,* 312–315. Memorandum of Conference, 24 June 1957, DDEL, AWF, DS, Staff Memo June 1957. News Conference, 24 June 1957, DDEL, OSAD, Box 6, Tests 1957 June-August (3). Eisenhower's metaphor recalls the famous speech by William Jennings Bryan at the 1896 Democratic National Convention. Bryan mesmerized his audience by asserting that advocates of the gold standard "shall not crucify mankind upon a cross of gold." Dwight D. Eisenhower's political ideology has never been confused with that of William Jennings Bryan. Eisenhower did, however, grow up in Kansas during the height of the Populist revolt, and likely studied Bryan's famous "Cross of Gold" speech along with countless others of his generation.

25. Telephone Call, Eisenhower and Dulles, 25 June 1957, DDEL, AWF, DS, Phone Calls, June 1957; Hewlett and Holl, *Atoms for Peace and War,* 398–402. Despite substantial evidence that Eisenhower's attitude changed drastically, albeit temporarily, after the meeting, he later argued that he was not impressed with the arguments of the scientists. See Memorandum of Conversation, 17 Apr. 1958, *FRUS, 1958–60,* 3:603–4.

26. Telephone Conversation, Cutler and Dulles, 1 July 1957, DDEL, JFD, TC (microfilm), 6:636.

27. Telegram, Dulles to Stassen, 1 July 1957, DDEL, AWF, OFA, Stassen 1957 (2) (microfilm), 28:308.

28. Memorandum of Conversation, 30 July 1957, DDEL, CH, CCS (microfilm), 15:162; see also Editorial Note, *FRUS, 1955–57*, 20: 664–65; Telegram, Dulles to Herter, 29 July 1957, *FRUS, 1955–57*, 20:666; Telegram, Herter to Dulles, 30 July 1957, *FRUS, 1955–57*, 20:667–68.

29. Divine, *Blowing on the Wind*, 144–47; Hewlett and Holl, *Atoms for Peace and War*, 394–97.

30. Divine, *Blowing on the Wind*, 155–56.

31. The director of the AEC's Division of Information Services, Morse Salisbury, informed Eisenhower's press secretary that Strauss replied to "more than a thousand letters" to Eisenhower expressing concerns about nuclear tests. Strauss offered to answer these letters on behalf of the president as a routine matter of bureaucratic efficiency. See Salisbury to Hagerty, 21 June 1957, DDEL, WHCF, OF, Box 526, OF 108-A (3). Although it was likely a common practice for one of Eisenhower's advisors to respond on the president's behalf, this procedure further shielded Eisenhower from the growing concerns among American citizens about testing. Eisenhower approved the practice of Strauss replying on his behalf after Strauss informed the president that Strauss's standard responses often received, in turn, a favorable reply. See Eisenhower's initials indicating his approval of this practice, Strauss to Eisenhower, 23 July 1957, DDEL, AWF, OFA (microfilm), 4:417.

32. Norman Cousins, *Dr. Schweitzer of Lambarene* (New York: Harper, 1960); it is unclear if Schweitzer's message had a significant impact on the President. Although he cautiously passed along Schweitzer and Cousins's letters to Dulles, Eisenhower otherwise carefully observed Schweitzer's earnest request for secrecy. See Telephone Conversation, Dulles and Eisenhower, 6 Feb. 1957, DDEL, AWF, DS, Feb. 1957 Phone Calls; Eisenhower to Dulles, 6 Feb. 1957, DDEL, AWF, DS, Feb. 1957 Misc (3); Phyllis Bernau (Dulles's Secretary) to Ann Whitman, 7 Feb. 1957, DDEL, JFD, WHMS (microfilm), 4:092; Divine, *Blowing on the Wind*, 121–22; *NYT*, 24 Apr. 1957; Hewlett and Holl, *Atoms for Peace and War*, 390. For an analysis of the administration's response to Schweitzer, see Lawrence Wittner, "Blacklisting Schweitzer" *BAS* 51 (May/June 1995): 55–61.

33. Divine, *Blowing on the Wind*, 121–22; *NYT*, 24 Apr. 1957; Hewlett and Holl, *Atoms for Peace and War*, 390. During the campaign debate in October 1956 only 24 percent favored a *unilateral* test ban as Democratic challenger Adlai Stevenson initially proposed. In a differently phrased poll at the end of April, 52 percent of Americans thought that fallout from testing presented a "real danger," while only 28 percent found no danger in testing. During the same period, 63 percent favored a *multilateral* test ban while only 28 percent opposed. See Gallup, *The Gallup Poll*, 2:1452, 1487–88; Eugene J. Rosi, "Mass Attentive Opinion on Nuclear Weapons Tests and Fallout, 1954–1963," *Public Opinion Quarterly* 29 (Summer 1965): 280–97.

34. Divine, *Blowing on the Wind*, 125–29, 182–83. For Pauling's petition and letter to Eisenhower see Pauling to Eisenhower, 4 June 1957, DDEL, WHCF, OF, Box 526, OF108-A (3). Strauss drafted a reply for Sherman Adams, rather

than Eisenhower, to send to Pauling. In it, Adams indicated that the recent congressional hearings revealed that there was "little or no uniformity of opinion" on the hazards of fallout. See Strauss to Goodpaster, 28 June 1957 and Adams to Pauling, 29 June 1957, ibid.

35. Divine, *Blowing on the Wind*, 125–26, 321.

36. *NYT*, 6, 7 June 1957.

37. J. Edgar Hoover to Robert Cutler, 19 June 1957, *DDRS*, 1988–155 (12 Jan. 2001).

38. Other prominent test-ban advocates assessed in the report included Bentley Glass, David Hill, Ralph Lapp, and Hermann Muller. See J. Edgar Hoover to Robert Cutler, 19 June 1957, *DDRS*, 1988–155 (12 Jan. 2001). The CIA also monitored the international communist propaganda campaign to end testing. See for example "Communist Propaganda in Policy Perspective," 31 May 1957; DDEL, OFA, Allen Dulles (3).

39. "What's Back of the 'Fall-out' Scare," *US News and World Report* (7 June 1957): 25–28.

40. Strauss to David Lawrence, 5 June 1957, LLS, AEC, DDE, Box 26G, Fallout.

41. J. Edgar Hoover to Cutler, 31 July 1957, DDEL, OSANSA, FBI, Box 1, A-B (1).

42. "Scientists and the Fall-Out Scare," *US News and World Report* (21 June 1957): 52.

43. Everett Holles (Strauss's assistant) to Hagerty, 12 June 1957, DDEL, WHCF, OF, Box 526, OF 108-A (3).

44. Strauss suggestions for Eisenhower Press Conference, 5 June 1957, LLS, AEC, DDE, Box 26E, Eisenhower. Strauss to Hagerty, 12 June 1957, DDEL, WHCF, OF, Box 526, OF-108 (A). Strauss informed Eisenhower that he was responding to the high volume of letters sent to the President on the test issue. Suggesting communist influence, Strauss asserted that many were sufficiently uniform to "make it apparent that they are the result of a campaign." See Strauss to Eisenhower, 23 July 1957, DDEL, AWF, OFA (microfilm), 4:417.

45. The President's Press Conference, 5 June 1957, *PPP: Eisenhower,1957*, 429–45.

46. Cousins to the President, 7 June 1957, DDEL, AWF, NS, Box 7, Cousins, Norman (1); Whitman to Strauss, 11 June 1957, DDEL, AWF, OFA (microfilm), 4:434; Eisenhower to Cousins, 21 June 1957, DDEL, AWF, DS, Misc (1) June 1957 (microfilm), 13:153; *US News and World Report* 42 (21 June 1957), 52.

47. *NYT*, 26, 27, 30 June 1957; Cousins to Eisenhower, 27 June 1957, DDEL, AWF, NS, Box 7, Cousins (1).

48. Eisenhower to Strauss, 2 July 1957, DDEL, AWF, OFA (microfilm), 4:422.

49. Strauss to Eisenhower, 3 July 1957, DDEL, AWF, OFA (microfilm), 4:420.

50. Press Release, 23 July 1957, NAII, RG59, en3009B, Box 32, File 2.222; *NYT*, 24 July 1957. The FAS position illustrates a division among test-ban advocates. Many physicists discounted the hazards from testing alone and abhorred

the dire warnings of test-ban advocates who stressed the hazards of fallout. Strauss and the AEC were able to draw attention to such sensationalist accounts and associate them with all test-ban advocates. This overshadowed the sober arguments of atomic scientists who favored a test ban primarily as a means to ease tensions and slow the arms race.

51. Quoted by Herken, *Brotherhood*, 314–15. See also Herken's expanded online notes on this episode, Chapter 19, note 24 at www.brotherhoodofthe-bomb.com. Overjoyed with the results of the scientists' misleading presentation to the president, Strauss attempted to spread their misinformation to the United Nations. He proposed to Henry Cabot Lodge, the U.S. Representative to the United Nations, to have Lawrence and Teller meet with leaders of friendly or neutral delegations to convince them of the necessity to continue testing. Lodge, perhaps more attentive to the skeptical press and negative international reaction to the scientists' argument, replied to Strauss that bringing the scientists to the UN "would be bad tactics and would defeat its own purpose." Lodge perhaps formed these views after meeting with Lawrence and Teller in September. See Strauss to Lodge, 19 Sep. 1957 and Lodge to Strauss, 1 Oct. 1957 both in LLS, AEC, Box 61, Lodge, H. C. Morse to Strauss, 7 Feb. 1958, LLS, AEC, Box 69, Morse.

52. Strauss, Memorandum for File, 1 Jan. 1958, LLS, AEC, Box 67, MFR 1958.

53. Ambrose, *Eisenhower*, 2: 400; Memorandum of Discussion, 299th Mtg of NSC, 4 Oct. 1956, *DDRS*, 1994–189 (12 Jan. 2001); *PPP, Eisenhower: 1960*, 1035–40; Damms, 57–78.

54. Memorandum of Conference, 24 Apr. 1957, DDEL, AWF, DS, Staff Memo (1) Apr. 1957.

55. Memorandum of Conference, 25 May 1957, *FRUS, 1955–57*, 20: 551–55; Hewlett and Holl, *Atoms for Peace and War*, 392–94; For Strauss's account of the meeting, see his Memorandum for Files, 25 May 1957, LLS, AEC, Box 26E, Eisenhower.

56. *NYT*, 30 June 1957; Divine, *Blowing on the Wind*, 152; *PPP: Eisenhower, 1957*, 551.

57. Memorandum of Conversation, 30 July 1957, DDEL, CH, CCS (microfilm), 15:162; Herter to Dulles, 30 July 1957, *FRUS, 1955–57*, 20: 666–68; according to Herken, "Strauss determined not only the kind of advice that Eisenhower would receive on nuclear weapons, but also to a large extent, the policies that followed from it"; see Herken, *Cardinal Choices*, 78.

58. Dulles, Addendum to Memorandum of Conversation with the President, 3 Aug. 1957, DDEL, JFD, WHMS (4:191).

59. John S. D. Eisenhower, Memorandum of Conference, 9 Aug. 1957, DDEL, AWF, DS, Memoranda on Appointments (2), Aug. 1957; John S. D. Eisenhower, Memorandum of Conference, 16 Aug. 1957, DDEL, AWF, DS, Memoranda on Appointments (1), Aug. 1957.

60. Cutler, Memorandum of Conference, 9 Aug. 1957, *FRUS, 1955–57*, 20: 694–95; the original with less exemptions in some areas is in DDEL, OSANSA, NSC, Subject Subseries, Box 1, Atom Weapons and Classified Intelligence-Misc

1955–1957 (1). Cutler, Memorandum of Conference, 9 Aug. 1957, *FRUS, 1955–57*, 20:698.

61. John S. D. Eisenhower, Memorandum of Conference, 9 Aug. 1957, *FRUS, 1955–57*, 20:699–701. Strauss, Memorandum for Files, 9 Aug. 1957, LLS, AEC, Box 26E, Eisenhower.

62. Strauss, Memorandum for Files, 9 Aug. 1957, LLS, AEC, Box 26E, Eisenhower.

63. For analyses of Eisenhower's response to *Sputnik* and the its apparent strategic implications, see Divine, *The Sputnik Challenge: Eisenhower's Response to the Soviet Satellite* (Oxford: Oxford University Press, 1993) and David L. Snead, *The Gaither Committee, Eisenhower, and the Cold War* (Columbus: Ohio University Press, 1999).

64. Smith, "The Nuclear Testing Policies of the Eisenhower Administration, 1953–1960," 336–40.

65. Ironically, Gordon Gray, who served as the chairman of the Personnel Security Board during the Oppenheimer case, became in March 1957 the Director of the ODM, giving him supervisory responsibility over SAC, whose members included Rabi, Bethe, and several other scientists who remained deeply bitter about the case. Gray later became Eisenhower's national security advisor from July 1958 until the end of his presidency.

66. Memorandum of Conversation, 15 Oct. 1957, DDEL, AWF, DS, Box 27, Stf Notes Oct '57 [2]; Herken, *Cardinal Choices*, 101–7.

67. Memorandum of Conversation, 8 Oct. 1957, *FRUS, 1955–57*, 20:739–40.

68. Memorandum of Conversation, 8 Oct. 1957, DDEL, JFD, WHMS, Box 5 MWPres '57(3). The week before, Dulles told Eisenhower that he thought they were reaching "the end of the road" in terms of Stassen's position in the administration. Dulles believed that Stassen could not be trusted to loyally or effectively implement administration policies. Eisenhower responded that he had "rather reluctantly come to the same conclusion," realizing that Stassen had lost the confidence of the administration. See Memorandum of Conversation, 1 Oct. 1957, DDEL, JFD, WHMS, Box 5, Mtgs w/President, 1957 (3).

69. Stassen's plan envisioned eight to ten control posts. Rabi believed as few as six would be effective. Memorandum of Conversation, 29 Oct. 1957, DDEL, OSS, SA, Box 3, AEC11(1).

Chapter 7

EPIGRAPHS: Quoted in Strauss's Memorandum for File, 1 May 1958, LLS, AEC, Box 68, Memo for the Record 1958. Pre-press notes, 6 Aug. 1958, DDEL, AWF, DS, Staff Notes August 1958 (3).

1. Smith, "The Nuclear Testing Policies of the Eisenhower Administration, 1953–1960," 412–14; Smith-Norris, "The Eisenhower Administration and the Nuclear Test Ban Talks, 1958–1960," 503–4, 512.

2. Divine, *Blowing on the Wind*, 212; Hewlett and Holl, *Atoms for Peace and War*, 542–45.

3. Rabi to Gordon Gray, 28 Oct. 1957, DDEL, AWF, NS, Box 26, Rabi; Memorandum of Conference, 30 Oct. 1957, DDEL, AWF, DS, Staff Notes Feb. 1957 (1). Ironically, Bethe advocated this early version of an anti-ballistic missile system, but soon discovered that it was impractical. He vigorously opposed the Strategic Defensive Initiative (SDI) during the Reagan administration, a position that once again placed him at odds with a cause that Edward Teller championed.

4. Rabi to Gordon Gray, 28 Oct. 1957, DDEL, AWF, NS, Box 26, Rabi; Memorandum of Conference, 30 Oct. 1957, DDEL, AWF, DS, Staff Notes Feb. 1957 (1); Eisenhower diary entry, 29 Oct. 1957, DDEL, AWF, DS, Box 27, DDE Diary: Oct. 1957.

5. Memorandum of Conference, 30 Oct. 1957, DDEL, AWF, DS, Staff Notes Feb. 1957 (1).

6. Strauss made a note to remind himself to tell Lawrence about Rabi's comment to Eisenhower, see his note, 6 Nov. 1957, LLS, AEC, Box 59, Lawrence—1957–58.

7. Eisenhower diary entry, 29 Oct. 1957, DDEL, AWF, DS, Box 27, DDE Diary: Oct. 1957.

8. Herken, *Brotherhood*, 291, 298.

9. Eisenhower diary entry, 29 Oct. 1957, DDEL, AWF, DS, Box 27, DDE Diary: Oct. 1957.

10. Memorandum of Conference, 30 Oct. 1957, DDEL, AWF, DS, Staff Notes Oct. 1957 (1).

11. Eisenhower to Strauss, 25 Nov. 1957, DDEL, AWF, DS, Staff Notes, Nov. 1957 (microfilm), 15:064; Telephone Conversation, Eisenhower and Strauss, 25 Nov. 1957, DDEL, AWF, DS, Phone Calls 1957; *NYT*, 25 Nov. 1957.

12. 6 Jan. 1958, NAII, RG59, S/AE, Disarmament, 12A.282.

13. Lodge to Dulles, 31 Mar. 1958, NAII, RG59, 600.0012/3–3158.

14. Memorandum of Conversation, 26 Dec. 1957, DDEL, JFD, WHMS, (microfilm) 4:093. After his meeting with Eisenhower, Dulles asked Philip Farley, who replaced Gerald Smith in October as Dulles's Special Assistant for Atomic Energy Affairs, to assess the attitude of the French and British attitudes on proposing a test ban separate from other disarmament measures. See Record of Telephone Conversation, 26 Dec. 1957, DDEL, JFD, TC, (microfilm) 7:007. Dulles also indicated that he was considering a policy revision on testing when he asked his assistants to provide him excerpts of his and Eisenhower's recent public statements on testing; see Farley to Dulles, 3 Jan. 1958, NAII, RG59, S/AE, Disarmament, 12A.282.

15. Dulles informed Stassen on 3 January that he would oppose his proposal before the NSC for a separate test ban without telling him that he had directed his own advisors to consider a similar proposal after Eisenhower indicated his interest a separate test ban in late December. See Memorandum of Conversation, 3 Jan. 1958, NAII, RG59, 600.0012/1–258.

16. Record of Telephone Conversation, Dulles and Adams, 8 Jan. 1958, DDEL, JFD, TC, WH, Jan-Mar. 1958 (2).

17. Stassen to Killian, 10 Dec. 1957, DDEL, OSAST, Box 7, Disarmament-General (1); Killian to Stassen, 26 Dec. 1957, ibid.

18. James R. Killian, Jr., *Sputnik, Scientists, and Eisenhower: A Memoir of the First Special Assistant to the President for Science and Technology* (Cambridge: MIT Press, 1977), 150.

19. Memorandum of Discussion at the 350th Meeting of the NSC, 6 Jan. 1958, *FRUS, 1958–60*, 3: 533–45. Killian, *Sputnik, Scientists, and Eisenhower*, 154.

20. Memorandum of Discussion at the 350th Meeting of the NSC, 6 Jan. 1958, *FRUS, 1958–60*, 3:533–45.

21. Ibid. Six days later Eisenhower, perhaps encouraged by PSAC's study of the matter, proposed joint technical studies on disarmament to the USSR. See Eisenhower letter to Nikolai Bulganin, 13 Jan. 1958, *PPP, Eisenhower, 1957*: 75–84.

22. Edward Teller, "Alternatives for Security," *Foreign Affairs* (Jan. 1958): 201–208. Memorandum of Discussion at the 350th Meeting of the NSC, 6 Jan. 1958, *FRUS, 1958–60*, 3:533–45.

23. Memorandum for the Files, 7 Jan. 1958, LLS, AEC, Box 26E, Eisenhower.

24. Strauss to the President, 9 Jan. 1958, LLS, AEC, Box 26E, Eisenhower. According to Eisenhower, Rabi in October 1957 believed that "a half dozen or so" inspection posts within the Soviet Union would be sufficient to detect any significant explosions. See Eisenhower Diary Entry, 29 Oct. 1957, DDEL, AWF, DS, Box 27, DDE Diary-Oct. 1957.

25. Memorandum of Conversation, 22 Jan. 1958, DDEL, AWF, DS, Staff Notes, Jan. 1958.

26. Although Teller wrote the letter several weeks after Strauss made his proposal to Eisenhower, Strauss was already familiar with Teller's views and certainly shared his concerns about a test moratorium. See Teller to Strauss, 20 Mar. 1958, LLS, AEC, Box 111, Teller 1957–58.

27. Strauss to Goodpaster, 29 Jan. 1958, DDEL, OSS, SA, Box 5, Atomic Energy Matters-Presidential Actions (2); Strauss to Eisenhower, 29 Jan. 1958, ibid.

28. Dearborn to the President, 14 Feb. 1958, DDEL, AWF, OFA, Dearborn (microfilm), 9:882.

29. Edward Teller and Albert Latter, "The Compelling Need for Nuclear Tests," *Life* (10 Feb. 1958): 65–72.

30. "CIA Suggestions Relating to the International Posture of the United States," DDEL, OSANSA, OCB Series, Admin Subseries, Box 5, FM Dearborn File—Jan. 1958 (2)

31. For State Department warnings of a unilateral Soviet moratorium, see Sonnenfeldt to Farley, 13 Mar. 1958, NAII, RG59, Rec Rel A/E Matters, Lot 57D688, 3008B, Box 349; Record of Telephone Conversation, Dulles and Strauss, 23 Mar. 1958, DDEL, JFD, TC, (microfilm), 7:266; Record of Telephone Conversation, Dulles and the President, 23 Mar. 1958, DDEL, JFD, TC, WH (microfilm), 10:274. For Dulles's draft of a presidential announcement of a test moratorium, see DDEL, AWF, DS, Staff Notes, March 1958 (1).

32. Dulles had already asked his atomic energy advisors to consider revisions to the administration's disarmament policy. See Farley to Dulles, 22 Mar. 1958, NAII, RG59, S/AE, Disarm, 12A.282.

33. Memorandum of Conference with the President, 24 Mar. 1958, *FRUS, 1958–1960*, 3: 567–72. Smith-Norris characterizes Eisenhower's response to Dulles's proposal as "unenthusiastic." See Smith-Norris, "The Eisenhower Administration and the Nuclear Test Ban Talks, 1958–1960," 508. In an effort to defang the criticism it knew would accompany the Soviet announcement of a moratorium, the administration on 26 March announced that it would invite the United Nations to select scientific observers to witness a test of a clean bomb in the Pacific that demonstrated its concern with reducing fallout from testing. See the President's News Conference of 26 Mar. 1958, *PPP, Eisenhower, 1958*: 232–33. The administration quietly cancelled this test when it became clear that the shot would be neither clean nor tactical. See Herken, *Brotherhood*, 324–26.

34. Divine, *Blowing on the Wind*, 200.

35. Major General Richard Coiner, who was the air force's assistant deputy chief of staff for atomic energy operations, and Colonel Lester Woodward also served on the panel as representatives from Defense. Bethe recalled in an oral history interview that Carson Mark of Los Alamos favored a test ban. See interview with Bethe, 3 Nov. 1977, DDEL, Oral History 483, 12–13.

36. "Report of the NSC Ad Hoc Working Group (Bethe Panel) on the Technical Feasibility of a Cessation of Nuclear Testing," 27 Mar. 1958, DDEL, OSANSA, NSC, Briefing Notes, Box 2, Atomic Testing Killian Report.

37. Ibid. The panel proposed 32 seismic and 20 acoustic monitoring stations within the Soviet Union. Stassen, based upon Bethe's previous analysis, advocated a system with 8 to 12 stations. The larger figure likely reflected the panel's compromise between the higher estimates of the AEC and DOD and the lower estimates of Bethe and the CIA.

38. Memorandum of Discussion at the 361st Meeting of the NSC, 3 Apr. 1958, *FRUS, 1958–60*, 3: 585–89.

39. *NYT*, 9 Apr. 1958.

40. Eisenhower to Khrushchev, 8 Apr. 1958, *PPP, Eisenhower, 1958*: 290–93.

41. The President's News Conference, 9 Apr. 1958, ibid., 298–99.

42. Record of Telephone Conversation, Dulles and Strauss, 9 Apr. 1958, DDEL, JFD, TC (microfilm), 7:700.

43. It is unclear if Strauss desired a reappointment as the AEC's chairman. His letter of resignation to Eisenhower acknowledged that he had become a political liability within the administration and his nomination would face a difficult challenge from his critics on the JCAE, primarily its chairman, Senator Clinton P. Anderson (D-N.M.), whom Strauss claimed had an "almost psychopathic dislike for me." See Strauss to Eisenhower, 31 Mar. 1958, LLS, AEC, DDE, Box 26E. Strauss's political observation proved prescient, as the Senate rejected his later nomination as Secretary of Commerce.

44. Record of Telephone Conversation, Dulles and Strauss, 9 Apr. 1958, DDEL, JFD, TC (microfilm), 7:700. Hewlett and Holl, *Atoms for Peace and War*, 479–80.

45. Strauss to Reston, 9 Apr. 1958, LLS, AEC, Box 113, Tests and Testing—

1958 (April-August); see also Strauss's notes on his meeting with Lippmann, 14 Apr. 1958, LLS, AEC, Box 68, Monitoring of Soviet Tests (1958–1971).

46. James R. Killian, Jr. *The Education of a College President* (Cambridge: MIT Press, 1985).

47. Columbia University, Oral History Project, Butler Library, New York, Columbia University Sesquibicentennial Project, I. I. Rabi, 737–38.

48. The original members of PSAC who had served on the ODM's advisory committee were Berkner, Bethe, Bronk, Fisk, Haskins, Killian, Land, Rabi, and Zacharias.

49. Killian, *Sputnik, Scientists, and Eisenhower*, 277–79.

50. Ibid., 150–58.

51. Ibid., 157.

52. Herbert York, director of Livermore Laboratory from 1952 to 1958 originally voted against the conclusion that a test ban would be militarily advantageous. Pressured by the other scientists, he changed his mind the following day. See ibid; and York, *Making Weapons, Talking Peace*, 117–19.

53. Herken, *Cardinal Choices*, 109–110. Scoville was the assistant director of the CIA's scientific intelligence branch and a firm test-ban advocate.

54. Hewlett and Holl, *Atoms for Peace and War*, 480–81.

55. Memorandum of Conversation, 17 Apr. 1958, *FRUS, 1958–60*, 3:603–4.

56. Ibid.

57. Herken, *Cardinal Choices*, 110–11.

58. Memorandum of Conversation, 11 Apr. 1958, *FRUS, 1958–60*, 3:597–99.

59. Record of Telephone Conversation, Dulles and Adams, 19 Feb. 1958, *FRUS, 1958–60*, 3 (microfiche supplement), 291.

60. For more on the Gaither Committee, see Snead, *The Gaither Committee, Eisenhower, and the Cold War*.

61. Memorandum of Conversation with the President, 23 Sep. 1958, DDEL, OSANSA, SAS, Pres Sub, Box 3, Mtgs w/the President, 1958 [3].

62. Sprague to Eisenhower, 14 Nov. 1957, NAII, RG59 Dec File, 600.0012, 1955–59, 11–1457.

63. Eisenhower to Dulles, 19 Nov. 1957, NAII, RG59 Dec File, 600.0012, 1955–59, 11–1957.

64. Memorandum of Conversation, 8 Apr. 1958, *FRUS, 1958–60*, 3:590–97. Lovett was unable to attend this session.

65. Record of Telephone Conversation, Dulles and Strauss, 27 Sep. 1957, DDEL, JFD, TC, Box 7, TM Sep-Oct [3].

66. Ibid.

67. Memorandum of Conversation, 8 Apr. 1958, *FRUS, 1958–60*, 3: 590–97.

68. Memorandum of Conversation, 26 Apr. 1958, NAII, RG59 Dec File, 600.0012, 1955–59, Box 2269, 4–2858.

69. Emphasis added. Strauss, Memorandum for the Files, 28 Apr. 1958, LLS, AEC, Box 26A, JF Dulles.

70. Ibid.

71. Ibid. Failing to convince Dulles's consultants as a group, Strauss sought to convince them individually. He lunched with Robert Lovett following the meeting at Dulles's house and informed Dulles's atomic energy advisor, Philip Farley, that he and Lovett were unsure how each of the consultants stood on the test suspension. Skeptical of Strauss's claims, Farley confirmed that each of the four consultants agreed with Dulles that the administration should seek an inspected test cessation agreement upon the conclusion of the *HARDTACK* series. See Farley to Dulles, 28 Apr. 1958, NAII, RG59, Rec Rel A/E Matters, Lot 57D688, Box 349.

72. Hewlett and Holl, *Atoms for Peace and War*, 481–82; Divine, *Blowing on the Wind*, 211.

73. Eisenhower letter to Khrushchev, 28 Apr. 1958, *PPP, Eisenhower, 1957*: 350–31.

74. For Divine, the 28 April letter "marked a reversal of the long-standing American policy that test-ban negotiations be linked to other disarmament goals." See Divine, *Blowing on the Wind*, 211–12. For Martha Smith, this temporary moratorium did not entail any fundamental shift in the U.S. position of testing, which she contends remained linked to a foolproof inspection system and progress on other disarmament measures; see Smith, "The Nuclear Testing Policies of the Eisenhower Administration, 1953–1960," 341–42. Smith neglects the significant contrary evidence, cited above, that Dulles considered a system that provided a 50–50 chance of detection to be adequate.

75. Dulles and Eisenhower had agreed to separate testing from a cutoff in production, but decided they could not publicly announce the change at least until Congress passed an amended Atomic Energy Act. See Pre-press Conference Briefing, 30 Apr. 1958, DDEL, AWF, DS, Staff Notes April 1958 (1). Eisenhower believed that if they publicly announced a separation of testing from a cutoff in production that Congress would never amend the AEA, see Record of Telephone Conversation, Dulles and Eisenhower, 1 May 1958, DDEL, JFD, TC, WH (microfilm), 10:530.

76. "Underground Test Error," *Science* 127 (18 Apr. 1958): 866.

77. "Detection of Nuclear Explosions," *BAS* (May 1958): 197–98. A JCAE investigation into the matter accepted the AEC's explanation that the mistake was unintentional. See "AEC Absolved on Test Reports," *NYT,* 16 Mar. 1958.

78. For more on the Humphrey subcommittee hearings, see Hewlett and Holl, *Atoms for Peace and War*, 473–76 and Divine, *Blowing on the Wind*, 180–92.

79. Edward Teller and Albert Latter, "The Compelling Need for Nuclear Tests," *Life* (10 Feb. 1958): 65–72.

80. Hewlett and Holl, *Atoms for Peace and War*, 473–76. Teller was sharply critical of Pauling's arguments, but respectful of Bethe's. Teller believed that Bethe was being "misled by his wishes" in minimizing the difficulties of detection. See Teller to Strauss, 25 Apr. 1958, LLS, AEC, Box 111, Teller 1957–58.

81. *NYT,* 30 Apr. 1958.

82. *Time* (28 April 1958): 17.

83. *Newsweek* (28 April 1958): 22.

84. Memorandum for File, 1 May 1958, LLS, AEC, Box 68, Memo for the Record 1958.

85. Strauss, undated notes, LLS, AEC, Box 92, Rabi. It remains unclear if Strauss ever sent a final version of this draft letter to Eisenhower or used it as a basis for a discussion. His comments are consistent, however, with remarks he made to Dulles's disarmament advisors in the 26 April meeting. In an effort to appeal to Eisenhower's sense of loyalty, Strauss also emphasized that Lawrence and Teller had issued public endorsements of his test-ban position during the 1956 campaign.

86. *NYT,* 11 May 1958.

87. Strauss to Eisenhower, 8 May 1958, DDEL, AWF, OFA (microfilm), 4:577.

88. Record of Telephone Conversation, Eisenhower and Dulles, 1 May 1958, DDEL, JFD, TC WH (microfilm), 10:530. Ironically, this dislike benefited Strauss's goals in the case. Passage of the AEA was a prerequisite for gaining British support for a test-ban agreement separate from a cutoff of fissionable material production. As long as those items remained linked, there was little chance of Soviet acceptance of the more extensive inspection measures necessary to monitor a production cutoff.

89. Memorandum of Conference, 14 May 1958, DDEL, AWF, DS, Staff Notes May 1958 (2). Eisenhower had previously considered Strauss for Secretary of Defense, but Dulles convinced Eisenhower that appointing Strauss, who was a deeply devout Jew, would alienate the Muslim nations in the Middle East. Eisenhower later considered him to replace Sherman Adams as his chief of staff before nominating him as Secretary of Commerce in November 1958. Strauss had made so many enemies that the Senate voted against his nomination in July 1959.

90. Ibid.

91. Minutes, 58th Meeting of the GAC, 5–7 May 1958, DOE/NTA, Accession No. 0073731. The most influential member of the GAC was Edward Teller. Joining Teller on the GAC were James B. Fisk (who was also a PSAC member), John C. Warner, Edwin M. McMillen, Jessie W. Beams, chairman Warren C. Johnson, T. Keith Glennan, and Robert E. Wilson. Fisk, the member of GAC who appeared most favorable to a test ban during the meetings, was not present when the others drafted their recommendations on testing.

92. Memorandum of Conference, 14 May 1958, DDEL, AWF, DS, Staff Notes May 1958 (2).

93. A poll in February 1958 asked individuals if they would support a *multilateral* test-ban agreement with the Soviet Union. The poll reported that 49 percent said yes, 36 percent said no, and 15 percent expressed no opinion. When asked in May 1958 if they would support a *unilateral* test-ban agreement, 29 percent responded yes, 60 percent responded no, and 11 percent expressed no opinion. The poll in May also found that 46 percent agreed that continued testing posed health risks to future generations, 27 percent disagreed, and 27 percent expressed no opinion. See Gallup, *Gallup Poll,* 2: 1541, 1552–53.

94. Memorandum of Conversation, Killian and Dulles, 14 May 1958, *FRUS, 1958–60,* 3: 607–8.

95. Record of Telephone Conversation, Dulles and Killian, 21 May 1958, DDEL, JFD, TC, WH (microfilm), 10:501.

96. Memorandum of Conversation, 19 May 1958, *FRUS, 1958–60*, 3: 609–12.

97. The list of nominations is in DDEL, JFD, WHMS, Box 6, Meetings with the President January–June 1958 (2).

98. Memorandum of Conversation with the President, 22 May 1958, ibid.

99. Record of Telephone Conversation, Dulles and Eisenhower, 21 May 1958, DDEL, AWF, DS, Phone Calls, May 1958.

100. Memorandum of Conversation with the President, 22 May 1958, DDEL, JFD, WHMS, Box 6, Meetings with the President January–June 1958 (2). Memorandum of Conversation, Dulles and Strauss, 22 May 1958, DDEL, JFD, CS, Box 16, JFD Chron. May 1958 (1). Strauss had earlier expressed to Dulles his strong opposition to Bethe, whom he claimed made a "garbled or distorted report." See Record of Telephone Conversation, Dulles and Killian, 21 May 1958, DDEL, JFD, TC, WH (microfilm), 10:500.

101. The *New York Times* commented on the balanced views of the group, depicting Bacher as favorably inclined toward a test ban, Lawrence as opposed, and Fisk without a firm position on the issue. *NYT*, 4 July 1958.

102. Divine, *Blowing on the Wind*, 215–16. Herken, *Brotherhood*, 322–23.

103. Memorandum of Conference, 18 June 1958, *FRUS, 1958–60*, 3:612–13.

104. Herken, *Brotherhood*, 324–27.

105. Strauss to Lawrence, 23 June 1958, LLS, AEC, Box 59, Lawrence 1957–58.

106. Strauss to Lawrence, 14 Oct. 1955, LLS, AEC, Box 59, Lawrence, 1946–56.

107. Gregg Herken suggests that Strauss's June letter reflected his concern that Lawrence's views had moderated considerably before the physicist departed for Geneva and that Lawrence was determined to develop a brotherhood between U.S. and Soviet scientists at Geneva as a means to slow the arms race. See Herken, *Brotherhood*, 319–29.

108. Strauss in 1960 commented to McCone that the Geneva discussions had turned out unfavorably due to Lawrence's premature departure. His comments thus reflected no concern that Lawrence had moderated his position on testing beyond limiting the yield and the number of weapons tests. See Strauss, Memorandum for Files, 31 Mar. 1960, LLS, AEC, Box 62, McCone.

109. Divine, *Blowing on the Wind*, 225–227; Hewlett and Holl, *Atoms for Peace and War*, 540–42.

110. Divine, *Blowing on the Wind*, 225–27.

111. The principals met at least four times in August to consider how the administration should respond to the successful Geneva conference of experts. Their views did not substantially change over the course of the meetings. See Memorandum of Conversation, 8 Aug. 1958, *FRUS, 1958–60*, 3:624–30. Memorandum of Conversation, 13 Aug. 1958, *FRUS, 1958–60*, 3:631–36. Memorandum of Conversation, 15 Aug. 1958, *FRUS, 1958–60*, 3:638–43. Memorandum of Conversation, 18 Aug. 1958, *FRUS, 1958–60*, 3:644–46.

112. Ibid.

113. Memorandum of Conversation, Dulles and Eisenhower, 10 July 1958, *FRUS, 1958–60*, 3:616.

114. Memorandum of Conference, 4 August 1958, *FRUS, 1958–60*, 3:617–18.

115. Pre-press notes, 6 Aug. 1958, DDEL, AWF, DS, Staff Notes August 1958 (3).

116. Memorandum for Files, 8 Aug. 1958, LLS, AEC, Box 62, McCone.

117. Memorandum of Conference, 12 Aug. 1958, DDEL, AWF, DS, Staff Notes August 1958 (2). Eisenhower wrote Teller on 21 August to inform him of his decision to suspend tests, but encouraged the staff at Livermore to "continue their research and development in this field [nuclear weapons] with their current vigor and devotion." See Eisenhower to Teller, 21 Aug. 1958, DDEL, WHCF, CF, Subject Series, Box 9, Atomic Weapons.

118. Hewlett and Holl, *Atoms for Peace and War*, 545.

119. Memorandum for Record, 13 Aug. 1958, DDEL, OSANSA, SAS, Subject Subseries, Box 6, MFR (1).

120. Dulles was in New York participating in discussions at the United Nations.

121. Goodpaster, Memorandum of Conference, 18 Aug. 1958, *FRUS, 1958–60*, 3:647–48. Gray, Memorandum of Meeting, 18 Aug. 1958, DDEL, OSANSA, SAS, Pres Sub, Box 3, Meetings with President—1958 (3).

122. Smith, "The Nuclear Testing Policies of the Eisenhower Administration, 1953–1960," 384.

123. Strauss, Memorandum For Files, 20 Aug. 1958, LLS, AEC, Box 67, MFR 1958.

124. Ibid.

125. Statement by the President Following the Geneva Meeting of Experts Proposing Negotiations on Nuclear Controls, 22 Aug. 1958, *PPP, Eisenhower, 1958*: 635–36.

126. Hewlett and Holl, *Atoms for Peace and War*, 546–47.

127. Smith, "The Nuclear Testing Policies of the Eisenhower Administration, 1953–1960," 412–14; Smith-Norris, "The Eisenhower Administration and the Nuclear Test Ban Talks, 1958–1960," 503–4, 512.

128. Record of Telephone Conversation, Herter and Eisenhower, 19 Aug. 1958, DDEL, CH, TC, Box 10, Telephone Conversations with the President—1958 (1).

129. Record of Telephone Conversation, Herter and Eisenhower, 19 Aug. 1958, DDEL, AWF, DS, Box 35, August 1958 Telephone Calls.

130. Divine, *Blowing on the Wind*, 222–25.

Chapter 8

EPIGRAPHS: Memorandum of Conference, 19 Mar. 1959, *FRUS, 1958–60*, 3: 716–18. Record of Telephone Conversation, Dillon and Herter, 8 Aug. 1959, DDEL, CH, TC (microfilm), 11:340. Memorandum of Conference, 20 Oct. 1959, DDEL, McC, Box 5, McCone Sealed File, 3.

1. According to Gordon Chang, the Soviet Union attempted to resolve the crisis before the 31 October test deadline. See Chang, *Friends and Enemies*, 182–202.

2. Smith-Norris, "The Eisenhower Administration and the Nuclear Test Ban Talks, 1958–1960," 538.

3. Joining Wadsworth in Geneva were scientists, representatives of the applicable government agencies, and two senators from the JCAE. Robert Bacher, one of the three lead scientists heading the U.S. delegation in 1958 to the Conference of Experts, served as Wadsworth's deputy. Hans Bethe attended the conference for three weeks as a consultant.

4. Teller to Strauss, 13 Sep. 1958, LLS, AEC, Box 111, Teller 1957–58. In the same letter, Teller mentioned the impression, based upon conversations with Richard Latter of the RAND Corporation and Harold Brown from Livermore, that Bacher made "a positive contribution. On the other hand, Fisk was quite weak and as the leader of our delegation had a great opportunity to do damage."

5. Memorandum of Conversation, 30 Sep. 1958, *FRUS, 1958–60*, 3:662–65.

6. Statement by the President Concerning the Continued Testing of Nuclear Weapons by the Soviet Union, 7 Nov. 1958, *PPP, Eisenhower, 1958*: 838–39.

7. The Soviet Union in September 1961 resumed testing.

8. Memorandum of Discussion at the 392nd Meeting of the NSC, 23 Dec. 1958, *FRUS, 1958–60*, 3:680–82.

9. Divine, *Blowing on the Wind*, 243–45. According to Martha Smith, the most contentious issue was the Eisenhower administration's continued insistence on linking a test ban with agreements on other disarmament issues. As discussed previously, Eisenhower and Dulles had already agreed to drop this link but not announce it publicly until absolutely necessary. Wadsworth announced this change at Geneva on 20 January 1959. See Smith, "The Nuclear Testing Policies of the Eisenhower Administration, 1953–1960," 398–402.

10. Jacobson and Stein, *Diplomats, Scientists, and Politicians*, 127.

11. Record of Telephone Conversation, Dulles and Herter, 25 Oct. 1958, DDEL, JFD, TC (microfilm), 7:1080. Dulles was concerned that Murray's attendance would sabotage the negotiations, but considered it "worse politics" to deny Gore's request. Dulles was unsure how Murray, as a "man of strong valued and fanatical convictions" who did not agree with some of the administration's policies, would act. Therefore, he was concerned that packing the delegation with those "unsympathetic to the administration" risked breaking up the negotiations. Dulles eventually allowed Murray to attend, but asked Herter to inform Gore that he had to be the "guarantor of Murray's proper conduct." Memorandum of Telephone Conversation, Herter and Gore, 26 Oct. 1958, DDEL, CH, CCS (microfilm), 20:237.

12. Memorandum of Conversation, Dulles and Murray, 28 Oct. 1958, DDEL, JFD, GCMS, Box 1, Memoranda of Conversation General L-M (4).

13. Bryce Harlow, Memorandum for Record, 18 Nov. 1958, DDEL, AWF, DS, Box 37, Staff Notes, Nov '58.

14. Gordon Gray to John Foster Dulles, McElroy, McCone, Allen Dulles, and Killian, 26 Nov. 1958, DDEL, OSANSA, NSC, Briefing Notes, Box 2, [Atomic Testing] Suspension of Nuclear Testing, 1958–1960 (2).

15. Memorandum of Conversation, 18 Nov. 1958, DDEL, JFD, CS, (microfilm), 13:036. Dulles also thought that Gore's "views probably reflect Murray's." See Record of Telephone Conversation, Dulles and McElroy, 18 Nov. 1958, DDEL, JFD, TC (microfilm), 8:322. PSAC's consideration of the issue referred to it alternately as the "Gore-Murray" proposal and the "Gore-Teller" proposal. Teller on 25 July had presented a similar proposal to allow underground tests to continue. See Skolnikoff to Killian, 18 Nov. 1958, DDEL, OSAST, Box 3, Disarmament—Nuclear Test Policy (2); and Record of Meetings, PSAC, 15–16 Dec. 1958, DDEL, US PSAC, Box 5, ROA & Meetings-PSAC.

16. Skolnikoff to Killian, 18 Nov. 1958, DDEL, OSAST, Box 3, Disarmament—Nuclear Test Policy (2).

17. Record of Special PSAC Meeting 21 Nov. 1958 on Nuclear Test Cessation Negotiations, 1 Dec. 1958, ibid. See also Skolnikoff to Killian, 21 Nov. 1958, ibid.

18. James J. Wadsworth, *The Price of Peace* (New York: Praeger, 1962), 24.

19. Panelists joining Berkner represented a cross section of opinion on the test-ban issue, from advocates, such as Bethe, to opponents, such as Albert Latter.

20. Memorandum of Conference, 12 Jan. 1959, *FRUS, 1958–60*, 3:683–87.

21. At this stage, Eisenhower believed that an adequate threshold could be set between 10kt and 20kt. Ibid. Eisenhower's commitment to a broad ban and rejection of McCone's call for an immediate atmospheric ban contradicts Smith-Norris's argument that Eisenhower sided with the AEC and Defense view. See Smith-Norris, "The Eisenhower Administration and the Nuclear Test Ban Talks, 1958–1960," 504. In fact, Eisenhower remained at odds with leaders of both organizations from January to March 1959.

22. Memorandum of Conference, 5 Jan. 1959, *FRUS, 1958–60*, 3:682–83.

23. Memorandum of Conference, 12 Jan. 1959, ibid., 683–87. For Eisenhower's letter to Macmillan notifying him of the change, see Eisenhower to Macmillan, 12 Jan. 1959, NAUK, FO 371/140433. Drafts of the message dated 11 Jan. 1959 reveal that Eisenhower had decided on the policy change before the meeting with his advisors on 12 Jan. 1959. See DDEL, AWF, D-H, Box 11, Dulles, Jan '59 [2].

24. Memorandum of Conference, 26 Jan. 1959, DDEL OSANSA, NSC, Briefing Notes, Box 6, Disarmament and Nuclear Test Ban Negotiations [1958–59].

25. Memorandum for Files, 10 Dec. 1958, LLS, AEC, Box 67, MFR 1958.

26. Strauss to Teller, 7 Jan. 1959, LLS, AEC, Box 111, Teller 1959–60.

27. Memorandum for Files, 10 Dec. 1958, LLS, AEC, Box 67, MFR 1958. Teller and Morse also had already appealed directly to Brigadier General Andrew J. Goodpaster, Eisenhower's staff secretary and one of his closest confidants, as he witnessed in October one of the nuclear tests in Nevada. Once again, Teller emphasized the possible loopholes in the Geneva system and stressed the neces-

sity of continued testing for peaceful purposes. See Gray, Memorandum of Conversation, 9 Oct. 1958, DDEL, OSANSA, SAS, Subject Sub, Box 11, Nuclear Testing. Goodpaster, Memorandum for Record, 10 Oct. 1958, DDEL, OSS, Subject Ser, Alpha Sub, Box 20, Nevada - Trip to Test Site [June-Oct 1958] [1].

28. Hewlett and Holl, *Atoms for Peace and War*, 489–90. McCone later became, to Eisenhower's great displeasure, Director of the CIA under Kennedy. McCone's suspicions in October 1962 about Soviet activities in Cuba were instrumental in authorizing the U-2 flights that discovered the installation of Soviet missiles.

29. Ibid., 497–98.

30. The *Bulletin of the Atomic Scientists* highlighted this episode as the "most significant part of the hearings for readers of the *Bulletin*." See "John McCone: New AEC Chairman," *BAS* (Oct. 1958): 334–35. *NYT*, 3 July 1958.

31. Memorandum of Conversation, 30 Jan. 1959, *FRUS, 1958–60*, 3:696–98.

32. Record of Telephone Conversation, Herter and McCone, 17 Jan. 1959, DDEL, CH, TC.

33. Charles J. V. Murphy, "Nuclear Inspection: A Near Miss," *Fortune* (Mar. 1959): 122–25, 155–62.

34. Bethe to Murphy, 19 Jan. 1959 and 20 Jan. 1959, HAB, Box 4, Folder 18 (Atomic Weapons Test Ban: Private Articles).

35. Memorandum of Meeting (27 Jan. 1959) with the President, 29 Jan. 1959, DDEL, OSANSA, SAS, Pres Sub, Box 4, Mtgs w/the President, 1959, [6]. McCone pressured Murphy to omit the specific details of the NSC discussion in April 1958, warning him that the administration would otherwise suppress the article. See Memorandum for File, 26 Jan. 1959, DDEL, OSANSA, NSC, Briefing Notes, Box 6, Disarmament and Nuclear Test Ban Negotiations [1958–59]. Murphy told McCone that the source of the NSC meeting details was Bethe, though he had also talked with Fisk, Teller, Gray, Dulles, and several others in the State Department. In contrast to Strauss, who often publicly dealt with personalities, McCone pressured Murphy not to emphasize the "division of opinion on doctrinaire or ideological grounds between the two groups of scientists." McCone emphatically told Murphy that he was doing an injustice to the administration by "digging up an old argument which we were all trying to bury." McCone threatened to call Henry Luce, the editor of Time-Life, to have the article suppressed if Murphy did not delete the emphasis on the divisions within the scientific community. See McCone, Memorandum for Files, 3 Feb. 1959, DDEL, McC, Com File, Box 1, COM 1-Chairman's Reading File - 1959 Jan-Mar.

36. Memorandum for Files, 10 Dec. 1958, LLS, AEC, Box 67, MFR 1958.

37. Memorandum of Conference, 26 Jan. 1959, DDEL, OSANSA, NSC, Briefing Notes, Box 6, Disarmament and Nuclear Test Ban Negotiations [1958–59].

38. Memorandum of Conversation, 30 Jan. 1959, *FRUS, 1958–60*, 3:696–98.

39. Memorandum of Conversation, 26 Mar. 1959, DDEL, OSAST, Box 8, Disarmament - Nuclear Test Policy [May '58 - Oct '60] [2].

40. Memorandum of Conversation, 21 Mar. 1959, *FRUS, 1958–60*, 3:720–25.

41. Strauss, Memorandum of Conversation, 7 Apr. 1958, LLS, AEC, Box 26A, JF Dulles.

42. Dulles to Hoegh, 2 Apr. 1958, DDEL, JFD, GCMS, Box 5, Misc Corr Nov 57 - Apr 58.

43. Memorandum of Conversation, 20 Mar. 1959, *FRUS, 1958–60*, 3:719–20.

44. Memorandum of Conversation, 26 Jan. 1959, DDEL, OSANSA, NSC, Briefing Notes, Box 6, Disarmament and Nuclear Test Ban Negotiations [1958–59].

45. Like Eisenhower, Dulles had approved this course several months before, but wanted to wait for a propitious moment to signal greater flexibility.

46. Dulles set the odds at Soviet acceptance of adequate inspection at 1:100. See Memorandum of Conversation, 30 Jan. 1959, *FRUS, 1958–60*, 3: 696–98.

47. Telegram, 5 Feb. 1959, ibid., 699–700; Memorandum of Conversation, 20 Mar. 1959, ibid., 719–20.

48. Dulles died on 24 May 1959. See Divine, *Blowing on the Wind*, 242–43, 255–56.

49. Ambrose, *Eisenhower*, 2: 524–26. At Dulles's urging, Eisenhower appointed Herter as his replacement. Eisenhower made his appointment contingent upon Herter receiving a full medical examination by "a whole bevy of doctors." See Memorandum of Conference, 13 Apr. 1959, DDEL, AWF, DS (microfilm), 21:240. Herter, who suffered badly from arthritis, passed the medical examination and became the Secretary of State on 21 April.

50. Memorandum of Conversation, 12 Feb. 1959, *FRUS, 1958–60*, 3:702–5.

51. Memorandum of Conversation, 21 Mar. 1959, ibid., 720–25. Killian's successor as Eisenhower's science advisor, George Kistiakowsky, eventually convinced Herter that Teller had greatly exaggerated the risks of a Soviet evasion. In time, Herter began to support Kistiakowsky over AEC and Defense.

52. Memorandum of Conference with the President, 22 Mar. 1959, ibid., 725–27; Memorandum of Conversation, 22 Mar. 1959, DDEL, OSAST, Box 3, Disarmament—Nuclear Test Policy (3).

53. Memorandum of Conversation, 26 Jan. 1959, *FRUS, 1958–60*, 3: 692–96.

54. Memorandum of Conversation, 2 Mar. 1959, DDEL, McC, Box 5, Mc-Cone Sealed File, 3.

55. Memorandum of Conversation, 26 Mar. 1959, DDEL, OSAST, Box 8, Disarmament-Nuclear Test Policy [May '58 - Oct '60] [2]. See also Killian's suggested modification of his comments to the record of the meeting, Killian to the Department of State, 31 Mar. 1959, ibid.

56. Memorandum of Conversation, 15 Apr. 1959, DDEL, OSANSA, NSC, Briefing Notes, Box 1, AEC—Nuclear Testing.

57. Memorandum of Conference, 25 Feb. 1959, DDEL, AWF, DS, Staff Notes February 1959 (1). Memorandum of Conference, 13 Mar. 1959, DDEL, AWF, DS, Staff Notes March 1959 (1).

58. Memorandum of Conference, 17 Mar. 1959, *FRUS, 1958–60*, 3: 714–16. See also the State Department record of this meeting at NAII, RG59, Dec File, 600.0012, 1955–1959, Box 2271, 3–1759. Three days later, Eisenhower indicated that he considered establishing the threshold above which underground tests would be prohibited at 100kt. This is significantly larger than the initial proposals for a threshold ban, which were based upon yields ranging from 10kt to 20kt. The larger threshold likely reflects the conclusions of the Berkner Panel. See Memorandum of Conference, 20 Mar. 1959, *FRUS, 1958–60*, 3:719–20.

59. Memorandum of Conference, 19 Mar. 1959, *FRUS, 1958–60*, 3:716–18.

60. See the Report of the Panel on Seismic Improvement (Berkner Panel), 16 Mar. 1959, DDEL, OSANSA, SAS, Subject Sub, Box 7, Science and Research-General (6). See also Spurgeon Keeny's summary of the report, Keeny to Killian, 13 Mar. 1959, DDEL, OSAST, Box 13, Nuclear Test Suspension - Seismic Data [Jan '58 - Apr '60] [2].

61. Report of the Panel on Seismic Improvement, 16 Mar. 1959, DDEL, OSANSA, SAS, Subject Sub, Box 7, Science and Research-General (6). See also Spurgeon Keeny's summary of the report, Keeny to Killian, 13 Mar. 1959, DDEL, OSAST, Box 13, Nuclear Test Suspension - Seismic Data [Jan '58 - Apr '60] [2]. Although the Panel on High Altitude Detection determined that it would be possible to evade a detection system by testing in space, it concluded that the cost to do so would be prohibitive.

62. Memorandum of Conference, 25 Feb. 1959, *FRUS, 1958–60*, 3:710–12.

63. Killian to Eisenhower, 31 Mar. 1959, DDEL, AWF, OFA, Killian (1).

64. Contrary to Smith, Eisenhower had yielded not to the pressure from the AEC and Defense, but to the weight of the counsel of his science advisors. Nevertheless, Eisenhower's movement toward an atmospheric ban was most pleasing to McCone, who was overjoyed that the administration was finally moving toward the basic AEC position he had outlined the previous December. See McCone, Memorandum to File, 9 Apr. 1959, DDEL, McC, Box 5, McCone Sealed File, 5, [2].

65. Killian also believed that he needed to return to his duties as the president of MIT. See Killian, *Sputnik, Scientists, and Eisenhower*, 205–7.

66. See for example Eisenhower's comments to Lawrence, Mills, and Teller, Memorandum of Conference, 24 June 1957, DDEL, AWF, DS, Staff Memo June 1957. Eisenhower in 1958 told Strauss that he believed that "testing is not evil, but the fact is that people have been brought to believe that it is." See Memorandum of Conference with the President, 24 Mar. 1958, *FRUS, 1958–60*, 3:570. See also Memorandum of Conversation, 12 Aug. 1958, DDEL, AWF, DS, Staff Notes August 1958 (2).

67. Libby minimized the hazards by stating that a person would have to consume a diet solely of wheat to approach the maximum tolerable level. Nevertheless, the fact that testing had reached near the maximum tolerable levels convinced Eisenhower not to authorize any atmospheric tests. 6 Mar. 1959, DDEL, AWF, DS, Staff Notes 1–15 Mar 59 (2); DDEL, OSS, Cabinet Series, Box 5, C-50 [1].

68. Divine, *Blowing on the Wind*, 271–75.

69. Memorandum of Conference, 17 Mar. 1959, *FRUS, 1958–60*, 3:714–16.

70. Memorandum, 17 Mar. 1959, NAII, RG59, Dec File, 600.0012, 1955–1959, Box 2271, 3–1759.

71. Record of Meeting with the Soviet Leaders at Semyonovskoye, 22 Feb. 1959, NAUK, PREM 11/2690. Record of Meeting in the Prime Minister's Dacha, 25 Feb. 1959, ibid.

72. Memorandum of Conference, 21 Mar. 1959, *FRUS, 1958–60*, 3:720–25.

73. Memorandum of Conference, 17 Mar. 1959, ibid., 714–16. Memorandum, 17 Mar. 1959, NAII, RG59, Dec File, 600.0012, 1955–1959, Box 2271, 3–1759.

74. Eisenhower to Macmillan, 23 Feb. 1959, DDEL, AWF, OFI, Box 24, Macmillan Oct '58 - Mar '59 [5].

75. Memorandum of Conference with the President, 19 Mar. 1959, *FRUS, 1958–60*, 3:716–18.

76. Memorandum of Conversation, 22 Mar. 1959, DDEL, JFD, WHMS, Box 7, WH Mtg w/ President 1959 [1].

77. See FRUS for several memoranda of conversations during Macmillan's visit. Memorandum of Conference, 20 Mar. 1959, *FRUS, 1958–60*, 3: 719–20. Memorandum of Conference, 21 Mar. 1959, ibid., 720–25. Memorandum of Conference, 22 Mar. 1959, ibid., 725–27. See also the editorial note on a second conversation with Dulles, ibid., 728.

78. Macmillan suggested pairing the inspected atmospheric ban with a temporarily uninspected ban on tests underground and at high altitudes. Eisenhower rejected offering this to his proposal to Khrushchev, but promised Macmillan that he would have his advisors study it and consider it as a future proposal if the Soviets rejected an inspected ban on underground tests. See Eisenhower to Macmillan, 4 Apr. 1959, NAUK, FO 371/140437; Macmillan to Eisenhower, 8 Apr. 1959, Ibid.; Eisenhower to Macmillan, 9 Apr. 1959, DDEL, AWF, DS, Box 40, DDE Dictation Apr. 1959; Macmillan to Eisenhower, 10 Apr. 1959, NAUK, FO 371/140437; Eisenhower to Macmillan, 11 Apr. 1959, ibid.; Macmillan to Eisenhower, 11 Apr. 1959, ibid. For the discussion of Macmillan's proposal see Memorandum of Conversation, 15 Apr. 1959, DDEL, OSANSA, NSC, Briefing Notes, Box 1, AEC—Nuclear Testing. For Herter's summary recommendation to Eisenhower see Memorandum for the President, 23 Apr. 1959, *FRUS, 1958–60*, 3: 733–34. For the detailed explanation attached to the cover letter to Eisenhower, see DDEL, OSAST, Box 8, Disarmament-Nuclear Test Policy [May '58 - Oct '60] [3]. When Gray informed Eisenhower that the Principals unanimously rejected Macmillan's proposal, Eisenhower, illustrating that his commitment to a ban ran ahead of his advisors, responded that he thought the "unanimous view" was "the wrong one." For Eisenhower's response, see Memorandum of Meeting with the President, 16 Apr. 1959, DDEL, OSANSA, SAS, Pres Sub, Box 4, Mtgs w/ the President, Jun-Dec 1959 [3]. In Eisenhower's view, there was not a pressing requirement to test in the near future, thus it would be worth accepting a temporary comprehensive ban without sufficient detection capabilities if that

was the cost of reaching an agreement on a permanent atmospheric ban with adequate controls. See Memorandum of Conversation, 13 Apr. 1959, DDEL, CH, Box 7, Chron File Apr '59 [2].

79. Eisenhower to Khrushchev, 13 Apr. 1959, DDEL, AWF, OFI, USSR Khrushchev April-November 1959 (4).

80. Divine, *Blowing on the Wind*, 257–59. Khrushchev to Eisenhower, 23 Apr. 1959, DDEL, AWF, OFI, USSR Khrushchev Apr.-Nov. 1959 (2).

81. Memorandum of Conversation, 17 June 1959, DDEL, OSANSA, NSC, Briefing Notes, Box 2, [Atomic Testing] Suspension of Nuclear Testing, 1958–1960 (5). According to Smith-Norris, Soviet negotiators subsequently indicated that they would accept somewhere between 3 and 20 inspections annually; see Smith-Norris, "The Eisenhower Administration and the Nuclear Test Ban Talks, 1958–1960," 526. According to PSAC's study, this fell well below what the Eisenhower administration would accept. Although Eisenhower had previously indicated that he would accept a system that provided a 90 percent assurance of detection, the gap between PSAC's assessment and the Soviet position proved too large to bridge. See Memorandum of Conversation, 2 May 1959, DDEL, OSS, Subj Series, DoS Sub, Box 3, State Dept. May-Sep 1959 [1].

82. Memorandum of Conference with the President, 2 May 1959, DDEL, OSS, Subj Series, DoS Sub, Box 3, State Dept. May-Sep 1959 [1]. Memorandum of Conversation with the President, 2 May 1959, DDE, CH, CCS (microfilm) 9:1068. Herter respectfully declined to reprimand McCone, citing Dulles's practice of allowing agencies to present their opposing views to the president in person.

83. Memorandum of Conversation, 5 May 1959, *FRUS, 1958–60*, 3: 737–42; Memorandum for the Files, 5 May 1959, DDEL, McC, Com File, Box 1, COM 1-Chairman's Memo for File through Dec '59; Memorandum of Conference with the President, 5 May 1959, DDEL, AWF, DS (microfilm), 21: 550.

84. Killian responded that in PSAC's view a test ban would still be advantageous to the United States.

85. Memorandum of Conference with the President, 5 May 1959, DDEL, AWF, DS (microfilm), 21:550.

86. Memorandum of Conversation, 5 May 1959, *FRUS, 1958–60*, 3: 737–42; Memorandum for the Files, 5 May 1959, DDEL, McC, Com File, Box 1, COM 1-Chairman's Memo for File through Dec '59; Memorandum of Conference with the President, 5 May 1959, DDEL, AWF, DS (microfilm), 21:550.

87. Memorandum of Conference with the President, 8 June 1959, DDEL, OSS, Subj Series, DoS Sub, Box 3, State Dept - 1959 [May-Sep] [3].

88. Notes on pre-press briefing, 3 June 1959, DDEL, AWF, DS (microfilm), 21:907.

89. See, for example, Eisenhower's comment in March 1959 to Dulles that in this "terrific armament race we must . . . have some little bit of hope—even if only in controlling atmospheric tests . . . In the long run there is nothing but war—if we give up all hope of a peaceful solution." Importantly, Eisenhower at this stage believed that an atmospheric ban would still include a few control

posts within Soviet soil. See Record of Telephone Conversation, Eisenhower and Dulles, 7 Apr. 1959, DDEL, AWF, DS, (microfilm), 21:118.

90. Memorandum of Meeting with the President, 1 June 1959, DDEL, OSANSA, SAS, Pres Sub, Box 4, Mtgs w/the President, 1959 [1].

91. According to Kistiakowsky, the panelists unduly yielded to aggressive arguments of Harold Brown, Teller's deputy at Livermore. Brown provided an especially negative assessment of the effectiveness of on-site inspection. See Kistiakowsky, *A Scientist at the White House*, 6. David Beckler, PSAC's executive officer, wrote Killian several years later that the Bacher Panel limited their discussions to technical issues and was not unduly influenced by Brown. See Beckler to Killian, 28 July 1975, JRK, Box 13, JRK Book, B.D. A-N.

92. See Record of Meetings, 1–2 July 1959, DDEL, OSAST, Box 8, Disarmament-Nuclear (Feb '58 - Apr '60).

93. For a summary of the Bacher Panel conclusions, see Luedtke to McCone, 8 July 1959, DDEL, McC, Box 6, Testing File #2 Eyes Only [4]. For a discussion of the report's implications, see Meeting of the Principals, 9 July 1959, DDEL, OSANSA, NSC, Briefing Notes, Box 2, [Atomic Testing] Suspension of Nuclear Testing, 1958–1960 (4).

94. The State Department's initial proposal, similar to Harold Macmillan's April framework, combined a ban on atmospheric tests with a temporary uninspected ban on underground tests while joint studies determined the ability to adequately detect tests in that environment. Meeting of the Principals, 16 July 1959, DDEL, OSANSA, NSC, Briefing Notes, Box 2, [Atomic Testing] Suspension of Nuclear Testing, 1958–1960 (4). The State Department proposal would ban tests in the atmosphere as well as those at high-altitudes. Although the Soviet Union remained unwilling to reconsider the underground detection issues, they had participated in the successful "Technical Working Group I" discussions on high-altitude testing, held from 22 June to 10 July 1959. Their agreement on these issues prompted the administration to extend the atmospheric ban to high-altitude tests. The State Department proposal also recommended a threshold ban on atmospheric tests below 10–25kt. Kistiakowsky to the President, DDEL, OSAST, Box 8, Disarmament-Nuclear Test Policy May 1959-October 1960 (4); McCone, Memorandum for the Files, DDEL, McC, Com File, Box 1, COM 1-Chairman's Memo for File [1959]. Memorandum of Conference with the President, 23 July 1959, *FRUS, 1958–60*, 3: 759–63.

95. Kistiakowsky, *A Scientist at the White House*, 17.

96. Killian to Eisenhower, 20 Apr. 1959, DDEL, OSS, Subj Series, White House Sub, Box 4, Dr. Killian [3]; Goodpaster, Memorandum for Record, 27 Apr. 1959, ibid.

97. Kistiakowsky, *A Scientist at the White House*, 10–11.

98. Ibid., 23.

99. Ibid., 9–11.

100. Meeting of the Principals, 16 July 1959, DDEL, OSANSA, NSC, Briefing Notes, Box 2, [Atomic Testing] Suspension of Nuclear Testing, 1958–1960 (4).

101. Kistiakowsky, *A Scientist at the White House*, 22.

102. Ibid., 17.

103. Bethe to Kistiakowsky, 22 July 1959, DDEL, OSAST, Box 8, Disarmament-Nuclear Test Policy [May '58 - Oct '60] [3].

104. Kistiakowsky, *A Scientist at the White House*, 21.

105. Memorandum of Conference with the President, 4 Aug. 1959, DDEL, AWF, DS (microfilm), 22:812; Kistiakowsky to the President, 4 Aug. 1959, ibid., 22:814.

106. Memorandum of Conversation, 10 Aug. 1959, DDEL, AWF, DS (microfilm), 22:774.

107. Kistiakowsky, *A Scientist at the White House*, 36–37.

108. Ibid., 16 July 1959, 11. Discussion at the 413th Meeting of the NSC, 16 July 1959, DDEL, AWF, NSC Series, Box 11, 413th Mtg of NSC 7/16/59.

109. McRae was the vice president of the Western Electric Company and a former president of the Sandia Corporation. The McRae Panel's report acknowledged a requirement to conduct some "safety" tests to ensure that nuclear weapons did not detonate accidentally. These tests posed little risk of releasing nuclear components. Report, Ad Hoc Panel on Nuclear Test Requirements, 18 Aug. 1959, DDEL, OSAST, Box 2, Ad Hoc Panel on Nuclear Requirements, Aug '59 - Apr '60.

110. Kistiakowsky, *A Scientist at the White House*, 42–46.

111. Twining to McElroy, 21 Aug. 1959, DDEL, OSAST, Box 3, Disarmament—Nuclear Test Policy (3); McElroy to Eisenhower, 14 Sep. 1959, DDEL, AWF, OFA, McElroy 1959 (1).

112. Kistiakowsky, *A Scientist at the White House*, 73.

113. Ibid., 48–49.

114. Ibid., 23.

115. Khrushchev Speech to United Nations, *NYT*, 19 Sep. 1959.

116. Previously, the Soviet Union insisted that twenty-eight of the thirty technicians staffing the control posts were Soviet citizens. The West proposed ten from the West, ten from the Soviet Union, and ten from neutral nations. Lodge speculated that Khrushchev would accept a 50–50 split between Soviet and Western technicians. See Lodge, Memorandum of Conversation, 17 Sep. 1959, DDEL, AWF, OFI, USSR-Khrushchev Visit 15–27 September 1959 (1) and Lodge, Memorandum of Conversation, 18 Sep. 1959, ibid. Khrushchev later suggested that his intransigence was due to his awareness that the Soviets were behind in strategic striking power. He feared that Western inspectors would have also discovered this. See Divine, *Blowing on the Wind*, 287. See also Khrushchev, *Khrushchev Remembers*, 410–11, 536. Herter and Gromyko also briefly discussed the test-ban negotiations. Gromyko indicated that the number of inspections and the staffing of the control posts were the only major unresolved issues. See Editorial Note, *FRUS, 1958–60*, 3:776.

117. Eisenhower to Macmillan, 1 Oct. 1959, NAUK, PREM 11/2675; Memorandum, President Eisenhower's talks with Chairman Khrushchev at Camp David, ibid.

118. Eisenhower to Macmillan, 29 Sep. 1959, NAUK, PREM 11/2675.

119. Memorandum of Conversation, 9 Oct. 1959, DDEL, AWF, DS, Box 45, Stf Notes—Oct '59 [2].

120. Memorandum of Conference with the President, 16 Oct. 1959, DDEL, AWF, DS (microfilm), 23:498.

121. The delegates originally agreed to resume the negotiations on 12 October, but later agreed to extend the recess until 27 October to provide sufficient time between the British elections and the resumption of the test talks.

122. Memorandum of Conversation, 6 Oct. 1959, *FRUS, 1958–60*, 3:777–89.

123. Ironically, it may have been John McCone who convinced the Soviet Union to accept the talks, which most test-ban opponents feared would lead to further delays in the resumption of testing. McCone met with Soviet diplomat K. V. Novikov in Vienna emphasizing the importance of the new technical data for detecting underground tests. McCone also suggested that the administration would accept a quota of around 200 annual on-site inspections. McCone was in Vienna attending a conference of the International Atomic Energy Agency. Memorandum of Discussions, 2 Oct. 1959, DDEL, McC, Box 6, Testing File #2 Eyes Only [2]. In McCone's view, technical talks would "reveal to any reasonable man the futility of safeguarding an underground cessation." Memorandum of Conversation, 6 Oct. 1959, *FRUS, 1958–60*, 3: 777–89.

124. Record of Telephone Conversation, Herter and Kistiakowsky, 11 Nov. 1959, DDEL, CH, TC (microfilm), 11:231.

125. Rabi was recovering from a recent heart attack. See Kistiakowsky, *A Scientist at the White House*, 150–51.

126. Kistiakowsky Diary, 5 Nov. 1959, DDEL.

127. Record of Telephone Conversation, Herter and Bacher, 10 Nov. 1959, DDEL, CH, TC (microfilm), 11:235.

128. Kistiakowsky, *A Scientist at the White House*, 147.

129. Memorandum of Discussion with the President, 11 Nov. 1959, DDEL, OSAST, Box 8, Disarmament-Nuclear Test Policy [May '58 - Oct '60] [4].

130. Fisk to Herter, 19 Dec. 1959, GBK, Cor 59–60, Box 29, GBK—Miscell Corre from Wash, file 3 of 8.

131. After the initial success of the 1958 Geneva Conference of Experts, Eugene Rabinowitch commented that the conference had "confirmed the belief of scientists that once an international problem had been formulated in scientifically significant terms, scientists from all countries, despite their different political or ideological backgrounds, will be able to find a common language and an agreed solution." See Rabinowitch, "Nuclear Bomb Tests," *BAS* (Oct. 1958): 282–87.

132. Kistiakowsky, *A Scientist at the White House*, 150.

Chapter 9

EPIGRAPHS: Memorandum of Conference with the President, 18 May 1960, DDEL, OSS, SA, AEC v.III (4). Herter to Wadsworth, 28 June 1960, DDEL, CH, Box 20, Letters M-Z Official-Classified (3).

1. Memorandum of Conversation, 23 Dec. 1959, DDEL, OSANSA, SAS, Pres Sub, Box 4, Mtgs w/the President, Jun-Dec 1959 [1].

2. Statement by the President on the Expiration of the Voluntary Moratorium on Nuclear Weapons Testing, 29 Dec. 1959, *PPP, Eisenhower, 1959*: 883.

3. Memorandum of Conference, 3 Feb. 1960, *FRUS, 1958–60*, 3:835–36.

4. Memorandum of Conversation, 2 Feb. 1960, *FRUS, 1958–60*, 3:833–34.

5. Kistiakowsky, *A Scientist in the White House*, 198–99.

6. Ibid., 228.

7. Ibid., 197–98.

8. Memorandum of Conversation, 16 Dec. 1959, DDEL, OSAST, Box 8, Disarmament-Nuclear Test Policy [May '58—Oct '60] [4].

9. Ibid.

10. Kistiakowsky, *A Scientist in the White House*, 197–98.

11. Memorandum of Conversation, 28 Dec. 1959, DDEL, OSANSA, NSC, Briefing Notes, Box 2, [Atomic Testing] Suspension of Nuclear Testing, 1958–1960 (3). The Principals also discussed how Eisenhower should address the end of the temporary test moratorium. Eisenhower's conversation with Gordon Gray on 23 December, however, showed that he had already decided to extend the moratorium for an unspecified time. See Memorandum of Conversation, 23 Dec. 1959, DDEL, OSANSA, SAS, Pres Sub, Box 4, Mtgs w/the President, Jun-Dec 1959 [1].

12. Kistiakowsky, *A Scientist in the White House*, 211–14.

13. Memorandum of Conversation, 29 Dec. 1959, DDEL, OSAST, Box 8, Disarmament-Nuclear Test Policy [May '58—Oct '60] [5].

14. Memorandum of Conference, 29 Dec. 1959, *FRUS, 1958–60*, 3:816–19.

15. Telegram, Gore to Eisenhower, 28 Dec. 1959, DDEL, WHCF, OF, Box 526, OF 108-A (5). Eisenhower to Gore, 13 Jan. 1960, ibid.

16. For an account of Strauss's confirmation battle, see Pfau, *No Sacrifice Too Great* , 222–41.

17. LLS, AEC, Box 113, Tests and Testing 1959–1960.

18. Strauss's handwritten note indicates that he read this memo to the president during their meeting. Memorandum to the President, 22 Jan. 1960, LLS, AEC, Box 26E, Eisenhower.

19. The navy wanted to conduct underwater tests to determine if underwater nuclear depth charges would destroy the ships that dropped them. Kistiakowsky strongly protested these tests as unnecessary and feared that radioactive materials would rise to the surface and contaminate the atmosphere. Although he conceded that there may be difficulties detecting tests in large lakes, Kistiakowsky was certain of the ability to detect oceanic tests. Record of Telephone Conversations, Herter and Kistiakowsky, 9 Feb. 1960, DDEL, CH, TC (microfilm), 11:495. The threshold proposal that Eisenhower read on 11 February included a ban on "all weapons tests in the oceans." See *PPP, Eisenhower, 1960*: 166–67.

20. Record of Telephone Conversation, Goodpaster and Herter, 9 Feb. 1960, DDEL, CH, TC, WH, (microfilm) 10:987. Goodpaster, Memorandum for Record, 9 Feb. 1960, DDEL, OSS, Subj Series, DoS Sub, Box 4, State Dept—Oct '59-Feb '60 [7].

21. Kistiakowsky, *A Scientist in the White House*, 232–33.

22. Record of Telephone Conversation, Herter and McCone, 3 Feb. 1960, DDEL, CH, TC (microfilm), 11:513.

23. Memorandum of Conversation, 3 Feb. 1960, *FRUS, 1958–60*, 3:835–36.

24. Memorandum of Conversation, 30 Jan. 1960, DDEL, McC, Box 5, McCone Sealed File, 5, [2].

25. Memorandum of Conversation, 3 Feb. 1960, *FRUS, 1958–60*, 3:835–36.

26. Memorandum of Conversation, 30 Jan. 1960, DDEL, McC, Box 5, McCone Sealed File, 5, [2].

27. *PPP, Eisenhower, 1960*: 166–67.

28. Memorandum of Conference with the President, 11 Mar. 1960, DDEL, AWF, DS, Box 48, Stf Notes, Mar '60 [3]. See also Goodpaster's supplementary note, dated 15 March, to the meeting above, ibid.

29. Record of Telephone Conversation, 21 Mar. 1960, DDEL, CH, TC (microfilm), 11:409.

30. Memorandum of Discussion at a Special Meeting of the NSC, 18 Feb. 1960, *FRUS, 1958–60*, 3:842.

31. Memorandum of Conference with the President, 10 Mar. 1960, *FRUS 1958–60*, 3 (microfiche supplement), 540. The press release announced Project Gnome, a 10kt "peaceful" nuclear device detonated 1,200 feet below the surface in a salt cavern near Carlsbad, New Mexico. The Eisenhower and Kennedy administrations delayed the shot until 10 December 1961. See Jacobson and Stein, *Diplomats, Scientists, and Politicians*, 351–52.

32. Along with a suspension of testing, Eisenhower also urged progress on disarmament measures, such as ceasing the production of materials for nuclear weapons production. Eisenhower implored Dillon and McCone to make progress on slowing the arms race as a means of "freeing the people of the world from the dreadful fear that now hangs over them." After McCone commented that the creation of armaments was as old as civilization, Eisenhower responded, "there is a distinct difference now between the present and the past insofar as in past wars there had always been a victor-now there would be none as all parties engaged in war and a large segment of humanity not engaged would be destroyed." McCone, Notes for the Files, 10 Mar. 1960, *FRUS, 1958–60*, 3:842.

33. Eisenhower, *Waging Peace*, 480.

34. Kistiakowsky and Killian considered the Soviet acknowledgement of the problems detecting underground tests a real breakthrough. Record of Telephone Conversation, Herter and Goodpaster, 21 Mar. 1960, DDEL, CH, TC, WH (microfilm), 10: 969. Record of Telephone Conversation, Herter and Kistiakowsky, 21 Mar. 1960, DDEL, CH, TC (microfilm), 11:409.

35. Record of Telephone Conversation, Eisenhower and Macmillan, 21 Mar. 1960, DDEL, AWF, DS, Box 48, Telephone Calls March 1960; NAUK, PREM 11/2994.

36. Curiously, Eisenhower did not seem to be concerned that the Soviets may not accept an agreement that was not binding. Memorandum of Conference with

the President, 23 Mar. 1960, *FRUS, 1958–60,* 3:848–49. For a legal interpretation of this issue from William Rogers, Eisenhower's Attorney General, see Rogers to Eisenhower, 6 May 1960, DDEL, AWF, OFA, Rogers 1960–61 (2).

37. The Principals met on consecutive days to formulate a recommendation for a president who had already made up his mind. Records of the meetings reveal that Kistiakowsky, Herter, and Dillon favored accepting a temporary moratorium, while McCone and some DOD officials vigorously objected. See Memorandum of Conversation, 22 Mar. 1960, DDEL, OSANSA, NSC, Briefing Notes, Box 2, [Atomic Testing] Suspension of Nuclear Testing, 1958–1960 (3) and Memorandum of Conversation, 23 Mar. 1960, *FRUS, 1958–60,* 3: 850–54. For Kistiakowsky's record of the meetings, see Kistiakowsky, *A Scientist in the White House,* 279, 281.

38. Joining Herter and Eisenhower were Goodpaster and Allen Dulles, Memorandum of Conference with the President, 24 Mar. 1960, DDEL, OSS, Subj Series, DoS Sub, Box 4, State Dept—1960 [Mar-May] [2].

39. McCone, Memorandum for the Files, 24 Mar. 1960, DDEL, McC, Box 5, McCone Sealed File, 5, [1].

40. Gray, Memorandum of Meeting with the President, 24 Mar. 1960, DDEL, OSANSA, SAS, Presid Sub, Box 4, 1960 Mtgs w/the President, Vol I [5].

41. Memorandum of Conference with the President, 24 Mar. 1960, *FRUS, 1958–60,* 3:861–63.

42. Kistiakowsky, *A Scientist in the White House,* 282.

43. Nixon told Strauss that Eisenhower was "extremely angry" with McCone's continued objections to his test moratorium decision. According to Nixon, Eisenhower believed that McCone was leaking information to the press on the internal test-ban debate in an effort to build support for his views. See Strauss, Memorandum of Conversation, 31 Mar. 1960, LLS, AEC, Box 54, Kennedy.

44. Kistiakowsky, *A Scientist in the White House,* 285.

45. Memorandum of Discussion, 28 Mar. 1960, *FRUS, 1958–60,* 3:864–66. Note by the Prime Minister, 28 Mar. 1960, NAUK, PREM 11/2994.

46. Memorandum of Discussion, 29 Mar. 1960, DDEL, OSAST, Box 8, Disarmament-Nuclear Test Policy [May '58-Oct '60] [6].

47. Kistiakowsky, *A Scientist in the White House,* 285–89.

48. Joint Declaration by the President and Prime Minister Macmillan on Nuclear Weapons Tests, 29 Mar. 1960, *PPP, Eisenhower, 1960–61:* 318–19. Eisenhower's private reply to Khrushchev emphasized that a four- to five-year temporary moratorium was unacceptable. Hopeful for an agreement, Eisenhower commented that the outstanding issues on control were "few, but they are of great importance." See Eisenhower to Khrushchev, 1 Apr. 1960, DDEL, AWF, OFI, USSR Khrushchev November 1959 (4).

49. Kistiakowsky, *A Scientist in the White House,* 288–89.

50. Strauss, Memorandum for the Files, 31 Mar. 1960, LLS, AEC, Box 62, McCone.

51. McCone claimed that State Department officials had planted articles with James Reston of the *New York Times,* Joseph and Stewart Alsop of the *New York Herald-Tribune* and Marquis Childs of the *Washington Post.* See ibid.

52. By this time, Teller and Bethe were publicly debating the test-ban issue in a series of essays. See Bethe's letter to the editor of the *New York Times* advocating acceptance of Khrushchev's counterproposal, *NYT*, 29 Mar. 1960. Several months later, he published an important essay advocating a test ban. See Hans A. Bethe, "The Case for Ending Nuclear Tests" *Atlantic Monthly* (Aug. 1960): 43–51. Teller's articles in the popular media include Edward Teller and Albert Latter, "The Compelling Need for Nuclear Tests." *Life* (10 Feb. 1958): 64–72. See also Teller, "Alternatives for Security," *Foreign Affairs* (Jan. 1958): 201–8. Bethe declined Teller's challenge to a debate with him on television; see Kistiakowsky, *A Scientist in the White House*, 398–99.

53. In an earlier book, Teller and Latter wrote, "It is almost certain that in the competition between prohibition and bootlegging, the bootlegger will win." See Edward Teller and Albert Latter, *Our Nuclear Future: Facts, Dangers, and Opportunities* (New York: Criterion Books, 1958), 140–41.

54. Divine, *Blowing on the Wind*, 306–9.

55. Kistiakowsky, *A Scientist in the White House*, 308. York was originally the only member of PSAC to oppose in 1958, presenting to Eisenhower a recommendation to seek a test-ban agreement. Since leaving Livermore, York's views moderated considerably. Once firmly tied to Teller's view of the importance of testing, York became a leading advocate for arms control. See York, *Making Weapons, Talking Peace*, 116–21.

56. Wadsworth to Herter, 7 May 1960, DDEL, CH, Box 20, Letters M-Z Official-Classified [3].

57. Position Paper: Nuclear Testing, 8 May 1960, DDEL, McC, Box 4, O&M 15–1 Visits by the Chairman Summit Meeting—May 1960.

58. Divine, *Blowing on the Wind*, 309–10.

59. Ibid., 311. *NYT*, 28 Apr. 1960.

60. A Gallup Poll released on 8 April found that 64 percent approved of Eisenhower's performance, 22 disapproved, and 14 had no opinion. Two months later following the U-2 incident and the failed Paris summit, 68 percent approved of Eisenhower's performance, 21 disapproved, and 11 remained undecided. See Gallup, *The Gallup Poll*, 2: 1661, 1672.

61. Telegram, U.S. Delegation at Geneva to the State Department, 3 May 1960, DDEL, OSS, Subject Series, DoS Sub, Box 4, State Dept—1960 March-May (5). Eisenhower, *Waging Peace*, 481.

62. Divine contends that Eisenhower left Paris "saddened by the realization that the unfortunate U-2 incident had destroyed the promising Paris conference and with it his fond hopes for agreement on at least the essentials of a test ban agreement." See Divine, *Blowing on the Wind*, 313–14. Writing a few years later, Divine assessed the chances for a "genuine breakthrough" at the Paris summit as "mixed," but maintained that Eisenhower "was ready to negotiate a comprehensive test ban treaty which would be a significant first step toward bringing the runaway arms race under control." See Divine, *Eisenhower and the Cold War*, 146; Stephen Ambrose assessed Eisenhower's determination to reach an agreement and the chances of reaching it even greater. According to Ambrose, the test-ban treaty, to be followed by some actual disarmament had become "the

major goal of his Presidency." For Ambrose, Eisenhower went to Paris genuinely seeking an accord with the Soviet Union and was willing to "take some risks and make some concessions" to achieve it. See Ambrose, *Eisenhower*, 2: 563–70, 579–80. According to Michael Beschloss, Eisenhower was determined to reach a limited test-ban treaty at the Paris summit. See Beschloss, *Mayday*, 7.

63. According to Martha Smith, several members of the administration, including State Department officials, PSAC, and the U.S. delegation in Geneva genuinely sought a test-ban agreement, but Eisenhower showed "little interest." Instead, Smith contends that Eisenhower approved AEC and DOD plans to resume underground testing. She fails to mention that these were not nuclear weapons tests. In fact, they were detonations using high explosives as part of the seismic improvement research program designed to extend the test moratorium to tests below the 4.75 threshold. See Smith, "The Nuclear Testing Policies of the Eisenhower Administration," 502.

64. Eisenhower, *Waging Peace*, 558.

65. 30 Mar. 1960, *PPP, Eisenhower, 1960–61*: 326.

66. Author's emphasis quoting his diary entry of 29 March 1960, Harold Macmillan, *Pointing the Way, 1959–1961* (New York: Harper and Row, 1972), 191. Charles de Gaulle also depicted Eisenhower as very hopeful of reaching an agreement with Khrushchev that would ease East-West tensions and serve as a "splendid exit" for the conclusion of his term in office. See Charles de Gaulle, *Memoirs of Hope: Renewal and Endeavor,* trans. Terence Kilmartin (New York: Simon and Schuster, 1971), 243–44. According to William Taubman, Khrushchev immediately after his trip to the United States in 1959 considered agreement on a test-ban accord likely, but that events in early 1960 at home strictly limited his ability to grant concessions at Paris. See Taubman, *Khrushchev: The Man and His Era* (New York: W. W. Norton & Co., 2003): 448–55.

67. Eisenhower specifically mentioned that he expected agreement on the joint study of underground tests below the 4.75 level. Despite the U-2 incident, scientists from the first three nuclear powers met in Geneva on 11 May to exchange information on the seismic research activities of the three nations to determine areas of future coordinated or joint research. Memorandum for the President's Personal Secretary, 11 May 1960, *FRUS, 1958–60*, 9:389–90.

68. Memorandum of Conversation, 5 May 1960, DDEL, OSAST, Box 8, Disarmament-Nuclear Test Policy [May '58—Oct '60] [6]. Kistiakowsky, who deeply desired a test-ban agreement, rested his hopes in the ability of scientists to find the means to improve the system of detection within the two-year period rather than wage a difficult battle to extend the temporary moratorium.

69. Position Paper: Nuclear Testing, 8 May 1960, DDEL, McC, Box 4, O&M 15–1 Visits by the Chairman Summit Meeting—May 1960. Memorandum of Conversation, 14 May 1960, *FRUS, 1958–60*, 3: 874–78. Telegram, UK Delegation to Geneva to Foreign Office, 23 Apr. 1960, NAUK, FO371/149285.

70. A RAND Corporation study concluded on the eve of the summit offered tremendous hope for improving the ability to distinguish between seismic events and weapons tests. Incorporating that study's findings, the position paper recom-

mended accepting ten to fifteen annual inspections if the Soviet Union accepted four or five additional control posts or accepted the rearrangement of some of the twenty-one agreed upon control posts to concentrate some in the areas of the greatest seismic activity within the USSR. See Position Paper: Nuclear Testing, 8 May 1960, DDEL, McC, Box 4, O&M 15-1 Visits by the Chairman Summit Meeting—May 1960. None of the Principals considered Soviet acceptance of either of these terms likely. For a discussion of this and the implications of the RAND study, see Memorandum of Conversation, 10 May 1960, *FRUS, 1958–60*, 3 (microfiche supplement) 564. Memorandum of Conversation, 14 May 1960, *FRUS, 1958–60*, 3:874–78.

71. The quota of on-site inspections remained an unresolved issue through 1963, when the Soviets would accept no more than five and the West would accept no fewer than seven. See Kistiakowsky, *A Scientist in the White House*, 423–24.

72. Kistiakowsky feared that his absence at the Paris summit would allow test-ban opponents such as McCone and DOD officials to dominate Herter at the Paris summit and greatly diminish the chances of reaching an agreement with the Soviet Union. See ibid., 322–23. The possibility remains that Kistiakowsky could have been called to join the talks at Paris if they ever reached an advanced state on such technical issues. On the other hand, unlike the Geneva summit 1955, where Eisenhower had already prepared his Open Skies proposal and instructed his disarmament advisors to remain close by until he decided to issue it, he had no such plans to present a significant proposal at the Paris summit.

73. Eisenhower, *Waging Peace*, 481.

74. According to Kistiakowsky, Eisenhower also said that the "scientists had failed him." Kistiakowsky responded that they had, in fact, repeatedly warned of the U-2's vulnerability to air defense weapons and that the management of the project had failed. Kistiakowsky did not record this conversation in his original diary. He included his account of this exchange, as he remembered it fifteen years later, as an editorial comment to his published diary. See Kistiakowksy, *A Scientist in the White House*, 375.

75. Hewlett and Holl, *Atoms for Peace and War*, 561.

76. Memorandum for the Files, 18 May 1960, *FRUS, 1958–60*, 3:879–80. Gates and the JCS also pressed for the resumption of testing after the Paris summit. See Twining to Gates, 13 Jun. 1960, DDEL, OSANSA, NSC, Briefing Notes, Box 2, [Atomic Testing] Suspension of Nuclear Testing, 1958–1960 (1); Memorandum of Conversation, 30 June 1960, DDEL, OSANSA, NSC, Briefing Notes, Box 2, [Atomic Testing] Suspension of Nuclear Testing, 1958–60 (1); Kistiakowsky, *A Scientist in the White House*, 360–61.

77. Memorandum of Conference with the President, 18 May 1960, DDEL, OSS, SA, AEC v.III (4).

78. Editorial Note, *FRUS, 1958–60*, 3:880–81.

79. "The President's News Conference of 17 Aug. 1960," *PPP, Eisenhower, 1960–61*, 641–42.

80. Memorandum of Conference with the President, 7 July 1960, *FRUS, 1958–60*, 3:889–93.

81. Memorandum of Conference with the President, 12 Aug. 1960, ibid., 897–901.

82. Memorandum of Conference with the President, 27 June 1960, DDEL, OSS, SA, AEC v.III (4).

83. "The President's News Conference of 10 August 1960," PPP, Eisenhower, 1960–61, 626–27.

84. Kistiakowsky, A Scientist in the White House, 289–91.

85. Memorandum of Conference with the President, 30 Mar. 1960, DDEL, OSS, SA, Box 16, Dr. Kistiakowsky [3].

86. Memorandum of Conference with the President, 22 Apr. 1960, DDEL, OSS, SA, AEC v.III (4); McCone, Memorandum for Files, 22 Apr. 1960, DDEL, McC, Box 5, McCone Sealed File, 5, [1]

87. Ibid.

88. McCone pressed for decisive actions in Geneva that would end the protracted de facto moratorium without adequate safeguards. See Memorandum of Conference with the President, 15 Aug. 1960, DDEL, OSS, SA, AEC v.III (4); McCone to Herter, 14 Sep. 1960, DDEL, McC, Box 4, RES&D 1–2—Testing—Aug-Dec 1960 [Folder 2] [1].

89. Memorandum of Discussion at the 455th Meeting of the NSC, 12 Aug. 1960, FRUS, 1958–60, 3:897–901.

90. Memorandum of Conference with the President, 19 Aug. 1960, FRUS, 1958–60, 3:901–4.

91. Memorandum of Discussion at the 455th Meeting of the NSC, 12 Aug. 1960, FRUS, 1958–60, 3:897–901.

92. Ibid. Eisenhower firmly stated that the seismic improvement experiments would not involve any experimental weapons. See also Memorandum of Conference with the President, 19 Aug. 1960 FRUS, 1958–60, 3:901–4.

93. Herter believed as early as June that the talks offered little chance of progress. See Memorandum of Conversation, 23 June 1960, DDEL, OSANSA, NSC, Briefing Notes, Box 2 [Atomic Testing] Suspension of Nuclear Testing, 1958–60 (1). Wadsworth lamented the "frightful dilemma" of finding a system for conducting seismic improvement experiments that satisfied both the U.S. and the Soviet Union. See Wadsworth to Herter, 1 July 1960, DDEL, CH, Box 20, Letters M-Z Offic-Class [3].

94. Memorandum of Conference with the President, 12 Aug. 1960, FRUS, 1958–60, 3:897–901. Administration officials suggested that twenty annual inspections were acceptable.

95. Memorandum of Conversation, 2 Aug. 1960, DDEL, OSANSA, NSC, Briefing Notes, Box 2 [Atomic Testing] Suspension of Nuclear Testing, 1958–60 (1).

96. Kistiakowsky, A Scientist in the White House, 372–74.

97. Strauss, Memorandum for the Files, 3 Nov. 1960, LLS, AEC, Box 67, MFR 1959–62.

98. Kistiakowsky, A Scientist in the White House, 331.

99. Ibid., 344. Record of Telephone Conversation, Herter and Kistiakowsky, 22 July 1960, DDEL, CH, TC (microfilm) 11:817.

100. Kistiakowsky, *A Scientist in the White House*, 391.

101. Kistiakowsky also considered the effort to assess weapons effects as contrary to Eisenhower's public comments on 11 May that announced the beginning of planning for the research program. See ibid., 345–46, 348–49, 360–61.

102. "Nuclear Test Ban Negotiations," 12 July 1960, DDEL, OSANSA, NSC, Briefing Notes, Box 2, [Atomic Testing] Suspension of Nuclear Testing, 1958–1960 (1).

103. Notes on the Meeting of PSAC with the President, 12 July 1960, DDEL, USPSAC, Box 3, Meetings with the President.

104. Kistiakowsky, *A Scientist in the White House*, 372–74. Record of Telephone Conversation, Herter and Gray, 22 July 1960, DDEL, CH. TC (microfilm) 11:823.

105. Memorandum for the Files, 1 Nov. 1960, LLS, AEC, Box 9, Bethe 1960–67.

106. Memorandum for the Files, 3 Nov. 1960, LLS, AEC, Box 67, MFR 1959–62.

107. Kistiakowsky, *A Scientist in the White House*, 368–69.

108. Ibid., 367.

109. Ibid., 364–65.

110. Kennedy to Eisenhower, 30 Mar. 1960, DDEL, WHCF, OF, Box 526, OF 108-A(5).

111. Memorandum of Conference with the President, 11 Mar. 1960, DDEL, AWF, DS, Box 48, Stf Notes, Mar '60 [3].

112. According to Kistiakowsky, Eisenhower referred to Johnson as "the most tricky and unreliable politician in Congress." See Kistiakowsky, *A Scientist in the White House*, 402.

113. Memorandum of Conference with the President, 7 July 1960, *FRUS, 1958–60*, 3:889–93.

114. *NYT*, 6 Sep. 1960.

115. For an analysis of the candidates' position on the test ban, see *NYT*, 1 Nov. 1960.

116. For Kennedy's response to Murray, see *NYT*, 10 Oct. 1960.

117. Nixon pledged that, if elected, he would urge Eisenhower to send Henry Cabot Lodge to Geneva to take charge of negotiations until February. Nixon considered the resolution of the test-ban negotiations "a question of the highest priority of American policy." See the text of his 26 October speech in Toledo, *NYT*, 27 Oct. 1960.

118. Eisenhower, *Waging Peace*, 481–82.

119. McCone, Memorandum of the Files, 28 June 1960, *FRUS, 1958–60*, 3 (microfiche supplement), 575. Goodpaster's record of this conversation, held on 27 June, does not indicate that Eisenhower was interested in clandestine testing. He simply recorded that Eisenhower "had no present intention of resuming tests." See Memorandum of Conference with the President, 27 June 1960, DDEL, OSS, SA, AEC v.III(4).

120. Memorandum of Conference with the President, 19 Aug. 1960, *FRUS, 1958–60*, 3:901–4. Although Eisenhower's comments in the historical record are

consistent with the recollection in his memoirs that he became convinced of the necessity of resuming tests, this provocative suggestion could also have simply been an effort to convince McCone that he was genuinely troubled by the continued test moratorium and to defang McCone's public calls for a resumption of testing. This interpretation admittedly rests solely upon the intuition gained from the review of thousands of documents on the subject.

121. Notes on the Meeting of the PSAC with the President, 12 July 1960, DDEL, USPSAC, Box 3, Meetings with the President.

122. Memorandum of Conference with the President, 19 Dec. 1960, DDEL, AWF, DS, Box 55, Staff Notes December 1960.

123. Kistiakowsky to Schulz, 13 Aug. 1963, GBK, Cor 61–65, Box 32, General Eisenhower.

124. One notable exception to the general lack of immediate concern in Eisenhower's warning was *The Nation,* which dedicated a special issue to consider whether the military-industrial complex already imperiled civilian control of the military. See *The Nation* 193 (28 Oct. 1961). For a discussion of the rising interest in Eisenhower's warning in the late 1960s, see Douglas Brinkley, "Eisenhower the Dove," *American Heritage* 52 (Sep. 2001): 58–65.

125. Oliver Stone, *JFK* (Warner Brothers Studios, 1991).

126. For an analysis of the origins of the warning in Eisenhower's farewell address, see Charles, J. G. Griffin, "New Light on Eisenhower's Farewell Address," *Presidential Studies Quarterly* 22, no. 3 (1992): 469–79. Griffin's analysis is based primarily upon oral history interviews with two of Eisenhower's speechwriters, Malcolm Moos, a Johns Hopkins political scientist, and Ralph Williams, a naval officer who assisted Moos. See also Martin J. Medhurst, "Reconceptualizing Rhetorical History: Eisenhower's Farewell Address," *Quarterly Journal of Speech* 80 (1994): 195–218. For an interpretation of Eisenhower's purpose for including the term, see Brinkley, "Eisenhower the Dove." For an analysis of the contemporary relevance of the term, see William D. Hartung, "Eisenhower's Warning: The Military-Industrial Complex Forty Years Later," *World Policy Journal,* 18 (Spring 2001): 39–44. See also James Fallows, "The Dustbin of History: The Military-Industrial Complex," *Foreign Policy* (Nov./Dec. 2002): 46–48.

127. Brands and Sherry have previously noted the irony of Eisenhower's warning, but without analyzing its origins or meaning. See Brands, "The Age of Vulnerability," 988–89, and Michael S. Sherry, *In the Shadow of War: The United States since the 1930s* (New Haven: Yale University Press, 1995), 233–36. For Richard Damms, the Eisenhower's Scientific-Technological elite referred to Killian and the members of PSAC; see Damms, "James Killian, the Technological Capabilities Panel, and the Emergence of President Eisenhower's 'Scientific-Technological Elite,'" 57–78. Gregg Herken adds members of the Gaither panel to test-ban opponents as possible inspirations for Eisenhower's warning; see Herken, "Commentary: In the Service of the State," *Diplomatic History* 24 (Winter 2000): 110–13. See also Walter McDougall, "Commentary: The Cold War Excursion of Science," *Diplomatic History* 24 (Winter 2000): 121–24.

128. Speech draft, 8 Jan. 1961, DDEL, AWF, Speech Series, Box 38, Final TV Talk-Jan. 17, 1961 (3). Unlike the passage on disarmament, it appears that Moos and Williams drafted the first versions of Eisenhower's twin warnings. See Griffin, "New Light on Eisenhower's Farewell Address," 469–79.

129. Eisenhower, "Farewell Radio and Television Address to the American People," 17 Jan. 1961. *PPP, Eisenhower, 1960–61:* 1039–40. See also Eisenhower's comments in his memoirs about his disappointment at his lack of success in the field of disarmament, Eisenhower, *Waging Peace,* 653.

130. Eisenhower, "Farewell Radio and Television Address," 1038–39.

131. Eisenhower's handwritten comments in a draft of the address dated 9 Jan. 1961 reveals him as the source of this sentence. On this draft, Eisenhower inserted "A government contract now seems to substitute for intellectual curiosity." See DDEL, AWF, Speech Series, Box 38, Final TV Talk—Jan. 17, 1961 (2).

132. Eisenhower, "Farewell Radio and Television Address," 1038–39.

133. Kistiakowsky, *A Scientist in the White House,* 424–25.

134. "Footnote to History," *Science* 133 (10 Feb. 1961): 355.

135. The President's News Conference of 18 Jan. 1961, *PPP, Eisenhower, 1960–61:* 1045–46.

136. "Footnote to History," *Science* 133 (10 Feb. 1961): 355.

137. Eisenhower to Kistiakowsky, 3 Feb. 1961, GBK, Cor 61–65, Box 32, General Eisenhower.

138. Eisenhower, *Waging Peace,* 614–16.

139. York, *Making Weapons, Talking Peace,* 125.

140. Herken, *Cardinal Choices,* 298 n. 104.

141. York, *Making Weapons, Talking Peace,* 125–27. For an earlier account that expresses a similar view, see York, *Race to Oblivion: A Participant's View of the Arms Race* (New York: Simon and Schuster, 1970), 9–14. See also York, "Eisenhower's Other Warning" (Letter to the Editor), *Physics Today* (Jan. 1977): 9–11. Killian agreed with both Kistiakowsky and York's earlier interpretations, recalling that he "repeatedly" witnessed Eisenhower angered by the issues that they raised. See Killian, *Sputnik, Scientists, and Eisenhower,* 237–39. Eugene Rabinowitch, writing shortly after Eisenhower's farewell address, believed that Eisenhower "did not fully understand or trust" his science advisors even though he accepted their advice on the test-ban issue. In Rabinowitch's view, Eisenhower considered scientists (along with armaments makers, technologists and, curiously, the military) as "disturbing alien forces" who had gained undue power and influence due to the imperatives of waging the Cold War. See Eugene Rabinowitch, "Hail and Farewell," *BAS* (Mar. 1961): 86–91.

142. Eisenhower to Strauss, 25 Nov. 1957, DDEL, AWF, DS, Staff Notes, Nov. 1957; Telephone Conversation, Eisenhower and Strauss, 25 Nov. 1957, DDEL, AWF, DS, Phone Calls 1957.

143. Telephone Call, Eisenhower and Dulles, 25 June 1957, DDEL, AWF, DS, Phone Calls, June 1957.

144. Memorandum of Conference, 19 Mar. 1959, *FRUS, 1958–60,* 3:716–18.

Epilogue

EPIGRAPHS: Bethe, "Disarmament and Strategy," *BAS* (Sep. 1962): 19. 22 Oct. 1963; *PPP, Kennedy, 1963*: 803.

1. *NYT*, 10 Oct. 1960.
2. Memorandum of Conversation, 19 Jan. 1961, DDEL, DDE Post-Presid, Augusta-WR Series, Box 2, JFK 60–61 [2].
3. Glenn T. Seaborg, *Kennedy, Khrushchev, and the Test Ban* (Berkeley: University of California Press, 1981), 35–36.
4. Chang, *Friends and Enemies*, 228–52.
5. Seaborg was also one of the scientists at Chicago who in 1945 signed the Franck Report. For Seaborg's explanation of his initial ambivalence toward the test ban; see Seaborg, *Kennedy, Khrushchev, and the Test Ban*, 35.
6. Herken, *Cardinal Choices*, 128.
7. Kennedy to McCloy, 27 Jan. 1961, *FRUS, 1961–63* 7:7–8.
8. Members of Fisk's interagency panel included both opponents and advocates of a test ban. Joining Fisk on the panel were Hans Bethe, General Austin Betts, Harold Brown, Spurgeon Keeny, Richard Latter, General Herbert Loper, Carson Mark, Doyle Lorthrup, Wolfgang Panofsky, Frank Press, Hebert Scoville, General Alfred Starbird, and Herbert York. See Report of the Ad Hoc Panel on the Technical Capabilities and Implications of the Geneva System (Fisk Report), 2 Mar. 1961, *FRUS, 1961–63* 7: (microfiche supplement).
9. McCloy to Kennedy, 8 Mar. 1961, *FRUS, 1961–63* 7:14–16.
10. Seaborg, *Kennedy, Khrushchev, and the Test Ban*, 57–59.
11. Memorandum of Conversation, Kennedy and Khrushchev, 4 June 1961, *FRUS, 1961–63* 7:86–91.
12. Memorandum of Conversation with the President and the Congressional Leadership, 6 June 1961, *FRUS, 1961–63*, 7:92–93.
13. Editorial Note, 31 Aug. 1961 Meetings, *FRUS, 1961–63*, 7:152–57. "Joint Statement With Prime Minister Macmillan Proposing a Three-Power Agreement To End Atmospheric Nuclear Tests," 3 Sep. 1961, *PPP, Kennedy, 1961*: 587. The Soviets rejected the Kennedy-Macmillan offer on 10 September because it was not part of a general disarmament treaty.
14. Statement by the President on Ordering Resumption of Underground Nuclear Tests, 5 Sep. 1961, *PPP, Kennedy, 1961*: 589–90.
15. Strauss to Kennedy, 6 Sep. 1961, LLS, AEC, Box 54, Kennedy.
16. Air Force General Lyman L. Lemnitzer was the chairman of the JCS until 30 Sep. 1962. Army general Maxwell D. Taylor was his successor. William C. Foster served as the director of the ACDA.
17. Summary of the Report of the Foreign Weapons Evaluation Group, 16 Jan. 1962, *FRUS, 61–63*, 7 (microfiche supplement). Joining Bethe on the evaluation group were three scientists from Livermore (Foster, Goeckermann, and Street) and four from Los Alamos (Mark, Spence, Cowan, and Goad).
18. Memorandum for the Record, 6 Mar. 1962, *FRUS, 61–63*, 7:362–65. Minutes of Meeting with the President, 9 Mar. 1962, *FRUS, 61–63*, 7:369–72. Seaborg, *Kennedy, Khrushchev, and the Test Ban*, 140–42.

19. Editorial Note, *FRUS, 61–63*, 7:487–88.

20. Robert Dallek, *An Unfinished Life: John F. Kennedy, 1917–1963* (New York: Little, Brown, 2003): 615–18. Dean might have again made an unauthorized suggestion in October of a willingness to accept as few as two to four on-site inspections. See Editorial Note, *FRUS, 61–63*, 7:623–25. His independent offers, similar to the actions of Stassen in 1957, may have created strong pressures within the administration for his resignation, which he submitted in late December 1962. See Editorial Note, *FRUS, 61–63*, 7:625. Much later, Seaborg learned from Wiesner that the Soviet belief that the U.S. might accept two to four inspections came from Kennedy's science advisor. See Seaborg, *Kennedy, Khrushchev, and the Test Ban,* 180–81.

21. For details of the Kennedy administration's evaluation of the new technical data and its consideration of a revised negotiating position, see Memorandum of Conversation, 26 July 1962, *FRUS, 61–63*, 7:499–507; Foster to Kennedy, 26 July 1962, *FRUS, 61–63*, 7:507–9; Memorandum of Meeting with President Kennedy, 27 July 1962, *FRUS, 61–63*, 7:510–14; Foster to Kennedy, 30 July 1962, *FRUS, 61–63*, 7:517–19; Memorandum of Meeting with President Kennedy, 30 July 1962, *FRUS, 61–63*, 7:520–24; Report of the Inspection Study Group (Foster Panel), July 1962, *FRUS, 61–63*, 7:524–27; Memorandum of Meeting with President Kennedy, 1 Aug. 1962, *FRUS, 61–63*, 7:527–30; Editorial Note, *FRUS, 61–63*, 7:560–61.

22. George Bunn, *Arms Control by Committee: Managing Negotiations with the Russians* (Stanford: Stanford University Press, 1992), 31–32.

23. See for example Theodore C. Sorenson, *Kennedy* (New York: Harper and Row, 1965), 727–28.

24. Bunn, *Arms Control by Committee,* 32–33.

25. For an account of the relationship between Kennedy and Macmillan on the test issue, see Kendrick Oliver, *Kennedy, Macmillan and the Nuclear Test-Ban Debate, 1961–1963* (New York: St. Martin's Press, 1998). For an analysis of Kennedy's concerns about the Chinese nuclear program, see Chang, *Friends and Enemies,* 228–52.

26. Seaborg, *Kennedy, Khrushchev, and the Test Ban,* 207–18.

27. For example, see Dallek, 619–21; Lawrence Freedman, *Kennedy's Wars: Berlin, Cuba, Laos, and Vietnam.* (New York: Oxford University Press, 2000), 267–68; Michael R. Beschloss, *The Crisis Years: Kennedy and Khrushchev, 1960–1963* (New York: Harper Collins, 1991), 598–601.

28. 10 June 1963, *PPP, Kennedy, 1963*: No 232.

29. Bunn, *Arms Control by Committee,* 35–36.

30. Kennedy sent a personal note with Harriman to Khrushchev emphasizing the president's interest in a comprehensive ban. See telegram, Bundy to Harriman, 12 July 1963, *FRUS, 61–63*, 7:797–98.

31. Instructions for the Honorable W. Averell Harriman, 10 July 1963, *FRUS, 61–63*, 7:785–88. Memorandum for Record, 10 July 1963, *FRUS, 61–63*, 7:789–90.

32. Chang, *Friends and Enemies,* 236–47.

33. Khrushchev definitively withdrew the previous Soviet offer of two to

three on-site inspections, foreclosing any progress on a comprehensive ban. See Telegram, Harriman to Department of State, 15 July 1963, *FRUS, 61–63*, 7:799–801.

34. Telegram, Harriman and Kaysen to the Department of State, 18 July 1963, *FRUS, 61–63*, 7:807. Seaborg, *Kennedy, Khrushchev, and the Test Ban*, 240–42.

35. Seaborg, *Kennedy, Khrushchev, and the Test Ban*, 244–49; Bunn, *Arms Control by Committee*, 37–39.

36. 26 July 1963, *PPP, Kennedy, 1963*: No. 316.

37. Rabi to Kennedy, 6 Feb. 1961, IIR, Box 4, JFK.

38. Kistiakowsky to Eisenhower, 30 July 1963, GBK, Cor 61–65, Box 32, General Eisenhower.

39. Inglis to Rabi, 30 Mar. 1963, IIR, Box 12, ACDA, GAC Rep, 61–63. Rabi to Inglis, 2 Apr. 1963, IIR, Box 12, ACDA, GAC Rep, 61–63.

40. Rabi to McCloy, 11 June 1962, IIR, Box 12, ACDA, GAC Corr, 1961–63.

41. "Teller Opposes Test Ban Treaty," *NYT*, 15 Aug. 1963.

42. Rabi to Senator Mansfield, 14 Aug. 1963, IIR, Box 42, NTBT, Gen, '63. *NYT*, 15 Aug. 1963.

43. Summary of the Report of the Foreign Weapons Evaluation Group, 16 Jan. 1962, *FRUS, 61–63*, 7 (microfiche supplement). Bethe agreed in early 1962 with the "Twining Committee" (a fourteen-member panel that included Edward Teller), that a test-ban treaty would not be to the military or technological advantage of the United States. Bethe conceded that some atmospheric tests were necessary. See Bundy to Kennedy, 17 Jan. 1962, *FRUS, 61–63*, 7:306.

44. Bethe to Bruno Rossi, 9 May 1962, HAB, Box 5, F44 (correspondence related to Rossi and N. Rockefeller).

45. Bethe, "Disarmament and Strategy," *BAS* (Sep. 1962):19. Bethe originally submitted this article to the *Saturday Evening Post* in an effort to reach the widest possible audience, but a new editor rejected the final version of his article. See Bethe, 7 Sep. 1962, HAB, Box 9, F22 (correspondence related to article in Sat Eve Post –1962). For an example of how test-ban opponents exaggerated Bethe's moderation on the test issue to bolster their own arguments, see Charles J. V. Murphy, "Now the President Will Decide on His Own," *Life* 52 (16 Feb. 1962): 71–83.

46. Wiesner to Kennedy, 6 Oct. 1963, *FRUS, 61–63*, 7:584; Report of the Foreign Weapons Evaluation Group Meeting of 2–3 Oct. 1962, 4 Oct. 1962, *FRUS, 61–63*, 7 (microfiche supplement).

47. Senate Committee on Foreign Relations, *Nuclear Test Ban Treaty*, 88th Cong., 1st sess., 1963, 1007–8.

48. *NYT*, 13 Sep. 1963.

49. Kistiakowsky, *A Scientist in the White House*, 423–24.

50. For background on the Pugwash conferences, see Lawrence S. Wittner, *The Struggle Against the Bomb: Resisting the Bomb - A History of the World Nuclear Disarmament Movement, 1954–1970* (Stanford: Stanford University Press, 1998), 33–37.

51. Kistiakowsky, Record of Conversation, 16 Mar. 1963, GBK, Cor 61–65, Box 35, Nuclear Test Ban.

52. Kistiakowsky, *A Scientist in the White House*, 423–24.

53. For Kistiakowsky's testimony in favor of ratification, see Senate Committee on Foreign Relations, *Nuclear Test Ban Treaty*, 88th Cong., 1st sess., 1963, 851–78.

54. Kistiakowsky to Eisenhower, 30 Nov. 1961, GBK, Cor 61–65, Box 32, General Eisenhower.

55. Strauss to McCloy, 18 Jan. 1961, LLS, AEC, Box 62, McCloy.

56. Strauss, Memorandum for Files, 28 Aug. 1962, LLS, AEC, Box 63, McCone.

57. Lewis L. Strauss, "Why Nuclear Testing is a Must for Freedom," *Reader's Digest* 79 (Sep. 1961): 54–61; *NYT*, 22 June 1961. "No Doubt USSR Testing," *US News and World Report* 51 (11 Sep. 1961): 40–42.

58. *NYT*, 12 Nov. 1961; *NYT*, 1 Feb. 1963.

59. Teller with Allen Brown, "Plan for Survival," *Saturday Evening Post* 235 (3 Feb. 1962):11–15; (10 Feb. 1962): 34–6; (17 Feb. 1962): 32–7. See also a rebuttal from eight scientists, "An Answer to Teller," *Saturday Evening Post* 235 (14 Apr. 1962): 69–73. The first two articles also appeared in *Reader's Digest;* see Teller with Allen Brown, "Plan for Survival," *Reader's Digest* 80 (Apr. 1962): 106–10; (May 1962): 49–53. Teller's series of articles were excerpts from a book on atomic policy. See Edward Teller with Allen Brown, *The Legacy of Hiroshima* (Garden City, N.J.: Doubleday, 1962).

60. Fuoss to Eisenhower, 25 Jan. 1962 and Eisenhower to Fuoss, 29 Jan. 1962, both in DDEL, DDE Post-Presid, Signature File 1962–63, Box38, Fu—.

61. "Eisenhower Urges Action," *NYT*, 13 June 1961.

62. Strauss to John S. D. Eisenhower, 12 June 1961, LLS, AEC, Box 26E, JSD Eisenhower.

63. Eisenhower indicated that he was sending identical letters to Gray, Goodpaster, McCone, and Strauss. He sent an identical letter to Herter two days later. Eisenhower to Gordon Gray, 14 June 1961, DDEL, DDE Post-Presid, Special Name Series, Box 5, Gray [1961]; Eisenhower to Strauss, 14 June 1961, LLS, AEC, Box 26E, Eisenhower; Eisenhower to Herter, 16 June 1961, DDEL, DDE Post-Presid, Special Name Series, Box 8, Herter [1961].

64. Gray to Eisenhower, 21 June 1961, DDEL, DDE Post-Presid, Special Name Series, Box 5, Gray [1961]; Strauss, Memorandum for Files, 15 June 1961, LLS, AEC, Box 113, Tests and Testing 1961 (March-June). Herter to Eisenhower, 22 June 1961, DDEL, DDE Post-Presid, Principle File, 1961, Box 6, Disarmament 1961. McCone to Eisenhower, 23 June 1961, LLS, AEC, Box 113, Tests and Testing 1961 (March-June). A written response from Goodpaster has not been found.

65. Strauss to John S. D. Eisenhower, 20 July 1961, DDEL, DDE Post-Presid, Special Name Series, Box 18, Strauss [1961].

66. John S. D. Eisenhower, Memorandum for the Record, 8 Sep. 1961, DDEL, DDE Post-Presid, Augusta-WR Series, Box 2, Mem of Conf, 1961–63 [2].

67. Strauss, Memorandum for the Files, 15 Dec. 1961, LLS, AEC, Box 26E, Eisenhower. Strauss's memoirs were sharply critical of Bethe's "naïveté" in believing that a test moratorium would benefit the United States because the Soviet Union would not attempt to test clandestinely. See Strauss, *Men and Decisions*, 421–24. Two months later, Strauss contacted Eisenhower again and charged Bethe with compromising "much secret data" in a public lecture. Strauss characterized Bethe as "the same naïve fellow" who considered the Soviets incapable of cheating. See Strauss to Eisenhower, 7 Feb. 1962, DDEL, DDE Post-Presid, Special Name Series, Box 18, Strauss [1962].

68. Eisenhower to Killian, 23 Nov. 1962, DDEL, DDE Post-Presid, Principle File, 1962, Box 37, Ki.

69. *NYT*, 4 Mar. 1962.

70. See for example Dean Rusk's briefing on the Berlin crisis and the test-ban talks. Memorandum of Conversation, 22 May 1962, DDEL, DDE Post-Presid, Augusta-WR Series, Box 2, Mem of Conf, 1961–63 [2].

71. Ambrose, *Eisenhower*, 2: 637–43.

72. McCone's identification of Libby as a test-ban supporter surprised Eisenhower, who had his son confirm Libby's position on the treaty with Strauss. See Memorandum of Conference, 24 July 1963, DDEL, DDE Post-Presid, Augusta-WR Series, Box 2, Mem of Conf, 1961–63 [3]. According to Strauss, Libby was profoundly concerned, worried, and unhappy about the treaty, but was under "unbelievable pressures" not to oppose the treaty. Strauss, Memorandum for the Files, 26 July 1963, LLS, AEC, Box 63, McCone. Strauss, Memorandum for the Files, 30 July 1963, LLS, AEC, Box 26E, Eisenhower. Strauss, telephone message to Eisenhower, 20 Aug. 1963, LLS, AEC, Box 114, Tests and Testing, 1962–66. Libby expressed concern in a Senate hearing over the impact of the treaty on laboratory personnel, the prohibition of Plowshare experiments outside of U.S. territory, and the lack of a 100mt weapon in the nation's arsenal, but concluded that he favored the treaty. See Senate Committee on Foreign Relations, *Nuclear Test Ban Treaty*, 88th Cong., 1st sess., 1963, 640–70.

73. Memorandum of Conference, 24 July 1963, DDEL, DDE Post-Presid, Augusta-WR Series, Box 2, Mem of Conf, 1961–63 [3].

74. Emphasis in the original. Macmillan to Eisenhower, 26 July 1963, DDEL, DDE Post-Presid, Principle File, 1963, Box 54, Ma [2].

75. Stassen to Eisenhower, 14 Aug. 1963, DDEL, DDE Post-Presid, Principle File, 1963, Box 65, Test Ban Treaty [2].

76. Telegram, Fulbright to Eisenhower, 14 Aug. 1963, DDEL, DDE Post-Presid, Principle File, 1963, Box 65, Test Ban Treaty [4].

77. *NYT*, Aug. 1, 1963. Kistiakowsky to R. L. Schulz, 13 Aug. 1963, GBK, Cor 61–65, Box 32, General Eisenhower. Strauss to Eisenhower, 14 Aug. 1963, DDEL, DDE Post-Presid, Principle File, 1963, Box 65, Test Ban Treaty [2].

78. Marine Radiogram, McCone to Eisenhower, 14 Aug. 1963, DDEL, DDE Post-Presid, Principle File, 1963, Box 65, Test Ban Treaty [4]. Eisenhower, Memorandum for the Record, 15 Aug. 1963, ibid.

79. Kistiakowsky to R. L. Schulz, 13 Aug. 1963, GBK, Cor 61–65, Box 32, General Eisenhower. Strauss to Teller, 1 Aug. 1963, LLS, AEC, Box 111, Teller

Feb-Aug 1963. Strauss to Eisenhower, 14 Aug. 1963, DDEL, DDE Post-Presid, Principle File, 1963, Box 65, Test Ban Treaty [2].

80. Kistiakowsky to Eisenhower, 18 Aug. 1963, GBK, Cor 61–65, Box 32, General Eisenhower.

81. Strauss to Eisenhower, 14 Aug. 1963, DDEL, DDE Post-Presid, Principle File, 1963, Box 65, Test Ban Treaty [2].

82. Strauss to Teller, 3 Sep. 1963, LLS, AEC, Box 111, Teller Feb-Aug 1963.

83. Trevor Gardner, a former assistant secretary of the air force, was the only member of the GAC who opposed ratification. See Kistiakowsky to Eisenhower, 30 July 1963, GBK, Cor 61–65, Box 32, General Eisenhower.

84. Eisenhower to Kistiakowsky, 10 Aug. 1963, GBK, Cor 61–65, Box 32, General Eisenhower. Kistiakowsky to Eisenhower, 18 Aug. 1963, GBK, Cor 61–65, Box 32, General Eisenhower.

85. Ibid.

86. Ibid.

87. Eisenhower to Fulbright, 23 Aug, 1963, DDEL, DDE Post-Presid, Secretary's Series, Box 10, Fa—. The *New York Times* printed Eisenhower's full response, see *NYT*, 27 Aug. 1963.

88. Ibid.

89. Ibid.

90. Eisenhower to Larson, 31 Aug. 1963, DDEL, DDE Post-Presid, Secretary's Series, Box 10, La—. Fulbright to Eisenhower, 4 Sep. 1963, DDEL, DDE Post-Presid, Principle File, 1963, Box 46, Fu—. See also *NYT*, 8 Sep. 1963. Memorandum of Conference, Sep. 19, 1963, DDEL, DDE Post-Presid, Special Name Series, Box 12, McCone 1963–66 [4].

91. Strauss to Teller, 3 Sep. 1963, LLS, AEC, Box 111, Teller Feb-Aug 1963.

92. Teller to Strauss, 12 Sep. 1963, LLS, AEC, Box 111, Teller Feb-Aug 1963.

93. Senate Committee on Foreign Relations, *Nuclear Test Ban Treaty*, 88th Cong., 1st sess., 1963. *NYT*, 15, 27, Aug. 1963.

94. Beckler to Kistiakowsky, 12 Aug. 1963, GBK, Cor 61–65, Box 35, Nuclear Test Ban.

95. Of the four listed, only Kistiakowsky was a full member of PSAC; the other three, all former members, served as consultants. Wiesner to Kennedy, 19 Aug. 1963, JFKL, President's Office Files, Box 85, OST, 1963.

96. Bundy to Humphrey, 10 Sep. 1963, JFKL, White House Central Subject Files, Box 204, PSAC.

97. Those who voted against the treaty included southern Democrats, such as Strom Thurmond from South Carolina, who voted against the treaty to protest Kennedy's recent civil rights initiatives, and conservative Republicans, such as Barry Goldwater from Arizona, who held worldviews similar to Strauss and Teller and shared their dire assessments of the treaty.

98. Eisenhower to Herter, 16 June 1961, DDEL, DDE Post-Presid, Special Name Series, Box 8, Herter [1961]. Divine, *Blowing on the Wind*, 318–21. Kennedy commented in April 1963 that Americans, based upon White House mail rather than any specific poll data, were against a ban by a ratio of fifteen to one.

See Dallek, *An Unfinished Life* , 618. A Gallup poll in August 1963 concluded that 63 percent of Americans favored ratification of the Limited Test-Ban Treaty, 17 percent opposed, and 20 percent had no opinion. See Gallup, *The Gallup Poll*, 2: 1837.

99. Eisenhower to Mayer, 29 Aug. 1963, DDEL, DDE Post-Presid, Principle File, 1963, Box 65, Test Ban Treaty [1].

100. Eisenhower to Arthur Larson, 12 Aug. 1963, DDEL, DDE Post-Presid, Secretary's Series, Box 10, La—.

101. See for example, Memorandum of Conference with the President, 19 Mar. 1959, *FRUS, 1958–60* 3:716–18.

102. In his memoirs, Eisenhower claimed no credit for the 1963 treaty and did not even present it as a major accomplishment. He simply commented, in a footnote, that some features of the 1963 treaty were "similar to the proposal we had made in the spring of 1959." See Eisenhower, *Waging Peace*, 482, n. 10.

103. Telegram, Killian, Kistiakowsky, and Rabi to Eisenhower, 16 Feb. 1968, JRK, Box. 13, Book Backup, G-N.

104. Killian, *Sputnik, Scientists, and Eisenhower*, 239–40.

Conclusion

EPIGRAPH: Eisenhower, *Waging Peace*, 480.

1. Mrs. Allen Jones to Eisenhower, 19 Sep. 1961 and Eisenhower to Freeman Gosden, 25 Sep. 1961, both in DDEL, DDE Post-Presid, Special Name Series, Box 4, Gosden, F 1961. Freeman Gosden was a golfing partner of Eisenhower's and a radio performer famous from the show "Amos and Andy."

2. Ambrose, *Eisenhower*, 2: 563–64. Divine, *Blowing on the Wind*, 314, 321–22. Divine, *Eisenhower and the Cold War*, 105, 124–25.

3. Smith, "The Nuclear Testing Policies of the Eisenhower Administration," 8.

4. Memorandum of Conference with the President, 11 July 1960, DDEL, OSS, Subj Series, DoS Sub, Box 4, State Dept—1960 [Jun-Jul] [3].

5. Erdmann, "War No Longer Has Any Logic Whatever,"91–92

6. Smith, 384, 514–20; Smith-Norris, "The Eisenhower Administration and the Nuclear Test Ban Talks, 1958–1960," 503–4.

7. Kistiakowsky to Bethe, 22 May 1975, GBK, Corr 1965–76, Box 38, B (2 of 3).

8. For example, see Ambrose, *Eisenhower*, 2: 570, 621.

9. Macmillan, *Pointing the Way*, 191.

10. Taubman, *Khrushchev*, 448, 454–55.

11. Eisenhower, *Waging Peace*, 482.

12. Memorandum of Conference, 29 Dec. 1959, *FRUS, 1958–60*, 3:816–19.

13. Charles Appleby Jr. concludes that Eisenhower's greatest contribution was establishing the notion that arms control was a balance of risks. See Appleby, "Eisenhower and Arms Control, 1953–1961," 442.

Sources

Manuscript Collections

Bancroft Library, University of California, Berkeley
  Ernest O. Lawrence Papers
California Institute of Technology Archives, Pasadena, California
  Robert F. Bacher Papers
Columbia University, Oral History Project, Butler Library, New York, New York
  Eisenhower Administration Project
    Anderson, Dillon
    Bowie, Robert
    Brownell, Herbert
    Eisenhower, Dwight D.
    Eisenhower, John S. D.
    Goodpaster, Andrew
    Hauge, Gabriel
    Killian, James R.
    McCone, John
    Moos, Malcolm
    Schulz, Robert
    Stassen, Harold
    Strauss, Lewis L.
    Wadsworth, James
  Columbia University Sesquibicentennial Project
    Rabi, I. I.
Cornell University Rare and Manuscript Collections, Ithaca, New York
    Hans A. Bethe Papers
Dwight D. Eisenhower Library, Abilene, Kansas
  John Foster Dulles Papers

Dwight D. Eisenhower, Papers as President of the United States, 1953–61
(Ann Whitman File)
 Dwight D. Eisenhower, Pre-Presidential Papers, 1916–52
 Dwight D. Eisenhower, Post-Presidential Papers, 1961–69
 Gordon Gray Papers
 Christian A. Herter Papers
 John A. McCone Papers
 Gerald C. Smith Papers
 White House Central Files
 White House Office Files
 Oral Histories
  Bethe, Hans A. (OH 483)
  Bowie, Robert R. (OH 102)
  Kistiakowsky, George B. (OH 412)
  McCone, John A. (OH 396)
  Smith, Gerald (OH 513)
  Stassen, Harold A. (OH 519)
  Williams, Ralph (OH 503)
Harvard University Archives, Cambridge, Massachusetts
 George B. Kistiakowsky Papers
Herbert Hoover Library, West Branch, Iowa
 Lewis L. Strauss Papers
Hoover Institution Archives, Stanford, California
 Edward Teller Papers
John F. Kennedy Library, Boston, Massachusetts
 President's Office Files
 National Security Files
 Office of Science and Technology
 White House Central Subject Files
Library of Congress. Washington, D.C.
 Clinton P. Anderson Papers
 J. Robert Oppenheimer Papers
 I. I. Rabi Papers
Massachusetts Institute of Technology Archives, Cambridge, Massachusetts
 James R. Killian, Jr. Papers
 Records of the Office of the President, 1930–59 (Compton-Killian Papers)

Government Archives

Department of Energy, Nuclear Testing Archive, Las Vegas, Nevada
National Archives II, College Park, Maryland
 Atomic Energy Commission (RG-326)
 Central Intelligence Agency (RG-262)
 Department of State (RG-59)
 Joint Chiefs of Staff (RG-218)
 National Security Council (RG-273)

The National Archives of United Kingdom, Public Record Office, Kew, United
  Kingdom
  Records of the Cabinet Office (CAB)
  Records created and inherited by the Foreign Office (FO)
  Records of the Prime Minister's Office (PREM)

Books

Adams, Sherman. *Firsthand Report: The Story of the Eisenhower Administration.* New York: Harper and Brothers, 1961.
Aldous, Richard. *Macmillan, Eisenhower and the Cold War.* Portland: Four Courts Press, 2005.
Ambrose, Stephen E. *Eisenhower.* Vol. 1, *Solider, General of the Army, President-Elect, 1890–1952.* New York: Simon and Schuster, 1983.
———. *Eisenhower.* Vol. 2, *The President.* New York: Simon and Schuster, 1984.
Arnold, Lorna, with Katherine Pyne. *Britain and the H-Bomb.* New York: St. Martin's Press, 2001.
Badash, Lawrence. *Scientists and the Development of Nuclear Weapons: From Fission to the Limited Nuclear Test Ban Treaty, 1939–1963.* New York: Prometheus, 1995.
Ball, Howard. *Justice Downwind: America's Atomic Testing Program in the 1950s.* Oxford: Oxford University Press, 1986.
Bechhoefer, Bernard G. *Postwar Negotiations for Arms Control.* Washington, D.C.: Brookings Institution, 1961.
Beschloss, Michael R. *The Crisis Years: Kennedy and Khrushchev, 1960–1963.* New York: Harper Collins, 1991.
———. *Mayday: The U-2 Affair.* New York: Harper and Row, 1986.
Bird, Kai, and Martin J. Sherwin. *American Prometheus: The Triumph and Tragedy of J. Robert Oppenheimer.* New York: Knopf, 2005.
Bischof, Günter, and Saki Dockrill, eds. *Cold War Respite: The Geneva Summit of 1955.* Baton Rouge: Louisiana State University Press, 2000.
Bose, Meena. *Shaping and Signaling Presidential Policy: The National Security Decision Making of Eisenhower and Kennedy.* College Station: Texas A&M University Press, 1998.
Bowie, Robert R., and Richard H. Immerman. *Waging Peace: How Eisenhower Forged an Enduring Cold War Strategy.* New York: Oxford University Press, 1998.
Brands, H. W., Jr. *Cold Warriors: Eisenhower's Generation and American Foreign Policy.* New York: Columbia University Press, 1989.
Brodie, Bernard, ed. *The Absolute Weapon: Atomic Power and World Order.* New York: Harcourt, Brace and Company, 1946.
Bundy, McGeorge. *Danger and Survival: Choices about the Bomb in the First Fifty Years.* New York: Random House, 1988.
Bunn, George. *Arms Control by Committee: Managing Negotiations with the Russians.* Stanford: Stanford University Press, 1992.

Blumberg, Stanley A., and Gwinn Owens. *Energy and Conflict: The Life and Times of Edward Teller.* New York: Putnam, 1976.

Chandler, Jr., Alfred D., and Louis Galambos, eds. *The Papers of Dwight D. Eisenhower.* 21 vols. Baltimore: The Johns Hopkins University Press, 1978.

Chang, Gordon H. *Friends and Enemies: The United States, China, and the Soviet Union, 1948–1972.* Stanford: Stanford University Press, 1990.

Chernus, Ira. *Eisenhower's Atoms for Peace.* College Station: Texas A&M University Press, 2002.

———. *General Eisenhower: Ideology and Discourse.* East Lansing: Michigan State University Press, 2002.

Childs, Herbert. *An American Genius: The Life of Ernest Orlando Lawrence.* New York: Dutton, 1968.

Clarfield, Gerald H. *Security with Solvency: Dwight D. Eisenhower and the Shaping of the American Military Establishment.* Westport, Conn.: Praeger, 1999.

Cousins, Norman. *Albert Schweitzer's Mission: Healing and Peace.* New York: Norton and Company, 1985.

Craig, Campbell. *Destroying the Village: Eisenhower and Thermonuclear War.* New York: Columbia University Press, 1998.

Culter, Robert. *No Time for Rest.* Boston: Little, Brown, & Co., 1965.

Dallek, Robert. *An Unfinished Life: John F. Kennedy, 1917–1963.* New York: Little, Brown, & Co., 2003.

Dean, Arthur H. *The Test Ban and Disarmament: The Path of Negotiation.* New York: Harper and Row, 1966.

Dean, Gordon E. *Forging the Atomic Shield: Excerpts from the Office Diary of Gordon E. Dean.* Edited by Roger M. Anders. Chapel Hill: University of North Carolina Press, 1987.

De Gaulle, Charles. *Memoirs of Hope: Renewal and Endeavor.* Translated by Terence Kilmartin. New York: Simon and Schuster, 1971.

Divine, Robert. *Blowing on the Wind: The Nuclear Test Ban Debate, 1954–1960.* New York: Oxford University Press, 1978.

———. *Eisenhower and the Cold War.* New York: Oxford University Press, 1981.

———. *The Sputnik Challenge: Eisenhower's Response to the Soviet Satellite.* New York: Oxford University Press, 1993.

Eisenhower, Dwight D. *At Ease: Stories I Tell to Friends.* Garden City: Doubleday, 1967.

———. *Crusade in Europe.* Garden City: Doubleday, 1948.

———. *Mandate for Change: The White House Years, 1953–1956.* Garden City: Doubleday, 1963.

———. *Waging Peace: The White House Years, 1956–1961.* Garden City: Doubleday, 1965.

Eisenhower, John S. D. *Strictly Personal.* Garden City: Doubleday, 1974.

Eisenhower Speaks: Dwight D. Eisenhower in His Messages and Speeches. Edited by Rudolph L. Treuenfels. New York: Farrar, Strauss & Company, 1948.

Evangelista, Matthew. *Unarmed Forces: The Transnational Movement to End the Cold War*. Ithaca: Cornell University Press, 1999.

Ferrell, Robert H., ed. *The Eisenhower Diaries*. New York: W. W. Norton, 1981.

Freedman, Lawrence. *Kennedy's Wars: Berlin, Cuba, Laos, and Vietnam*. New York: Oxford University Press, 2000.

Freeman, J. P. G. *Britain's Nuclear Arms Control Policy in the Context of Anglo-American Relations, 1957–58*. London: Palgrave Macmillan, 1986.

Gallup, George H., ed. *The Gallup International Public Opinion Polls: Great Britain, 1937–1975*. 2 vols. New York: Random House, 1976.

Gallup, George H., ed. *The Gallup Poll: Public Opinion, 1935–1971*. 3 vols. New York: Random House, 1972.

Garthoff, Raymond L. *Assessing the Adversary: Estimates by the Eisenhower Administration of Soviet Intentions and Capabilities*. Washington: Brookings Institution, 1991.

Geelhoed, E. Bruce, and Anthony O. Edmonds. *Eisenhower, Macmillan, and Allied Unity, 1957–1961*. New York: Palgrave Macmillan, 2003.

Gentile, Gian P. *How Effective is Strategic Bombing? Lessons Learned From World War II to Kosovo*. New York: New York University Press, 2001.

Gilpin, Robert. *American Scientists and Nuclear Weapons Policy*. Princeton: Princeton University Press, 1962.

Goodchild, Peter. *Edward Teller: The Real Dr. Strangelove*. Cambridge: Harvard University Press, 2004.

Greenstein, Fred I. *The Hidden-Hand Presidency: Eisenhower as Leader*. New York: Basic Books, 1982.

Hacker, Barton C. *Elements of Controversy: The Atomic Energy Commission and Radiation Safety in Nuclear Weapons Testing, 1947–1974*. Berkeley: University of California Press, 1994.

Hagerty, James C. *The Diary of James C. Hagerty: Eisenhower in Mid-Course, 1954–55*. Edited by Robert H. Ferrell. Bloomington: Indiana University Press, 1983.

Herken, Gregg. *Brotherhood of the Bomb: The Tangled Lives and Loyalties of Robert Oppenheimer, Ernest Lawrence, and Edward Teller*. New York: Holt, 2002.

———. *Cardinal Choices: Presidential Science Advising from the Atomic Bomb to SDI*. Rev. ed. Stanford: Stanford University Press, 2000.

Hershberg, James. *James B. Conant: Harvard to Hiroshima and the Making of the Nuclear Age*. New York: Alfred A. Knopf, 1993.

Hewlett Richard G., and Oscar E. Anderson, Jr. *A History of the United States Atomic Energy Commission*. Vol. I. *The New World, 1939–1946*. University Park: Pennsylvania State University Press, 1962.

Hewlett, Richard G., and Frances Duncan. *A History of the United States Atomic Energy Commission*. Vol. II. *Atomic Shield, 1947–1952*. University Park: Pennsylvania State University Press, 1969.

Hewlett, Richard G., and Jack M. Holl, *Atoms for Peace and War 1953–1961:*

Eisenhower and the Atomic Energy Commission. Berkeley: University of California Press, 1989.

Holloway, David. *Stalin and the Bomb: The Soviet Union and Atomic Energy, 1939–56.* New Haven: Yale University Press, 1994.

Hughes, Emmet J. *The Ordeal of Power: A Political Memoir of the Eisenhower Years.* New York: Atheneum, 1963.

Immerman, Richard H. *John Foster Dulles: Piety, Pragmatism, and Power in U.S. Foreign Policy.* Wilmington, Del.: Scholarly Resources, 1999.

Immerman, Richard H., ed. *John Foster Dulles and the Diplomacy of the Cold War.* Princeton: Princeton University Press, 1990.

Jacobs, Travis Beal. *Eisenhower at Columbia.* New Brunswick, N.J.: Transaction Publishers, 2001.

Jacobson, Harold K., and Eric Stein, *Diplomats, Scientists and Politicians: The United States and the Nuclear Test Ban Negotiations.* Ann Arbor: University of Michigan Press, 1966.

Johnson, Walter, ed. *The Papers of Adlai E. Stevenson: Toward a New America, 1955–1957.* Boston: Little, Brown, 1972.

Khrushchev, Nikita A. *Khrushchev Remembers: The Last Testament.* Translated and edited by Strobe Talbott. Boston: Little, Brown & Co., 1974.

Killian, James R., Jr. *The Education of a College President.* Cambridge: MIT Press, 1985.

———. *Sputnik, Scientists, and Eisenhower: A Memoir of the First Special Assistant to the President for Science and Technology.* Cambridge: MIT Press, 1977.

Kinnard, Douglas. *President Eisenhower and Strategy Management: A Study in Defense Politics.* Washington: Pergamon-Brassey's, 1989.

Kistiakowsky, George B. *A Scientist in the White House: The Private Diary of President Eisenhower's Special Assistant for Science and Technology.* Cambridge: Harvard University Press, 1976.

Knopf, Jeffrey W. *Domestic Society and International Cooperation: The Impact of Protest on US Arms Control Policy.* New York: Cambridge University Press, 1998.

Lapp, Ralph E. *The New Priesthood: The Scientific Elite and the Uses of Power.* New York: Harper and Row, 1965.

———. *The Voyage of the Lucky Dragon.* New York: Harper and Row, 1958.

Lepper, Mary M. *Foreign Policy Formulation: A Case Study of the Nuclear Test Ban Treaty of 1963.* Columbus: C. E. Merrill, 1971.

Macmillan, Harold. *Pointing the Way, 1959–1961.* New York: Harper and Row, 1972.

———. *Riding the Storm, 1956–1959.* New York: Harper and Row, 1971.

Mandelbaum, Michael, ed. *The Other Side of the Table: The Soviet Approach to Arms Control.* New York: Council of Foreign Relations Press, 1990.

Marks, Frederick W., III. *Power and Peace: The Diplomacy of John Foster Dulles.* Westport, Conn.: Praeger, 1993.

Melanson, Richard A., and David Mayers, eds. *Reevaluating Eisenhower: American Foreign Policy in the 1950s.* Urbana: University of Illinois Press, 1987.

McMillan, Priscilla J. *The Ruin of J. Robert Oppenheimer and the Birth of the Modern Arms Race.* New York: Viking, 2005.

Miller, Richard L. *Under the Cloud: The Decades of Nuclear Testing.* New York: Free Press, 1986.

Murray, Thomas E. *Nuclear Policy for War and Peace.* New York: World Publishers, 1960.

Noble, George B. *Christian A. Herter.* New York: Cooper Square Publishers, 1970.

Oliver, Kendrick. *Kennedy, Macmillan and the Nuclear Test-Ban Debate, 1961–1963.* New York: St. Martin's Press, 1998.

Pach, Chester J., Jr., and Elmo Richardson. *The Presidency of Dwight D. Eisenhower.* Rev. ed. Lawrence: University Press of Kansas, 1991.

Pauling, Linus. *No More War!* New York: Dodd, Mead, 1962.

Perret, Geoffrey. *Eisenhower.* New York: Random House, 1999.

Pfau, Richard. *No Sacrifice Too Great: The Life of Lewis L. Strauss.* Charlottesville: University of Virginia Press, 1984.

Pilat, Joseph F., and others, eds. *Atoms for Peace: An Analysis after 30 Years.* Boulder, Col.: Westview Press, 1985.

Rigden, John. *Rabi: Scientist and Citizen.* New York: Basic Books, 1987.

Roman, Peter J. *Eisenhower and the Missile Gap.* Ithaca: Cornell University Press, 1995.

Rose, Kenneth D. *One Nation Underground: The Fallout Shelter in American Culture.* New York: New York University, 2001.

Rosenberg, Victor. *Soviet-American Relations, 1953–1960: Diplomacy and Cultural Exchange During the Eisenhower Presidency.* Jefferson, N.C.: McFarland & Company, 2005.

Ross, Stephen T. *American War Plans, 1945–1950.* London: Frank Cass, 1996.

Ross, Steven T., and David Alan Rosenberg, eds. *America's Plans For War Against The Soviet Union, 1945–1950.* Vol. 11. *The Limits of Nuclear Strategy.* New York: Garland Publishing, 1989.

Rostow, W. W. *Europe after Stalin: Eisenhower's Three Decisions of March 11, 1953.* Austin: University of Texas Press, 1982.

——*Open Skies: Eisenhower's Proposal of July 21, 1955.* Austin: University of Texas Press, 1982.

Sakharov, Andrei. *Memoirs.* New York: Knopf, 1990.

Schweber, S. S. *In The Shadow of the Bomb: Bethe, Oppenheimer, and the Moral Responsibility of the Scientist.* Princeton: Princeton University Press, 2000.

Seaborg, Glenn T. *Kennedy, Khrushchev, and the Test Ban.* Berkeley: University of California Press, 1981.

Sherry, Michael S. *In the Shadow of War: The United States since the 1930s.* New Haven: Yale University Press, 1995.

Shurcliff, W. A. *Bombs at Bikini: The Official Report of Operation Crossroads.* New York: W. H. Wise and Co., 1947.

Snead, David L. *The Gaither Committee, Eisenhower, and the Cold War.* Columbus: Ohio State University Press, 1999.

Sorenson, Theodore C. *Kennedy.* New York: Harper and Row, 1965.

Stassen, Harold, and Marshall Houts. *Eisenhower: Turning the World Toward Peace.* St. Paul, Minn.: Merrill, 1990.

Strauss, Lewis L. *Men and Decisions.* Garden City: Doubleday, 1962.

Taubman, Philip. *Secret Empire: Eisenhower, the CIA, and the Hidden Story of America's Space Espionage.* New York: Simon and Schuster, 2003.

Taubman, William. *Khrushchev: The Man and His Era.* New York: Norton and Company, 2003.

Teller, Edward, with Allen Brown. *The Legacy of Hiroshima.* Garden City: Doubleday, 1962.

Teller, Edward, and Albert Latter. *Our Nuclear Future: Facts, Dangers, and Opportunities.* New York: Criterion Books, 1958.

Teller, Edward, with Judith L. Shoolery. *Memoirs: A Twentieth-Century Journey in Science and Politics.* Cambridge, Mass.: Perseus, 2001.

Trachtenberg, Marc. *A Constructed Peace: The Making of the European Settlement, 1945–1963.* Princeton: Princeton University Press, 1999.

Vanderbilt, Tom. *Survival City: Adventures Among the Ruins of Atomic America.* Princeton: Architectural Press, 2002.

Voss, Earl H. *Nuclear Ambush: The Test-Ban Trap.* Chicago: Henry Regnery Co., 1963.

Wadsworth, James J. *The Price of Peace.* New York: Praeger, 1962.

Watson, Robert J. *History of the Office of the Secretary of Defense.* Vol. 4, *Into the Missile Age, 1956–1960.* Washington, D.C.: OSD, 1997.

Wicker, Tom. *Eisenhower.* New York: Times Books, 2002.

Wiesner, Jerome B. *Where Science and Politics Meet.* New York: McGraw Hill, 1965.

Wittner, Lawrence S. *The Struggle Against the Bomb: One World of None: A History of the World Nuclear Disarmament Movement Through 1953.* Stanford: Stanford University Press, 1995.

———. *The Struggle Against the Bomb: Resisting the Bomb—A History of the World Nuclear Disarmament Movement, 1954–1970.* Stanford: Stanford University Press, 1998.

York, Herbert F. *Arms and the Physicist.* Woodbury, N.Y.: American Institute of Physics Press, 1995.

———. *Making Weapons, Talking Peace.* New York: Basic Books, Inc. 1987.

———. *Race to Oblivion: A Participant's View of the Arms Race.* New York: Simon and Schuster, 1970.

Zubok, Vladislav M., and Constantine Pleshakov. *Inside The Kremlin's Cold War: From Stalin to Khrushchev.* Cambridge: Harvard University Press, 1996.

Articles

Bernstein, Barton J. "Crossing the Rubicon: A Missed Opportunity to Stop the H-bomb?" *International Security* 14 (Fall 1989): 132–60.

———. "Four Physicists and the Bomb: The Early Years, 1945–1950." *Historical Studies in the Physical and Biological Sciences* 18, no. 2 (1988): 231–63.

———. "Ike and Hiroshima: Did He Oppose It?" *Journal of Strategic Studies* 10 (September 1987): 377–89.

———. "The Quest for Security: American Foreign Policy and International Control of Atomic Energy, 1942–1946." *Journal of American History* 60 (March 1974): 1003–44.

———. "Seizing the Contested Terrain of Early Nuclear History: Stimson, Conant, and the Their Allies Explain the Decision to Use the Atomic Bomb." *Diplomatic History* 17 (Winter 1993): 35–72.

———. "Truman and the H-Bomb." *Bulletin of the Atomic Scientists* 40 (March 1984): 12–16.

Bethe, Hans A. "The Case for Ending Nuclear Tests." *Atlantic Monthly* 206 (August 1960): 43–51.

Brands, H. W. "The Age of Vulnerability: Eisenhower and the National Insecurity State." *American Historical Review* 94 (October 1989): 963–89.

Brennan, Donald A., and Morton H. Halperin. "Policy Considerations of a Nuclear-Test Ban." In *Arms Control, Disarmament, and National Security,* edited by Donald A. Brennan. New York: Braziller, 1961.

Brinkley, Douglas. "Eisenhower the Dove." *American Heritage* 52 (September 2001): 58–65.

Buhite, Russell D., and Wm. Christopher Hamel. "War for Peace: The Question of an American Preventive War against the Soviet Union, 1945–1955." *Diplomatic History* 14 (Summer 1990): 367–84.

Bundy, McGeorge. "The Missed Chance to Stop the H-Bomb." *New York Review of Books* 29 (13 May 1982): 13–22.

Chernus, Ira. "Operation Candor: Fear, Faith, and Flexibility." *Diplomatic History* 29 (November 2005): 779–808.

"Congress Is Told How Pressures Grew to Ban Tests." *U.S. News and World Report* 42 (14 June 1957): 75–79.

Cousins, Norman. "Dr. Teller and the Spirit of Adventure." *Saturday Review* 41 (15 March 1958): 26, 63.

Damms, Richard V. "James Killian, the Technological Capabilities Panel, and the Emergence of President Eisenhower's 'Scientific-Technological Elite.'" *Diplomatic History* 24 (Winter 2000): 57–78.

Dingman, Roger. "Atomic Diplomacy During the Korean War." *International Security* 13 (Winter 1988/89): 50–91.

———. "Alliance in Crisis: The Lucky Dragon Incident and Japanese-American Relations." In *The Great Powers in East Asia, 1953–1960,* edited by Warren Cohen and Akira Iriye. New York: Columbia University Press, 1990.

Divine, Robert A. "Early Record on Test Moratoriums," *Bulletin of the Atomic Scientists* 42 (May 1986): 24–26.

Dulles, John Foster. "A Policy of Boldness." *Life* 32 (19 May 1952): 146–60.

———. "Challenge and Response in United States Policy." *Foreign Affairs* 36 (October 1957): 25–43.

———. "Policy for Security and Peace." *Foreign Affairs* 32 (April 1954): 353–64.

Dyson, Freeman J. "The Future Development of Nuclear Weapons." *Foreign Affairs* 38 (April 1960): 457–64.

Erdman, Andrew P. N. "'War No Longer Has Any Logic Whatever': Dwight D. Eisenhower and the Thermonuclear Revolution." In *Cold War Statesmen Confront the Bomb: Nuclear Diplomacy since 1945,* edited by John Lewis Gaddis and others. New York: Oxford University Press, 1999.

Evangelista, Matthew. "Cooperation Theory and Disarmament Negotiations in the 1950s." *World Politics* 42 (June 1990): 502–28.

"Facts About A-Bomb 'Fall-out': Not a Word of Truth in Scare Stories Over Tests." *U.S. News and World Report* 38 (25 March 1955): 21–26.

Fallows, James. "The Dustbin of History: The Military-Industrial Complex." *Foreign Policy* (November/December 2002): 46–48.

Foot, Rosemary J. "Nuclear Coercion and the Ending of the Korean Conflict." *International Security* 13 (Winter 1988/89): 92–112.

Gaddis, John Lewis. "The Unexpected John Foster Dulles." In *John Foster Dulles and the Diplomacy of the Cold War,* edited by Richard Immerman. Princeton: University Press, 1990.

Gehron, William J. "Geneva Conference and the Discontinuance of Nuclear Weapons Tests: History of Political and Technical Developments of the Negotiations from October 31, 1958 to August 22, 1960." *U.S. Department of State Bulletin* (September 26, 1960): 482–97.

Glass, H. Bentley. "The Hazards of Atomic Radiation to Man: British and American Reports." *Bulletin of the Atomic Scientists* 12 (October 1956): 312–17.

Graybar, Lloyd J. "The 1946 Atomic Bomb Tests: Atomic Diplomacy or Bureaucratic Infighting?" *Journal of American History* 72 (March 1986): 888–907.

Greene, Benjamin P. "Eisenhower, Science and the Nuclear Test Ban Debate, 1953–1956." *Journal of Strategic Studies* 26 (December 2003): 156–85.

Greene, John Robert. "Bibliographic Essay: Eisenhower Revisionism, 1952–1992, A Reappraisal." In *Reexamining the Eisenhower Presidency,* edited by Shirley Anne Warshaw. Westport, Conn.: Greenwood Press, 1993.

Greenstein, Fred I. "Eisenhower as an Activist President: A Look at New Evidence." *Political* Science *Quarterly* 94 (Winter 1979–80): 575–99.

Griffin, Charles J. G. "New Light on Eisenhower's Farewell Address." *Presidential Studies Quarterly* 22, no. 3 (1992): 469–79.

Hartung, William D. "Eisenhower's Warning: The Military-Industrial Complex Forty Years Later." *World Policy Journal* 18 (Spring 2001): 39–44.

Henderson, Philip O. "Organizing the Presidency for Effective Leadership: Lessons from the Eisenhower Years." *Presidential Studies Quarterly* 17 (Winter 1987): 43–69.

Holl, Jack M. "Eisenhower's Peaceful Diplomacy: Atoms for Peace and the Western Alliance." *Materials and Society* 7 (1982): 365–78.

Hopmann, P. Terrence. "Internal and External Influences on Arms Control Negotiations: The Partial Test Ban." In *Peace, War, and Numbers,* edited by Bruce N. Russett. Beverly Hills: Sage Publications, 1972.

Immerman, Richard H. "Eisenhower and Dulles: Who Made the Decisions?" *Political Psychology* (Autumn 1979): 3–20.

Immerman, Richard H. "Confessions of an Eisenhower Revisionist: An Agonizing Reappraisal." *Diplomatic History* 14 (Summer 1990): 319–42.

Keefer, Edward C. "President Dwight D. Eisenhower and the End of the Korean War." *Diplomatic History* 10 (Summer 1986): 267–89.

Kissinger, Henry A. "Nuclear Testing and the Problems of Peace." *Foreign Affairs* 37 (October 1958): 1–18.

Kistiakowsky, George, and Herbert York. "Strategic Arms Race Showdown Through Test Limitations." *Science* (August 2, 1974): 404.

Leffler, Melvyn P. "The American Conception of National Security and the Beginnings of the Cold War, 1945–48." *American Historical Review* 89 (April 1984): 346–381.

Loeb, Benjamin S. "Ratification of the Limited Test Ban Treaty." In *The Politics of Arms Control Treaty Ratification,* edited by Micheal Krepon and Dan Caldwell. New York: St. Martin's Press, 1991.

Magraw, Katherine. "Teller and the 'Clean Bomb' Episode." *Bulletin of the Atomic Scientists* 44 (May 1988): 32–37.

Malloy, Sean L. "A 'Paper Tiger?' Nuclear Weapons, Atomic Diplomacy, and the Korean War." *The New England Journal of History* 60 (Fall 2003-Spring 2004): 227–52.

Manning, Mary. "Atomic Vets Battle Time." *Bulletin of the Atomic Scientists* 51 (January/February 1995): 54–60.

Marine, Gene. "McCone of the AEC." *Nation* 188 (1 April 1959): 307–10.

McAuliffe, Mary S. "Commentary/Eisenhower the President." *Journal of American History* 68 (December 1981): 625–32.

Medhurst, Martin J. "Atoms for Peace and Nuclear Hegemony: The Rhetorical Structure of a Cold War Campaign." *Armed Forces and Society* 23 (Summer 1997): 569–92.

———. "Reconceptualizing Rhetorical History: Eisenhower's Farewell Address." *Quarterly Journal of Speech* 80, no. 2 (1994): 195–218.

Miller, Steven E. "Politics over Promise: Domestic Impediments to Arms Control." *International Security* 84 (Spring 1984): 67–90.

Murphy, Charles J. V. "The Atom and the Balance of Power." *Fortune* 48 (August 1953): 97, 202.

———. "The Case for Resuming Nuclear Tests." *Fortune* 61 (April 1960): 148–50, 178, 183–4, 188, 190.

———. "Now the President Will Decide on His Own." *Life* 52 (February 16, 1962): 71–83.

———. "Nuclear Inspection: A Near Miss." *Fortune* 59 (March 1959): 122–25, 155–63.

Murray, Thomas. "Reliance on the H-Bomb and Its Dangers." *Life* 42 (6 May 1957): 181–98.

Norris, Robert S., and William N. Arkin. "Known Nuclear Tests Worldwide, 1945–1995." *Bulletin of the Atomic Scientists* 52 (May/June 1996): 61–63.

Norton-Taylor, Duncan. "The Controversial Mr. Strauss." *Fortune* 51 (January 1955): 110–12, 164–70.

"Nuclear Tests: World Debate." *Time* 71 (7 April 1958): 16.

Oppenheimer, J. Robert. "Atomic Weapons and American Policy." *Foreign Affairs* 31 (July 1953): 525–35.

Orear, Jay. "Detection of Nuclear Weapons Testing." *Bulletin of the Atomic Scientists* 14 (March 1958): 98–101.

Patterson, David S. "President Eisenhower and Arms Control." *Peace and Change* 11, no. 3–4 (1986): 3–24.

Rabe, Stephen. "Eisenhower Revisionism: A Decade of Scholarship." *Diplomatic History* 17 (Winter 1993): 97–115.

Roberts, Chalmers N. "The Hopes and Fears of an Atomic Test Ban." *Reporter* 22 (28 April 1960): 20–23.

Roman, Peter J. "Eisenhower and Ballistic Missiles Arms Control, 1957–1960: A Missed Opportunity?" *Journal of Strategic Studies* 19 (September 1996): 365–80.

Rosenberg, David Alan. "The Origins of Overkill: Nuclear Weapons and American Strategy." In *The National Security: Its Theory and Practice, 1945–1960*, edited by Norman A. Graebner. New York: Oxford University Press, 1986.

———. "A Smoking Radiating Ruin at the End of Two Hours: Documents of American Plans for Nuclear War with the Soviet Union, 1954–1955." *International Security* 6 (Winter 1981–82): 3–38.

Sawyer, Roland. "The H-Bomb Chronology." *Bulletin of* the *Atomic Scientists* 10 (September 1954): 287–90.

Schilling, Warner A. "Scientists, Foreign Policy, and Politics." *American Political Science Review* 56 (June 1962): 287–300.

Smirnmov, Yuri, and Vladislav Zubok. "Nuclear Weapons after Stalin's Death: Moscow Enters the H-Bomb Age." *Cold War International History Bulletin* No. 4 (Fall 1994): 1, 14–18.

Smith-Norris, Martha. "Only as Dust in the Face of the Wind: An Analysis of the BRAVO Nuclear Incident in the Pacific, 1954." *Journal of American-East Asian Relations* 6 (Spring 1997): 1–34.

———. "The Eisenhower Administration and the Nuclear Test Ban Talks, 1958–1960: Another Challenge to 'Revisionism.'" *Diplomatic History* 27 (September 2003): 503–41.

Soapes, Thomas F. "A Cold Warrior Seeks Peace: Eisenhower's Strategy for Nuclear Disarmament." *Diplomatic History* 4 (Winter 1980): 57–71.

"Some Senate Views on Test Ban and Inspection." *Bulletin of the Atomic Scientists* 13 (September 1957): 267.

Spencer, Steven N. "Fallout: The Silent Killer." *Saturday Evening Post* 232 (29 August 1959): 28, 87–90, and (September 5, 1959): 25, 84–86.

Stevenson, Adlai E. "Why I Raised the H-Bomb Question." *Look* 21 (5 February 1957): 23–25.

Strauss, Lewis L. "Why Nuclear Testing is a Must for Freedom." *Reader's Digest* 79 (September 1961): 54–61.

Strong, Robert A. "Eisenhower and Arms Control." In *Reevaluating Eisenhower: American Foreign Policy in the 1950s*, edited by Richard A. Melanson and David Mayers. Urbana: University of Illinois Press, 1987.

Suri, Jeremy. "America's Search for a Technological Solution to the Arms Race:

The Surprise Attack Conference of 1958 and a Challenge for 'Eisenhower Revisionists.'" *Diplomatic History* 21 (Summer 1997): 417–51.

Teller, Edward. "Alternatives for Security." *Foreign Affairs* 76 (January 1958): 201–8.

Teller, Edward with Albert Brown. "Plan for Survival," *Saturday Evening Post* 235 (3 February 1962): 11–15.

Teller, Edward and Albert Latter. "The Compelling Need for Nuclear Tests." *Life* (10 February 1958): 64–72.

Wells, Samuel F. Jr. "The Origins of Massive Retaliation." *Political Science Quarterly* 96 (Spring 1981): 31–52.

"What Scientists 'Agree'?" *National Review* 5 (5 April 1958): 318.

"Why Nuclear Tests Go On: AEC Gives Official Reasons." *U.S. News and World Report* 42 (14 June 1957): 136–37.

Wittner, Lawrence. "Blacklisting Schweitzer." *Bulletin of the Atomic Scientists* 51 (May/June 1995): 55–61.

York, Herbert F. "Eisenhower's Other Warning." *Physics Today* 30 (January 1977): 9–11.

———. "The Great Test-Ban Debate." *Scientific American* 227 (November 1972): 15–23.

Government Documents

United States, Arms Control and Disarmament Agency. *Documents on Disarmament, 1945–1959.* Washington: G.P.O., 1961.

———, Department of State, *Bulletin*, 1945–63.

———, *Foreign Relations of the United States.* 1947–63.

———, House, Subcommittee of the Committee on Appropriations. *Hearings on the Military Establishment Appropriations Bill for 1947*, 79: II.

———, *Public Papers of the Presidents: Dwight D. Eisenhower, 1953–1961. John F. Kennedy, 1961–1963.*

———, Senate, Committee on Foreign Relations. *Nuclear Test Ban Treaty: Hearings*, 88: I, 1963.

Dissertations

Appleby, Charles Albert. "Eisenhower and Arms Control, 1953–1961: A Balance of Risks." Ph.D. diss., Johns Hopkins University, 1987.

Davis, Zachary S. "Eisenhower's Worldview and Nuclear Strategy." Ph.D. diss., University of Virginia, 1989.

Greene, Benjamin P. "'Crucified on a Cross of Atoms:' Eisenhower, Science, and the Nuclear Test-Ban Debate, 1945–1963." Ph.D. diss., Stanford University, 2004.

Rosi, Eugene J. "Public Opinion and Foreign Policy: Nongovernmental Opinion Concerning the Cessation of Nuclear Weapons Tests, 1954–1958." Ph.D. diss., Columbia University, 1967.

Smith, Martha J. "The Nuclear Testing Policies of the Eisenhower Administration, 1953–1960." Ph. D. diss., University of Toronto, 1997.

Index

In this index an "f" after a number indicates a separate reference on the next page, and an "ff" indicates separate references on the next two pages. A continuous discussion over two or more pages is indicated by a span of page numbers, e.g., "57–59." *Passim* is used for a cluster of references in close but not consecutive sequence.